Key Events in African History

Key Events in African History

A Reference Guide

Toyin Falola

An Oryx Book

Greenwood Press
Westport, Connecticut • London

Library of Congress Cataloging-in-Publication Data

Falola, Toyin.
    Key events in African history : a reference guide / Toyin Falola.
      p. cm.
    Includes bibliographical references and index.
    ISBN 0–313–31323–7 (alk. paper)
    1. Africa—History. I. Title
  DT20.F34 2002
   960—dc21   2001058644

British Library Cataloguing in Publication Data is available.

Library of Congress Catalog Card Number: 2001058644
ISBN: 978–0–313–36122–7

First published in 2002

Greenwood Press, 88 Post Road West, Westport, CT 06881
An imprint of Greenwood Publishing Group, Inc.
www.greenwood.com

Printed in the United States of America

The paper used in this book complies with the
Permanent Paper Standard issued by the National
Information Standards Organization (Z39.48–1984).

10 9 8 7 6 5

To three creative interpreters of Africa:
Akinwunmi Isola, poet and playwright
Dele Jegede, artist
Oyekan Owomoyela, folklorist

Contents

Part II. The Nineteenth-Century Period

Part III. The Twentieth-Century Period

Preface

This is a reference work containing chapters on thirty-six significant events in African history, from the earliest historic times to the present. It is directed toward high school and college libraries as a research tool for students who are taking survey courses in African history. This work should be used alongside a reader in African history. The presentations recognize that the majority of readers and students have little or no knowledge of African history. It is not a textbook—the idea is not to present extensive discussions of economics, political development, and contemporary history but to present an analysis of singular events that shaped the history of the continent.

A timeline of key events in African history opens the book, with entries chosen for overall relevancy to the text matter. Some of the initial dates (B.C.) are approximations. The timeline of the premodern era is more detailed because this represents the longest period in African history, a period that is often ignored in the literature. Then comes an overview of the history of Africa that puts all of the events in their proper historical context. Thirty-six chapters follow, arranged in chronological order. Each chapter discusses a watershed event and consists of a comprehensive essay on the event; its historical, social, and geographic context; and its long-term significance. Suggestions for further reading are presented at the end of each chapter, drawing mainly on books that are accessible to students and teachers, that are easily understood, and that can serve as reference material for detailed research. Many of the illustrations are from my personal collections and photographs of replicas of ancient pieces.

This book explores many of the research findings of the last eight decades. The major events are analyzed in all their wide ramifications, and they reveal just how ancient and diverse the history of the continent is. Thus, some events deal with ancient times, showing the high points in a long history. Others deal with the periods of the Arab and Western incursions, showing those powerful moments when Africa became drawn into the global world. It was from Africa that blacks in the

United States, Europe, the Caribbean, and Central and South America came. The definition of the Americas, as well as their history and that of the politics of race relations, can never be given without including Africa. The remainder of the book explores modern history. All the periods are related: The march of African history unfolds while the connection between the past and present is clear to see. The modern period does not stand in isolation from the past. If some of the events of the early periods show how Africans struggled to master their environments, later events reveal the history of conquest by others. The impact of the outside world is multifold and profound, as Africans were connected with others and their world was transformed in the others' image. Old Africa has never disappeared, and indigenous traditions shape responses to imported cultures.

Acknowledgments

This book benefited from suggestions from various people, from my children to colleagues in various American universities. My eagerness to consult others reminded me of the sayings by the Maasai of East Africa: "One head does not consume all knowledge" and "It is the eye which has traveled that is clever." In developing a comprehensive timeline and arriving at the events to include, I received valuable advice from the following professors: George Ndege, Funso Afolayan, Akanmu Adebayo, Kwabena Parry, Femi Kolapo, Steven Salm, Jonathan Reynolds, Saheed Adejumobi, Jackie Woodfork, Femi Vaughan, Andrew Barnes, Ehiedu Iweriebor, and Ugo Nwokeji. Dr. Barbara Rader, the Executive Editor at Greenwood, added suggestions as well. Comments on the initial drafts were received from a host of scholars: George Ndege, Joel Tishken, Kirsten Walles, Ann O'Hear, Edmund Abaka, Jonathan Reynolds, Wilson Ogbomo, and Funso Afolayan.

All the maps were prepared by Sam Saverance, a student in my seminar on Nigeria who took a keen interest in the manuscript. Sam is a mature student, dedicated and brilliant. Words are inadequate to express my gratitude to Sam, but I can at least pray for him: May he fulfill all his life's ambitions and become an elder.

I must thank three staff members in my department. Lisa Vera was generous in her assistance, adding a number of editorial changes to the master copy. She embodies the spirit that the Swahili celebrate in their proverb "Haraka haraka haina baraka"—which means to work with devotion and to do things properly at a steady pace. Laura Flack is always kind and efficient in meeting my needs, always requested when they are urgent—"The stomach does not wait for a pot that is cooking!" Sister Laura, as I call her, is able to understand the language of my stomach. Last but not least, Michael Montaque helped with the illustrations, in addition to feeding me occasionally. I can only pray that Michael does not leave me to rejoin his ancestors in France.

I cannot but also thank the members of my family and a number of friends, as well as note some key events during the writing moment. My wife lost her father, Pa Peter Olusola, an event that showed the continuity of modern Africa with its past in the respect for elders, the role of children, and the importance of funeral rites. Condolences and gifts were received from all over the world, and we will forever remain grateful. My wife's brother, Dr. Bola Olusola, joined us in Texas to take up a medical practice, thus adding to the size of the kinship group. My daughter, Bisola Falola, entered college to begin the initiation to adulthood. The children have grown so quickly that I blame myself for having just a few! Two of my students, Jackie Woodfork and Saheed Adejumobi, completed their Ph.D. degrees and moved to comfortable academic positions. May they prosper in life and remember to take care of me in old age! The family continues to be blessed with good friends, and we particularly rejoice in the accomplishments of Bayo and Sade Oyebade of Nashville, Femi and Tinu Babarinde of Phoenix, and Alusine and Christiana Jalloh of Arlington. Finally, I wish to express my heartfelt gratitude to my wife and friend O'Bisi.

I hope that readers will appreciate the rule that guided the writing of this book—clear, not fancy!

Timeline of Historical Events

There is no consensus on the periodization of African history, but I have adopted the most common. Many dates before the fifteenth century are approximations, some based on scientific carbon-14 dating techniques. Written Arabic and European documentation improved historical records after the fifteenth century, although dates are not always precise. This list is by no means exhaustive; it is offered only as a guide to better understand the material in this book.

ANCIENT PERIOD

40,000 B.C.   Prehistory: *Homo sapiens sapiens* ("modern man") emerged.

5000 B.C.+   The Agricultural Revolution occurred, with profound consequences for African civilization.

                Early states such as Egypt began to be created.

4000 B.C.   Metalworking (copper) was known in Sinai.

3100 B.C.   Egypt developed a centralized government. The states of Upper and Lower Egypt were unified, and the civilization of Pharaonic Egypt emerged.

                The Sahara was in its last wet phase, before it became a desert.

1800 B.C.   Agriculture, urbanization, and centralized political authority were now established in many parts of North Africa.

1650 B.C.   The Hyksos invaded and governed Egypt until ca. 1500 B.C.

                Horses and chariots were used in Egypt.

1000 B.C.   The Berber civilization arose in North Africa.

                Horses and donkeys were used to drive carts and chariots to cross the Sahara between North and West Africa.

950 B.C.   The Nubians (Kush) regained independence from Egypt.

            Palestine also broke away from the Egyptian empire.

814 B.C.   Carthage was founded by the Phoenicians in Tunisia.

730 B.C.   Kush rose to power in northeast Africa. The first "Iron Age" kingdom developed. Kush became powerful enough to invade Egypt successfully.

670 B.C.   The Assyrians invaded Egypt, forcing the Kushite kings to withdraw to Nubia permanently.

500 B.C.   Ideas of iron-working began to spread in West, central, eastern, and southern Africa, largely in association with the dispersal of the Bantu-speaking people.

            Trade continued between West Africa and North Africa.

            The Nok culture in Nigeria was a successful example of the use of iron.

332 B.C.   The native Egyptian dynasty ended when the Greeks invaded Egypt and established the Ptolemaic dynasty, which lasted for 300 years.

146 B.C.   The Romans conquered Carthage and began their control of the coastal parts of North Africa.

100 B.C.   Iron-working spread to many parts of southern Africa.

            Camels were now replacing horses and donkeys in the trans-Saharan trade.

30 B.C.   Egypt was conquered by the Romans.

23 B.C.   A Roman army invaded Kush and sacked the city of Napata.

PRECOLONIAL PERIOD

A.D. 100   The kingdom of Aksum was established.

            The use of camels transformed the trans-Saharan trade.

            The East African coast was part of an international trade with the states of the Persian Gulf and western India.

300   The knowledge of iron-working was now firmly established in many parts of Africa.

            Prosperous cities emerged in Roman North Africa.

            Ghana had probably emerged as a small state.

320+   The Ethiopian Orthodox Church was founded in the reign of King Ezana, A.D. 320–56

350   Aksum attacked Meroë to put an end to a kingdom that had lasted for centuries.

429   The Vandals, a group of Germanic warriors, overran the Maghrib and ended Roman rule.

| 622 | The Islamic calendar started at year zero. The new religion of Islam was established. |

| 640 | An Arab army entered Egypt, and the spread of Islam in North Africa followed. |

| 710 | Aksum army was defeated by Arab Muslims. |

| 800 | The empire of Ghana in West Africa became powerful and controlled the gold and salt trade across the Sahara; Gao emerged as a major center in West Africa. |

The Muslim conquests in North Africa and Spain recorded great successes.

Egypt became a great center of Islamic civilization.

The state of Kanem was founded in the Eastern Sudan.

| 945 | Arab settlers reached the East African coast. |

| 969–1171 | The Fatimid caliphate in Egypt existed from 969 to 1171. |

| 1000+ | Ghana was at the height of its power. |

The king of Gao accepted Islam in ca. A.D. 1010.

A number of Hausa and Yoruba states were founded; the empire of Kanem expanded.

Coastal cities in East Africa were part of the Indian Ocean trade.

Iron-working was known in many parts of West Africa.

| 1054 | The Almoravids captured Audaghost from Ghana. |

| 1061–117 | The Almoravids established new Muslim states in Morocco and Spain. |

| 1076 | Ghana began to collapse under the Almoravid attacks. |

Arts and sciences flourished in North Africa.

| 1086 | The king of Kanem (Hume) accepted Islam, thus drawing parts of the Eastern Sudan and the Lake Chad region into the Islamic world. |

| 1150 | The Zagwe dynasty was founded in Ethiopia. It adopted Christianity as a state religion and governed till 1270. |

Swahili culture and city–states had emerged, with such notable coastal cities as Mogadishu, Mombasa, and Kilwa.

| 1200 | Political confusion reigned in the Western Sudan, leading to the fall of the Ghana empire. The Benin kingdom came under the Eweka dynasty. The Almohads established a new Muslim state in North Africa and Spain (1147–1289). |

| 1230 | Sundiata became the king of the Mandinka state of Kangaba. A legendary and cult hero, he defeated Sumanguru and other neighbors to found the kingdom of Mali in about 1235. |

The Christian kingdom of Nubia fell.

1255	Mamluk soldier–kings ruled in Egypt from 1250 to 1517.
	Gao attained great commercial power.
	The first Kanem-Borno empire rose around Lake Chad.
1270	The Solomonid dynasty emerged in Ethiopia and governed till 1550.
1300	Wolof states were founded in Senegal.
	The kingdom of Ife among the Yoruba was flourishing.
1315	The Mossi kingdom was founded.
	The Nubian king converted to Islam.
1324	Mansa Musa of Mali went on a pilgrimage to Mecca.
1327	Sankore University in Timbuktu, Mali, was founded.
1325–53	Ibn Battuta was traveling in different parts of Africa.
1375	The kingdom of Adal was founded.
1415	East African trading ambassadors visited the capital of the Chinese empire.
	The Portuguese captured the port of Ceuta in northwestern Morocco.
	Timbuktu and Jenne in West Africa became famous centers of Islamic scholarship.
1434	Mamluk sultans were in control of Egypt.
	Benin was a strong empire in West Africa.
	The Portuguese reached the West African coast.
1450s	The trans-Atlantic slave trade began.
1464	The Zimbabwe empire was in existence.
1468	Sunni Ali established the Songhay empire.
1472	Morocco was attacked by the Portuguese and Spanish; the Portuguese reached the Bight of Benin.
1480s	Portuguese missionaries arrived in Kongo.
1482	The Portuguese built a fort at El-Mina (later called Elmina), on the Gold Coast, in West Africa.
1491	King Nzinga Nkuwu, the Manikongo, became a Christian and adopted the name Joao 1 (John 1).
1505	The Portuguese reached Mwene Mutapa (or Monomatapa). Christianity was established there.
	The Portuguese destroyed the notable Swahili city–state of Kilwa.
1506	Henrico, the son of King Afonso I of the Kongo, became the bishop of Utica. He was the first black Catholic bishop in Africa.

1509	The Bunyoro kingdom was established in Uganda.
1517	The Ottoman Turks conquered Egypt.
1519	Mahmud el-Kati began writing his famous history of the Sudan, *Chronicle of the Seeker after Knowledge.*
1520	A Portuguese expedition reached Ethiopia and established diplomatic relations.
1525	The Turks took control of Algiers.
1529	Ethiopia was conquered for the first time by an external power, in an Islamic jihad led by Ahmad ibn Ghazi, a Somali Muslim. Muslim control lasted till 1541.
1530	Christianity was introduced in Benin.
1540	King Andriamanelo and the Imerian kingdom were in power in Madagascar.
1571	Portugal conquered Angola to establish its first African colony.
1591	The Moroccans invaded Songhay.
1614	Idris Alooma of the Kanem-Borno empire introduced the use of guns.
1625	The foundation of the kingdom of Dahomey was established.
1630	Nzinga led a resistance struggle against the Portuguese in Angola.
1650	The Portuguese government sent settlers to Mozambique.
	Wegbaja became the first king of Dahomey.
1652	The first Dutch settlement in South Africa was established. The Dutch East Indies Company established Cape Town as a "refreshment center" and a fort.
1659	The French occupied St. Louis in Senegal. St. Louis became the first French colony in sub-Saharan Africa.
	The first Dutch-Khoi war in South Africa was fought.
ca. 1670	Osei Tutu founded the Asante empire.
1690s	Osei Tutu established the Asante Confederation.
1705	Asante became a strong empire under Osei Tutu.
1713	Britain was now the biggest slave buyer and carrier in Africa; the Bambara state of Segu was established.
1722	French settlers and slaves arrived in Mauritius.
1723	A series of frontier wars began between the Boers and the Bantu-speaking Xhosa of South Africa.
1725	The imamate of Futa Jallon was established.
1750	Islamic revival movement spread in the Western Sudan.
	Euro-African trade expanded in the Niger Delta.

1765   The British established a colony in Senegambia that lasted till 1783.

1784   The Omani Arabs gained control of the Swahili city–states.

1791   Freetown (Sierra Leone) was founded.

1797   Mungo Park, a European explorer, attempted to locate the source of the River Niger in West Africa.

1804   The jihad of Uthman dan Fodio began.

         The Church Missionary Society established a mission in Sierra Leone.

1806   The British took over the Cape Colony.

1811   Muhammad Ali attained power in Egypt.

1814   The first European-type school was established in West Africa: the Christian Institution, at Leicester, for recaptive children.

1816   The first church was established among Africans in Kissy, Sierra Leone, by a Nova Scotian settler, Rev. C.F. Wenzel, a Baptist. In 1817 it became St. Patrick's Church.

1817   The Yoruba Wars began.

1819   Shaka founded the Zulu empire.

1820s   Lesotho emerged as a leading state in southern Africa.

1822   Liberia was founded by 12,000 liberated slaves.

1827   Fourah Bay College was founded in Sierra Leone, the first Western college in West Africa.

1828   Merina rulers established control in Madagascar.

1830   The French attacked Algeria.

         The Oyo empire fell, and Ibadan began to rise.

1830–32 The Rivers Niger and Nile were mapped.

1834   The Boers began their "Great Trek" into the interior of southern Africa.

1840s   The Ndebele state emerged in the area of modern-day Zimbabwe.

1842   The Orange Free State, the first Boer republic in the interior of southern Africa, was established.

1845   The first grammar school in West Africa was established in Sierra Leone.

1847   Abd el-Kadr of Algeria surrendered to the French.

1851   The French established Libreville to resettle freed slaves.

1853   Botswana forces defeated Boer invaders.

1853–79 Egypt expanded.

1855   Emperor Tewodros founded modern Ethiopia.

1858   Martin Delany, an African American, negotiated the foundation of an African American colony in Nigeria. This potentially important project never got off the ground.

1861   The British annexed the colony of Lagos.

1864   Samuel Ajayi Crowther was appointed the second bishop of a Christian church in Africa.

1867   Diamonds were discovered in South Africa. Gold was discovered twenty years later, and both minerals transformed the economy of this region.

1873–74   The Anglo-Asante war was fought.

1880   Almost half a million converted to Christianity in Uganda when the Kabaka (king) was converted.

1881   The Mahdist revolt in Sudan began.

COLONIAL PERIOD

1882   Egypt was conquered by the British.

1884–85   The Berlin Conference took place and the Scramble for Africa began.

1885   King Leopold proclaimed his authority over the Congo.

1890s   Black-controlled Ethiopian Christian Churches in south Africa were formed.

1891   Bishop Samuel Ajayi Crowther died.

1892   Dahomey was conquered by the French, and a French protectorate was declared.

1893   The Yoruba Wars ended.

1895   The Battle of Fashoda was fought.

1896   Ethiopia defeated Italy at the Battle of Adowa.

            The French acquired Upper Volta.

1897   The British invaded Benin City, in what they called a "Punitive Expedition."

1898   Samori Toure's resistance against the French ended in defeat.

1899–1902   The Boer War was fought in South Africa.

1900   British colonists began to settle in the highlands of Kenya.

            The first Pan-African Conference was held.

            The Buganda Agreement was signed between the British and Buganda. This enhanced the power of the Kabaka, king of Buganda, whose agents were used to extend British authority to other areas of Uganda.

1901   The Yaa Asantewa War was fought between the Asante and the British.

1903   The Seychelles were separated from Mauritius to become a British crown colony.

1905   The Maji Maji Rebellion in Tanganyika (Tanzania) was suppressed by the Germans.

1908   The Congo was formally annexed by Belgium after reports of brutality by private companies.

1910   The Middle Congo became part of French Equatorial Africa.

        White minorities acquired power in South Africa.

1912   The African National Congress (ANC) was formed in South Africa.

        Edward Wilmot Blyden died.

        The French took control of Morocco.

1914   The First World War began.

        Blaise Diagne was elected as the first African in the French National Assembly.

        The Universal Negro Improvement Association was formed.

1916   Belgium acquired control in Rwanda and Burundi as mandated by the League of Nations.

1917–19 The Influenza Pandemic took place.

1919   Clements Kadalie of South Africa organized a union of mine workers, numbering almost 100,000, the largest in the continent.

1920   The National Congress of British West Africa was established.

1921   Simon Kimbangu founded the Kinbagu Church, Africa's largest independent church.

1922   An Anglo-Egyptian treaty declared Egypt to be no longer a British colony, although independence was in name only.

1924   The South African Nationalist Party came to power and began to institute a policy of racial discrimination against Africans.

1929   An economic depression began and lasted for at least five years.

        The Aba Women Riots occurred in Nigeria, organized by women to protest tax increases.

1935   The Italian invasion of Ethiopia provoked an international crisis.

1939   The Second World War broke out.

1941   British troops liberated Ethiopia.

1944   The Brazzaville Conference was held. This was the conference that de Gaulle called to "liberalize" colonial rule in French Africa, but its tepid reforms demonstrated that Africans would not be rewarded for their participation in the war and that de Gaulle had no intention of letting the colonies go.

1945 Post–World War II ideas of liberation and self-determination put colonialism in crisis.

1948 Apartheid became official in South Africa.

1951 Libya became independent of Italy.

1952 Mau Mau resistance against the British in Kenya began.

Egypt became the first African country to gain independence from European rule.

1954 Nasser came to power in a military coup in Egypt.

The Algerian War of Independence began.

1955 At the first interracial conference in South Africa, the South African Freedom Charter was created.

1956 Morocco, Sudan, and Tunisia became independent.

1957 Ghana became independent.

1958 Guinea became independent.

POSTCOLONIAL PERIOD

1958 The United Nations Economic Commission for Africa (ECA) was set up.

1960 This was the Year of African Independence. Gabon, Senegal, Mali, Burkina Faso, Democratic Republic of the Congo, Congo, Côte d'Ivoire, Chad, Cameroon, the Central African Republic (CAR), Benin, Mauritania, Niger, Madagascar, Togo, Nigeria, Somalia and Congo-Brazzaville obtained their independence.

A civil war began in Congo and lasted till 1965.

1961 Patrice Lumumba was murdered in the Congo.

The Eritrean liberation struggles began.

Sierra Leone and Tanzania became independent.

The Republic of South Africa was established, independent of the British Commonwealth.

1962 Algeria, Rwanda, Uganda, and Burundi became independent countries.

Nelson Mandela, the leader of the ANC, was jailed for treason. He would not be released until 1990.

1963 The Organization of African Unity was founded in Addis Ababa, Ethiopia.

A military coup took place in Togo, the first in sub-Saharan Africa.

Kenya became independent. Nationalists in Guinea-Bissau began armed struggles.

1964   The Tanganyika African National Union (TANU) became the only legal party in Tanzania.

        Malawi and Zambia became independent.

1965   The Unilateral Declaration of Independence was made in Rhodesia (now Zimbabwe)—a white minority government declared itself free of Britain.

        Gambia became independent.

1966   The First Festival of Negro Arts (later known as FESTAC) was held in Dakar, Senegal.

        Military coups took place in Nigeria and Ghana.

        The Namibian War of Independence began.

        Basutoland became independent as Lesotho, while Bechuanaland became Botswana.

1967   The Arusha Declaration in Tanzania established a socialist program.

1968   Equatorial Guinea, Swaziland, and Mauritius became independent.

1969   Eduardo Mondlane, leader of the FRELIMO (Front for Liberation of Mozambique) independence movement in Mozambique, was assassinated.

1970   The Nigerian Civil War ended.

        In Egypt, the Aswan Dam was completed, and Nasser died.

1971   Hastings Kamuzu Banda became president-for-life of Malawi.

1972   Zambia became a one-party state under the United National Independence Party.

1973   Amilcar Cabral of Guinea-Bissau was assassinated.

1974   The imperial government of Haile Selassie was overthrown in Ethiopia.

1974–75 The Portuguese colonies of Guinea-Bissau, Angola, Mozambique, São Tomé, Cape Verde, and Comoros (without Mayotte) became independent.

1975   The Economic Community of West African States was formed.

1976   The Soweto uprising took place in South Africa.

        Ethiopia and Somalia went to war over the Ogaden province.

        The Seychelles became independent.

1977   Djibouti became independent.

1978   The African National Congress recorded success in its armed attacks on some targets in South Africa.

1979   Jean-Bédel Bokassa, self-crowned emperor of the Central African Republic, was deposed.

        Tanzania invaded Uganda and ended the dictatorship of Idi Amin.

Jimmy Carter visited sub-Saharan Africa, the first American president to undertake an official visit.

1980   The Lancaster House Agreement ended white minority rule in Rhodesia. The country was renamed Zimbabwe.

The Lagos Plan of Action for Continental Development was drawn up.

1981   The World Bank (Berg) Report for the Recolonization of Africa was published.

1982   AIDS (acquired immunodeficiency syndrome) was reported in Africa.

The Southern African Development Co-ordination Conference was established.

The Sahrawi Democratic African Republic (formerly Spanish Sahara) was recognized as independent by the Organization of African Unity.

1983–85 The World Bank/International Monetary Fund Structural Adjustment Programs (SAPs) began to be imposed on African countries.

1989   The ECA's African Alternative Framework–Structural Adjustment Program was published.

The Liberian Civil War began in December.

1990   Namibia became the last colony to gain independence.

1992   The United Nations intervened in Somalia to restore order. The administration of President George Bush authorized U.S. troops to enter Somalia on a humanitarian mission.

The civil war in Sierra Leone began.

1993   Eritrea became independent.

1994   Apartheid ended, and Nelson Mandela was elected president in South Africa.

Genocide occurred in Rwanda.

1999   Presidential elections were held in Nigeria and Algeria.

2000   Africans from West Africa living in Libya complained of racial discrimination by Arabs, and hundreds of them returned to their countries. The crisis had implications for continental solidarity and reopened old wounds in regional conflicts.

2001   The Africa Union was created to replace the Organization of African Unity.

PART I

The Ancient
and Precolonial Period

/

Africa: An Overview

We have mentioned very little, passing over much from fear of being lengthy and verbose. But the sensible reader will understand that beyond the stream there is the sea.

Ahmad Ibn Fartua, A.D. 1575

Africa is no vast island, separated by an immense ocean from other portions of the globe, and cut off through the ages from the men who have made and influenced the destinies of mankind. She has been closely connected, both as source and nourisher, with some of the most potent influences which have affected for good the history of the world.

Edward Wilmot Blyden, 1880

PERCEPTION AND KNOWLEDGE

The contents of this book reveal the richness of African history. Even a century ago, a book as rich as this was not possible; there were those who still believed that Africans had no history worth writing about. Indeed, the world knew little of African history at the beginning of the last century and Africans were treated as inferior people who could not have contributed to civilization. In spite of the trade relations existing between the European nations and Africa since the fifteenth century, it took a while for knowledge of its people and places to grow. Writing in the early eighteenth century, English satirist Jonathan Swift wrote a poem about the continent:

So geographers in Afric maps
With savage pictures fill the gaps
And o'r uninhabitable downs
Placed elephants for lack of towns.[1]

A century later, Africa was still regarded as a "dark continent." And even today, there are many Americans who cannot locate many African countries on a map. Most modern maps actually show Africa as smaller than it is. Thus, Greenland, which is smaller than the African countries of Sudan and the Democratic Republic of the Congo (formerly Zaire), appears bigger on most maps than the entire African continent. Areas far away from the equator, such as Canada, also appear much larger in many map projections. Africa is vast, and the distance between the north and south of the continent (similar to the distance between east and west) is almost 4,660 miles (7,500 kilometers). The United States of America can be fitted more than three times into this huge continent. Africa is the second largest continent, following Asia, and its nations comprise a quarter of the membership of the United Nations.

If Western subjective opinions and racism were unkind to Africa, Western science and technology have been kinder by revealing rich sources of impressive and ancient history and civilization in Africa. The discipline of archaeology has liberated Africa from its long obscurity and revealed the records of the prehistoric period. New sources of knowledge from other disciplines contribute to the rapidly unfolding knowledge about Africa. Even the unwritten statements of African elders, previously dismissed, are now understood to be rich libraries with information of limitless value.

GEOGRAPHY AND PEOPLE

Africa is diverse in its geography and people. An extensive rain forest, a huge savanna, the largest desert in the world, and many mountains and rivers are among the notable features of a diverse landscape. The continent is divided by the equator, with much of it falling into the tropical zone. Africa looks like a giant plateau, broken up by hills, lakes, and rivers. The plateau can be as low as 1,600 feet above sea level in many areas but is close to 4,000 feet in the east and south. The continent faces the Antarctic in the south and the Mediterranean Sea in the north. The coastline has few peninsulas or navigable inlets, which limited the development of navigation for a long time.

There are five major climate zones: Mediterranean, desert, savanna, forest, and highland. The northern part of Africa lies along the southern coast of the Mediterranean Sea, a narrow coastal strip with a climate similar to that of southern Europe. In the northwest corner is the area known to the Arabs as the Maghrib (that is, the west), home to the Berbers and now containing the countries of Morocco, Algeria, and Tunisia. In the northeast is the River Nile, Africa's longest river, with two sources in the south—the Blue Nile starts in the highlands of Ethiopia,

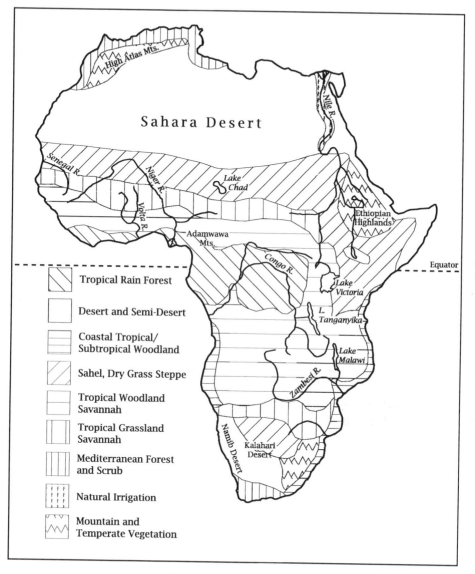

Topography of Africa.

and the White Nile in the lake region of East Africa. The rains in both source areas cause the Nile to overflow its banks each year, depositing rich mud carried down from the Ethiopian Highlands. The narrow strip of land along its banks is so rich that it is able to support a dense population.

South of the Mediterranean coastal area is the Sahara Desert, the world's most extensive desert, larger in size than Europe, and occupying almost a quarter of the surface of Africa itself. Initially wet in its climate, it has been a dry area for thousands of years. Except for the oases—areas with water—the desert is largely uninhabited. For centuries, the oases served as resting places for the trade caravans that connected North and West Africa. In the western and central parts of the Sahara are three mountain areas—Aïr, Hoggar, and Tibesti—that capture rain and thus support agriculture. The desert edge is called the Sahel, an Arabic word for "shore." Then come the grasslands, the savanna that stretches across Africa, known in the historical record as the Sudanic area.

South of the savanna is the forest land, which becomes tropical rain forest in some areas. With the West African forest joining that of Zaire, Africa has the largest tropical forests in the world. Jungles are few and scattered. To the south of the forest is yet another area of savanna. In the south, this savanna is interrupted by the Kalahari and Namib Deserts. At the southern tip of the continent, we have another Mediterranean-like climate, due largely to higher rainfalls.

Four large rivers have played a major role in African history—the Nile, Niger, Congo, and Zambezi. These and their tributaries flow through the interior before draining into the sea. Some of the rivers have rich silt, as in the case of the Nile, providing excellent opportunities for agriculture. Rapids and waterfalls make these rivers hard to navigate, except for short distances.

In central and southern Africa, a plateau straddles the equator. At the eastern edge of this plateau is the Great Rift Valley with very high steep sides. Below the Rift Valley are small lakes. Notable highlands in Africa include the Drakensburg Mountains in the southeast, the Atlas Mountains in the northwest, the Fouta Djallon Mountains in the west, and the Ethiopian Highlands in the northeast. Active volcanoes are found in the eastern part of central Africa and in Gabon.

THE AFRICAN HERITAGE

Africans have always shown a remarkable ability to adapt to their environment. Not only have they eked out a living from the environment; they have also created economic and political organizations based on local resources and ideas. Even people's diets are affected by where they live—if those in the forest prefer root crops such as yam and potatoes, those in the savanna choose grains such as sorghum and millet. In areas where the deserts and savannas meet, the land is very well suited to cattle herding. Here, there have always been many nomadic groups, such as the Maasai of modern Kenya.

Africans speak a variety of languages, over a thousand, mainly indigenous to them. These languages are very much connected to their cultures and identities.

A language group could constitute a nation—not a tribe, which is sometimes used in a derogatory way to mean an inferior language and people. Speakers of a language can run into millions, but there are also languages spoken by smaller numbers. The majority of the languages are old, evidence that many groups and cultures have habited the continent for centuries.

Contacts with outsiders have led to the use of additional languages, such as Arabic, and European languages, notably English, French, and Portuguese, in areas formerly colonized by European powers. In the past, a number of languages were understood over wide areas, notably Arabic, Hausa, Fulfulde, and Swahili. Since the beginning of the twentieth century, English and French have spread rapidly in many countries, thus enabling Africans who have received Western education to communicate with one another.

In spite of the variations in language and environment, Africans have a number of characteristics in common. They identify themselves with kinship groups—combinations of many nuclear families tracing descent from one ancestor—and they expect that family members will support one another. In the past, large families were common—a man could have two or more wives and many children. Children are expected to work for their parents and take care of them in old age in a situation where there are no nursing homes or insurance policies. Elders are respected, for their contribution to the progress of others and for their wisdom in resolving conflicts. Land is highly valued, not just for farming and herding but as creating a tie that holds many generations together.

Religion has always been important as well. Indigenous religious beliefs were well established before the spread of Islam and Christianity. Traditional beliefs in many areas assigned power to a number of gods and goddesses, the spirits of the ancestors, and the creator. Many Africans also believed in the power of magic and witchcraft and might attribute death or disease to curses. Many groups also believed in the idea of a God with supreme power. From their religion flowed morality, justice, and sanctions. The gods and other unseen forces would punish and reward, according to a person's actions and morality. The earthly world had its complexities and evils, but they could be controlled by magical powers and sacrifices to the gods.

The introduction of Western science, Islam, and Christianity has not destroyed many of the old religious ideas and beliefs. Even today, people still consult diviners, Islamic priests, and "medicine men" for charms to cure a variety of illnesses or merely to seek good fortune. Africans have also redefined Islam and Christianity, adapting them to their own traditional beliefs and practices. An awareness of the importance of both the family and religion is also shown in the way Africans have defined their identity. Kinship and religious traditions have combined with other beliefs to define groups and people. To retain their identity, Africans have developed a strong sense of historical consciousness. Proverbs, stories, idioms, and other verbally communicated statements are part of what we now call African oral traditions, which have enabled scholars to understand the past of Africa. The majority of African people shared the colonial experience—the imposition of European rule—which introduced many aspects of Western culture to them. However, while accepting the new changes coming from the West, they have succeeded in retaining many older values and indigenous practices.

THE REGIONS OF AFRICA

The continent can also be divided into regions—north, west, central, east, and south, each comprising different countries and characteristics. To start with the areas north of the Sahara, including areas facing the Mediterranean Sea and the delta and lower reaches of the Nile, this region was inhabited by the Berbers and ancient Egyptians. In appearance, its people look like southern Europeans, and their languages indicate connections with Arabia and Mesopotamia. In the region of the Upper Nile, people of this stock intermarried with blacks and became known as Ethiopians, meaning "people with the burnt face." Ancient Egypt, one of the earliest human civilizations, emerged here. The modern countries of North Africa include Tunisia, Egypt, Algeria, Libya, and Morocco. The Sudan may be classified as part of either North or East Africa. Although most of the countries are big, they also include desert areas that are largely uninhabited. The tendency is to live close to areas with water, the Mediterranean in the case of Tunisia, Libya, and Algeria, the Nile in the case of Egypt, and the Atlantic Ocean in the case of Morocco. The people are united by Arab-Islamic culture, which also marks them as different in many ways from the rest of the continent.

In West Africa, nomadic groups are among those living in the savanna. The forest dwellers are mainly farmers. The people of West Africa developed cities and villages and participated in long-distance trade, which brought considerable wealth. Their ability to use iron, cultivate crops, and herd animals enabled them to acquire the resources to build large settlements, increase their population, and colonize the forest. It was from West Africa that the Bantu-speaking peoples originated and subsequently migrated to settle in central, eastern, and southern Africa, acting as the pioneers that opened up the continent for human habitation and development. The Rivers Niger and Benue, gold deposits, trade contacts with North Africa through the Sahara, and other advantages enabled West Africa to develop many great kingdoms. One of the earliest was the powerful trading state of Ghana, which flourished from the eighth to the eleventh century A.D. Ghana profited from its abundant resources of gold as well as from control of the southern end of the trans-Saharan trade. The Mali and Songhay empires attained fame in the same region after the thirteenth century. To the east of Songhay were the Hausa city–states and the Kanem-Borno empire northeast of Lake Chad. In the forest region and its fringes, a host of impressive kingdoms also emerged at various periods, notably the empires of Oyo among the Yoruba, Benin among the Edo, Dahomey in the area of modern-day Benin, and Asante among the Akan. Modern West Africa comprises sixteen countries: Benin, Burkina Faso, Cape Verde, Côte d'Ivoire, Gambia, Ghana, Guinea, Guinea-Bissau, Liberia, Mauritania, Niger, Nigeria, Senegal, Sierra Leone, Western Sahara, and

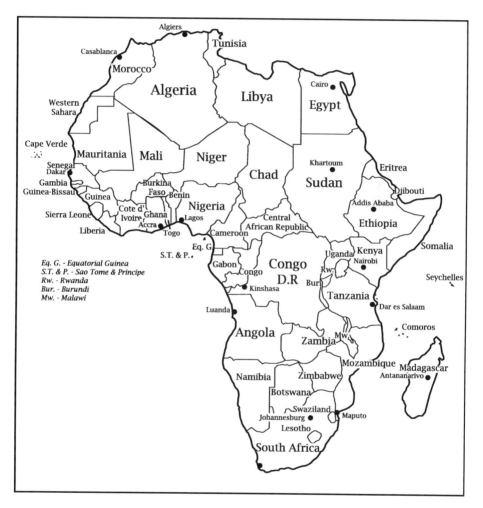

Countries making up the African continent.

Togo. Nigeria is the largest in size and population. Although some are English-speaking and others are French-speaking (while Portuguese is used in Guinea-Bissau), intraregional movements among the people have been common for centuries.

In East Africa, a strong tradition of cattle keeping has existed for centuries, thereby affecting the people's lifestyles. The region was also connected with the Indian Ocean from a very early period. Arab and Persian refugees settled along the coast and intermarried with the African population. A chain of small towns developed along the coast, from Mogadishu in modern Somalia to Sofala in modern Mozambique. It was along the coast that the Swahili culture and language developed, as a mixture of the cultures of Bantu speakers and Arabs. International commerce linked East Africa with the Arab world, India, and China, and many of the coastal cities prospered from it. In the interior, the area saw the rise and fall of such notable kingdoms as Bunyoro, Nkore, Buganda, Toro, and Busoga. Modern East Africa is made up of Kenya, Uganda, Tanzania, Sudan, Rwanda, and Burundi, the countries of the Horn of Africa (Somalia, Djibouti, Ethiopia, and Eritrea), and the islands (the Comoros, Madagascar, Mauritius, and the Seychelles). This is a highly diversified region, with long historic connections to other peoples in Africa, the Middle East, and Asia.

Central Africa also shared the history of Bantu migrations and the development of agriculture. The region is dominated by equatorial rain forests. The land is hard to clear, and the climate is hot and moist, which probably explains the low population densities in many areas. The people tend to concentrate around riverbanks. Here the complex and powerful kingdom of Kongo developed south of the Zaire River. In the interior, the Luba people also developed their own state, and other kingdoms, such as those of the Lunda and Kuba, emerged. Islam has had little influence in this region, except in northern Cameroon and Chad. Christianity and traditional beliefs are strong. The impact of the people's worldview can be seen in their wooden sculptures and other art forms that reveal the importance the people attach to spiritual forces. Today, central Africa comprises the following countries: Congo, Chad, Cameroon, the Democratic Republic of the Congo, Equatorial Guinea, Gabon, and São Tomé and Príncipe. The majority of them have long-established ties with France, and the French language is widely spoken.

To the south of the Zambezi (modern Zimbabwe) arose the empire of Mwene Mutapa, famous for building the Great Zimbabwe stone buildings. As in other parts of Africa, both internal and external trade were extensive. The modern countries of southern Africa include Angola, Botswana, Lesotho, Malawi, Mozambique, Namibia, South Africa, Swaziland, Zambia, and Zimbabwe. The region suffered a great deal from European domination, and many of the worst cases of racial discrimination occurred here.

HISTORICAL PHASES

Africa is an ancient continent, with a long history. Archaeologists have concluded that it is the original home of humankind. Evidence of human evolution

The Zimbabwe ruins.

makes it possible to reach some conclusions about the characteristics of the prehistoric period of 40,000 years ago. Great changes followed in the development
of stone tools. As early as 5000 B.C., Africans were able to farm and domesticate
animals. Some 4,000 years later, the continent entered an Iron Age, enabling societies to grow and states to emerge. Trade expanded, generating wealth for
members of the political class. Through a series of migrations that lasted hundreds of years, Africa south of the Sahara was dominated by Bantu speakers who
introduced iron and agriculture to various places. The economy and politics also
grew in scale and scope.

At various times in history hundreds of states and peoples emerged, with different adaptations to their environments, languages, and economic lifestyles. If
some groups survived for long periods as hunters and gatherers (such as the San
of southern Africa), many others took to farming, and others chose a life of no-
madism. Many towns and villages emerged, many of which were combined into
large kingdoms. And there were also groups, such as the Dinka and Nuer, who
did not live in such kingdoms but in political systems based on family bonds and
the authority of elders.

Civilization had emerged in the ancient period. The kingdoms of Egypt and Kush antedated the Christian era. The Nile valley was able to support agriculture and a dense population, both of which contributed to the emergence of Ancient Egypt. By 3100 B.C., this powerful state was able to control the use of water and land and to tax the farmers who made use of both. A centralized administration, headed by a powerful king, the pharaoh, was able to manage revenues, promote arts and culture, and trade with other areas. Egypt was a leading world power in ancient times. Egypt itself was to be conquered by other powers—the Assyrians, Persians, Greeks, Romans, and Arabs. Since the Arab conquest in A.D. 640, Islam has remained the principal religion in Egypt.

On the Upper Nile, another civilization emerged, borrowing from Egyptian culture but developing local traditions. This was the kingdom of Kush, with its famous capital at Meroë, which had become powerful by the seventh century B.C. After Kush declined, another kingdom—Aksum—became famous by the fourth century A.D. Aksum successfully established the foundation of the Ethiopian empire.

In the Maghrib, home to the Berbers, those who lived in fertile areas around the mountains were agriculturalists, and those in the desert and desert fringes were nomads. Along the coast, agriculture was more intensive, and big cities developed. The Phoenicians were establishing trading stations along the North African coast as early as 1000 B.C. The early stations grew into independent settlements by 800 B.C. Carthage, one of these colonies, located in the area of modern Tunisia, was established in about 614 B.C. and later developed into a powerful empire. The Carthaginians contributed to the spread of the use of iron, the development of agriculture, and the expansion of trade along the North African coast. By 600 B.C., Carthage had become the wealthiest city in the western Mediterranean. Wealthy merchant families dominated politics, and an urban culture emerged. As with most other empires on the continent, a period of decline later set in. In the case of Carthage, the resistance of the Berbers, the indigenous population, as well as an attack by the Romans brought the empire to an end.

Carthage struggled with the Greeks for control of southern Spain and Sicily but was ultimately incorporated into the Roman Empire in 146 B.C. The region prospered from agriculture and trade, and Christianity spread to some areas. The era of Roman rule was ended in A.D. 429 by the Vandals, whose kingdom was in turn destroyed in A.D. 534 by the Byzantine Empire. In A.D. 670, the Arabs began a series of difficult military campaigns that ended in their political conquest in A.D. 709. A cultural revolution followed, as the region became Islamized and Arabized. As noted above, many other kingdoms were established in different parts of the continent, such as Ghana, Mali, Songhay, Kongo, and Great Zimbabwe.

Contacts with outsiders shaped some aspects of the history of the continent. Before the seventh century A.D., notable contacts, mainly with North Africa, were established by the Phoenicians, Greeks, and Romans. These contacts enabled the spread of ideas and technology and the promotion of trade. From the point of view of contemporary history, the two most enduring contacts were those made by the Arab Muslims and the Europeans. After the seventh century, the Arabs introduced Islam to North Africa, and through various agencies and jihads, the religion spread to other parts of Africa. This brought many changes, such as the spread of the Islamic religion, Islamic education, the Arabic language and literacy, ideas about political centralization, and various aspects of culture such as the wearing of the turban. The Arabs conquered Egypt in A.D. 640, and ever since the country has been predominantly Islamic. Islamic laws took deep root, and Arabic became the national language. From Egypt, Islam spread up the Nile to the Funj sultanate in the northern part of modern Sudan. West of Egypt, Islam gained dominance in North Africa, from where it traveled through trans-Saharan trade to West Africa. Islam reached East Africa through the activities of Arab refugees and traders living in the coastal city–states.

Christianity is the second major religion on the continent. Its spread actually predated the rise of Islam, although it was only able to reach a small part of the continent before the nineteenth century. Christianity spread in North and northeast Africa during Roman rule, but the Arab conquest halted its growth, and Islam was able to displace Christianity, except in Ethiopia.

Other changes came from association with the West. These contacts began during the fifteenth century but were restricted for many years to the coastal areas. The Portuguese were the earliest to reach sub-Saharan Africa, motivated by a combination of religious, political, and economic reasons. The Portuguese were seeking a route to the gold-producing region of West Africa that would avoid areas controlled by their Muslim enemies in North Africa and the Sahara Desert. The Portuguese believed that the Muslims could be attacked from the rear if the Portuguese discovered a legendary Christian king, the so-called Prester John, who would be a valuable ally. If they were able to convert Africans to Christianity, they hoped that this would boost their trade and military strength. In 1482 their voyages led them to West Africa, where they established a fort, São Jorge da Mina (now Elmina Castle), where they were able to trade in gold. Later, they established contacts with the Benin empire and colonized the islands of São Tomé and Príncipe. The quest to spread Christianity collapsed, and they diverted their full attention to trade. In due course, this trade was dominated by slaves. In Angola, the Portuguese established a permanent base after 1571, from which slaves were exported to Brazil. The Portuguese traveled further south, reaching the Cape of Good Hope and later East Africa. Their attacks on the Swahili city–states destroyed the prosperity of these states. The Portuguese established permanent settlements in Angola and Mozambique, introduced new crops to Africa (e.g., cassava, maize, peanuts, and tobacco), and promoted an extensive trade in human beings. Other European countries joined the Portuguese in the lucrative slave trade: the British, Dutch, Danes, Spanish, Swedes, and French. The slave trade contributed to the underdevelopment of Africa.

Great changes occurred in Africa during the nineteenth century. The slave trade was abolished and replaced by a trade in raw materials. More European traders came to the continent, driven by the desire for profit. Missionaries of different denominations flocked to Africa to spread Christianity. Western education began to spread with the new religion. A number of European traders and missionaries began to urge their governments to play a more direct role in African affairs. Gradually, Europeans began to move from the coast to the hinterland. By the 1880s, the European nations were competing in the great Scramble for Africa. Colonial rule was established in many areas after 1885. This brought many changes, such as the creation of the African countries as we know them today, the establishment of Western schools and hospitals, the expansion of cities, and the creation of an economy that was solely dependent on exports.

During the twentieth century, African countries struggled for independence and won it at different times. For instance, in 1960, seventeen African countries obtained their independence, and the continent moved into the postcolonial era. Africans inherited power, the flags and anthems were changed, and a new era began. The first generation of African leaders made sweeping promises to their people—talking as idealists rather than pragmatists, they anticipated immediate positive changes for their people and an important role for their countries and continent in global politics. Modern Africa has witnessed changes in many areas. People move from one place to another, creating cities with larger populations and greater needs. New institutions and occupations have been created in response to modernization. Since their independence, the countries have had to face the problems of overcoming economic underdevelopment and building strong and independent nation–states.

CONTEMPORARY CHALLENGES

Africa entered the twenty-first century in miserable conditions. Independence failed to lead to economic empowerment and political stability but led instead to intense struggles for survival and growing poverty among the majority of the people. As unpleasant to Africans as it may be, the Western media carry stories of failures rather than of successes, with the theme of a continent in a permanent state of crisis.

Most of Africa's crises relate to economic underdevelopment. Poverty is pervasive, as millions of people find it almost impossible to obtain basic human needs, including nutritious food and clean water. Although it was a continent self-sufficient in food production for centuries, Africa now has countries that are dependent on external food aid. Healthy people underpin the economies that grow—but here, too, there is a problem with the failure to find answers to the old diseases of malaria and cholera and the newer AIDS (acquired immunodeficiency syndrome). The environment is being degraded by excessive tree felling, increasing desertification, and drought. External debts keep mounting and now amount to well over $200 billion. The annual economic growth rate, the lowest in the world, is 1.5 percent, well below the annual population growth rate.

Many other problems involve political instability and struggles for power. A tiny minority, members of the political class and the military, have taken to politics primarily to enrich themselves. There are too many authoritarian leaders who misgovern their countries. Elections are hard to conduct, and opposition forces tend to be treated as enemies. It is not that Africans are hard to govern—indeed, they are resilient and tolerant. The problems lie squarely with the political leaders who manipulate the divisions in society for personal interest. Many countries have experienced wars, leading to the deaths of over 2 million people, the creation of millions of refugees, and the ruination of economies.

The continent has tried most of the commonly used political models and types of government with limited positive results. An American-style presidential system was tried in Nigeria between 1979 and 1983, but it ended in a military coup. The one-party state is common, but it does not put an end to the bitter struggles for power. Military regimes have dominated many countries, but they have only succeeded in destroying political and economic institutions. In recent years, so-called democratic parties are emerging, even when elections are conducted in a manner that does not generate public confidence.

The problems have unleashed an endless search for solutions, secular and religious. Various economic ideologies—capitalism, socialism, African socialism, African communism—have been tried without much success. In terms of religion, the search for salvation does not concern just the unseen spiritual world but also the overcoming of poverty, disease, and emotional problems. Islam, Christianity, and indigenous religions are all represented in the faith-driven answers to problems. In terms of secular ideologies, socialism was tried and abandoned, but capitalism is yet to deliver.

Africa is a continent on the move. The failure of the last four decades has not destroyed the people and their hopes for a greater future. Change is a common feature of life and history. People continue to press for democracy. Impressive

Modern post office. Part of the landscape in modern cities.

success has been recorded since the 1990s, with the rise of multiparty systems and the holding of elections in various places, including Nigeria, Ghana, South Africa, Benin, Cape Verde, São Tomé and Príncipe, Zambia, Madagascar, Mali, the Central African Republic, Niger, and Malawi. A sharing of power between the established ruling classes and the opposition forces has occurred in a number of places. Military regimes still exist in a number of countries, but they are unpopular. Since the end of the Cold War, countries outside Africa no longer need to support bad leaders for ideological reasons. Energies are now being channeled to privatization of enterprises, in the hope that individuals will manage them better than governments. Religious and nongovernmental organizations within and outside Africa are calling on Western countries and lending institutions to write off the bulk of Africa's debt so that its people will have greater resources to alleviate poverty.

The expectations of most Africans are clear enough: They want sustainable development and stable politics that will increase their standards of living. The conditions to realize this goal are present. Millions of women are active and industrious, the youthful population is high, the sense of communal identity and the support networks have not been completely destroyed, natural endowments are abundant, and the number of educated people continues to grow. In addition, the African market is large and expanding, wars between countries are rare, life expectancy is increasing in many countries, and the majority of Africans want democracy to thrive. Effective and committed leadership should be able to fully exploit all these advantages and solve many of the continent's lingering economic and political problems.

NOTE

1. Quoted in Robert Stock, *Africa South of the Sahara: A Geographical Interpretation* (New York: The Guilford Press, 1995), p. 13.

SUGGESTIONS FOR FURTHER READING

Ajayi, J.F. Ade, and Michael Crowder, eds. *Historical Atlas of Africa*. London: Longman, 1985.

Curtin, P.S., L. Feierman, L. Thompson, and J. Vansina. *African History*. 2nd ed. New York: Longman, 1995.

Davidson, Basil. *African Civilization Revisited*. 4th printing. Trenton, N.J.: Africa World Press, 1998.

Fage, J.D. *A History of Africa*. 3rd ed. London: Routledge, 1995.

Falola, Toyin, ed. *Africa*. 5 vols. Durham, N.C.: Carolina Academic Press, 2000–2002.

Griffiths, Ieuan L.L. *An Atlas of African Affairs*. London: Methuen and Co., 1984.

Harris, J.E. *Africans and Their History*. 2nd ed. New York: Penguin, 1998.

July, Robert W. *A History of the African People*. 4th ed. Prospect Heights, Ill.: Waveland Press, 1992.

McCarthy, Michael. *Dark Continent: Africa as Seen by Americans*. Westport, Conn.: Greenwood Press, 1983.

McEvedy, Colin. *The Penguin Atlas of African History*. New York: Penguin, 1995.

Morrison, Donald G., Robert C. Mitchell, and John N. Paden. *Black Africa: A Comparative Handbook*. 2nd ed. New York: Paragon House, 1989.

Newman, James L. *The Africans: A Triple Heritage*. Boston: Little, Brown, 1986.

Ramsay, F. Jeffress. *Africa*. 6th ed. Guilford, Conn.: Dushkin Publishing/Brown & Benchmark Publishers, 1995.

UNESCO General History of Africa. Vols. 1–8. Berkeley: University of California Press, 1981–92.

1

The Prehistoric Past:
The Evolution of *Homo sapiens sapiens*, 40,000 B.C.

The consensus of opinion is that human beings evolved in Africa and migrated to other parts of the world. This idea was expressed as early as 1859 by Charles Darwin in *The Origin of Species* and reaffirmed by him in 1871 in *The Descent of Man*. Darwin was ignored by those who held to biblical origin stories, whereas those who regarded Europeans as racially superior to others could not accept that their own ancestors had an African origin.

Science, especially archaeology, and linguistic research have come to validate the view that Africa is the birthplace of humankind. The examination of ancient objects of stone and bone as well as many other artifacts and fossils from various parts of the continent have shed light on human evolution. The sequence of events can be determined by stratigraphy—the idea that objects found below layers of earth are older than those above. A dating technique, radiocarbon dating (carbon-14), has also made it possible to provide an approximate age for a variety of organic materials, such as charcoal and bones, that are as much as 50,000 years old. The more recent technique involving mitochondrial DNA (deoxyribonucleic acid)—the analysis of the genetic material in a cell that is passed unchanged from a mother to her child—has also confirmed the archaeological evidence that modern humans originated in Africa and began to move elsewhere about 150,000 years ago. This chapter traces human evolution, with the emphasis on *Homo sapiens sapiens* who emerged about 40,000 years ago.

Africa is an ancient continent, one of the oldest. It contributed to the prehistoric development of humankind. The history of *Homo sapiens sapiens* and those before them shows how humans emerged and developed the first tools and technology, how they lived in a difficult environment, and how they survived on gathering, fishing, and hunting. This is a long history during which people and the objects they valued both emerged, a time when variations in climate, skin color, way of life, and beliefs began to occur in various parts of Africa and the rest of the world. The success of these people in taming the huge and difficult continent of Africa is an integral aspect of world history.

Homo sapiens sapiens ("modern man" or "thinking thinking man") was a stage in the development of "hominids"—primates who had enlarged brains and the capacity to walk on two legs. How the earliest hominids evolved over 3 million years ago is still a subject of great speculation. There are archaeological records of the earliest humans in East and southern Africa, including hominids that could stand and walk on two legs. These two-legged beings could use their hands to protect themselves, use simple tools, and carry a few items. Their fingers, too, became elongated, thus giving them an advantage in making tools.

The first clues to what the early hominids looked like, and which of them are connected to "modern man," are derived from many skeletons found in eastern and southern Africa. When the first one was discovered in 1925, it was given the name *Australopithecus* (the "southern ape"). A major find was also discovered in 1974 in Ethiopia, the remains of a young female, now known as "Lucy" in archaeological circles. Not more than the size of an eight-year-old child, *Australopithecus* was slender and walked on two legs. In appearance, such beings were like apes; in behavior, like human beings. Lucy was able to walk upright, a major progress in human development that made it possible to free the hands to make tools.

About 100,000 years ago, the modern human (*Homo sapiens*) began to displace the archaic hominids. Even if some anatomical features of the previous hominids were retained, the emphasis now shifted to cultural and intellectual changes, such as the ability to use tools and live in groups.

THE FAMILY *HOMO* (MAN)

Hominid skulls found in Tanzania and Ethiopia reveal those with better brain capacity than *Australopithecus*. A generation of hominids known as *Homo habilis* ("handy man" or "clever man") emerged 1.5 million years ago. *Homo habilis* had larger brains than the Australopithecines and a greater ability to use simple stone tools. *Homo habilis* was followed by *Homo erectus* ("upright man"), with a brain capacity of 1,100 cubic centimeters (67.1 cubic inches) and a more erect posture. *Homo erectus* lived over a million years ago, mainly in savanna environments and close to water, and they used stone tools known as "hand axes," found in various parts of the world. *Homo sapiens* ("wise man") has been described as the early form of modern man. *Homo sapiens* evolved over 100,000 years ago, reaching a brain capacity of 1,300 to 1,400 cubic centimeters

(79.3 to 85.4 cubic inches). What is regarded as the final evolution is *Homo sapiens sapiens*, "modern man," which forms the main subject of this chapter.

Homo sapiens sapiens appeared by 40,000 B.C., with a brain capacity of almost 1,450 cubic centimeters (88.4 cubic inches). By 10,000 B.C., these beings could be found in all the major regions of the world. What did they look like? What did they do for a living? What was their stage of technology? Do specific examples of people actually exist that demonstrate some of the features of this early history? Archaeology has provided significant answers to some of these questions. As more discoveries unfold, the answers will be modified or affirmed in future years.

Homo sapiens sapiens looked similar to many modern-day Africans but was originally brown-skinned. The change in color was a process of adaptation to the environment and changing climate. In Africa with its tropical sun, *Homo sapiens sapiens* developed a dark coloration as a protection from the powerful rays of the sun. In cooler climates, skins tended to become paler in order to absorb more rays.

Technology in the early years was dependent on stone. If animals like the chimpanzees could use implements to search for food, only *Homo* could make tools, shape them to their desired needs, and use the tools to forage and hunt. *Homo sapiens sapiens* and its immediate predecessors belonged to a Stone Age era that endured till 6,000 years ago when metals were discovered in some parts of the world, notably western Asia and Sinai. Even then, the use of stone survived. Our early history and that of the entire *Homo* line are very much tied to the use of stone tools.

"STONE AGE" TECHNOLOGY

Stone tool technology evolved over time, reaching sophistication with *Homo sapiens sapiens*. There were three stages in the development of stone technology and culture: the Early Stone Age, or the Paleolithic; the Middle Stone Age, or the Mesolithic; and the Later Stone Age, or the Neolithic. The earliest stone tools are the Oldowan, basic cutting and chopping tools associated with the Early Stone Age. Flakes were chipped off a volcanic pebble to create sharp edges. The flakes were not refined but served the useful purposes of scraping skins, whittling sticks, and cutting various objects. These early tools were inefficient for hunting but seem well adapted to a scavenging lifestyle.

"Acheulian" tools followed, the second major development in the Early Stone Age, mainly scrapers and axes cut to desired shapes for digging, chopping, or slicing. The hand ax was a rugged tool, heavy to carry, chipped on two sides, and having a sharp point. In all the regions where hand axes have been discovered, they reveal similarities and clearly show that long hours must have been spent to make them. The toolmakers lived in camps, engaged in some cooperative enterprises, buried their dead, and used fire to roast animals and warm themselves.

The march of civilization advanced to the Middle Stone Age about 150,000 years ago, with *Homo sapiens'* ability to use bone tools in addition to stones. The stone tools improved in design, and they became more precise. Regional variations and styles began to appear, as we have evidence of well-cut stone tools that looked like knives and scrapers. In southern Africa where some evidence dates as far back as 200,000 years ago, some stone tools show that the makers carefully selected the stones and made tools with a great deal of ingenuity. The *Homo sapiens* of the Middle Stone Age lived in caves or built shelters of stones and tree branches, used fire, organized camps, hunted, and socialized.

The most advanced era came with the Later Stone Age, the period of *Homo sapiens sapiens* 40,000 years ago. The stone tools reached their most impressive level of sophistication, most notably in the development of microliths, that is, "tiny stones." The edges were sharp, so the tools were efficient. Their shapes, crescents and triangles, reveal an early understanding of geometry. The handles were stronger, and some stone tools were connected to wooden shafts to make powerful arrows and spears. A greater use of bows and arrows was made for hunting purposes. Creative uses were made of bone materials, for such tools as barbs for harpoons, awls, needles, and fishhooks.

THE LIFESTYLES OF *HOMO SAPIENS SAPIENS*

These beings were both versatile and creative. They made use of inherited stone tools and added various new tools and styles. They lived and worked in a highly imaginative manner. They invented bows and arrows and improved hunting techniques. They created art works, making use of various materials, including egg shells, to draw, paint, adorn the body, and engrave walls. Tools were beautified. The dead were buried with respect, and there were even cases of ritual performance. Paintings and engravings decorated rocks and shelters, revealing an interest in art and the activities that dominated the time. In areas where some of the paintings and engravings have survived, we find a preference for yellow, orange, white, and red. Paints were made from animal fats and vegetable dyes, and they were applied to rock and other objects with feathers and sticks. These paintings were both natural and abstract. The abstract paintings derived inspiration from the environment, from beliefs about life and death and rituals. Other paintings portrayed animals and people and events such as dancing, hunting, and fishing.

The people were able to adapt to their environments, leading to the development of regional variations in tools and lifestyles. As shown below, their occupations were dependent on their immediate environment, but they showed creativity in producing the resources to sustain themselves and multiply.

Many of them lived in camps. The camps could be seasonal, in cases where it was necessary to migrate. Overhanging rocks and caves provided shelter, and windbreaks could also be made from grass, branches, and stones. Many shelters were conical in shape, held together by sticks and covered with grass thatch. For food, they relied on wild fruits, seeds, nuts, insects, and dead animals.

As the camp sites were small, families or groups also tended to be small in size. Evidence suggests that small bands of twenty people could occupy an area in dry zones, while the size tended to double in wetter areas that had more food and game. As to the size of the entire African population, we will never know the precise figure, but some estimates put it at 200,000 about 40,000 years ago. This was a large number in view of the limited access to food, the difficulty of reproduction, and the fragility of people and their shelters. Nevertheless, so creative were the people that they overcame severe limitations, and their population grew to about 3 million around 3,000 years ago. They learned how to hunt, cooperate, and communicate, all activities that ultimately led to the ability to use language. Many languages separated from the original ones, and it is clear that many languages in Africa are indeed ancient. As the population of *Homo sapiens sapiens* increased and as they dispersed to various places and different ecological regions, so too cultural variations began to show. By about 3,000 years ago, at least thirty-seven distinct languages had arisen in Africa.

The social organization was rather loose, based largely on family units. Members of different families interacted and intermarried. The need for survival was paramount—to obtain food and protect themselves from powerful animals. The people probably practiced a division of labor between men and women, but status distinctions were apparently less marked. Rather, we have evidence of cooperative labor among the people—they looked for food and shared it in small groups. Individuals needed the group to be able to survive, thereby engendering a community based on interdependence and the ability to cooperate. The barriers imposed by ecology and the problems of disease created the conditions that bonded people into groups.

Possibilities for conflicts also existed. Competition for camps, food, and materials to make tools could lead to the need to create safety and security networks. One group might seek the means to protect itself against another or even simply to dominate in order to ensure its own survival. As the population grew, the awareness of "frontiers" and "boundaries"—between groups and communities— probably led to conflicts.

MAJOR OCCUPATIONS OF *HOMO SAPIENS SAPIENS*

Three occupations dominated the society: gathering, hunting, and fishing. Thus, most members of *Homo sapiens sapiens* have been described as hunter–gatherers and fishermen/women. Africans and others at this stage of civilization were still unable to tame animals or to grow food crops and store them. Instead, they relied on gathering wild plants and animals, hunting those animals that their tools could kill. Between 40,000 and 10,000 years ago, the skills of hunting, fishing, and gathering grew to a high level of efficiency.

Archaeological evidence derived from various locations in Africa and observation of the hunting and gathering tradition among the Khoisan-speaking people of the Kalahari in modern-day Botswana have revealed important information about early occupations and interactions with the environment.

Gathering was the most important occupation, since over one-third of the food needed for survival was obtained by wandering about collecting a variety of fruits, nuts, melons, roots, and tubers. Insects were delicacies, notably termites, caterpillars, and locusts. It appeared that more women engaged in gathering than men, although both sexes used similar methods: They dug with sticks and put the contents in small bags.

As difficult and backbreaking as gathering might be, and as unromantic as it appears to us today, it had great merits as an economic enterprise and lifestyle. Gathering ensured survival, as the best available way to obtain food. Without the ability to grow crops, and given the difficulties associated with hunting, gathering was the most reliable method. Adults and children, women and men, indeed the majority of people in society, could take part in gathering without putting their lives at risk. Unlike hunting, where one could work for days without a major success, gathering offered assured opportunities of food. By simply following the seasons, the gatherers could always obtain fruits, tubers, and roots. A pattern emerged in which the gatherers could move from one location to another, knowing ahead of time what was available.

Fishing communities evolved in areas close to lakes, seas, and rivers. Shellfish could be collected on banks and coasts. When fishhooks and other tools were invented, *Homo sapiens sapiens* could catch fish in large quantities without any risk to life. They could also kill stranded seals. Fish is rich in protein and probably contributed to improved nutrition and population growth.

Fishing created distinct communities based around rivers and lakes. Even the southern reaches of the Sahara, which are now dry, used to be favorable to fishing. *Homo sapiens sapiens* developed fishing equipment and technology, including nets, bone-tipped harpoons, and tidal traps. Harpoon barbs and fishhooks were made from bone, and baskets and nets from reeds. Baked-clay pottery was made in its earliest forms in an industry that became widespread in many parts of the continent.

The evidence of pottery has led to the suggestion that settled communities were emerging, even if they were small in size. Food must be available to allow for time to make clay pots. Pots enabled the storage of water, food, and other necessities. In addition, pottery allowed people to carry items including cooked food and water. Since pottery is heavy and bulky, and thereby inconvenient for gatherers who survived by moving from place to place, the making of pottery tends to suggest that the people were staying in one place for a much longer period than before. When the long time needed to make and dry pottery is considered, it is additional evidence that *Homo sapiens sapiens* could consider the advantages of creating some semipermanent settlements. Fishing and pottery instigated both technology and settlement.

Vivid and dramatic evidence provides information on yet another important occupation: hunting. Stone artifacts, animal bones, arrows, and bows all show that animals were hunted on a regular basis. Multibarbed spears, arrows, and bows were invented to kill small and large animals. Indeed, small bands of hunters were able to pursue buffalo and antelope and to share their harvests in a communal way. In the tropical forest where arrows and bows were less effective, the people used traps, axes, pits, and spears to hunt game. Catching small animals such as rats and snakes relied on nets, snares, and traps. Poison was obtained from plants and insects and pasted on arrow heads.

Hunting supplied food of high quality. Animal protein supplemented the vegetables derived from gathering. But there was more to hunting than food. Animal skins provided the raw material for clothes, bags, slings, leather thongs, shelter, and a variety of other needs. Bones were used for tools and ornaments. Hunting bands were social and community organizations that enabled people to interact and to practice leadership. Indeed, oral stories in many African villages and towns associate the foundation of settlements with the bravery and leadership of hunters. Hunters were also associated with rituals and magical powers.

The tools that *Homo sapiens sapiens* relied on were made of natural materials, stone and bone. Survival was dependent on the natural growth of animals and plants. For their shelters, people relied on caves, trees, and overhanging hills. As people's needs and knowledge grew, they created specialized chipped stones, bows and arrows, nets, harpoons, fishhooks, and fish spears. Observation of the environment contributed to the development of religion, art, and identity. Prehistoric people were able to develop culture—they painted on cave walls, carved figures out of stone and bone, and had ideas about nature as reflected in their artwork. The role that the environment played during that time continued in later periods. Human progress in Africa, population increase, and urbanization have been partly dependent on the environment.

As on other continents, Africa has witnessed major environmental changes in the last 20,000 years. The Sahara Desert used to be green—it saw its last wet period in about 9000 to 3000 B.C. The dry period that followed created the largest desert on the continent. Lake Chad was bigger than it is today, probably overflowing as far south as the Atlantic Ocean. Rivers from the Sahara flowed into the lake. In East Africa, Lake Turkana was connected with the Nile, and Lake Nakuru overflowed into the Great Rift Valley. In the Christian era, the environment began to acquire many of the characteristics that we now associate with Africa. *Homo sapiens sapiens* and associated social organizations survived. Not only did humans multiply; they advanced in their technologies and developed agriculture and states (see Chapters 3 and 4).

SUGGESTIONS FOR FURTHER READING

Bahn, Paul G., ed. *Cambridge Illustrated History of Archaeology*. Cambridge: Cambridge University Press, 1996.

Clark, J.D. *The Prehistory of Africa*. New York: Praeger, 1970.

Connah, Graham. *African Civilizations*. Cambridge: Cambridge University Press, 1993.

Fagan, Brian. *People of the Earth: An Introduction to World History*. Boston: Little, Brown, 1983.

Falola, Toyin, ed. *Africa*, Vol. 1, *African History before 1885*. Durham, N.C.: Carolina Academic Press, 2000. Chapter 3.

Leakey, R., and R. Lewin. *Origins: What New Discoveries Reveal about the Emergence of Our Species and Its Possible Future.* New York: Dutton, 1977.

Phillipson, D.W. *African Archaeology.* New York: Cambridge University Press, 1985.

Schmidt, Peter R. *Historical Archaeology: A Structural Approach in African Culture.* Westport, Conn.: Greenwood Press, 1978.

Wenke, Robert J. *Patterns in Prehistory. Humankind's First Three Million Years.* 4th ed. New York: Oxford University Press, 1999.

Wilson, A. *Origins Reconsidered.* New York: Little, Brown, 1992.

2

The Agricultural Revolution, 5000 B.C.+

It was not only human beings that evolved in Africa. Goods, objects, and tools developed there as well. Africa also provides evidence of how early people struggled to control their environments, moving beyond a gathering economy to domesticate and herd animals and cultivate food crops. The Agricultural Revolution—the transition from food gathering to food production—was one of the most profound innovations in world history. The shift from gathering to farming and pastoralism occurred during the Neolithic era (the Later Stone Age).

Agriculture created the basis for what can be called the beginning of civilization. Humans could live in settlements, domesticate animals, cultivate plants, and develop ideas about political institutions. Associated with the development of agriculture were a greater knowledge of the environment, the use of more efficient tools, even when they were originally made of stone, and the formation of religious ideas shaped by nature.

In Africa, the move toward an Agricultural Revolution occurred about 5,000 years ago, toward the end of the Later Stone Age. Three major characteristics defined this revolution. First, plants and animals were domesticated. The ability to domesticate animals led to pastoralism, a dependence on animals as sources of food, notably milk and meat. Second, the revolution entailed the use of improved tools and led to the shift from stone to metal. Third, society was transformed in many ways: The increased availability of food instigated a population increase; camp dwellers began to live in villages, complex societies that had to be managed; and division of labor allowed many people to devote themselves to agriculture and other occupations.

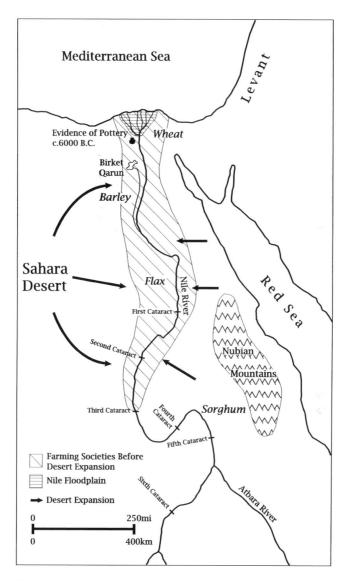

Cultivation of the Nile floodplain.

THE EARLY HISTORY OF FARMING

The Agricultural Revolution occurred in five major culture hearths in Africa: the Nile valley, the Ethiopian Plateau, the forest-savanna boundary in west-central Africa, the West African savanna, and the West African forest. Each region produced methods of cultivation and cultivated crops suitable to its environment. From these five areas, the ideas of farming and pastoralism spread to other parts of the continent. Migrations facilitated the spread of agriculture, especially the series of Bantu migrations from West Africa to central and southern Africa (see Chapter 4).

The speculation has been that "cereals" were the first plants to be cultivated. Wild sorghum and millets in the savanna and wheat and barley in the northeast were originally obtained through gathering activities. The need to protect them in areas where they grew well probably led to collecting their seeds and scattering them in arable land. To help the new crops survive, hoeing and plowing were done to remove weeds, and deliberate efforts were made to protect the stronger plants and their seeds. With respect to animal domestication, the need arose to protect the weaker animals from predators and to put animals to effective use in a variety of ways. Cattle, sheep, and goats were to become the three major types of domestic animals.

Evidence of early agriculture has been found in the Nile valley. Some strains of wild barley were tended in Egypt and Nubia by 10,000 B.C. By 6000 B.C., types of millet and sorghum that were indigenous to Africa were cultivated and harvested on the Upper Nile. Changing climatic conditions in some parts of Africa led to a drier environment, the Sahara Desert spread, and the people in the northeast had to depend on the Nile River. The exploitation of the Nile transformed farming into a full-time occupation and led to the establishment of permanent settlements by 5000 B.C. In the Nile valley, the Egyptians recorded spectacular success in exploiting the seasonal flooding of the river to irrigate their fields. From here and from western Asia, the cultivation of wheat and barley spread in North Africa, notably along the Mediterranean margins.

The cultivation of African crops also developed and grew in the savanna grasslands, south of the Sahara Desert. A number of key objects have been discovered: baked-clay pottery used for cooking and storing water, sickle blades made of stone and used to harvest grasses, grinding stones used to produce flour, and a few plants and seeds. The cultivation of cereals spread gradually after 4000 B.C. The desert spread, the margins of Lakes Chad and Turkana retreated, and river flows also declined. Previous reliance on fishing and gathering had to either give way or be supplemented with cultivation for the population to survive. From around 3000 to 1000 B.C., "Neolithic" farming spread in the savanna from the Upper Nile in the east to Senegambia in the west. Sorghums and millets were the major crops—guinea sorghum in areas west of Lake Chad, bicolar sorghum to the east, and drought-resistant pearl millet in areas close to the Sahara. Rice was grown in the forest areas of Guinea, Côte d'Ivoire, and Liberia and in the wetlands of the Upper Niger delta.

Neolithic farming also developed in the tropical forest, but rather than involving cereals, it involved the planting of root crops and the harvesting of trees. Yam, a tuber, and oil-producing trees were important in the forest zone between Côte d'Ivoire and Cameroon. Archaeological evidence from Cameroon shows that Stone Age farming existed there by 1000 B.C., with people growing and/or harvesting yams, fruits, and palm nuts. In addition, they kept goats and made pottery. Archaeologists have also concluded that it was from the Cameroon regions that the Bantu-speaking peoples spread out to the south and east of Africa, seeking out new areas in the forest to develop. By 1000 B.C. when farming was well established in different parts of the forest region, the production of bananas and root crops was becoming increasingly specialized.

A distinctive practice emerged in eastern Africa, in the Ethiopian Highlands where three crops were grown: *enset*, with bananalike fibrous stalks; *noog*, a species of oil plant; and *tef*, a small-seeded cereal that has survived till today. Among the people of northern Kenya and Uganda, the preference was for pastoralism, although they, too, cultivated millets. Farming experienced a late development in areas south of the equator, almost waiting for the introduction of iron 2,000 years ago.

THE EARLY HISTORY OF PASTORALISM

Pastoralism was being practiced in the East African savanna by 5000 B.C. The bones of domesticated cattle have been recovered in the Great Rift Valley and the Serengeti plains. By 2000 B.C., cattle herding had become an established occupation from the Serengeti to eastern Turkana. Cattle herders interacted with hunter–gatherers and probably exchanged some goods. The pastoralists made use of such stone tools as knives, spearheads, and scrapers. They made baked-clay pottery, distinctive stone bowls, reed baskets, and beads made out of stones and ostrich-egg shells.

Further south, in southern Africa, Stone Age people herded domestic cattle long before the iron-using mixed farmers of later years. Probably the ancestors of the Khoisan who now inhabit the desert parts of Namibia and Botswana, these pastoralists had lighter skin and were shorter than their descendants. They herded sheep, a practice inherited by the Khoisan, who were to spread it to other parts of southern Africa. Cattle herding began much later.

Evidence from the Sahara suggests that pastoralism preceded farming. In the area of the Sahara Desert, the climate was moist from the sixth to the fourth millennium B.C., with sufficient grass to support animal herding. Sheep and goats were domesticated as far back as 7000 B.C. in the northern Sahara (areas of modern Algeria and Libya), and cattle were added in about 4000 B.C. The Saharan pastoralists took to rock painting, and some of their surviving paintings have been dated to between 3500 and 2500 B.C. These paintings clearly reveal a preoccupation with animals such as sheep and long-horned cattle. Also depicted were valuable tools and objects such as pack-oxen used to carry goods, skin bags used as water containers, and pots used to store water and milk. The human beings in the paintings appeared as a mixture of black and Mediterranean races and wore woven clothes, decorated their bodies, and used ornaments. Cattle herders moved out of the Sahara Desert from the fourth millennium B.C. They reached the edge of the tropical rain forest by 1500 B.C. and were able to continue to herd cattle, which developed an immunity to trypanosomiasis (sleeping sickness).

The spread of pastoralism to other parts of the continent was curtailed by nature. Where tsetse flies, bloodsucking insects, existed, it was hard for animal herding to survive. A bite from the fly would transmit a parasite that caused "sleeping sickness," which could kill both animals and humans. Immunity to the parasite could be developed over time, but tsetse-infested areas were not useful to wandering pastoralists. The areas preferred by these flies—thickly wooded and low-lying valleys—were avoided. Specialized pastoralism developed in the open savanna grasslands of southern and eastern Africa and the southern Sahara, areas the tsetse fly avoided.

THE CONSEQUENCES OF AGRICULTURE

Farming had many major effects on Africa. To start with, it made a variety of foods available to the population. Among the crops that were successfully domesticated were cereals (e.g., African rice, *tef*, bulrush millet, finger millet, sorghum), fiber plants (e.g., cotton), tubers and roots (e.g., yams), stimulants (e.g., coffee, kola), pulses (e.g., cowpeas, Bambara peanuts), oil crops (e.g., shea butter, palm oil, castor oil), starch and sugar plants (e.g., *enset*), vegetables (e.g., eggplants, okra), and fruits (watermelons, tamarind).

Second, farming turned wandering food gatherers into creators of more enduring settlements. Rather than being perpetually on the move in search of wild plants, they now settled close to their farms. The choice of settlements was strategic: They were close to fertile land and water. The settlements grew into villages. Egypt is a good example—food production transformed it into the most densely populated place in the world. Not only did Egypt grow in population, but it was able to create a state (see Chapter 3).

Third, the construction of permanent houses went along with the creation of settlements. Prehistoric caves and camps were abandoned for simple houses made of woven reeds, mud, and poles, with roofs thatched with plants. More durable houses were built of stone, while settlements could be enclosed by stone walls for defensive purposes.

Fourth, a population increase followed, made possible by improved nutrition and greater access to food. In addition, living in settlements enhanced the opportunities to reproduce—women had more time to nurture their babies, while other members of the community could also contribute to child rearing. The connection between agriculture and families was even stronger: More hands were needed to till, weed, and harvest; young children could be engaged in scaring away birds or tending domestic animals. A larger household had the resources to create larger farms and thus in turn to produce the food to feed its members and further expand family size.

Fifth, the varied tasks of planting and building called for the invention of new tools and a host of other necessary objects. In addition, cultivators had to create storage for their surpluses and tools. One artifact commonly found in archaeological discoveries has been pottery. Baked-clay pottery was useful for storage of water and food, transport of food from farms to houses, cooking, and storage of domestic objects. The wide range of uses to which pottery was put meant that more and more people devoted themselves to its production.

Stone tools were refined. The use of the ground stone ax defined the era. A selected stone was ground against another, harder rock to create a smooth-looking surface and a sharp edge. Called "Neolithic" ("new stones") tools, these axes looked like modern metal ax heads.

Sixth, significant social changes followed, notably in cooperation to produce food and manage surpluses. Planting and harvesting required advanced planning and notification of members of the household. Which seeds would grow where and when? When was the right time to harvest? How large would the harvest be, and where would the surplus be kept? Ideas of time and sequence of events were necessary to manage people and resources. Adequate plans must be in place to store food and protect it from insects.

The ability to produce surplus food meant that a person or household could produce more than was needed at a particular time. The producer had an insurance against hunger and could use his or her time on other ventures. More important, a small percentage of the population could be released from farming to do other things. Thus, a seventh consequence became possible: the emergence of other occupations and specialists in them. Among the most skilled and notable were priests and other religious and ritual specialists.

Two other types of specialists emerged, which led to yet another impact: Administrators and rulers became managers of the settlements. The use of power entailed settling conflicts and planning other aspects of community activity that required the cooperation of many people. It was likely that the early rulers began as "rainmakers," priests or hunters who were able to protect others in the settlement, cure diseases, and control pests. As their power and settlements grew, so too did their authority and influence, until some of them—like the pharaohs of Egypt—began to claim that they were gods or descendants of gods.

The generation of surpluses and the ability to manage settlements led to the promotion of relations among people who lived in separate areas and villages. Early forms of trade began, in tools, raw materials, and some luxury goods. Thus, agriculture contributed to the emergence of trade.

Another major impact was a growing division in society: the small farmer and the big farmer; the poor and the rich; the priest and the uninitiated; the ruler and the subjects. The scale and extent of these divisions varied from one society to another. The communal sharing and sense of egalitarianism that defined the previous hunter–gatherer societies were beginning to yield to a more competitive and hierarchical order.

The development of pastoralism created additional impacts, some similar to those that have already been described. Herding animals provided milk and food.

Other than for social occasions or to meet emergency needs, the animals were rarely slaughtered for meat. Animal domestication produced not less than three agricultural approaches. First, there were mixed farmers, who cultivated crops and herded animals. The mixed farmers lived in permanent or semipermanent settlements. Then there were cultivators who kept a few domestic animals. Essentially, they were farmers, and animal rearing was secondary. Finally, there were pastoralists whose major occupation was herding animals. Pastoralists did not necessarily create permanent settlements, since they needed to move in search of pastures. Their movements did not, however, prevent the creation of communities. They and their animals could carry essential materials, including items needed to build shelters. The availability of food and surpluses also enabled them to create large communities in areas suitable for both human habitation and animal grazing.

As ancient as the development of agriculture appears today, certain themes have persisted in African history ever since. The majority of the population still consists of farmers and pastoralists. The ability to generate surpluses continues to have implications for the economy and politics. The factors that affect food supply are shared by ancient and modern Africans. The basic practices of planting, harvesting, and storing are similar, but the system that produces those practices has varied over the years, from subsistence agriculture to highly mechanized production.

Ancient agriculture shares many characteristics with modern subsistence systems. The tools used were simple. Originally, they were even slow and inefficient, for example, the stone tools. The use of metal in later years improved the technology. With minimal mechanization there was an almost total dependence on human labor. The need to expand areas under cultivation eventually led to the development of ways to expand the size of the household through marriage or social networks. The farmers also consumed a large part of what they produced, stored some in anticipation of food scarcity or drought, and exchanged the rest for other items.

If food supply was one of the major aims of agriculture, it was affected by a number of factors, some of which are also found in later times. To start with, agriculture depended on arable land. People moved into areas that could support the production of crops and created settlements there. The land reserve was huge, but the tasks of clearing, planting, harvesting, and weeding were onerous. Related to land was the factor of water supply, which explains efforts to live close to sources of water and to develop irrigation methods. Weather and climatic conditions were and are important. Many Africans abandoned the Sahara region when it became a desert. Areas infested with tsetse flies made large-scale animal herding impossible. Atmospheric conditions determined cropping. Africans understood the impact of weather, and they responded in creative ways, even migrating to newer areas that were more conducive to agriculture. Finally, crops and farms could be attacked by pests. Annual crop losses to pests could be as high as 50 percent. Over time, Africans cultivated crops that resisted some pests or practiced farming methods that minimized the dangers of disease.

The Agricultural Revolution did not put an end to other economic activities such as fishing, hunting, and even gathering. Certainly, there were Africans who lived in areas unsuitable for crop cultivation, and there were groups who did not immediately adopt a settled lifestyle. However, crop cultivation and animal domestication created a profound revolution in the way people lived and organized society. The development of the Egyptian civilization is one example of the impact of agriculture.

SUGGESTIONS FOR FURTHER READING

Fagan, Brian. *Africa in the Iron Age*. Cambridge: Cambridge University Press, 1975.

Falola, Toyin, ed. *Africa*. Vol. 1, *African History before 1885*. Durham, N.C.: Carolina Academic Press, 2000. Chapter 3.

Gailey, Harry A., Jr. *History of Africa*. Vol. 1, *From Earliest Times to 1800*. Malabar, Fla.: Krieger, 1999.

Harlan, J.R., J. de Wet, and A. Stemler, eds. *Origins of African Plant Domestication*. The Hague: Mouton, 1976.

McCann, James. *Green Land, Brown Land, Black Land*. Portsmouth, N.H.: Heinemann, 1999.

Robertshaw, Peter. *Early Pastoralists of South-western Kenya*. Nairobi: British Institute in Eastern Africa, 1990.

3

The Civilization of Ancient Egypt, 3100 B.C.+

The development of farming and the domestication of animals enabled a number of Neolithic groups to establish settlements that grew into villages and towns. This was a major transition to civilization—the abandonment of a wandering lifestyle and the formation of settled village communities and states. The Neolithic farmers, in the process of controlling water supplies to promote agriculture, created the earliest civilizations in such places as the banks of the Tigris and Euphrates Rivers in Asia and the Nile in Africa.

The Egyptian civilization developed and prospered along the River Nile. Ancient Egypt was a powerful and united state, governed by leaders who presided over a complex bureaucracy. The legacy of Egypt is long and monumental.

EARLY FOUNDATIONS

There could have been no Egypt without the Nile, the longest river in Africa. In the Neolithic era, the Nile valley was marshier and wetter than it is today. It was probably a home to hunter–gatherers as far back as 12,000 B.C. The successors of these people made the transition to farming and built small villages along the Nile. The principle on which their agriculture depended was consistent: The Nile flooded each year about the same time; the flood provided water for the fields; and as the water receded, a rich deposit of silt was left behind to renew the soil. Thus, the areas along the Nile were rich enough to support agriculture and settlements.

From clusters of settlements, Egypt was gradually united to form a kingdom. The initial unification was into two kingdoms: the kingdom of Lower Egypt in the Nile Delta close to the Mediterranean Sea and the kingdom of Upper Egypt, located to the south along the Nile valley.

A decisive moment came in about 3100 B.C. when the kingdoms of Lower Egypt and Upper Egypt were united into one big state. The architect of this unity was King Menes of Upper Egypt, who also established a dynasty, with power based within the same family and passed from father to son or daughter. About thirty dynasties rose and fell in Ancient Egypt, from about 3100 to 332 B.C. These various dynasties have been grouped into three major phases: the Old Kingdom, the Middle Kingdom, and the New Kingdom. These phases were long, full of events that led to the fall and rise of kingdoms. However, over its 3,000-year history, Ancient Egypt was able to sustain the idea of a centralized political system.

THE OLD KINGDOM, 2685–2200 B.C.

The Old Kingdom was headed by the pharaoh, believed to be divine, that is, a god on earth. Below the king were members of the dynastic family, priests, and government officials. Over time, the government officials developed into a powerful hereditary nobility. At a lower level were the peasants. This period witnessed the rule of eleven dynasties that established and consolidated the authority of the pharaoh, fought major wars, and engaged in trade with Lebanon and the Phoenicians. The oldest major stone building, a pyramid, was built at Saqqara, in addition to some other pyramids. The unity and stability established in about 3100 B.C. lasted for almost a thousand years.

Toward the end of the Old Kingdom, power rivalry developed between the pharaohs and the nobility, on the one hand, and among the members of the nobility, on the other hand. The nobles acquired power at the expense of the pharaohs. Starting in ca. 2160 B.C., a civil war led to the collapse of the central government, and Egypt entered a period of decline. There was another major development, to the west of the Nile, that probably affected Egyptian politics and stability for some time. The Sahara Desert was drying up, forcing many of its peoples to migrate to the Nile valley. They may have disrupted the lives of their host farming communities. The evidence relating to the period 2200 to 2040 B.C. suggests that many people failed to pay their taxes, trade declined, and no pyramids were constructed. Unity was to be restored around 2100 B.C.

THE MIDDLE KINGDOM, 2040–1785 B.C.

In about 2040 B.C., a new dynasty of pharaohs was created in the city of Thebes. Egypt was reunited, and the Middle Kingdom lasted for three centuries. The kingdom was strong and peaceful. Political stability and prosperity contributed to the greater development of art, architecture, and literature. The

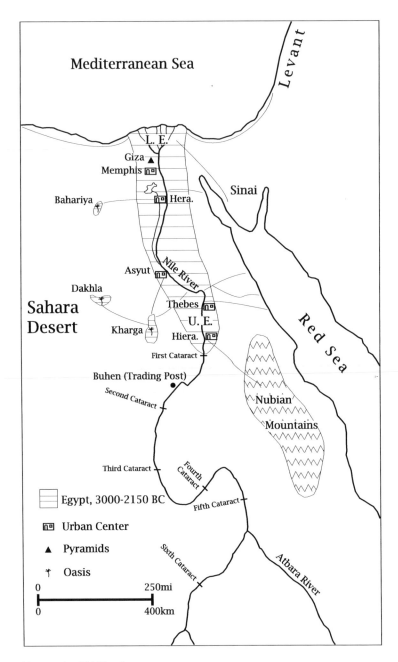

Mediterranean Sea

Levant

L. E.

Giza ▲
Memphis 🏠

Bahariya 🕆

Hera. 🏠

Sinai

Baharíya

Asyut 🏠

Nile River

Dakhla 🕆

Sahara
Desert

Thebes 🏠

Kharga 🕆

U. E.

Hiera. 🏠

First Cataract

Red Sea

Buhen (Trading Post) ●

Second Cataract

Nubian

Mountains

Third Cataract

Fourth
Cataract

Fifth Cataract

Egypt, 3000-2150 BC

🏠 Urban Center

▲ Pyramids

🕆 Oasis

Sixth Cataract

Atbara River

0   250mi

0   400km

Egypt—the Old Kingdom.

building of pyramids was restored, taxes were paid, and trade relations were revived. More land was put under cultivation, and irrigation expanded. Egypt established control as far as the second obstacle in the Nile to easy passage/travel by conquering Nubia.

Decline set in from the 1780s B.C. onward. The power of the king declined, while that of the priests and nobles was strengthened. Power rivalry led to chaos. In addition, Egypt began to witness attacks from external invaders. The Egyptian civilization was known to its neighbors, some of whom began to seek its advantages and land for themselves. Foreign invaders attacked Egypt and governed it for many years. The first attack came from the Hyksos—a semitic-speaking people who migrated to the Nile Delta from the northeast. By 1650 B.C., the Hyksos had overthrown the ruling Egyptian dynasty and established what is now known as the New Kingdom. In about 1570 B.C., the Hyksos were driven out of Egypt.

Imperial expansion marked this period of Egyptian history. The Hyksos had a superior military technology, based on horse-drawn chariots, and they also knew how to work bronze, a harder substance than the copper that the Egyptians used. A large and powerful army was used to create an empire.

The Hyksos adopted Egyptian civilization and ruled as the pharaohs did, but they were regarded as outsiders by the people. They were unable to control the entire Nile valley, but only the northeast. Upper Egypt was ruled by Nubian princes, and the middle portion of the Nile valley was ruled by a Theban prince. A war of liberation was conducted by the Theban princes who mastered the Hyksos' technology and led a successful attack by 1500 B.C.

THE NEW KINGDOM, 1570–1085 B.C.

Egypt improved on its standing army and engaged in successful wars against Palestine, Syria, and Nubia to the fourth cataract. Wars were also fought with the Hittites of Turkey and the Libyans. Egypt became a world power. It moved its capital from Memphis in Lower Egypt to Thebes in Upper Egypt. The Israelites left Egypt under the leadership of Moses. The period saw the erection of massive palaces, temples, and statues by King Rameses II. Trade, too, expanded, especially in hardwoods, gold, incense, and ivory. The Somali coast in East Africa was drawn into a lucrative regional and international commerce.

What followed this era is known as the "Late Period," a time when Egypt experienced more external invasions from various quarters. After 1100 B.C., the empire was attacked from the north and west. Palestine and Nubia attained independence. A host of foreign invaders included the Libyans, Nubians, Persians, and Assyrians. When the attacks were successful, foreign dynasties came to power. Instability was interrupted by eras of peace (664–525 B.C.) that allowed for the expansion of trade. The last Egyptian dynasty ended in 332 B.C. when Alexander of Macedon (also known as "Alexander the Great") conquered Egypt and placed it under the control of his general, Ptolemy. Greek control lasted until 30 B.C., when the Romans took over.

THE CIVILIZATION OF ANCIENT EGYPT

The rise and fall of kingdoms did not destroy the stability of many aspects of Egyptian culture, while its agriculture and trade were stable for most of the time. The authority of the pharaoh was acknowledged, and the economic basis of power was the exploitation of the labor of the poor.

Egypt was a centralized state, one of the earliest in world history. At the apex of the political system was the pharaoh, a powerful king whose claim to divinity ensured that he was obeyed and respected. Below the king came the nobles who managed a large and complex bureaucracy. Thanks to the Nile, a transportation system based on reed and timber boats made many settlements accessible to the agents of the pharaohs. Although the kingdom was vast, extending almost 1,000 kilometers (621 miles) from the first cataract, only a rather narrow area was occupied by the people. Until the time of the New Kingdom, there was no need to build a standing army, and the kingdom enjoyed peace and stability for almost 1,500 years. The areas to the east and west were mainly desert, which offered protection, and the population was mainly rural.

The Nile was so central to the economy and society that the river was worshipped as a god. The economy depended on agriculture. The chief grains were barley and wheat. The people also grew flax (which was spun and woven into linen), vegetables, and fruits such as grapes and figs. Large quantities of these products were harvested, because the land was fertile and farmworkers were plentiful. They reared animals, notably goats and cattle, and they also fished and hunted animals.

The arable land was broken up into estates. The estates were farmed by the peasants who depended on rudimentary wooden plows and hoes, lived in mud houses, and were supervised by the officers of the king. The harvests were shared between the peasants and the pharaoh, who took the lion's share in the form of taxes and rents. The vast majority of the population consisted of peasants who sustained the wealth of the few—the pharaoh and the nobles. Although the peasants had access to fish and meat, they ate little of it, again because they had to pay taxes. The estates and the peasants were supervised by scribes and tax collectors who represented the pharaoh. Taxes were imposed according to the annual level of the Nile. The king and his officials could also conscript people to work on public projects. The surpluses acquired from the peasants were kept in government stores and used to generate resources to maintain the grand lifestyles of the kings and the bureaucrats, pay the civil servants, feed the population in time of shortage, and support the priests and their shrines.

So successful was the agricultural system that it generated a considerable surplus that promoted trade in the region and beyond. Egyptian merchants were members of the great caravans that traveled in Africa and Asia. Still more impressive was the building of ships that sailed on the Red, Aegean, and Mediterranean Seas. Egyptian goods (grain and gold) were traded in exchange for raw materials and luxury items produced elsewhere. Imported items included precious stones, incense, and spices from western Asia; ostrich feathers, ebony, and ivory from the Nubians to the south; and timber, a scarce product in the Nile valley, from Byblos in Palestine. During the time of the Old Kingdom, the king established a monopoly on foreign trade.

Religion had a prominent place in society, and through it we have an understanding of the people's major beliefs and ideas. Life was seen essentially in religious terms, with the physical world as a mere extension of the spiritual. As it did on agriculture, the River Nile exerted a major influence on religion. The principal gods captured the gentle and predictable features of life along the Nile. The river itself was a god. The well-known "Hymn to the Nile" attests to the strong belief held by many people:

Hail to thee, O Nile, that issues from the earth and comes to keep Egypt alive! . . .

When the Nile floods, offering is made to thee, oxen are sacrificed to thee . . . birds are fattened for thee, lions are hunted for thee in the desert, fire is provided for thee. And offering is made to every other god, as is done for the Nile. . . . So it is "Verdant art thou!" So it is "Verdant art thou!"

So it is "O Nile, verdant art thou, who makest man and cattle to live!"[1]

As with the ebb and flow of the Nile, so too with life—a cycle of birth, life, death, and rebirth or regeneration. Death was not the end of a person but the start of a new life in a spiritual world. Based on the belief that the physical body was still needed in the "next world," Egyptians developed the science of mummification—the application of chemicals to dry the body and preserve it for hundreds of years. The mummy was treated with dignity, preserved in a tomb, and provided with all essential needs (food, tools, clothing, weapons, and jewelry). Also in the tomb were servants, represented by painted or sculpted figures, in case the mummy required errands to be run. This burial arrangement reflected the social and political division in society. The pharaohs enjoyed the most lavish burials—the pyramids that housed their corpses were massive, filled with chambers full of goods that reflected their status. The graves of the poor contained just a few items.

The sun, regarded as a guardian spirit, was yet another major god. There were many other gods and goddesses, as each district and village had local deities, associated with a variety of sacred animal symbols such as those of the cat, bull, crocodile, jackal, and scarab (a type of beetle). For example, the goddess Bastet had the head of a cat and the body of a woman, and her statues were worshipped in many homes. Animals were believed to have special powers.

Just as Egyptians were united by the pharaohs, so too were their gods and goddesses. For example, Re, the great sun god, united all the other gods and goddesses associated with guardianship during the Old Kingdom. During the period of the Middle Kingdom, Re became known as Amon Re, after the principal sun god of Thebes, the capital city. To take another example, all the gods and goddesses associated with fertility and the vegetation of the Nile were united as one god, Osiris. The pharaoh, too, could be treated as a god. During the dynastic era, the belief was that the pharaoh was the human representation of Amon Re or Osiris.

Progress was made in other important areas such as art, architecture, and education. Ancient Egypt was famous for its monuments, notably the pyramids and the Great Sphinx. Over 4,000 years old, the Sphinx has the head of a man and the body of a lion and was probably a representation of the sun god. The pyramids were tombs made for the pharaohs. Today, about eighty of these pyramids can be found along the west bank of the Nile. The most famous, which include the Great Pyramid, are located at Giza. Herodotus, the Greek historian of the fifth century B.C., described the construction of the Great Pyramid built for Cheops, also known as Khufu, the first pharaoh of the first dynasty, in about 2600 B.C. According to Herodotus, the king forced thousands of Egyptians to work. The stones were obtained from the Arabian mountains, transported across the Nile, and then dragged to the location of the pyramids on a road that took ten years to build. The pyramid took twenty years to construct, with a heavy cost in resources and people.

Burial in pyramids was abandoned during the New Kingdom and was replaced by burial in huge stone caves carved out from mountains in a special area known as the "Valley of the Kings" near Thebes. One of these impressive stone caves, that of Tutankhamun, a minor pharaoh of the eighteenth dynasty, was discovered in the 1920s, and its contents are now preserved in the Cairo Museum.

The monuments and pyramids provide evidence on architecture and engineering. Talented engineers and architects designed and constructed these structures as well as others. Among the most famous architects of the Old Kingdom was Imhotep, credited with having designed the step pyramid of King Djoser and worshipped as a god after his death. The monuments and pyramids bore the stamp of religion—each god had its own shrine or temple. The pharaohs devoted considerable resources and time to building their tombs. Talented artists and artisans were retained on a full-time basis to create the gold ornaments, jewelry, and pottery that were placed in the tombs. The walls of the tombs could also be painted with multiple scenes showing the occupations and people of the time.

Astronomy and mathematics developed, in part in order to control irrigation and extend the arable land. The floodplain was measured, with results that showed an understanding of geometry and arithmetic. To understand the season and the timing of the flood, Egyptians had to study the stars, moon, and sun, and they eventually came up with the first annual calendar, based on twelve months and 365 days. Furthermore, they were able to create a water clock to measure the time of day, and a "Nilometer," which recorded the rise and fall of the waters of the Nile.

Education and the bureaucracy were connected. A complex government was managed by civil servants in charge of various responsibilities. Many scribes were required for record keeping. These scribes, all males, were honored. Women of the upper class might also be literate. In the days of the Old Kingdom,

Girl musicians, tomb of Nakht, Egypt.

the scribes trained their sons to read and write. During the Middle Kingdom, the training was carried out in schools.

By 3000 B.C., the Egyptians had developed a system of writing known as hieroglyphics, based on the use of over 600 symbols, signs, and pictures to communicate sounds and words. Hieroglyphics were initially carved on tombs and monuments but later inscribed on papyrus, which presented better writing opportunities. Papyrus was a light, paperlike material made from the pulp of the papyrus plant, which was found in large quantities along the Nile. It was not complicated to make, even with the limited tools available. It was easy to transport, which meant that written words could travel. Hieroglyphics were used initially to estimate taxes and record crop yields but later to record other events, such as the activities of the pharaohs, and for diplomatic correspondence. Thanks to hieroglyphics and the tombs, we have evidence to analyze the civilization of Ancient Egypt.

NOTE

1. Quoted in William Travis Haines III, *World History: Continuity and Change* (New York: Holt, Rinehart and Winston, 1997), p. 15.

SUGGESTIONS FOR FURTHER READING

Asante, Molefi. *Classical Africa*. Rochelle Park, N.J.: Peoples' Publishing Group, 1994.
Bernal, Martin. *Black Athena: The Afro-Asiatic Roots of Classical Civilization*. London: Free Association Press, 1987.
Breasted, Jerry Henry. *Ancient Records of Egypt: Historical Documents from the Earlier Times to the Persian Conquest*. Chicago: University of Chicago Press, 1906–7.
Brier, Bob and Hoyt Hobbs. *Daily Life of the Ancient Egyptians*. Westport, Conn.: Greenwood Press, 1999.
Diop, Cheikk Anta. *The African Origin of Civilization: Myth or Reality*. Edited and translated by Mercer Cook. Chicago: Lawrence Hill Books, 1974.
Falola, Toyin, ed. *Africa*. Vol. 1, *African History before 1885*. Durham, N.C.: Carolina Academic Press, 2000. Chapter 4.
Hilliard, Constance B. *Intellectual Traditions of Pre-Colonial Africa*. Boston: McGraw-Hill, 1998.
Kaster, Joseph. *The Wisdom of Ancient Egypt: Writings from the Time of the Pharaohs*. New York: Barnes and Noble Books, 1993.
Morenz, Siegfried. *Egyptian Religion*. Translated by Ann E. Keep. London: Methuen & Co. Ltd., 1973.
Simpson, William Kelly. *The Literature of Ancient Egypt: An Anthology of Stories, Instructions, and Poetry*. New Haven, Conn.: Yale University Press, 1973.

4

The Iron Age and the Spread of Bantu Speakers, 730 B.C.+

Next in importance to the Agricultural Revolution was the revolution involving the use of iron. One of the early centers of iron production, in about 500 B.C., was Meroë, the capital of the powerful kingdom of Kush in the area of modern-day Sudan. Other major centers were in central Nigeria and in the area of Lake Victoria. Other than in the Nile valley, Africa did not experience a Bronze Age as an intermediary period between its Stone Age and Iron Age. The leap to an Iron Age was a revolution with monumental consequences: Better weapons and tools were made; state-building was possible as iron-using people were able to conquer their stone-using neighbors and establish political control over them; the construction of settlements and houses was facilitated by the use of metal technology; and mastery of the harsh environment was made easier. With iron, Africa became a leader in innovations and adaptations to the environment.

METALWORKING: HISTORY AND SIGNIFICANCE

The use of metal accelerated the pace of the growth of civilization, contributing in no small measure to the improvement of the techniques and methods used to farm and to domesticate animals. Iron is far superior to stones for making tools, ornaments, and weapons. It is also more manipulable than stone: It can be made into items of various shapes and sizes, used in combination with wood, sharpened to a desired edge, decorated, and refined.

Both copper and bronze were used in Ancient Egypt. Copper was mined in Sinai, located in the northeast of Egypt, as far back as 4000 B.C. The skills of the

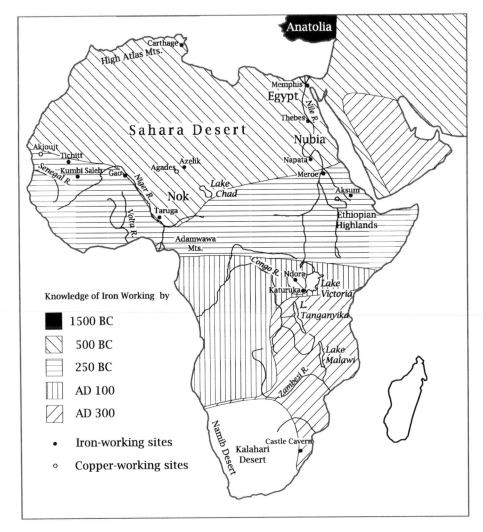

Spread of iron working in Africa.

Benin bronze head.

people of the Neolithic Age were adequate to mine copper, a "soft" metal available in a pure metallic form that could be hammered and shaped into various ornaments and implements. To extract it from the ore, people had to devise a system of heating in order to "melt" copper from rock. When tin and copper were smelted together, they produced an alloy, bronze, a harder metal also suitable for weapons, tools, and ornaments. Knowledge probably grew slowly, but once acquired it became highly valued.

Metals were valuable trade items, as they could only be produced in a few places. Having metals and the knowledge of working them was a great source of wealth, as metal objects could be sold in exchange for other important goods. A metal like gold was traded over long distances without losing its value and formed one of the sources of the wealth of Egypt and kingdoms in West Africa such as Ghana, Mali, and Songhay. When a metal was scarce, as in the case of gold, its value was further enhanced. From Ancient Egypt, the use of bronze spread along the coastline of North Africa. Early sites of copper-working have also been discovered on the southern edges of the Sahara and in central Niger, although the extent to which the peoples in these areas used this metal remains unclear.

Iron-working was far more complicated than the working of copper or gold, and it consumed a large amount of hardwood charcoal. Iron ore could not just be "melted" from rock; it has to be extracted in a chemical process. Smelting furnaces had to be made. Charcoal and crushed ore were mixed in the furnace, a fire would be lit, and air pumped into the furnace with bellows. The injected air formed part of the chemical process while it also raised the temperature of the furnace. Heating and adding air involved hours of intensive work. When the furnace was broken, the red iron was removed and then vigorously hammered to remove impurities. The process would leave behind waste slag, which is the main evidence that we have for the early sites, since the final products, iron tools and weapons, hardly survive because of rust.

Objects made of iron were superior to those of copper and bronze. Not only was iron ore widely available in many parts of Africa, but iron was a harder metal than copper and tin, and iron objects could be more finely sharpened. There were several early centers of iron production in Africa, and the idea may have evolved independently in several places. The specialized technique of production became known in many regions through the dispersal of knowledge over time.

One of the earliest world centers of iron-smelting was Anatolia in modern Turkey where iron was smelted by 1500 B.C. Although the knowledge was kept secret by the Hittites of Anatolia for a long time, to retain their military advantage over their neighbors, the technology later spread in western Asia and Ancient Egypt. Because it lacked adequate timber to produce charcoal, Egypt was at a disadvantage and had to remain dependent on bronze until 670 B.C. when the Assyrians successfully used iron weapons in their invasion. Thereafter, the Nubian rulers withdrew to the Upper Nile, below the second cataract, where they developed the first African kingdom based on iron. This was Kush, with its capital at Meroë, discussed in the next chapter.

IRON IN WEST AFRICA

It remains unclear whether the skill of smelting iron developed in various independent centers in West Africa. There were a number of early smelting centers in the Saharan areas of Mali, Mauritania, and Niger. But it is probable that the knowledge of iron-working spread from the Phoenicians in North Africa to the Sahara, then to West Africa. In the quest for trade, the Phoenicians (from the area of modern-day Lebanon) had moved to various parts of North Africa from about 1000 B.C. By 800 B.C., they had created independent settlements, most notably Carthage, in 814 B.C., in modern-day Tunisia. The Phoenicians brought the knowledge of iron-smelting with them, introduced it to the region, and engaged in trade within North Africa and beyond. There was also a trade across the Sahara, which brought products from West Africa (gold, ivory, and slaves) to North Africa in exchange for metal goods, books, cloth, and salt. Iron probably spread in the process of this interregional commerce. The Berbers of North Africa acted as the couriers, first learning how to smelt iron, then transmitting it to groups in the Sahara region.

Iron-smelting was practiced in central Niger, Nigeria, and southern Mali by 500 B.C. The Iron Age gave rise to what is now known as the "Nok culture," named after a site in Taruga in Nigeria's Middle Belt where ancient artifacts were discovered. Many figurines of terra-cotta—or baked clay—were found, in addition to baked-clay cooking pots and bowls. The figurines represented animals and human heads. Central Nigeria had been occupied before the Iron Age, thereby suggesting that a Stone Age population had made the transition to the use of iron. By A.D. 1000, the knowledge of iron-working had spread to most parts of West Africa and the rest of the continent, due in part to the migrations of the Bantu people that are discussed in the next section. Iron ore was abundant, and it was put to good use.

Iron had a revolutionary impact on the people of Nok and other early iron-working societies in West Africa. Iron created tools and weapons that were far stronger and more efficient than those made of stone, bones, and wood. Spears, hoes, machetes, and axes were powerful tools for farming and hunting, thereby making it possible to increase the food supply. More food improved nutrition and living standards. The population also increased.

As people became numerous, they needed more land on which to farm and build houses. Again, iron became useful in expanding the areas that human beings could inhabit. People like the Bantu of West Africa migrated in search of new areas to occupy. The forests could be penetrated, and human beings had the tools to defend themselves from dangerous animals. Succeeding generations built on the achievements of previous generations, while the population moved in various directions within the continent.

A process of state formation also began, leading to the emergence of the kingdom of Ghana and many other states. Iron was a source of military and political power. To have it and to keep the secret of making it was to have access to the means to destroy, subdue, and conquer others. Whether to conquer others or to defend oneself, the need to form a government became important. A village, a town, or a state had to think of security, and leaders emerged to organize the people. The ability to produce more food enabled the creation of specialists who could devote their time to administration, offer services, or produce a wide range of commodities. This division of labor in turn promoted the expansion of trade, from local to international commerce. Again, administrations had to manage trade, increasing specialization in society and growing populations.

As in other parts of the continent, the early iron-using states were small and had simple governments. Some were administered by clan elders and chiefs with little power. In other places, the leaders could be powerful kings and their counselors. There were also societies without chiefs, which created democratic arrangements to resolve conflicts. Over time, some areas became highly centralized (e.g., Ghana, Mali, and Songhay), whereas others chose segmentary political systems (e.g., the Igbo of Nigeria). The success of the Iron Age in West Africa contributed significantly to the spread of iron and population in the rest of Africa. The agents of this spread are known as the Bantu.

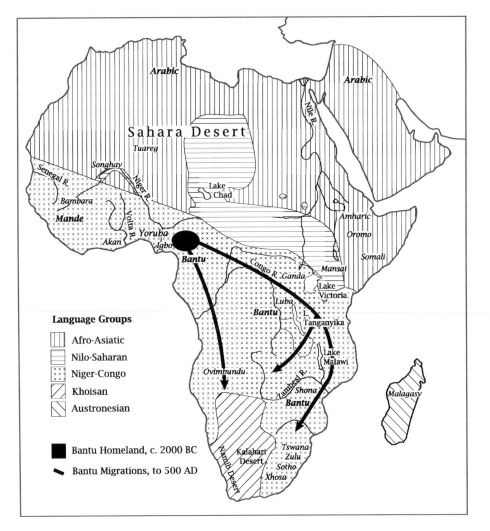

African languages and Bantu expansion.

BANTU MIGRATIONS

Irrespective of where the ideas of agriculture and iron-making originated, they had become widespread in all of sub-Saharan Africa by the fifth century A.D. This remarkable success has been attributed to one of the largest and most significant population movements in the human experience, that of the Bantu-speaking people. The Bantu were originally from West Africa, members of farming communities who had the skills to smelt and use iron.

The full details of the early history of the Bantu-speaking people and their contributions to prehistory may never be known, but broad patterns are gradually emerging. The movements of the Bantu to other parts of Africa lasted for many centuries. The migrations occurred in a series of waves. The people did not all go in the same direction but moved to various parts of eastern, central, and southern Africa. The migrations were uneven and gradual. An ambitious leader could initiate a movement by seceding from a group, leaving an established village with his own group of followers. Early movements are likely to have involved small groups of people, while the process of absorption of the previous hunter-gathering societies may also have been gradual. The series of Bantu migrations involved demography and the transfer of culture and technology through human agency.

The migrations occurred in two major streams: eastern and western. The eastern stream involved migrations from West Africa to the Lake District in East Africa, and from there to southeastern Africa. These series of migrations followed the savanna corridors. The western stream included various movements from the area of Cameroon to the region of the rain forests in west-central Africa. The Bantu migrations into the rain forests were completed by the third century A.D.

THE EVIDENCE

Theories of the Bantu migrations rely on linguistics and archaeology. The linguistic evidence has revealed an original parent of the Bantu languages. Linguistic scholars have traced the African language "family tree," with its various branches. The branches of the language are tied to the movement of people from a single homeland. There is a Bantu family of languages, all connected in various ways, showing that their original sources were similar. The Bantu language family covers what is known as the Niger-Congo language group, which spans most of sub-Saharan Africa. The word stem is *ntu*, and its variants are common to the languages in the Niger-Congo group. The prefix *ba* is also common in this language family, and the combination of *ba* and *ntu*, which is *ba-ntu*, means "people." "Bantu" itself does not refer to any single language in the Niger-Congo group.

Within the group, there are about 450 languages, which can all be traced to a single proto-Bantu language originally spoken in the area of modern-day Cameroon. The Bantu language spread from here eastward to the forest area and southward to the savanna. As the people moved in different directions, they lost touch with their original homeland, and they developed different languages in their various new homelands. New dialects, new words, and the incorporation of many loan words would transform their languages, moving them further away from the original to the extent that they might not even be able to understand the original language anymore. A new language evolved, although it still belonged to the family of the original parent. Linguistic evidence has affirmed that proto-Bantu gave birth to many languages.

When we turn to the other evidence—archaeology—we see that materials have been obtained from a number of early iron-using sites. Since plants, grains, and cooked meals usually do not survive for too many years, evidence of early agriculture tends to be direct. Among the most reliable artifacts are baked-clay pottery, slag deposits, and grinding stones. Broken pottery has been highly useful, as certain containers and decorated pots suggest the existence of settled

Ancient Yoruba terra-cotta head.

farming communities. The way the pots were made and the decorative patterns and grooves on them can yield valuable information on customs. Styles and methods of decoration could be similar, suggesting relationships among various groups.

THE SPREAD OF BANTU SETTLEMENTS

The movement of the Bantu speakers out of West Africa began as far back as the first millennium B.C. when some groups penetrated the Congo forest, where they established farming communities using stone tools. Their crops included yams, nuts, and palm oil, while they also tended animals. It remains unclear when and where the transition to the use of iron was made.

What is clear is that once iron was known, the spread of Bantu speakers to various parts of eastern, central, and southern Africa was rapid and successful during the early centuries of the first millennium A.D. The Asian yam and banana were introduced to Africa in the second century A.D., probably through Madagascar by Malayo-Polynesian sailors. These two crops did well and spread quickly, notably in Uganda and the Congo forest.

Furnace construction and pottery decorations have suggested some notable differences between western and eastern Bantu traditions. In southern Africa, both traditions combined to produce a mixed tradition. References in the literature to "western" and "eastern" are generally based on people's traditions and pottery styles. To start with a few examples of the eastern tradition, a pottery style known as Urewe ware has been dated to a period between the second and the fifth centuries A.D., although it is much older than this in its origins. At the base of the pots and bowls are indentations, and related pottery has been found in Kenya and Tanzania. From a study of Urewe ware and other distinctive decorative styles, it has been concluded that the Bantu reached many areas in the lakeland region, the Great Rift Valley, and the areas of modern-day Malawi, the Maputo region in Mozambique, Zimbabwe, and southern Africa. Following the western tradition, iron-working Bantu speakers were already in the Congo forest, northeastern Zambia, and Zimbabwe by the first or second century A.D. From Zimbabwe, they moved to the Transvaal rural land for farming or grazing in South Africa. What appears to be the dividing line between the eastern and western traditions is the Luangwa valley in eastern Zambia.

THE SIGNIFICANCE OF THE SPREAD OF THE BANTU

The spread of the Bantu speakers and of iron were inseparable. Indeed, the Bantu are also referred to in the literature as Iron Age farmers just to underscore the connection. Between the second and fifth centuries A.D., iron-working farmers spread rapidly to various parts in eastern, central, and southern Africa. Thereafter, their iron-working and farming were consolidated and improved upon, ultimately producing the ability to establish large empires. In the early centuries of expansion, the Bantu settled in areas that were fertile and easy to cultivate. This probably explains the preference for river valleys or high rainfall regions—southeast Africa rather than the southwest. As the population grew and new streams joined the migrations, other areas were occupied.

The Bantu speakers contributed to demographic changes in Africa, not just by being migrants to new areas but by creating conditions favorable to population increase. New cultures emerged where the Iron Age farmers established themselves. This involved a process of intermarriage and cultural fusion that led to the creation of new, distinctive cultures in many places.

The search for areas to settle also involved the availability of sources of raw materials. This involved the availability not only of ore but also of hardwood to produce sufficient charcoal to feed the fire in the furnaces. Other materials such as stone axes and clay to build furnaces were more readily available.

Bantu migrants transformed the indigenous Stone Age populations wherever they went. In some areas, they cohabited and exchanged products, as in the case of Bantu settlers and the Stone Age people in Tanzania. In some other areas, as in many parts of central and southern Africa, the Bantu were able to absorb into their groups a number of Khoisan hunter–gatherers. And there were also cases where hosts who could not adapt to Bantu culture and economic practices were forced to migrate elsewhere. The Bantu had the skills and knowledge of iron-working, farming, and animal domestication. Thus, they tended to be more culturally advanced than their hosts.

They introduced iron and farming to many areas. Farming was the major occupation. Sorghum and millets were the major crops, but the list of others was long, including beans, all kinds of fruits, and melons. A number of farmers kept a few domestic animals such as sheep, goats, chickens, and pigs. Fishing and hunting were done where circumstances permitted.

The use of space recognized the role of farming as the basis of the economy. The environment supplied most needs. The early settlements were mostly small villages, with fewer than fifteen houses. However, there were large villages as well, as in Natal in South Africa. People lived in round houses, built with clay and poles. Also within the village would be storage bins for seeds and surplus grains. Livestock pens to confine domestic animals would complete the landscape of the village, with all the buildings arranged in a circle.

The villages were mainly self-sufficient in access to many basic necessities. However, conditions for trade existed, especially to obtain commodities, such as salt, that could only be produced in certain places. When an area ran out of iron ore, its people had to depend on trade to obtain tools and weapons.

The Bantu speakers contributed to the formation of new forms of social and political organization. The village constituted the basis of government. In a small village, the political community was probably no more than a group of family members. The women not only took care of children; they also prepared the food and tended crops. Men were probably acquiring dominance, in part because of their control of iron and production. Men were the hunters and in many places also organized the trade between villages. In addition, the Bantu speakers contributed to the process of state formation and have been credited with the establishment of a number of kingdoms such as Zimbabwe and Kongo. The spread of Iron Age farmers in Africa ultimately brought the Stone Age to an end and instigated major changes in economy and politics.

SUGGESTIONS FOR FURTHER READING

Falola, Toyin, ed. *Africa*. Vol. 1, *African History before 1885*. Durham, N.C.: Carolina Academic Press, 2000. Chapter 5.

Greenberg, Joseph. *The Languages of Africa*. Bloomington: Indiana University Press, 1970.

Harlan, J.R.J. de Wet, and A. Stemler, eds. *Origins of African Plant Domestication*. The Hague: Mouton, 1976.

Herbert, W. Eugenia. *Iron, Gender, and Power: Rituals of Transformation in African Societies*. Bloomington: Indiana University Press, 1993.

Phillipson, D.W. *African Archaeology*. New York: Cambridge University Press, 1985.

Schmidt, Peter R. *Iron Technology in East Africa: Symbolism, Science, and Archaeology*. Bloomington: Indiana University Press, 1997.

Schmidt, Peter R., ed. *The Culture and Technology of African Iron Production*. Gainesville: University Press of Florida, 1996.

Shillington, Kevin. *History of Africa*. Rev. ed. New York: St. Martin's Press, 1995.

Vansina, J. *Paths in the Rainforest*. Madison: University of Wisconsin Press, 1990.

5

The Rise of Kush and Aksum, 730 B.C.+

THE FIRST IRON AGE KINGDOM: KUSH

Egypt was not the only civilization in the Nile valley (see Chapter 3). While Egypt grew in the Lower Nile valley, other states flourished in the Upper Nile valley in an area known as the Sudan. Both Kush and Aksum emerged in the regions of the Upper Nile and Ethiopia.

The Kush kingdom, with its famous capital at Meroë, was created by the Nubians located on the Upper Nile. This area was very closely connected with Ancient Egypt. Trade relations began during the Old Kingdom. However, by 1500 B.C., Egyptian rule had been extended over the Nubian hinterland, as far as the fourth cataract, in order to establish greater control of trade. Egyptian control lasted for about 500 years, during which time Egyptian temples, towns, and influence emerged in the region. The Nubian ruling class also adopted Egyptian culture, especially religion and art.

When the Egyptian dynasties of the New Kingdom collapsed, Egypt withdrew from the Nubian area. Starting from about 1000 B.C., the Nubian rulers began to build a new kingdom that the Egyptians called Kush. The Nubian rulers of Kush continued to use Egyptian ideas and culture, even modeling their kingdom after that of Egypt. By 730 B.C., they had become independent and powerful enough even to invade Egypt and establish control at Thebes. Known as the Ethiopian dynasty, the Nubians governed Egypt for sixty years. This political control did not translate into any cultural change, as the Nubian leaders worshipped Egyptian gods, used the double crown of Upper and Lower Egypt, and even inscribed their names on Egyptian temples.

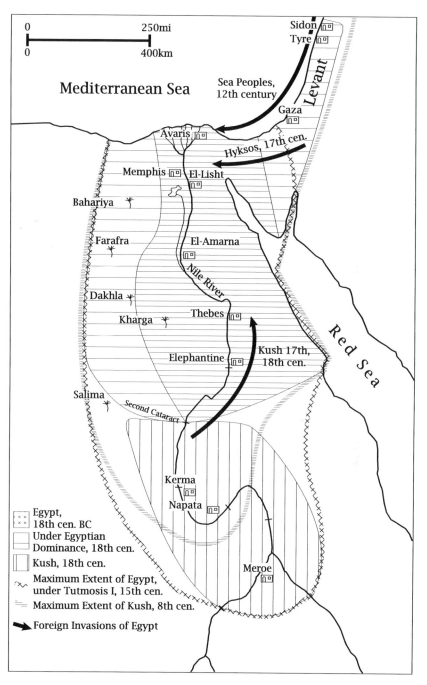

Kush and Middle Kingdom Egypt.

In 670 B.C., the Assyrians invaded Lower Egypt and forced the Kushites to withdraw to Nubia, where they established a new kingdom, located at Napata, close to the fourth cataract. Years later, the Kushites were forced to abandon Napata and move to Meroë, a decision that led to major consequences.

The "island of Meroë" was located between the Rivers Nile and Atbara. The location offered many advantages. It was more secure from attacks by Egypt. The threat of Egyptian invasion was real, and a decisive attack had been launched against Napata in 593 B.C. Meroë was located further south, near the sixth cataract, and had one advantage that could enhance its military capability: the availability of iron resources.

The Meroë region had both iron ore and hardwood timber. The Assyrians had shown the superiority of iron technology over that of copper and bronze. The Nubians knew that the security of their kingdom now depended on building an iron industry. Thus at Meroë, an iron-using state emerged. Iron improved their weapons and gave them better arrows and spears for hunting, hoes for ploughing, and axes for felling timber. The potential for the economy was enormous.

The Meroë region was also well suited to agriculture. Unlike Napata, Meroë provided access to a large expanse of land. Iron tools were, however, necessary in this tropical rainfall region. On the floodplain of the Lower Nile, such tools were not required. In Meroë, the floodplain was smaller and the Nile valley was narrower. In the older city of Napata, the land available was not even enough to support a growing population. At Meroë, iron tools enabled the people to "tame" the land, well beyond the areas close to the river, and also to develop an agricultural system that was later to become common in the African savanna. They were able to cultivate tropical millet and sorghum and graze cattle, thereby developing a successful mixed farming economy.

As with Egypt, where agriculture was also successful, Meroë was able to use its surplus to promote trade. Meroë also enjoyed a favorable location for trade. Trading parties going to Egypt could detour to Meroë and rejoin the Nile near the town now known as Faras. Such a detour actually enabled them to avoid the obstacles of the third and second cataracts on the Nile. Meroë also had an outlet to the Red Sea. Should relations with Egypt become strained, this provided an alternative trade route. As the Red Sea grew in importance as a major route between the Mediterranean, India, and the Far East, Meroë also profited immensely. Indeed, the extensive use of the Red Sea for trade purposes actually enhanced the prosperity of Meroë, which was able to export ostrich feathers, gold, ivory, ebony, and leopard skins. Meroë became a major city, supported by its iron industry and trade. Political and economic success enabled the creation of what is now known as the Meroitic civilization.

The use of iron created some new elements in the Meroitic economy, in contrast to that of Egypt. The major industrial occupations were iron-smelting and toolmaking. The success of the kingdom of Meroë resulted from its ability to produce large quantities of superior iron weapons and tools. It was not dependent on irrigation and a floodplain but on savanna land cleared with iron implements.

Its inhabitants concentrated on tropical cereals. Unlike the Egyptian farmers who lived in a densely populated land and were closely controlled by the agents of the pharaohs, the peasants of Meroë were scattered over a larger area, divided into many villages governed by less powerful officials. Although they paid taxes, their assessment was not as rigorous as in Egypt. The pastoralists had more land and enjoyed a greater degree of autonomy than their Egyptian counterparts.

The seat of government was the city of Meroë. The king, the bureaucrats, and the craftsmen who worked for the court all lived there. The king was an absolute monarch. Although there was a ruling family, a candidate had to be approved by the nobles and priests. A few unpopular monarchs were removed. The king's mother exercised tremendous influence. The king controlled trade and derived considerable revenues from the export of mining and hunting products. Hunting on behalf of the king produced elephants, leopards, and ostriches. Hunters also served as soldiers in war, and trained elephants were used in war.

MEROITIC CULTURE AND SOCIETY

Meroë passed through stages, including an initial stage of duplicating Egyptian culture and a later phase of indigenization and creativity that led to a distinctive Meroitic culture. In the early phase, Meroitic religion and politics were shaped by those of Egypt. The founding rulers described themselves as kings of Upper and Lower Egypt, although their influence was among the Nubians. The kings had pyramids built over their tombs. Egyptian hieroglyphics were adopted, and Egyptian was used as the official language. Egyptian gods were adopted.

The second stage saw the development of a distinctive Meroitic culture. The Meroitic language replaced the Egyptian one, and a Meroitic script was invented. In religion, while Egyptian gods were retained, new ones were added. The most notable addition was Apedemek, the Lion-God, associated with the southern Nile (that is, the Nubian area). A priesthood of Apedemek was created, which kept live lions as symbols. The priests of Apedemek and other gods were influential, rich, and powerful. The god himself was represented either by the head of a lion and the body of a snake or by the head of a lion and the body of a man. He was a warrior god and was also associated with wisdom and learning. One notable prayer to Apedemek has survived as an inscription written in Egyptian hieroglyphics:

Thou are greeted, Apedemek, lord of Naqa; great god, lord of Musawwarat-es-Sofra; splendid god, at the head of Nubia. Lion of the south, strong of arm. Great god, the one who comes to those who call him. The one who carries the secret, concealed in his being, who was not seen by any eye. Who is a companion for men and women, who will not be hindered in heaven and earth. Who procures nourishment for all men in this his name "Perfect Awakener." The one who hurls his hot breath against his enemy, in this his name "Great of Power." Who kills the enemy. . . . The one who punishes all who commit crimes against him. Who prepares the place for those who give themselves to him. Who gives to those who call to him. Lord of life, great in his sight.[1]

Meroitic art and architecture also had their own features. Statues, pictures, and engravings of tropical animals like giraffes, lions, elephants, and ostriches were made. So also was pottery, for domestic use and decoration. Meroitic pyramids were small in size and regular in shape.

THE END OF MEROË

Meroë use its iron weapons and trained elephants to stabilize its kingdom for many years. However, it eventually began to experience a decline. An ambition to expand the kingdom to Lower Nubia between the first and second cataracts led to wars with Egypt and its Roman rulers. A Roman counterattack in about 23 B.C. ended in disaster for Meroë. Not only did the Egyptian army reach Napata, but it ruined many areas and carried away thousands as captives, who were later sold into slavery. Meroë survived and was actually prosperous and stable again between 12 B.C. and A.D. 12. For another two centuries, relations with Egypt were peaceful, and Meroë profited from regional trade. The kingdom came to an end in about A.D. 300. It lost its advantages from producing iron, having overexploited its timber resources. Its land, too, became less productive for agriculture, perhaps due to erosion. It also lost considerable revenues from regional trade, due in part to the decline in demand for its exports and the vigorous competition and challenges offered by its neighbor, Aksum, for the control of the Red Sea trade to the Indian Ocean. In ca. A.D. 350, an attack by King Ezana of Aksum brought the city of Meroë to an inglorious end.

THE RISE OF AKSUM

The second impressive kingdom in the region was Aksum, which also built great structures, created a written language, adopted Christianity, and profited from international trade.

Aksum was located in the Ethiopian Highlands east and south of Kush. The area was populated in ancient times. By the first century A.D., Aksum had grown into a powerful kingdom. The king credited with the foundation of the kingdom is Ezana (A.D. 320–50). He was able to build a strong army that was used to establish control of various areas. Ezana's success in defeating Kush gave Aksum greater control of the Red Sea trade. Thereafter, Ezana consolidated both his own power and that of his kingdom and created a period of great prosperity. Control was established over a number of vassal states that sent tributes to the king. The kingdom continued to prosper long after Ezana died. It brought more areas under its control. Even during the sixth century A.D. when its fame was diminishing, it was able to extend beyond the Red Sea to incorporate the region of Saba, in modern Yemen.

AKSUM CULTURE AND SOCIETY

The kingdom was governed by a powerful king, who resided in the capital. The king exercised direct power in the capital territory, and he delegated power

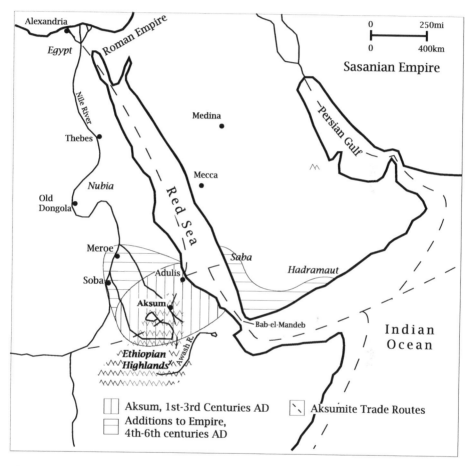

Kingdom of Aksum.

to regional leaders in the provincial areas. Leading chiefs as well as civil servants managed the administration. Levies and tributes were collected from the provinces. When areas asserted their independence, they also refused to remit the tributes. The king also derived revenues from the control of the import and export trade. In addition, the peasants who used the irrigated and terraced agricultural land had to pay for it.

Like Kush, Aksum drew substantial wealth from the Red Sea trade with India. Aksum was a center of long-distance commerce, able to dominate the African market of the Red Sea trade for over 300 years between the fourth and eighth centuries A.D. Aksum exported rhinoceros horn, war elephants, incense, and tortoiseshell to Mediterranean markets. As imports, it received olive oil, silk, muslins, wine, glass, and brass and copper objects. A thriving seaport was established at Adulis, growing to become the most famous ivory market in northeast Africa. Aksum was a prosperous kingdom. The king collected taxes on imports and exports, in addition to establishing control of foreign trade. The kingdom minted its own coins, which eased commercial transactions, especially at Adulis. A successful commercial economy did not mean that Aksum abandoned agriculture. It had people with skills in tropical agriculture, as well as skills in terracing and irrigating desert land. Many farmers exploited the fertile foothills and valleys of Tigré and Amhara.

A vibrant culture emerged. Many people were literate, and they were able to develop a written language, known as Ge'ez, which later evolved into the modern Amhara language in Ethiopia. Ezana was one of the earliest kings in Africa to become a Christian. In addition, he made Christianity the official religion of Aksum. Conversion was a major decision, made partly to use religion to unite the kingdom or maintain strong control over the people. According to the granite inscriptions on Ezana's monument, he probably also believed that the religion would improve the administration of his kingdom: "I will rule the people with righteousness and justice, and will not oppress them, and may they preserve this Throne which I have set up for the Lord of Heaven." The religious legacy has been enduring, lasting long after the collapse of the kingdom of Aksum. King Ezana established the foundation of what is now known as the Ethiopian Church. The adoption of Christianity enabled Aksum to strengthen its trade relations with the eastern Mediterranean, which was controlled by the Greeks. Christianity continued to grow throughout the life of the kingdom and developed its own distinctive traditions.

THE FALL OF AKSUM

The prosperity of Aksum began to decline from the seventh century A.D. for two major reasons. First, its agricultural and commercial production declined. This has been attributed to environmental degradation caused by uncontrollable erosion, excessive land use, and reckless deforestation.

The second and the more important reason was that Aksum lost its commercial power to Persia, a major trading rival, which was able to gain control of the Red Sea trade from about A.D. 600. The Persians expelled Aksum from the Arabian peninsula. A hundred years later, more losses were incurred when the Arabs began to take control of the African and Arabian sectors of the Red Sea trade. The spread of Islam in western Asia and northern Africa gave the Arabs a great political and commercial advantage. The trade between the Indian Ocean and the Mediterranean that used to pass through the Red Sea was diverted to Arabia through the Persian Gulf. Losing most of its lucrative trade, the kingdom of Aksum lacked the resources to compete. By about A.D. 800, Aksum had moved its capital south into the interior of the Ethiopian Highlands, and its kingdom had become very much reduced. Without the revenues to sustain the kings and nobles, the kingdom became dependent on agriculture. A landed aristocracy emerged, but they were not as rich as their predecessors who had depended on commerce. The kingdom was isolated, and Arab and Greek influence declined. The most enduring legacy became the Christian religion, which survived the end of the kingdom. Aksum was able to use its isolation to develop an African Christian culture and to escape the spread of Islam after the seventh century.

NOTE

1. Quoted in P. L. Shinnie, *Meroë: A Civilization of the Sudan* (New York: Praeger, 1967), p. 143.

SUGGESTIONS FOR FURTHER READING

Davidson, Basil. *African Civilization Revisited.* 4th printing. Trenton, N.J.: Africa World Press, 1998.

Falola, Toyin, ed. *Africa*, Vol. 1 *African History before 1885.* Durham, N.C.: Carolina Academic Press, 2000. Chapter 4.

Mokhtar, G., ed. *Ancient Civilizations of Africa.* Vol. 2 of *UNESCO General History of Africa.* Berkeley: University of California Press, 1981.

O'Connor, David. *Ancient Nubia: Egypt's Rival in Africa.* Philadelphia: University Museum of Archaeology and Anthropology, University of Pennsylvania, 1993.

Shinnie, P.L. *Meroë: A Civilization of the Sudan.* New York: Praeger, 1967.

Zabkar, L.V. *Apedemak: Lion God of Meroë.* Warminster, England: Aris & Phillips Ltd., 1975.

6

The Greeks and Romans in North Africa, 332 B.C.+

Today, so deep and prevalent is the Arab impact on North Africa that it is seldom remembered that the region witnessed the penetration and spread of Hellenic, Phoenician, and Roman cultures before the age of Islam in the seventh century A.D. The Greeks established a dynasty in Egypt in 332 B.C. that lasted till the Roman conquest in 30 B.C. The Greeks and the Romans had varying degrees of influence in other parts of North Africa.

EGYPT UNDER THE PTOLEMIES: ECONOMY

Ptolemy was the first of the fifteen Greek-speaking pharaohs who ruled Egypt during a period of 300 years. Trade was of paramount importance to the Greeks. Egypt was regarded as an important part of the international trading network: It was strategically located to tap the products of the Indian Ocean and the African interior in exchange for those of Mediterranean Europe. Egypt also had the fertile land to produce sufficient food for a large number of administrators and merchants stationed in the region. So important was the interest in trade that by 250 B.C. the dynasty had assembled a huge trading fleet of almost 4,000 ships. To maximize its trading advantages, the dynasty established Alexandria, a trading city suitably located in the Nile Delta, on the Mediterranean coast. Two other cities were equally famous: Naucratis, a Greek emporium, and Ptolemais. In addition, the Greek dynasty created the new port city of Paraetonium.

The various projects to promote trade achieved their desired results. A merchant class was established in Egypt, Alexandria grew into an important city, the

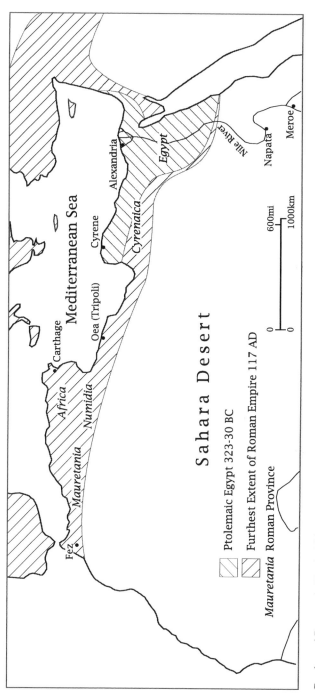

Greeks and Romans in North Africa.

Egyptian trading network expanded, and trade with the African interior flourished, contributing to the growth of Meroë and later Aksum. The Arabian camel, instead of the Egyptian donkey, became popular and effective as a pack animal used in crossing the desert between the Nile and the Red Sea. The camel was able to cope with water shortage and desert heat. The Greek-speaking leaders and the merchant class lived a comfortable life, maintained by the profits from the trade and the taxes collected from the Egyptian peasants.

Throughout the period of Greek and Roman rule, the port of Alexandria was the leading commercial center in the Mediterranean. From here, Egypt exported grains and other agricultural products, papyrus (the cheapest writing material at the time), perfumes, medicaments, linen, and jewelry. From India and Arabia came ships that docked on the Red Sea coast, bringing with them goods of oriental and African origins, such as ebony, ivory, pearls, precious stones, textiles, incense, and spices. These were carried overland, then down the Nile to Alexandria where they were again transported by sea to the west. Animals were among the most desired articles of trade—lions, camels, rhinoceroses, ostriches, crocodiles, and hippopotami were all taken to the major fighting arenas of the Roman world.

Agriculture grew as well. The Ptolemies were able to reclaim additional land in the fertile basin, which was distributed as agricultural land to peasants. However, the peasants experienced very harsh treatment. Not only did they have to pay more tax, but the system of collection could be draconian. The Greek-appointed tax collectors penetrated the nooks and crannies of the land to add to the list of taxpayers. They added to the tax as well, by remeasuring the floodplain in order to reevaluate taxes. They set peasants against each other, by rewarding with more land those who promised to pay additional taxes, thereby punishing those who, for one reason or another, were unable to farm large areas.

The Ptolemies tried to defend Egypt from their rivals, and they also attempted wars of expansion. In the third and second centuries B.C., they were constantly at war with their rivals, Macedonia and Syria, mainly to control the eastern Mediterranean. The Ptolemies were able to build a fleet that mastered the seas, conquered Cyprus and Cyrenaica, and imposed their garrisons in the Aegean islands and in some cities on the mainland of southern and western Asia Minor.

IMPACT OF GREEK CULTURE

This period was noted for cultural changes and the exchange of cultures between the Greeks and the Egyptians. The Greeks had long respected the Egyptians, holding their arts and religion in very high regard. Indeed, many notable Greek scholars regarded Egypt as the most civilized place, with an advanced religion, clean people, and orderly government. The Greeks actually invented the word "civilized," and its application to Egypt fitted what they had in mind: a politically stable society where arts and religion flourished. The Greeks knew that they had much to learn from Egypt. The Greeks exploited Egypt in a way that damaged many of its established cultural practices and beliefs. They were, however, able to borrow many aspects of Egyptian religion, arts, and sciences, which were integrated into the Greek cultural system.

First, the period saw an impact on languages and writing. The use of the ancient Egyptian language declined, as the use of the Greek language spread. Nobles and civil servants used Greeks for official transactions. As Egyptian scribes were replaced, the training of new scribes was conducted in Greek. Egyptian hieroglyphics were abandoned and replaced by the simpler Greek writing.

Second, an enduring legacy of this period can be found in two names—Ethiopia and Libya. The Greeks invented the words: "Ethiopian," to describe the blacks who lived to the south of Egypt, and "Libyan," to describe those who lived to the west of Egypt. Both names now refer to modern African countries.

Third, Alexandria emerged as a leading city of culture, a reputation that survived the fall of the Ptolemies. In Alexandria, many cultures intermixed and intermarried, and the cosmopolitan city became home to Egyptians, Greeks, and Jews. Many of the Egyptian Copts who adopted aspects of Greek culture became known as Alexandrians. A great library was built in Alexandria, reflecting the attention to scholarship and the pursuit of knowledge. The city was also famous for its book trade, which supplied the literate citizens of the Nile valley. Knowledge advanced in the fields of medicine, physics, mathematics, mechanics, and geography. The cumulative knowledge of the Egyptians over a 3,000-year period was built upon in many new and creative ways. Religious ideas received great attention. When Christianity was introduced, Alexandria became a leading center of theological discussions. It was also here that other leading philosophical ideas were developed, notably gnosticism. *Gnosis* is the Greek word for "knowledge," and gnosticism is the subconscious knowledge derived from insight and self-awareness rather than reason. Gnosticism was a way to seek knowledge about God and other spiritual powers. When Christianity began to spread, gnosticism was regarded as opposed to the new religion, and the movement was dismissed as a heresy.

Finally, Egyptian culture interacted with other Mediterranean cultures, taking from others but also giving to them. Reliance on the Greeks and Macedonians in the bureaucracy and armies attracted many people with their cultures. The Greeks did not ignore all Egyptian local customs or the religious roles of the pharaohs. They built new temples to the ancient Egyptian gods, and they employed Egyptians in their administration. A number of oriental cults spread in the Greco-Roman world. Even after the Romans had conquered Egypt, the fusion of Greek and Egyptian cultures—known as Hellenism—did not come to an end. The Ptolemies promoted the spread of the Egyptian cult of Osiris and Apis, which became popular in the west. The goddess Isis also became well known and was later adopted by the Romans as one of their official deities. Roman villas were decorated with ideas from the landscapes of Egypt. Obelisks from Egyptian temples as well as Egyptian granite were taken to adorn Roman buildings.

THE ROMAN ERA

The coastal areas of North Africa had experienced external invasions and control by the Phoenicians and Greeks. By the mid-first century A.D., the Romans were able to extend their empire to many parts of western Europe and the entire Mediterranean world. Rome conquered Carthage in 146 B.C. This North African extension was named "Afrika" by the Romans, a name that was later applied to the entire continent. Two centuries later, the Romans extended their control over the Berber populations to the west of Carthage, then known as the kingdoms of Numidia and Mauretania.

As with the Greeks in Egypt, the Romans regarded North Africa as an economic estate to be maximally exploited for grain and olive oil. Agricultural resources were fully tapped, especially the production of wheat in the coastal plains and olive trees in the dry areas of the hinterland. The land devoted to these two products was expanded and the products sent to Rome, not to be sold but to be distributed freely to privileged citizens.

In the case of Egypt, the major goal of Roman economic policy was to produce grains for Rome. The peasantry was heavily taxed to the point that it became unprofitable for many farmers to work on their lands; instead, they took to banditry. Africans were heavily taxed in order for the Roman elite to enjoy themselves. To protect the supply of grains from Egypt, the Romans ensured that troublemakers from Rome would not have access to the territory. The governor of Egypt itself was a prefect of equestrian rank, to ensure obedience to the emperor in Rome. The borders of Egypt were protected to prevent external attacks.

The Romans transferred to North Africa their ideas of class and privilege. Distinct class and occupational lines emerged in their colonies. The Roman administrators and wealthy people, mainly "Romanized Carthaginians" (a mixed group of Phoenicians and Berbers), lived in the major towns and coastal cities. Many of the members of this privileged class had huge farm estates where they used slave labor. The Romans built an urban culture, with about 500 cities having a total population of 2 million. Within the cities were great buildings, while a network of roads linked the cities with one another and with the ports along the coast.

The lower class, the vast majority of the population, lived outside the cities and estates. These were the indigenous Berbers, tenaciously clinging to their culture and language and eager to free themselves from the exploitative colonial rule. The Roman authorities promised to offer them protection against raids from desert nomads, but this was never provided. The Berbers were resentful of the Roman tax collectors. The Romans allowed the Berbers to stay on their land but imposed heavy taxes on them.

Other classes were treated by the Romans as low, poor, or outcasts. Slaves worked on the estates of the rich. Mainly Berbers, they were captured in the desert. The nomads constituted a class of their own, located outside the farming areas. They herded sheep, goats, and cattle. Their political allegiance was loose, sometimes to nomadic leaders, sometimes to Berber princes, and sometimes to the Romans. They did not necessarily consider themselves as part of the Roman Empire, and the majority of them actually lived outside the areas defined as Roman provinces.

Peace was difficult to maintain in areas far removed from towns and estates. The most unstable areas were the southern fringes of the empire, which Berbers from the Sahara Desert attacked at various times. All efforts to patrol these areas proved abortive. In addition, there were always Berber chieftains who were seeking independence. By the fourth century A.D., a number of chiefs in the areas known as Numidia and Mauretania had declared their independence. Early in the fifth century, the northern European Vandals attacked the Romans and drove them out of North Africa.

A NEW RELIGION: CHRISTIANITY

The period of Greco-Roman rule coincided with the spread of Christianity in many parts of North and northeast Africa from the first to the sixth century A.D. Although Christianity did not spread to many parts of Africa until the nineteenth century and later, the early beginnings were significant (see Chapter 15). Alexandria, the hub of commerce in Egypt, was also the most important center of Christendom during the first century A.D. The city was home to great theologians who defined the new religion, as well as a bishopric probably established by Mark, the disciple and gospel-writer. The Septuagint, the oldest Greek translation of the Bible, was made at Alexandria. Christianity also received some support from the people.

The new religion appealed to the urban poor and the peasants, perhaps because it offered hope, at least, of an afterlife. The people despised the Roman tax collectors. If the secular authorities could not save them, the message of Christianity told them that they would not suffer for long or, at least, their suffering would end on earth. To those who suffered hardships and oppression, the promise of a better afterlife drew them to Christianity.

In Egypt and other parts of Africa, Christianity offered an opportunity to express nationalist sentiments against Roman rule. The emperor, regarding himself as the pharaoh did, saw in Christianity a great challenge to his divine authority and power. Turning to Christianity was interpreted as turning against the emperor. Until the early fourth century, Christians suffered a great deal of persecution. Certain elements of Egyptian culture made Christianity appealing to the people. They had previously believed in some of the fundamentals of the new Christian theology such as the resurrection of the dead, an afterlife with punishments and rewards, the idea that a god (like Jesus Christ) could be put to death, and the idea that a child could have an earthly mother without a father (as in the birth of Jesus).

There was also the growth of a monastic culture, in part to escape oppression by the government officials and other worldly problems. A group of devout people would seclude themselves to dedicate themselves primarily to worship.

Rather than concerning themselves with worldly issues, they meditated on the spiritual.

Christianity spread westward, reaching the Berber-speaking peoples. Resentment to Roman rule became a reason why many converted, in spite of the threat of persecution. The Berber-speaking Christians were treated as enemies of the Roman Empire. The persecution of the early Christian Church ended in A.D. 302. Ten years later, Emperor Constantine converted to Christianity, which thus became the official religion.

Conversion to Christianity continued, but anti-Roman nationalism took another turn. The most notable rejection of the official Roman Church was the formation of the Donatists by about 400 North African bishops. The Donatists among the indigenous Berber population were able to blend with Christianity many of their local customs and beliefs. A number of new ceremonies and doctrines were added to Christian practices. Donatist Christianity was a source of unity among its members. The Donatist bishops and their followers were persecuted, but many refused to yield. Many even sought martyrdom because they believed that it would secure their salvation. Among the staunch supporters of the Roman Church was Aurelius Augustinus (A.D. 354–430), who became one of the most prominent founding fathers of the church and a saint, now known as Saint Augustine of Hippo.

A similar development occurred in Egypt where the Coptic Church (practicing Monophysitism) developed in spite of vigorous opposition by the Roman Church. Among the major beliefs of the Monophysites was that Jesus, being divine, could never have been a human being. The official Roman Church dismissed this belief as heretical and expelled those who subscribed to it. The majority of Egyptians took to Monophysitism, thus creating an identity for themselves with their own practices, including a monastic tradition and the use of the local Coptic language.

Egyptian Monophysite missionaries spread Christianity to the south, notably into Nubia, in the sixth and seventh centuries. Three Christian Nubian kingdoms emerged—Noba, Makurra, and Alwa—with prosperous Christians in power. Some of the wealth was spent on church buildings and monasteries.

SUGGESTIONS FOR FURTHER READING

Bernal, Martin. *Black Athena: The Afroasiatic Roots of Classical Civilization*. New Brunswick, N.J.: Rutgers University Press, 1987.

Falola, Toyin, ed. *Africa*. Vol. 1, *African History before 1885*. Durham, N.C.: Carolina Academic Press, 2000. Chapter 11.

Mokhtar, G., ed. *UNESCO General History of Africa*. Vol. 2, *Ancient Civilizations of Africa*. Berkeley: University of California Press, 1981.

Sharpe, Samuel. *Egyptian Mythology and Egyptian Christianity with Their Influences on the Opinions of Modern Christendom*. London: Carter Publishers, 1896.

7

Ethiopia: The Emergence of a Christian Kingdom, A.D. 1250+

The glory of Aksum (see Chapter 5) was restored in the central highlands of the Ethiopian interior during the twelfth century. Before 1150, Ethiopia was no more than an isolated Christian state, a farming society dominated by a landed aristocracy. It was militarily weak and unable to even withstand the forces of its southern neighbors in the Shawa (or Shoa) plateau. However, from the early eleventh century, its fortune began to change, partly because of the revival of the Red Sea trade. The Ethiopian economy now broadened to include participation in regional and international trade, as it established trade links north of Adulis (the old port of Aksum) through which it reached the islands of Dahlak. Two powerful dynasties emerged, the Zagwe and the Solomonid.

THE ZAGWE DYNASTY, 1150–1270

The revival of Ethiopia was due to the emergence of the Zagwe dynasty, founded by a commoner, Takla Haymanot. The Zagwe overthrew the Aksumite line of kings, centralized power, established a new capital at Adefa, built a large army, promoted Christianity, and embarked on aggressive territorial expansion that led to the creation of the Ethiopian kingdom.

The rulers of the Zagwe dynasty reorganized the administration and politics. First, they replaced many state officials. The old ruling families in many towns and villages were dropped in preference for associates and members of the royal family and military commanders who practiced Christianity. The provincial governors were charged with the responsibility of maintaining security, sending men to serve in the army whenever the capital called upon them to do so, ensuring that trade remained undisturbed and traders were secure, and generating resources (through taxation) to finance the central administration.

Second, the Zagwe spent time and resources on the army. From its safe location in the central highlands, the Ethiopian state conquered areas south of Lake Tana and the Shawa plateau. Conquered areas were administered by powerful governors who enjoyed a great deal of autonomy.

Third, they benefited from international trade, with Ethiopia becoming the most important supplier of myrrh and frankincense to the Muslim world. Ethiopia was also a major supplier of slaves, especially women who became domestics and concubines of Muslims in Yemen and southwestern Arabia. The trade was highly lucrative, and the slaves came mainly as war captives from the people around the south of Lake Tana. In addition, the trade supplied small quantities of ivory and gold to Egypt. Under King Lalibela during the thirteenth century, Ethiopia became prosperous and famous, able to maintain diplomatic relations with Cairo and finance expensive public projects.

The political and religious officials were rewarded in various ways. Many were appointed as provincial governors, with power to impose tax on the subject population and keep some of the proceeds. Leading officers of state were granted extensive personal estates where they put people to work for them producing food and other items. Christian missionaries were allowed to operate in conquered areas, being granted free land by the Zagwe kings and protected by the governors. The missionaries established churches and monasteries, spread a Christian culture, and provided religious education to many people.

Ethiopia's survival and progress depended on the monarchy and the church. When the king was strong, the kingdom was united and strong. When the king was weak or young, the aristocrats and noblemen took advantage, asserting themselves and even governing the districts as autonomous leaders. The church was involved in politics. The *abuna* (bishop) was a powerful force. When the monasteries and the *abuna* supported the emperor, the kingdom was united and strong. But there were times when competition was so intense that the position of *abuna* was vacant or powerful monasteries failed to fully support the king.

CHRISTIANITY

Ethiopia is one of the earliest and most successful centers of Christianity in Africa. Irrespective of the political fortune of the kingdom, it always maintained its Christian tradition. Ethiopia regarded itself as part of the Egyptian Coptic Church, an important part of the early archdiocese of Alexandria. Even with the rise of Islam in North Africa and the decline of the Coptic Church, Ethiopia was committed to the appointment of an Egyptian as its leading bishop.

The Zagwe kings supported the Ethiopian Church in maintaining relations with the Holy Land in Palestine and also contributed to the prestige of Christianity as a religion and way of life. Ethiopian missionaries and other Christians used the established trade routes with Egypt to travel to Jerusalem.

Ethiopian Christianity continued to develop in its own distinctive way. Its church leaders remained true to the monastic tradition that dated back to the sixth century. The missionaries of the Zagwe era continued to preach the old Monophysite religion. The theological influence was drawn from the Old Testament. Facing the growing power of Islam, and neighbors committed to indigenous religions, the Ethiopians used Christianity to forge an identity for themselves—they believed that they were the chosen people of God and the real descendants of ancient Israel. With its rituals and beliefs drawn from what was perceived to be uncorrupted Christianity, Ethiopia stood as an outpost of the religion. The church also contributed to the

Painted ceiling, Debra Berhan church, Ethiopia.

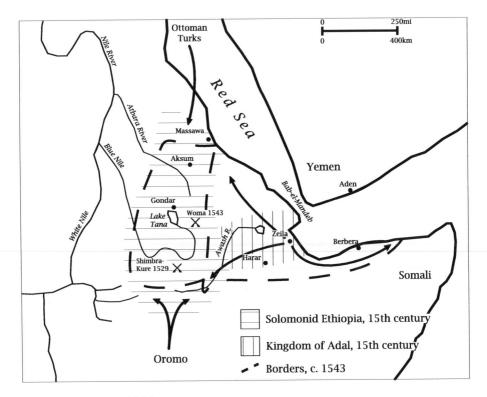

Solomonid Ethiopia and Adal.

development of education, literature, and the arts—the monasteries served as educational centers, and monks devoted considerable time to intellectual pursuits.

One legacy of the Zagwe era that has survived till today is the solid rock churches of Lalibela. A series of impressive churches, all monoliths, were created by the Ethiopian monks in the thirteenth century, during the reign of King Lalibela (1200–1250), the greatest of the Zagwe rulers. These churches, eleven of which have been discovered, were hewn out of rock in the Adefa region. A set of smaller churches, also carved out of mountains, have been discovered in Tigré. Given the slow and laborious process required, only the most dedicated could have contemplated such a project and carried it through to its conclusion. Each church was named after a site in Jerusalem—further evidence of the link— such as Golgotha (the tomb of Jesus Christ).

THE SOLOMONID DYNASTY, 1270–1550

A new line of kings was established in 1270. Known as the Solomonids, they based their claim to power on an old Aksum belief that a traditional union was cre-

Crown of Emperor Menelik II, Ethiopia.

ated with the marriage of King Solomon to the Aksumite queen of Sheba (Saba). They traced their descent from this union. Members of the dynasty originated in the Amhara region, in the central highlands, speaking the Amharic language, now widely used in modern Ethiopia.

In keeping with the traditions of their claims to power, the Solomonid kings created elaborate rituals, and kingship was regarded as divine. The *Kebra Nagast* (*Glory of Kings*), an older document, was refined to state the claim of this dynasty to power. Now one of the most important documents in Ethiopian history, the chronicle states that Yekuno Amlak and his successors were descendants of King Solomon of Israel. To narrate the story, which remains important even till today, Makeda, the Queen of Sheba, visited Jerusalem and later gave birth to Solomon's son Ebna-Hakim, who later became King Menelik I of Ethiopia, consecrated by his father. Unhappy about how his mother was treated, Menelik I stole the Ark of the Covenant and took it to Ethiopia. Thereafter, the laws of Israel were established in Ethiopia. Whether the legend is accurate or not is not the issue, but there is a strong belief that the Ark of the Covenant is still in Ethiopia and that all Ethiopian kings must trace their descent from Solomon.

The Solomonid dynasty brought many changes to Ethiopian politics and society. After a civil war in the 1290s, a system was put in place to check all ambitious members of the royal family. As soon as a new king was installed, a list of possible rivals to the throne was compiled, and they were then confined to Mount Gishen, a secure mountain fortress guarded by soldiers. The number of detained princes increased, as the practice continued for over 200 years. Detained on what was known as the "mountain of kings," the exiled princes enjoyed amenities within Mount Gishen, and many took to a life of serious religious meditation, writing, and composition of songs.

The Solomonid kings also exercised more power than many of their predecessors. A chronicle dealing with one of them, Emperor Zara Yaqob (1434–68), written about fifty years after his death, described the king as severe and authoritarian. He was so much opposed to "pagan worship" that many people were put to death. Monks who showed little devotion to Christianity were punished. Yaqob appointed his sisters as governors to administer the provinces, and "all the peoples trembled before the undaunted might of the king."[1] The account of his coronation showed that the Ethiopian kings had substantial wealth: "After arriving within the walls of Axum, the king had brought to him much gold which he scattered as far as the city gate on the carpets which were spread along his route. This amount of gold was more than a hundred ounces."[2] A sixteenth-century record indicated that the power of the king and members of his court was sometimes oppressive, and the citizens were not always happy with their rulers:

There would be much fruit and much more cultivation in the country, if the great men did not ill-treat the people, for they take whatever they have. The latter are thus not willing to provide more than they require and what is necessary for themselves.

In no part that we went about in were there butchers' shops, except at the Court, and nobody from the common people may kill a cow (even though it is his own) without leave from the lord of the country.

The people . . . are afraid of excommunication, and if they are ordered to do something that is to their disadvantage they do it from fear of excommunication.[3]

For instance, in the southern districts of Hadya, Ifat, and Shoa, the people were displeased with their governors. The majority of the farming population refused to adopt Christianity, and they regarded with hostility the Christian aristocrats who exploited them. Local governors created large estates, using the labor of the local population for their personal benefit.

As with most dynasties, the Solomonid kings protected the territories they already possessed while expanding into other areas and strengthening the central government at the same time. During the fourteenth and fifteenth centuries, they expanded southward. The aims of the expansion were to increase the size of the kingdom, obtain more revenues from conquered areas, control the trade routes of the Shawa plateau, and spread Christianity. They recorded significant successes, although they were to initiate a long and complicated rivalry with the Muslim sultanates in the Awash valley region.

Evidence of external relations clearly suggests that Ethiopia was strong and respected. During the fourteenth century, the Ethiopian emperor was the protector of the patriarchate of Alexandria. Relations with Egypt were cordial. Ethiopia also reopened contacts with Europe during the fifteenth century, with diplomatic exchanges with Spain, Portugal, and Venice. After 1493, the Portuguese established important contacts with Ethiopia.

Christianity remained the state religion. The Solomonid kings promoted faith; some even insisted on the recitation of prayers at canonical hours and prohibited many traditional religious practices. New monasteries were constructed, not hewn out of rock as before but as simple but efficient circular buildings constructed of mud and poles and covered with thatch. Attempts to create new monasteries and convert the so-called pagan population in the southerly areas of the kingdom were unsuccessful, in part because of the resistance of the people to the imposition of alien rule and religion but more because of the growing power of Islam. Ethiopia was committed to the Coptic Church in spite of attempts by the Portuguese to introduce Catholicism in the sixteenth and seventeenth centuries. A Catholic missionary recorded that Catholics were unwelcome, persecuted as "disturbers of the public tranquility, who had come into Ethiopia with no other intention than to abolish the ancient laws and customs of the country, to sow divisions between father and son, and preach up a revolution."[4]

The change in church architecture was reflected in residential architecture as well, as the Solomonid dynasty abandoned the Aksum style of rectangular buildings made of stone. Instead, they opted for the circular design that was common in the rest of the continent.

The Solomonid kings abandoned the previous tradition of living permanently in the stone palace at Adefa. Instead, they opted for mobile palaces of simple design, located in various parts of the kingdom. The palace was now a collection of tents, resembling a camp. Within a period of twelve months, the royal camp could be moved three times.

The constant relocation of the royal courts was motivated by political and economic considerations. The presence of the court in a province ensured loyalty to the kings, payment of taxation by the people, and direct administration for some months. In remote areas, the court was able to police the people and check possible acts of rebellion. However, the construction of new buildings and the feeding of a large number of state officials ruined an area in which the court was located. Resources in food and wood in a small area became quickly depleted and the environment so badly damaged that in some instances during the sixteenth century it took an area occupied by the court at least a decade to recover. Given its constant relocations, the court was consuming rather than producing, relying on the local population to supply its needs. The members of the court and the military were so numerous that a district could not meet their needs for too long a time, which explains in part why the court moved from place to place. It was difficult to obtain large regular quantities of food supplies from areas located in mountainous terrain unconducive to extensive farming.

ETHIOPIA AND ITS MUSLIM RIVALS

The push to the south brought the Solomonid kings into contact and conflict with the expanding Islamic frontiers. From the eighth century onward, the Swahili city–states (see Chapter 10) were drawn into the Indian Ocean trade. The Arabs were heavily involved in this trade. In their quest to make more profits, Muslim merchants of Arab origins began to penetrate the African interior. During the tenth and eleventh centuries, they were moving in the direction of the Ethiopian Highlands, in the area of the Awash valley. Here, they came in contact with Kushitic-speaking Africans, set up trading colonies, and made contact with African traders. Gradually, they began to control the economy of the Awash valley, especially the trade in ivory and slaves.

The Arabs' economic power and political interests were to conflict with those of the Solomonid dynasty, which was eager to extend its political control in the same region. During the twelfth and thirteenth centuries, the Muslims established a number of small states such as the sultanate of Shoa and the kingdom of Ifat. They penetrated further inland, to the south of the Blue Nile, in search of slaves, and they established a number of trading and raiding settlements such as Bali, Sharka, Hadya, and Dawara.

The Ethiopian kings were uncomfortable with the Muslim expansion into these areas. Under the Zagwe kings, Ethiopia was able to use its large army to check the Muslims. Between 1320 and 1340, Ethiopia was able to bring several small Muslim states, including Ifat, under its control. More interested in captives to sell, and with an army trained to capture people rather than to defend and expand a territory, the Muslim sultans were unable to match the Ethiopian army.

Failing to check Ethiopian power, the sultans of Ifat moved eastward, to the region of the Harar plateau, where they founded the new kingdom of Adal between the coastal port of Zeila and the Ethiopian Highlands. Far away from the Ethiopian kings and strategically located for trade and security, the Adal rulers rebuilt their power and prestige. They recruited their armies from among the Somali, thus drawing the Somali people into the conflict between Christian Ethiopia and Muslim Adal. Adal was also successful in converting the pastoral Somali to Islam. The Muslims were united, and Adal and Ethiopia engaged in a series of wars and competing raiding expeditions for captives and cattle for the greater part of the fifteenth century.

In 1526, under a Muslim general, Ahmad ibn Ibrahim, Adal decided on a jihad (holy war) against Ethiopia. Ahmad ibn Ibrahim was determined to reform Islam. He criticized the merchants for ignoring Islam and the political leaders for their debauchery, and he regarded the Christian kingdom of Ethiopia as an enemy. With access to modern firearms obtained from the Ottoman Turks, Adal was able to defeat the Ethiopian forces in 1529. The casualties on both sides were heavy, Ethiopian unity crumbled, and Adal overran southern Ethiopia and replaced the Christian governors with Islamic ones. The king of Ethiopia, the once confident Emperor Lebna-Dengel, was thoroughly humiliated, and the Muslims destroyed many churches and monasteries and much literature and artwork.

In the 1530s, Ethiopia had to reorganize its forces and also sought military assistance from the Portuguese with whom it had maintained contact since 1520. Meanwhile, Ahmad ibn Ibrahim was not consolidating his gains, many of his Somali soldiers had returned home, and the remainder of the Adal forces were left to police a large area. In 1543, Ethiopia was able to launch a successful retaliatory offensive that led to the death of Ahmad ibn Ibrahim and the collapse of his kingdom. In the years that followed, Ethiopia regained many of its territories in the south. However, the prolonged warfare with the Muslims led to the death of thousands of people, the destruction of valuable books, art treasures, and churches, and the conversion of many groups to Islam. In addition, the wars weakened both Ethiopia and Adal and left the southern region of Ethiopia militarily weak. The Oromo pastoralists to the northeast of Lake Turkana were able to expand into this region, although Ethiopia continued to maintain its unity and practice Christianity.

NOTES

1. Quoted in Basil Davidson, *African Civilization Revisited* (Trenton, N.J.: Africa World Press, 1991), p. 144.
2. Ibid., p. 145.
3. C.F. Beckingham and G.W.B. Huntingford, eds., *The Prester John of the Indies* (Cambridge: Hakluyt Society, 1961), p. 515.

4. Quoted in Robert O. Collins, *Eastern African History* (Princeton, N.J.: Markus Weiner, 1997), p. 87.

SUGGESTIONS FOR FURTHER READING

Falola, Toyin, ed. *Africa*. Vol. 1, *African History before 1885*. Durham, N.C.: Carolina Academic Press, 2000. Chapter 10.

Freeman-Grenville, G.S.P. *The East African Coast: Select Documents from the First to the Earlier Nineteenth Century*. 2nd ed. London: Rex Collins, 1975.

Ogot, B.A., and J.A. Kieran, eds. *Zamani: A Survey of East African History*. Nairobi, Kenya: East Africa Publishing House, 1968.

Samatar, Said, ed. *The Shadow of Conquest: Islam in Colonial Northeast Africa*. Trenton, N.J.: Red Sea Press, 1992.

Tamrat, T. *Church and State in Ethiopia, 1270–1527*. Oxford: Clarendon Press, 1972.

Ullendorff, Edward. *The Ethiopians*. London: Oxford University Press, 1960.

Zewde, Bahru. *A History of Modern Ethiopia, 1855–1974*. Addis Ababa, Ethiopia: Addis Ababa University Press, 1991.

8

The Spread of Islam, A.D. 622 Onward

In the Name of God,
the Merciful, the Compassionate
Praise belongs to God
the Lord of all Being
the All-merciful,
the All-compassionate,
the Master of the Day of Doom
Thee only we serve; to Thee alone we pray for succor.
Guide us in the straight path,
the path of those whom Thou hast blessed, not of those against whom
Thou art wrathful, nor of those who are astray.

> The opening statement of the *Holy Quran*

One of the most important events in African history was the spread of Islam from the seventh century onward. Initially associated with the Arab invasions of the Nile valley and the Maghrib (North Africa), the consequences of the spread of Islam and Arabic culture have remained important to this day. Not only is the entire North African region dominantly Islamic, but Islam also spread remarkably well in sub-Saharan Africa. Islam and Christianity are the two major universal religions in Africa, although there are more Muslims than Christians. Islam was also the first religion to profoundly change the majority of African societies, both incorporating new ideas into their lifestyles and blending indigenous

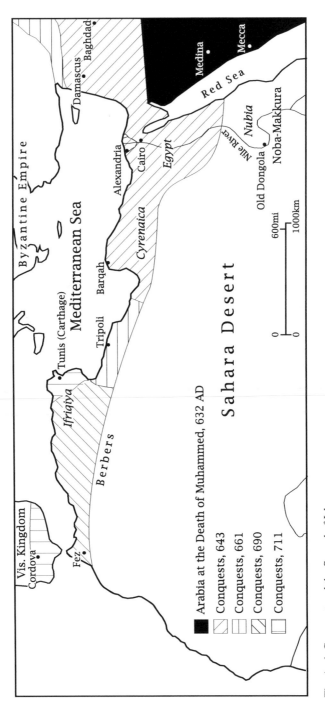

The Arab Conquest and the Spread of Islam.

practices with Islamic ones. As we shall see in the discussion of another major event, the Sokoto jihad, Islam also instigated a revolution in various parts of Africa (see Chapter 13). How did Islam start, how did it spread, and what were the consequences of its adoption?

THE PROPHET MUHAMMAD
AND THE ORIGINS OF ISLAM

The founder of Islam was the Holy Prophet Muhammad. He was born in Mecca in about A.D. 570. He started life as a trader before founding the religion of Islam. His personal conversion began at the age of forty, with the visions (divine revelations) that he received from Allah (God) through the Angel Jibreel (Gabriel). The Angel Jibreel commanded Muhammad to recite the following: "In the name of thy Lord who created, created Man of a blood-clot. And thy Lord is the Most Generous, who taught by the Pen, taught Man that he knew not." His messages were based on his visions and emphasize the oneness of God (monotheism) and social justice and equality. The idea of one God (Allah) was very important to the new religion: "Say God is One; God the Eternal: He did not beget and is not begotten, and no one is equal to Him." The will of Allah must be obeyed. This message went against previous beliefs in many gods. Those who obeyed God were enjoined to form a community of worshippers to promote Islam and help needy members, an idea that also went against the practice of relations based on families and clans.

These visions were compiled, without editing, into the *Quran*, the holy book of the Muslims recorded in the Arabic language. Every statement in the *Quran* is regarded as sacred, inspired by Allah. A number of other practices and beliefs became important. Muslims were enjoined to avoid alcohol and pork. They must "struggle for the faith," which meant participation in a jihad to attain personal religious perfection and contribute to the spread of Islam. Obeying Allah and fulfilling all the obligations of Islam will be rewarded with eternal salvation on the day of judgment, that is, at the end of the world. Those who disobey will be punished with eternal fire.

As the new religious leader preached his message and became known, he attracted hostility from established political, economic, and religious leaders who regarded his attacks on idol-worship and many of the social and business practices of the Arabs as a threat to their privileges and trade. Under the threat of persecution, in A.D. 622, Muhammad performed his *hijra* (withdrawal) from Mecca to Medina, a small oasis town in the Arabian desert. The flight is now regarded as the beginning of the Islamic calendar. At Medina, he established a religious community under his leadership, combining religious with political power. No distinction was made between civil and religious laws or between society and faith. In other words, the Prophet was both the religious and the political leader, a model that many others after him have either practiced or preached. He also proclaimed a jihad (holy war) and launched an attack against Mecca in 630.

Other areas were added to the new Islamic empire. So successful was he that by 632 when he died, he had not only established Islam but spread it among the majority of Arabs in Arabia. A century later, Islam had reached many lands, covering all of North Africa and other parts of the world.

Islam preached a commitment to one God (Allah), like Judaism and Christianity; both religions were well known in the region before the rise of the Prophet Muhammad. Muslims were expected to believe in Allah, and the revelations from Him passed through the Prophet Muhammad and were recorded in the *Quran*. If Christianity was too complicated in its theology, Islam was rather simple. And unlike Judaism, which preached an ideology of exclusiveness, Islam accepted anyone as long as he accepted the basic message of the One True God. Islam also minimized ceremonies and did away with hierarchies of priests. Rather, it stated religious expectations in very simple ways: fasting during Ramadan; saying prayers five times a day; displaying generosity and kindness to the poor and needy.

In the early years of Islam, Muslims regarded one another as members of the same community, united by religious beliefs and worship. The Prophet insisted that they must respect people of other faiths. Indeed, religions such as Christianity that believed in one God and had a written scripture were recognized, and their members did not need to be converted to Islam. However, they should pay tax, *jizya*, for their protection, and they should be excluded from serving in the Islamic army or administration.

The early Muslim community believed that religious affairs should not be separated from civil affairs. The Prophet was the leader, religious and political, and his successors, known as caliphs, also regarded themselves as such. They led their people in prayer, administered justice, and governed. The *sharia*, the body of basic law, must be respected by all the members of the Muslim community. The *sharia* comprises the words of the *Quran* and the sayings and practices of the Prophet Muhammad and his immediate successors as recorded in oral tradition. The *sharia* stipulates the correct practices to be followed by an Islamic government; the rules to regulate business, divorce, marriage, other social practices; and individual personal conduct. Religious leaders and learned men, *qadi*, were appointed to administer the *sharia*. The leadership of a mosque was vested in an *imam*, although anyone could lead prayer. The *qadis* and *imams* together constitute what is called the *ulema*, the men of ideas and learning, and one of the most powerful and respected groups in the Islamic community.

In theory, the Islamic community was supposed to have a single head, the caliph (or the deputy of the Prophet). In practice, after the death of the Prophet, the leading members disagreed over the criteria for the selection of the caliph. The selection of the fourth caliph in A.D. 656 led to a split. Ali, the son-in-law of the Prophet, was chosen in that year, but he was challenged by another religious leader, Muawiya, who overthrew him and established the Umayyad dynasty in A.D. 661. Since then, the split has affected the Islamic community. One group was composed of the Shi'ites, who believed that the caliphs should be members of the family of the Prophet, direct descendants of Ali and Fatima (the Prophet's daughter). The other group, the Sunni, believed that the caliph should be a person chosen by members of the Islamic community. Because the direct line of Ali's descendants was already broken, some Shi'ites believed that the true caliph would appear one day as the Mahdi, the savior, who would lead all Muslims and restore Islam to its original perfection. While the Sunni have been more successful in holding on to power, there have been occasions when the Shi'ites have acquired influence in Africa. Today, there are many Shi'ites in East Africa, and they constitute a powerful group in Iran. The political unity among the Muslims ended in A.D. 750, as separate caliphates emerged. Even the most powerful caliphs in Bagdad were later to be controlled by their Turkish commanders.

THE ARAB INVASIONS AND THE SPREAD OF ISLAM

Islam united the Arabs and empowered them not only to spread a religion and culture but to establish political control in areas far beyond their own land. By the beginning of the eighth century, Islamic political control stretched from Morocco and Spain in the west to the Indus River in the east.

Islam combined with commercial and political considerations in motivating the Arab followers of the Prophet Muhammad to invade areas beyond their Arabian homeland. They were not ignorant of the immense political and economic opportunities involved in creating empires and states. However, they were united only by language before the rise of the Prophet Muhammad. Islam united them and invested them with a notion of brotherhood and the will to fight for their beliefs. The Arabs used to be predominantly desert nomads. Before the seventh century, they had engaged in many small-scale migrations to fertile areas on the fringes of the desert, while many groups developed the military skills to control desert oases so as to ensure access to water for themselves and their animals. The unity provided by Islam turned them into successful conquerors, thereby giving them access to more land and greater economic opportunities. The rich resources of the lands of Egypt, Mesopotamia, and elsewhere were known to them, and the desire to control these places was as strong as the motivation to spread Islam.

Control of trade was equally important. The Arabian peninsula had been a major part of a vibrant international trade between Africa and Asia (between the Red Sea and the Persian Gulf) as well as between the Indian Ocean and the Mediterranean. Mecca and some Arab-controlled cities had served as trading centers, while many Arab traders had been involved in the trade networks in this region, especially in the caravan trade across the desert. Political control would facilitate this trade in addition to ensuring the dominance of Arabs in its most lucrative aspects.

Irrespective of their motives, religious or political, the Arab invasions were successful. The first major victory was the conquest of Egypt and other parts of the fertile areas of the Lower Nile by A.D. 640. The majority of Egyptians, suffering from oppression and persecution by the Coptic Church, were unwilling to resist the Arab armies. A new Islamic capital was built at Cairo, which enabled the Arabs to establish firm control of areas south of the Nile valley and to benefit from strong trade connections with Arabia and Syria. The Arab armies failed in their southward expansion to incorporate the Nubians but signed a treaty that enabled extensive trade relations between them.

Next was the conquest of the areas west of Egypt, called al-Maghrib ("the West") by the Arabs. The area was huge, and opposition by the Berbers and the Byzantine Empire (which had taken over from the Vandals) was strong. The Arabs built enough ships to finally defeat the Byzantine fleet in the 690s. They conquered and destroyed Carthage and built the new Arab city of Tunis. Conquering the Berbers was far more difficult, as both the Arabs and the Berbers were masters of the use of the camel and desert warfare. The strong solidarity among the Arabs, compared to the divisions among the Berber leaders, eventually led to the victory of the Arabs by A.D. 711 when they were able to reach the Atlantic coast of Morocco.

ARAB RULE AND ISLAM IN NORTH AFRICA

Administration evolved over time, since the Arabs were occupied with wars of conquest. They started as an army of occupation and created a distinction between Muslims and non-Muslims. Muslims were exempted from taxation, a policy that pleased the poor and the peasants. Non-Muslims could convert or pay the poll tax. No policy of forced conversion was pursued, and this enabled the Arabs to collect tax and their subjects to retain their old religious practices. For almost a century in North Africa, the Arabs confined themselves to the coastal cities where they practiced Islam and used slave labor on their farms. The slaves were obtained as war captives from the Berber population and from blacks in West Africa through trade or raiding expeditions in the Sahara.

In Egypt, the Arabs became the landlords, leading merchants, and administrators. Ever since, they have continued to consolidate their hold, and older traditions have been replaced. The Coptic Christians retained their land and religion. The Arabs collected taxes, mainly in food. The taxation policy was less exploitative than under the preceding Greek and Roman rule. The Egyptians who converted to Islam did not have to pay tax.

Arab rule led to the spread of Islam, although as a gradual process. However, by the tenth century, the majority of the people in Egypt and North Africa had become Muslims. A number of factors made this possible. To start with, in areas where Christianity had not been firmly established, for example, among the vast majority of the Berbers in North Africa, Islam had an opportunity to present an alternative and to gradually displace Christianity. Second, the recruitment of non-Arabs into the Arab army encouraged conversion to Islam. Among the Berbers, many joined the army voluntarily, while many others were conscripted. Once converted, they became strong defenders of Islam, and they benefited from the imposition of the Islamic empire. Third, local people who had been converted to

Islam worked as missionary agents among their own people. This was an effective means of peaceful and gradual propaganda. Over time, Islam became associated not only with the foreign Arabs but also with the local citizens. Finally, the advantages of the use of the Arabic language and Arabic education facilitated the expansion of Islam among those seeking new skills and opportunities. Arabic was the language of administration, religion, education, and commerce, and those who wanted access to any of these had to use the language and possibly convert to Islam. The education system and the spread of Islam were combined in the use of the *Quran*. In Egypt the Coptic language gradually became the language of the minority.

Arab rule in North Africa was affected by the power rivalry among the successors of the Prophet Muhammad and the emergence of competing dynasties that appointed the caliph (head of the Islamic world or caliphate) and interpreted the wishes of the Prophet Muhammad in different ways. The Umayyad dynasty seized power and moved the capital to Damascus in A.D. 680. Later, the Abbasids came to power and moved the capital to Bagdad in A.D. 750. Then arose the Shi'ites who believed that only the descendants of the Prophet Muhammad were qualified to rule.

There were also African Muslim leaders who wanted to reject the authority of the Arabs. The Berbers, for example, protested the arrogance of the Arabs among them and rejected the authority of the caliph based in Bagdad. Many Berbers joined the Shi'ites and other movements opposed to the Bagdad caliphate. The greatest threat to the caliphate in Bagdad came in the tenth century when a group of radical Muslims in the central Maghrib established the Fatimids dynasty. The Fatimid established control in North Africa and in A.D. 969 declared Egypt free of Bagdad.

ISLAM IN OTHER PARTS OF AFRICA

Islam reached other parts of Africa at different periods, not through Arab conquests but mainly through the peaceful work of missionaries and traders. Holy men and scholars traveled to various places to preach and teach. The migration of Muslim groups spread Islam to new areas. Muslim traders served as self-appointed missionaries, taking Islam to areas where they had established contacts. The process was slow, and it continued well into the twentieth century.

The Arab conquest and occupation of North Africa provided opportunities for Islam to reach areas to the south. From North Africa, Islam reached the Nubians, the people of the Fezzan, and the southern Berbers. Through these three groups Islam spread southward, to the Sahara Desert, the southern desert edges, and then the savanna. The settlement of Muslims in the Horn of Africa and on the East African coast led to the spread of Islam to the Somali people. By the tenth century, Islam had become established in many parts of the East African coast.

In the case of West Africa, the Sanhaja Berbers, who lived along the desert edges, up to the northern boundaries of the Senegal river, accepted Islam and served as its couriers. However, the most important agency in the spread of Islam was international trade. Through the trans-Saharan trade that linked North and West Africa, thousands of Muslim traders, including Arab and Berber merchants, visited the savanna areas of West Africa. Missionaries accompanied the traders, and both propagated Islam in the major market cities. By the eighth century, Islam had reached the northern edges of West Africa. A trading post was established at the oasis town of Sijilmasa, the northern "port" of the trans-Saharan trade routes that reached the empire of Ghana. The Muslim merchants established their own small colonies in places they visited, such as the capital of Ghana. Here, they practiced their religion, hosted preachers and missionaries, and converted many of those who came in contact with them.

When some states such as Mali in the Western Sudan and Kanem in the Eastern Sudan accepted Islam as an official religion, it spread among their elite and city dwellers. Thus, the conversion of rulers was the second major stage in the propagation of Islam. The conversion of the first kings was crucial, as they usually had influence on other chiefs, civil servants, and city dwellers.

Among the Africans that accepted Islam, some took to missionary work. This was the third stage in the process, one in which Africans served as agents to convert other Africans. A number of African merchant groups actually became notable missionaries, combining their trade with religious duties. Such groups include the Diakhanke of the Senegambia, the Dyula in the area of modern Ghana and Côte d'Ivoire, and the Hausa of northern Nigeria. Islam spread slowly in Africa, being originally confined to cities and commercial centers, until the rise of Islamic states during the nineteenth century.

THE IMPACT OF ISLAM

Their conquests gave the Arabs control of a huge area of land—Egypt and North Africa, the greater part of the eastern Roman Empire, and Persia. They were able to inherit the leading civilizations of the time. The Arabs were able to preserve what they inherited and to improve upon many aspects. They promoted Islamic education, developed the school system to the university level, built great libraries, and cultivated the arts. They paid serious attention to the sciences, mathematics, poetry, philosophy, architecture, and medicine. Among the notable contributions of the Muslims are Arabic numerals; the foundation of algebra; the use of the astrolabe, an instrument needed to ascertain the position of stars; the calculation of distances; and the creation of the first pharmacy school. They also devoted considerable time and knowledge to the codification of *sharia* law, leading to the emergence of four leading schools of law, each with its own interpretations but with respect for the others.

A concept of Islamic community and unity has developed since the seventh century. The conquests were vast and heterogeneous, but the idea of developing unity in the Islamic world was strong. Certain practices have made this possible, up to today, in spite of political divisions among Islamic countries. Muslims

Sankore mosque, Timbuktu.

perform the hajj (pilgrimage) to Mecca and Medina, enabling millions of people to interact every year, united by religious experience. The Arabic language is the language of Islamic learning and worship. In North Africa and other parts of the Muslim world, Arabic is also the language of daily communications. When Muslims pray, they must face Mecca, irrespective of where they live.

In spite of power struggles, the idea of unity among the members of the Islamic community became an integral part of Islam. This idea promoted the emergence of a uniform political arrangement in areas that accepted Islam. An Islamic community had a head, known as the caliph if he was the supreme head of all Muslims. If he was the head of a region or an area, he could be known as the sultan or the *amir* (emir), the shortened form of *Amir al-Muminin*, meaning the Commander of the Faithful. The caliph or emir had a prime minister, the *wazir*, as well as judges, the *qadis*, who administered the *sharia*. Where matters were not covered by the *sharia* or were merely administrative, the *wazir* could exercise great executive power.

Sufi brotherhoods, which can be described as Islamic associations, spread to various areas. Members of the brotherhoods dedicated themselves to religious contemplation, and some believed in mysticism. To the commands of Islam, Sufism would add love and deep devotion to God and worship, and commitment to a simple lifestyle. Some brotherhoods appealed to those who could not read and write in Arabic, while some others appealed to those who could strengthen their faith through rigorous scholarship. The brotherhoods were many, some local, others drawing membership from many cities and states. The members of a brotherhood developed a strong sense of community, and they respected their leader, who might even be treated as a saint. Members of different brotherhoods might compete and engage in feuds that were difficult to resolve. For instance, in West Africa, members of the Qadiriyya and Tijaniyya brotherhoods have had conflicts.

Islam was a bringer of change. Essentially, it represented a religious change, conversion from one religion to another, thereby shaping people's outlook and views about many things. New religious practices spread, such as praying in Arabic, fasting, worshipping in the mosque, and undertaking the pilgrimage to Mecca. As Islam spread, so did the idea of the "five pillars" that must be observed by Muslims: confession of the faith ("I bear witness that there is no deity except Allah and that Muhammad is His Servant and Messenger"); prayer five times a day; supporting the poor through alms; fasting during the month of Ramadan; and performing the hajj (pilgrimage) at least once in a lifetime.

Where the Arabs dominated, as in North Africa, Islam also resulted in the penetration of a new culture. Even where the Arabs did not dominate, as in most of sub-Saharan Africa, aspects of Arabic culture spread. For instance, the Arabic script and mode of dressing spread in areas that accepted Islam. Islamic areas were connected by religion, language, and diplomatic exchanges among their rulers.

Some material gains accompanied Islam, such as Islamic education, the acquisition of Arabic, and exposure to a new lifestyle influenced by Arab culture. Those who were interested in trade were able to use Islam as a means of identification with traders from other Islamic areas.

The pilgrimage to Mecca and Medina brought other advantages. The Muslim elite made valuable connections in different parts of Africa and Saudi Arabia, learned the leading ideas of the time, and used some of these ideas to change their own societies. Some of these ideas related to the use of firearms in warfare, the role of educated people in administration, and architectural innovations. Africans gained access to the documented knowledge of the Islamic world.

Islamic scholars and preachers also visited different parts of Africa, bringing with them new knowledge and education. Africans, too, began to write and to produce their own famous Islamic scholars, such as Ahmed Baba, a sixteenth-century author.

Islam affected African politics. Islam encouraged the trend toward political centralization—the king and the civil servants exercised more power. The use of Arabic enabled the keeping of records and exchange of written diplomatic correspondence. Islamic judges replaced traditional ones where the *sharia* was accepted as law.

SUGGESTIONS FOR FURTHER READING

Clarke, Peter B. *West Africa and Islam*. London: Edward Arnold, 1982.

Falola, Toyin. *Violence in Nigeria: The Crisis of Religious Politics and Secular Ideologies*. Rochester, N.Y.: University of Rochester Press, 1998.

Falola, Toyin, ed. *Africa*. Vol. 2, *African Cultures and Societies before 1885*. Durham, N.C.: Carolina Academic Press, 2000. Chapter 7.

Falola, Toyin, and A. Adediran. *Islam and Christianity in West Africa*. Ile-Ife, Nigeria: University of Ife Press, 1983.

Levtzion, Nehemia, and Randall L. Pouwels, eds. *The History of Islam in Africa*. Athens: Ohio University Press, 2000.

Lewis, I.M., ed. *Islam in Tropical Africa*. Oxford: Oxford University Press, 1964.

9

Kingdoms of West Africa: Ghana, Mali, and Songhay, A.D. 1000–1600

TRADING STATES

In the West African Sudan, along the desert fringe, three great kingdoms flourished between about A.D. 1000 and 1600, becoming powerful and wealthy from trans-Saharan trade. The earliest was Ghana, which was followed by Mali, then Songhay. They all shared certain things in common. They rose and fell in the same region, known to the Arabs as the Bilad al-Sudan ("the Southern Country"), an area that was fertile and accessible to the Niger River that nourished the soil and provided a means of communication. They were all Iron Age societies, which had access to metal to fashion agricultural tools and weapons to fight wars of expansion. They had all inherited an abundant corpus of ideas on religion, politics, and the economy and were able to build on these ideas. Islam was introduced to them, providing advantages to the kings of Mali and Songhay who embraced it.

They were all able to enforce law and order through a political system that centralized power in the king and a few major officials. The strength of their army and central authority determined the extent of the areas they controlled; when their strength diminished, their kingdoms would contract. They divided their administration into two sectors—the capital, where the king exercised direct power over the city; and the provinces supervised by governors sent by the king.

The three kingdoms built strong economies. Agriculture was the core of the economy, but substantial wealth came from international trade. Occupations and specializations were diverse—in all their leading cities could be found craftspeople, healers, and men of learning. The cities were noted for their markets, which catered to large regions. The cities and the kingdoms became part of an international network of commerce that connected West Africa with North Africa, the Middle East, and southern Europe. Information about the kings and their wealth reached other lands. The wealth and glory of the three kingdoms depended very much on the trans-Saharan trade.

THE TRANS-SAHARAN TRADE

The trans-Saharan trade was the principal agency of contact between North Africa and West Africa. It was more than a regional trade; it was an international trade that led to the exchange of goods between various parts of Africa, the Middle East, and Europe. The trade across the Sahara was an ancient one, dating as far back as 600 B.C. The trade was transformed in the first century A.D. with the use of the camel. Compared with the donkeys and horses that had previously been used as pack animals, camels could carry heavier loads, endure greater hardships including desert heat, and travel for longer periods without water. The camel was the "truck" of the desert, which facilitated travel on many routes. West Africa supplied gold and ivory, brought by the Berbers who crossed the desert and sold the products to North African merchants. The products found their way to many courts and homes of the wealthy in the cities on the Mediterranean coast. By the eighth century, the Arabs were able to inherit a well-developed international trade. They too profited from it, and trade expanded more than ever before.

West African gold, slaves, and copper were traded in exchange for salt from the Sahara and North African products such as salt, metal, beads, and cloth. The West African products were in turn sent to southwest Asia and Europe. All the regions involved in the trade benefited from it: North Africa and southern Europe needed West African gold for luxury items and later for coins. The West Africans needed salt, which the traders in the Sahara and beyond could supply from the desert sources in Taghaza and Bilma, and horses for their cavalry. However, many other goods were involved on both sides—West Africa received copper, books (after the introduction of Islam), metalware (e.g., pots, pans, and swords), dates, spices, and silk in exchange for their kola nuts, ivory, and slaves.

To cross the desert was risky. One needed large supplies of food, sometimes enough for four months, and had to deal with water scarcity and insect bites. Small parties could become lost, as reported by Ibn Battuta, the Arab traveler who crossed the Sahara in 1352:

We used to go ahead of the caravan, and when we found a place suitable for pasturage we would graze our beasts. We went on doing this until one of our party was lost in the desert; after that I neither went ahead nor lagged behind. We passed a caravan on the way, and they told us that some of their party had become separated from them. We found one of them dead under a shrub, of the sort that grows on the sand, with his clothes on and a whip in his hand.[1]

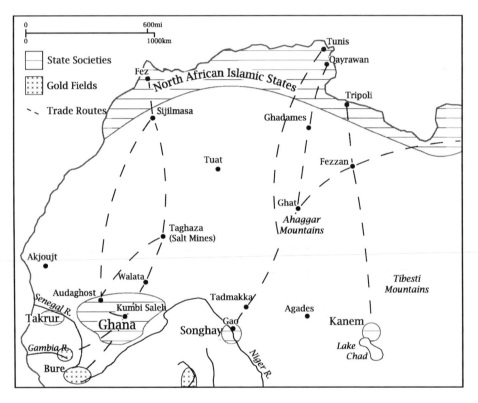

Early West African states and trans-Saharan trade.

The journey was also time-consuming, taking up to three months or more to cross the desert. The traders traveled in large caravans, which could include over a thousand camels.

The difficulties did not constitute a hindrance to the merchants, porters, and others connected with the business who profited from it until the trade collapsed in the early years of the twentieth century. The merchants in North Africa who financed the trade relied on the Berbers living in the Atlas Mountains and the northern Sahara to serve as intermediaries with the people of West Africa.

There were at least three leading routes that were used for centuries. The western route was from Sijilmasa in North Africa through the desert oases of Taghaza and Taodeni to the Niger bend in the Western Sudan. The central route began at Tunis and passed through Ghat and Agades, with one trail branching in the direction of the Niger bend and another to Hausaland. There was an eastern trail, from Tripoli and the Hoggar Mountains through the desert towns of Bilma and Murzuk to the Lake Chad region. Along these trails were oases that could supply water. Villages and towns grew around them; the passing traders rested here and conducted some small-scale trade. The southern termini, the commercial cities in West Africa, varied in their fortunes and included Audaghost, Kumbi, Walata, Jenne, Timbuktu, Gao, Kano, and Katsina.

The trade was of much consequence to the economy and society of the three great kingdoms. It made various imported goods available—some essentials such as salt and some luxury items such as cloths. The trade routes also brought Islam and other ideas from outside and spread the knowledge of West Africa to other parts of the world. The trade contributed to the emergence of cities and kingdoms through access to revenues, markets, and trade routes. Starting as small trading settlements, they grew bigger as their markets grew and more traders visited them. Other occupations grew, to supply products needed by city dwellers and visiting traders. Political administration became sophisticated in order to maintain order, regulate laws guiding commerce, and protect visiting traders. From the trade, administrators raised revenue that they used to finance their armies and administration. As the political leaders extended their power over adjoining areas, the cities grew, ultimately becoming centers of larger kingdoms or being incorporated into them. Ghana was the first success story.

GHANA, A.D. 1000+

Ghana was one of the earliest of the West African kingdoms, emerging around the fourth century A.D. It was located far to the northwest of the modern country of Ghana. The founders of the empire were the Soninke, who were able to use iron for farming and warfare. The use of iron gave them an advantage in subduing their neighbors and absorbing them into their empire. The area along the Upper Niger River was favorable to agriculture, and the Soninke and other groups were able to benefit by producing large quantities of food. Living in the western Sahel, an area accessible both to the goldfields south of the Senegal

River and to the salt-producing region of the Sahara, the Soninke were able to profit as middlemen in the trading network.

Powerful kings emerged among the Soninke. They were war leaders and traders, but they were also regarded as semidivine. Using their resources from trade and their ability to fight, they were able to conquer new areas and maintain their kingdom for a long time. They were able to purchase a large number of horses from North Africa to build a cavalry force. Ghana attained the height of its power in about—A.D. 1000 it was large, powerful, secure, and prosperous. It had abundant resources to equip a large army with iron weapons of war.

The empire controlled the lucrative salt and gold trade, which fed into the international trans-Saharan trade. The empire was close to the sources of gold production at Wangara and to the most active trade routes. It thus played a middleman role that enabled it to control and tax the products of the Western Sudan as well as those coming from North Africa and the Sahara. Ghana received traders and travelers from other lands, providing them with security, opportunities, and the freedom to practice their own religions.

The kings derived their wealth from the gold trade. By the eighth century, Ghana was already being described by the Arabs as "the land of Gold." The wealth of Ghana impressed Arab geographers and travelers, who left some records. One observer noted: "The king of Ghana was a great king. In his territory are mines of gold, and under him a number of kingdoms. . . . In all this country there is gold."[2] And another reported: "All pieces of native gold found in the mines of the empire belong to the sovereign, although he lets the public have the gold dust that everybody knows about; without this precaution, gold would become so abundant as practically to lose its value."[3]

The kings collected taxes on the import and export of major articles such as gold and salt, in addition to maintaining a monopoly on production. The wealth of the kings of Ghana enabled them to maintain their administration and army. The kings and his chiefs lived in comfort. In a book completed in 1068, al-Bakri, an Arab writer, reported on the splendor of the king:

When the king gives audience to his people, to listen to their complaints and to set them to rights, he sits in a pavilion around which stand ten pages holding shields and gold-mounted swords. On his right hand are the sons of the princes of his empire, splendidly clad and with gold plaited in their hair.

The governor of the city is seated on the ground in front of the king, and all around him are his counsellors in the same position. The gate of the chamber is guarded by dogs of an excellent breed. These dogs never leave their place of duty. They wear collars of gold and silver, ornamented with metals.

The beginning of a royal meeting is announced by the beating of a kind of drum they call *deba*. This drum is made of a long piece of hollowed wood. The people gather when they hear its sound.[4]

Ghana experienced a setback in the second half of the eleventh century, because of internal weakness and external attacks. A large empire, it contained people of diverse origins, many of whom were struggling to assert their independence. It was also unable to meet the challenges posed by external aggression. In about A.D. 1054, it was attacked by the Almoravids, a group of Berber Muslims from the northwest, in the Mauretanian desert. The Almoravids wanted to gain control of the trade routes, free themselves from the power of Ghana, and spread Islam. Although the Almoravids won the initial wars, they were unable to keep the Soninke and other groups loyal to them. In 1087, the Almoravids lost control. Ghana recovered toward the end of the eleventh century but found it hard to maintain control over many of its provinces. In the second half of the twelfth century, Ghana had to deal with more internal wars, disruption of trade routes, declining agricultural productivity, and conflicts for power. It also lost control of the salt trade to its neighbors, forcing many of the people in its capital city, Kumbi Saleh, to migrate elsewhere in search of opportunities. In about 1235, the Malinke people attacked Ghana and established the new empire of Mali.

MALI, A.D. 1230+

The Malinke-speaking people built the Mali empire. They were part of Ghana until they broke away in the thirteenth century to establish the Kangaba kingdom near the Upper Niger River. Their legendary hero is Sundiata who transformed Kangaba into the Mali empire. Epics telling of Sundiata have survived, crediting him with supernatural powers and great achievements. He emerged on the scene around 1230, leading a powerful army to conquer many areas and governing them until about 1260. He established a capital at Niani, located on the upper reaches of the Niger River. By gaining control of the gold-producing region, he acquired a source of immense wealth. His empire also became involved in the lucrative trans-Saharan trade and established control over the three great cities of Jenne, Gao, and Timbuktu. The king grew powerful, and the empire became prosperous. Sundiata also established an effective administration with the mansa (king) at its head. By the early fourteenth century, Mali had surpassed Ghana in fame, wealth, and territory. Writing about this period, Ibn Khaldun, the great North African historian of the fourteenth century, commented that "the power of Mali became mighty. All the nations of the Sudan stood in awe of Mali, and the merchants of North Africa traveled to his country."[5]

Under Mansa Musa (ca. 1312–37), Mali attained the height of its power. Mansa Musa expanded the empire through conquests, adding areas twice the size of the former kingdom of Ghana. Mali controlled the major markets and leading routes of the trans-Saharan trade. Niani, Gao, and Timbuktu were major commercial centers. The emperor and his empire were wealthy. A uniform system of law and order was imposed on a large area, and the people were secure. A combination of effective leadership, efficiency in the collection of revenues, and availability of resources to sustain an army made Mansa Musa one of the greatest statesmen of precolonial Africa.

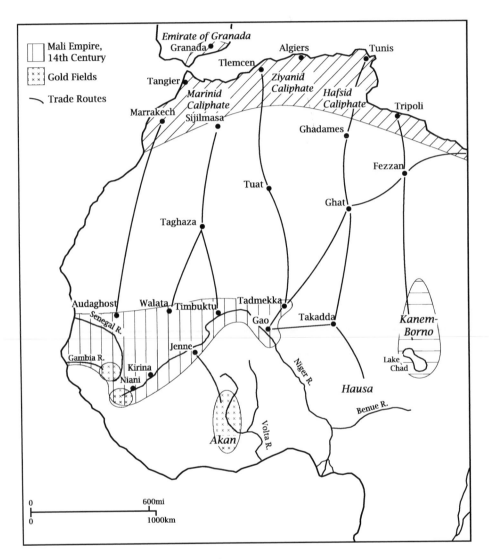

The Mali empire and North African connections.

The widespread fame enjoyed by Mansa Musa was also due to his conversion to Islam. This gave Islam a boost, although the majority of the population did not adopt the new religion. There was no official policy of imposition of Islam on the people. In 1324, Mansa Musa embarked on a pilgrimage to Mecca. This enabled him to display the wealth of his empire and establish friendly relations with rulers in North Africa and the Middle East. He arrived in Cairo with an estimated 80,000 attendants carrying sacks of gold dust and gold bars. The impact of his visit was such that the value of gold fell after his departure. Mali appeared on a European map in 1339, an indication of the interest in and knowledge of this important kingdom. A scholar who lived in Cairo after Musa's visit to the city praised him as "the most powerful, the richest, the most fortunate, the most feared by his enemies and the most able to do good to those around him."[6]

Mansa Musa returned from the pilgrimage with new ideas on various subjects. He was accompanied by Islamic teachers, architects, scholars, and legal experts who assisted him in establishing Islamic education in Mali. He built an Islamic university at Timbuktu, which was attended by students from far and wide. New mosques were built in the cities, enabling Muslims to worship as members of a community. Many more people accepted Islam, and Muslim scholars and traders were able to propagate their religion in new areas. Mali became a regional power. The empire sent ambassadors to countries such as Egypt and Morocco, while international scholars and travelers visited the capital of Mali. Niani, the capital, was described by the famous Moroccan traveler Leo Africanus as large and its people as "the most civilized, intelligent and respected" of West Africans.[7]

The emperor headed a centralized adiministration. He was chosen from among the families qualified to rule. He lived in the capital where he exercised direct power. He was assisted by a number of high-ranking chiefs, mainly members of the warrior elite who also belonged to important families. Some of the chiefs performed specific duties, such as supervising the use of land and forest or collecting revenues for the king. The revenues were derived from levies on farmers, dues collected from traders, and tributes from the provinces. The emperor appointed governors to rule the provinces. Mansa Musa appointed members of his own family and trusted associates to serve as provincial governors in order to guard against any disloyal leader organizing a rebellion against him. The administration was efficient, and order was maintained. In the words of Ibn Battuta, the Muslim traveler who remarked on Mali in the mid-1300s:

[The people] are seldom unjust, and have a greater horror of injustice than other people. Their sultan shows no mercy to anyone who is guilty of the least act of it. There is complete security in their country. Neither traveler nor inhabitant in it has anything to fear from robbers or men of violence.[8]

Mali began to decline during the second half of the fourteenth century. Failure to achieve workable rules of succession to the throne led to a series of struggles for power among members of the royal family. As one qualified candidate competed

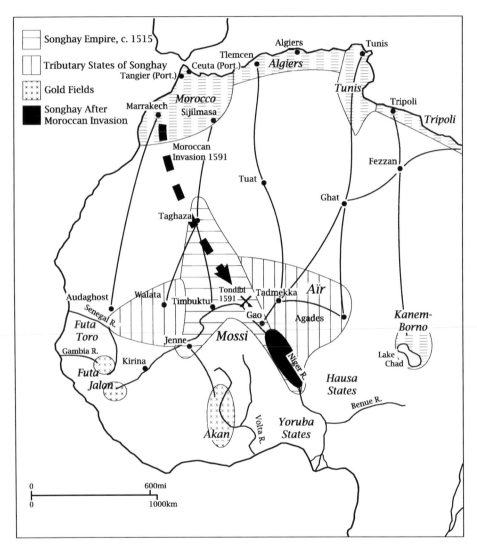

The rise and fall of Songhay.

with another, civil wars broke out, and the central authority of the empire became weakened. The empire struggled to survive until about 1400. Thereafter, it experienced one major political problem after another. The financial resources of the empire were reduced, and many provinces took the opportunity to free themselves from the power of the center. The important province of Gao rebelled, and the Tuaregs of the southern Sahara, a strong nomadic group, seized control of the famous city of Timbuktu and another important town, Walata. Three other groups rebelled, notably the Mossi in the southwest who later established their own independent kingdom. By the late 1400s, the empire had collapsed, but another powerful state emerged in its place.

SONGHAY, A.D. 1468+

In conditions similar to those that led to the founding of Ghana and Mali and in the same region, Sunni Ali established Songhay in about 1468. Songhay was originally a province of Mali, centered in the important city of Gao, but it later asserted its independence under the leadership of Sunni Ali. Gao was a major commercial center in the middle Niger region. For many years before the mid-fifteenth century, Gao served as one of the main centers of the trans-Saharan trade and of Islam and as the capital of a state. It was in view of its importance that the Mali empire, under Mansa Musa, imposed its rule over it. Gao later broke free of Mali, defended itself against various rivals, and embarked upon its own wars of expansion.

The remarkable wars of expansion and Gao's transition to an empire were made possible by Sunni Ali, a great warrior, political strategist, and leader. Oral traditions about Sunni Ali have survived, some portraying him as a great magician, just to attest to his power, courage, and intelligence. Ruling for a long period (1464–92), he was able to build a powerful army that conquered important cities and territories. Leading one expedition after another, he did not suffer a single defeat in a career dominated by wars. He conquered Timbuktu and Jenne, two great commercial cities. The Songhay empire later grew to become larger than Mali. It was also based on agriculture and control of the major trade routes, benefiting from its favorable location along the Niger River. Sunni Ali laid the foundation of the empire's administration, setting up a system similar to those of Ghana and Mali.

Emperor Muhammed Touré (also called Askia the Great) presided over the empire at its height. Like Sunni Ali, he ruled for a long period (1493–1528) and served as a successful empire builder. His wars of conquest expanded the empire to its widest territorial limits, incorporating virtually the whole of the former Mali empire and extending eastward to the boundaries of Hausaland in modern Nigeria. Songhay became the largest state in West Africa during the sixteenth century. Muhammed Touré divided the empire into provinces, each headed by a governor. The army and administration were financed by customs duties, tolls, tributes from the provinces, and sales of products from the royal estates.

Muhammed Touré was the first ruler of the empire to adopt Islam. His two pre-decessors, including Sunni Ali, the founder of the empire, practiced their tradi-tional religion. The Islamic scholars accepted Muhammed Touré as a leader. Touré broke with the past by his commitment to Islam. He made a pilgrimage to Mecca in 1495, a great accomplishment that endeared him to many Muslims and Islamic leaders. He was appointed by the sharif of Mecca (the spiritual leader of Islam) as the caliph of the Western Sudan, a position that he used to promote the spread of Islam. He made use of Islamic scholars in his administration and in promoting Is-lamic education and religion. He used Islam to unite many of his followers.

Timbuktu became the leading center of trade and culture in the Western Sudan. Imports came from North Africa, China, India, and Europe, brought through the trans-Saharan trade by merchants who included Arabs, Jews, Italians, and others. Songhay supplied gold and slaves. Under Askia the Great, the supply of slaves in-creased. His wars of expansion produced captives, who were sold in the market of Gao and then transported to Egypt, Turkey, and various areas of southwest Asia. Timbuktu became one of the wealthiest cities in West Africa.

Timbuktu was famed for its Islamic education. Muslim scholars were based in its Islamic university. Leo Africanus, a notable Muslim traveler, reported on Timbuktu at the turn of the sixteenth century:

Here are great numbers of religious teachers, judges, scholars and other learned persons, who are bountifully maintained at the king's expense. Here too are brought various manu-scripts or written books from Barbary, which are sold for more money than any other merchandise.[9]

Like Ghana and Mali, the empire of Songhay also collapsed. There were suc-cession struggles and power rivalries. New leaders emerged in many provinces, each seeking autonomy. The Malinke, Fulani, Hausa, Mossi, and other groups within the empire also rebelled. The empire was so large that it was difficult to govern without an effective system of communication and control. In the center, people struggled for power, and there were many succession disputes and even a civil war. Hostile neighbors launched frequent attacks.

If Songhay was able to survive its internal divisions, it found it very difficult to overcome the external aggression of the king of Morocco, Mulay al Mansur, whose army, with superior firearms, defeated the Songhay troops in 1591. The reason for the attack was Morocco's interest in the wealth of Songhay. Earlier in 1578, Morocco had defeated Portugal and halted the Portuguese ambition to con-quer North Africa. Morocco became stronger thereafter, but at considerable cost. To fill a fast diminishing treasury, Morocco looked southward, to Songhay, fa-mous for its wealth in gold. The Moroccan army, including a large number of mercenaries and ex-prisoners, marched south in December 1590, armed with arquebuses, the most modern weapons of war. Songhay lost one battle after another, suffering heavy casualties. Gao and Timbuktu were looted, and their wealth taken to Marrakech.

The defeat was devastating: Songhay's central authority collapsed, law and order broke down, many traders and scholars deserted the area, provinces seceded, Islam declined as a religion, and trade routes were disrupted. However, many other states emerged in the region, as in the case of the Mossi to the south, to continue the tradition of establishing and managing kingdoms. In other parts of the West African region, other large kingdoms, such as the Hausa states, Kanem-Borno, Oyo, Benin, Dahomey, and Asante, lasted for much longer.

CONCLUSION

The kingdoms demonstrate the capability of Africans to create large states and manage them for a long time. Armies were built, leaders emerged, revenues were generated, and various groups were united as members of the same kingdoms. Extensive regional and international commerce took place that connected West Africa with many other parts of the continent. Goods of various origins also reached West Africa. Through Islam, literacy in Arabic began to spread among many Muslims, especially those based in urban commercial centers.

NOTES

1. Quoted in Basil Davidson, *African Civilization Revisited* (Trenton, N.J.: Africa World Press, 1991), p. 97.
2. Ibid., p. 86.
3. Ibid., p. 87.
4. Ibid., pp. 86–87.
5. Ibid., p. 88.
6. Quoted in Basil Davidson, *West Africa before the Colonial Era* (New York: Longman, 1998), p. 43.
7. Ibid.
8. Quoted in Davidson, *African Civilization Revisited,* p. 99.
9. Quoted in Adu Boahen, *Topics in West African History* (New York: Longman, 1997), p. 38.

SUGGESTIONS FOR FURTHER READING

Ajayi, J.F.A., and Michael Crowder, eds. *History of West Africa.* Vol. 1. London: Longman, 1971.
Collins, Robert O. *African History in Documents: Western African History.* Princeton, N.J.: Markus Wiener, 1997.
Davidson, Basil. *West Africa before the Colonial Era. A History to 1850.* New York: Longman, 1998.
Falola, Toyin, and A.G. Adebayo. *A History of West Africa.* Lagos, Nigeria: Paico, 1987.
Falola, Toyin, ed. *Africa.* Vol. 1, *African History before 1885.* Durham, N.C.: Carolina Academic Press, 2000. Chapter 6.
Levtzion, N. *Medieval West Africa before 1400.* Princeton, N.J.: Markus Wiener, 1999.

10

The Rise of the Swahili City–States of East Africa, Tenth–Fourteenth Century A.D.

Between the tenth and fourteenth centuries A.D., a number of city–states emerged and flourished along the coast of East Africa. A new culture, including a language, developed. It became known as the Swahili (Afro-Arab) culture, and it has survived till today. *Swahili* is an Arabic word, derived from *sahil*, which means "coast." *Swahili* literally means "the people of the coast." Due to their location, the Swahili states became the gateway to the African interior and developed as international markets that drew traders and visitors from Asia, Arabia, and the Persian Gulf. Swahili society emerged in an area that had long been inhabited by the people of East Africa. "Swahili" is used to mean the following: a group of East African coastal cities whose religion and culture were Islamic; whose population included Africans and Arabs; whose cities were noted for their trading culture and economy; and whose inhabitants and language were mainly African. This chapter will consider the historical antecedents to the Swahili states and identify the features of Swahili society.

THE INDIAN OCEAN TRADE AND AZANIA

Navigation on the Indian Ocean led to the development of an international trade. Sailors studied and took advantage of the direction of the monsoon winds in the western Indian Ocean. From November to March, the monsoon winds blew from the Indian coast toward Africa, in a southwestern direction. During this period, sailors would travel to Africa. Then from May to September, the winds blew northeast, in the direction of the Persian Gulf and India, and the sailors would travel in this direction. This enabled East Africa to be integrated with traders from Southeast Asia, western India, and Arabia.

The trade began long before the rise of Islam in the seventh century. The island of Madagascar off the southeastern coast of Africa received visitors from the islands of Indonesia in ancient days. In the early centuries of the first millennium A.D., the Greeks called the East African coast "Azania." East Africa was then populated by Iron Age people, probably the descendants of the Bantu-speaking migrants. In a sailors' handbook, *The Periplus of the Erythraean*, written by an Egyptian-Greek during the first century A.D., the author mentioned a number of the cities along the coast and their trade items: In exchange for wheat, iron tools, weapons, and cotton cloths, the Azanians supplied coconut oil, ivory, and rhinoceros horn. The same source also described the Azanians as fishermen who were skilled enough to use small boats constructed from pieces of wood joined together by coconut fiber. Powerful chiefs protected commerce, governed the trading cities, and engaged in trade themselves. It was through these contacts that some food crops such as rice and bananas were brought to Africa from Southeast Asia. Many cities grew up along the coast, partly to serve as middlemen between the African hinterland and the overseas traders. The cities also absorbed foreigners, such as Arabs, who decided to settle on a permanent basis.

By A.D. 1000, the coastal cities had grown in size and wealth. Now called the land of Zenj by the Arabs, the coastal cities were notable markets visited by traders from Persia, Arabia, and India. When the Islamic capital was located in Bagdad in A.D. 750, the Persian Gulf began to enjoy more visibility in the Indian Ocean trade. This brought more Arab traders and settlers to the East African coast. The presence of the Arabs promoted trade and political relations with the Muslim world. The Arab settlers also intermarried with the African population. Mogadishu and Lamu were two of the most important cities, accessible to traders who continued to use the monsoon winds. One of the earliest written accounts, by an Arab traveler, described the area:

The sea of Zanj reaches down to the country of Sofola . . . which produces gold in abundance and other marvels; its climate is warm and its soil fertile. . . . The Zanj speak elegantly, and they have orators in their own language. . . . These peoples have no code of religion; their kings follow custom and . . . a few political rules. . . . Each worships what he pleases, a plant, an animal, a mineral. They possess a great number of islands where the coconut grows, a fruit that is eaten by all the peoples of the Zanj.[1]

The trade patterns followed by the Arabs became well established. As before, they depended on the seasonal monsoon winds to cross the ocean between western Asia and East Africa. The Arabs used a sailing ship known as a dhow, and the journey was usually of long duration. Having to spend so much time on the sea, and depending on the changes in the direction of the wind, they could not afford to stay for too long in Africa. The most convenient places for the Arab traders to stay were the islands of Mogadishu, Barawa, and Lamu. The East African traders would bring the products of the interior and those manufactured in the coastal cities to sell to the visiting Arab traders, who wasted no time in procuring them. The East African cities exported raw materials, notably gold, copper, leopard skins, coconut oil, shells, ivory, mangrove poles with which to build houses in the Persian Gulf, and slaves. Their imports comprised a variety of imported items and luxuries, such as East Asian pottery, Indian silk and cotton, and glassware.

As the trade expanded and became more steady and lucrative, a number of Arab Muslims began to settle permanently along the coast in order to derive more profit from African products and serve as middlemen. The Arab settlers intermarried with the local populations and developed colonies that hosted foreign traders. By A.D. 1000, many towns including Arab immigrants had developed on the islands of Lamu, Kilwa, Comoro, and Zanzibar. Trade and wealth transformed small settlements into large Swahili city–states.

THE SWAHILI CITY–STATES

By the late tenth century, a new culture and society was already emerging, a multicultural mix of people and ideas from three sources—African, Asian, and Islamic. While people from Indonesia settled in Madagascar, waves of Arabian and Persian Muslims arrived on the East African coast as permanent settlers. The intermingling between settlers and Africans resulted in the formation of Swahili society.

The Swahili states were located along the coast. They were all trading cities. Kilwa, Mogadishu, Sofala, and Mombasa were some of the leading Swahili cities. The economy was dominated by the trade across the Indian Ocean. From the tenth to the mid-eleventh century, the trade grew, due in part to the increasing demand for African gold and ivory in Egypt and Europe. The trade reached its peak during the fourteenth century, the cities prospered, and some produced specialized products for export. For instance, at Sofala, dyed textiles were produced to exchange for gold from the interior. Wealthy traders minted their own coinage in silver and copper for local exchange while using gold (the Fatimid dinar in the tenth and eleventh centuries) for international transactions. The most successful of the cities was Kilwa, which grew in prosperity between the late eleventh century and the fifteenth century. Kilwa controlled the trade of the southern interior, where its merchants were able to obtain gold brought from around the Zimbabwe plateau and the Limpopo valley. A regular supply of gold ensured active participation in the overseas trade and a visible role for the wealthy merchants.

Altogether, there were about forty Swahili city–states, small and large. The small states contained small populations, mainly Africans who were not Muslims and who were treated as subject people. The small states contained a few

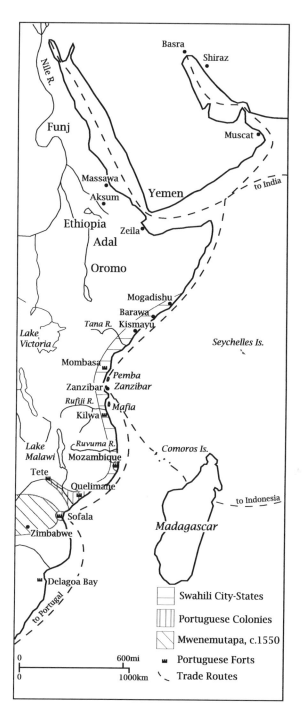

Swahili states and Portuguese control.

Muslims, including the ruling family. The cities included a mosque and some stone houses. The large states, Kilwa, Mogadishu, Mombasa, Pate, Zanzibar, and Malindi, were prosperous, and the majority of the houses were built of coral. Relations among the various Swahili states were peaceful, in spite of the competition for trade.

Whether small or large, the cities had their own rulers, largely drawn from Muslim dynasties that claimed Arab or Persian ancestry. The cities also generally enjoyed political autonomy, although there was a moment in the late fourteenth and early fifteenth centuries when the sultans of Kilwa controlled a number of small cities. All the cities had to maintain relations with African states in the interior. The primary interest was commerce. From the interior came key products, gold, ivory, and skins. Without these products, the coastal cities would not have been prosperous. Imported goods were carried from the coastal cities to the interior, mainly luxury goods including cloth, beads, and pottery.

Commercial interests could also lead to complicated rivalries and wars. In the search for goods, cattle, and slaves, the wealthy merchants and rulers of the coastal cities often organized raiding expeditions into the interior. A Kilwa sultan in the early fourteenth century was notorious for raiding the interior for war booty, some of which he kept to himself and some of which he gave as gifts to his friends and guests. However, relations were generally more peaceful than antagonistic.

THE SWAHILI CULTURE AND SOCIETY

Kiswahili evolved as a language, growing to become the most widely used language in East Africa, not just along the coast but also in the interior. Today, it is the official language of Tanzania. Kiswahili is a Bantu language with many Arabic loan words. The Arab settlers along the coast donated the Arabic words. Originally, they would use Kiswahili in their oral transactions but Arabic in written communications. In due course, Kiswahili became a written language, using the Arabic script.

More and more Arabs visited the East African coast, and they acquired influence in politics and religion. In the twelfth century, a number of Arabs were becoming rulers. Islam spread, not just among the settler populations but also among Africans. Islam became the most important religion. It spread peaceably. As the religion of both foreign merchants and Swahili rulers and merchants, Islam appealed to those who wanted to emulate their lifestyles or engage in trade. It was also a religion that defined identity: For those who wanted to avoid appearing to be members of the lower class, the adoption of Islam made it possible.

A new architectural style became popular—a rectangular design built of blocks made from coral. The cities grew in size and wealth. Part of the wealth was spent on building mosques. Houses of two or three stories were also built. Interior decorations included Persian and Chinese porcelain used to adorn vaults and cupolas. Ceramic lamps were used, and furniture included mats, carpets, stools, and beds adorned with gold, silver, and ivory.

Swahili society was stratified into at least three classes. On the lowest rung of the ladder were the slaves, who were also non-Muslims. They were taken from the interior, either through trade or as war booty. They worked as domestics and as factory workers, producing glass and cotton cloth.

Next were the free Africans, lacking claim to any Persian or Arab ancestry. They constituted the majority, used the Kiswahili language, and practiced Islam. They could be found in a variety of occupations, many of which revolved around trade or production. Many worked as artisans, craftspeople, administrators, and clerks.

At the very top were the wealthy merchants and men of power and status. These were Kiswahili- and Arabic-speaking people. They were generally of Persian or Arabian ancestry and Muslims. Among them were the members of the ruling families, merchants, successful Muslim preachers, visiting Muslim traders, and diplomats. Among the symbols of wealth were expensive cloth made of silk and cotton, imported porcelain from China, Iran, Iraq, Egypt, and Syria, silver and gold jewelry, and large stone houses and palaces. The rulers collected import and export dues, which ran as high as 50 percent, on all goods that passed through their cities. Trade was the primary occupation of the members of the wealthy class. In Mombasa and Kilwa, a number of wealthy merchants also organized the production of items sold to the African hinterland, notably glass, shell beads, and cloth. Many among them took to farming as well, on estates where their slaves grew millet, cotton, fruits, and vegetables.

THE END OF SWAHILI CIVILIZATION

> From our ships the fine houses, terraces, minarets, with the palms and trees in the orchards, made the city [Kilwa] look so beautiful that our men were eager to land and overcome the pride of this barbarian, who spent all that night bringing into the island archers from the mainland.[2]

The above quotation is from the opening account of a Portuguese eyewitness to the destruction, in 1505, of Kilwa, the most important Swahili city–state. Like the Songhay empire in West Africa, the glory of the Swahili was brought to an end by external invaders.

The Portuguese sailed along the East African coast in 1498, the first Europeans to take a southern route to the Indian Ocean. The Portuguese were seeking an alternative route to India, via the south, in order to avoid their powerful Muslim rivals in the eastern Mediterranean and North Africa. The Portuguese had no knowledge of the trade and prosperity of the Swahili states, and their original goal was to replace their Muslim rivals in controlling the rich trade with India, in highly valued goods such as silks, perfumes, spices, and other luxuries.

It was in the process of traveling to India that the Portuguese discovered the Swahili cities. Their ambition changed, as they decided to seize control of these prosperous states and their trade. The Portuguese decided to attack and plunder the Indian Ocean trade, force the city–states to pay heavy tributes, and seize the valuables of the wealthy merchants and the ordinary people.

The Portuguese deployed a strategy that left few or no diplomatic options for the Swahili city–states to pursue. The Portuguese would arrive in the harbors of the Swahili, heavily armed. An ultimatum was then presented to the rulers demanding unreasonable annual tributes to the king of Portugal. A refusal would be met with an attack, regarded as a "holy war" of Christians against Muslims: The Muslims who resisted would be killed, the city would be destroyed, and its valuable possessions would be confiscated. The Portuguese were successful because the Swahili city–states had not previously cooperated to fight external aggression, and they had not been faced with an enemy coming from the sea.

Except for Malindi, all the Swahili city–states refused the conditions set by Portugal. In 1503, Zanzibar became the first to suffer an attack and to be forced to accept the payment of an annual tribute. In the same year, the Portuguese became pirates on the Indian Ocean: They seized ships and forced them to pay ransom in gold. Two years later, it was the turn of Kilwa. The city was plundered of its valuables. Then the Portuguese moved to Mombasa, where they started a fire that destroyed many houses. An eyewitness reported on the event:

Once the fire was started it raged all night long, and many houses collapsed and a large quantity of goods was destroyed. For from this town trade is carried on with Sofala and with Cambay [located in western India] by sea. There were three ships from Cambay and even these did not escape the fury of the attack. It was a moonless night.[3]

Many of those who escaped the inferno were killed by the Portuguese on the following day. Mombasa was raided by an angry Portuguese mob with a desire for wealth:

The Grand-Captain ordered that the town should be sacked and that each man should carry off to his ship whatever he found: so that at the end there would be a division of the spoil, each man to receive a twentieth of what he found. The same rule was made for gold, silver, and pearls. Then everyone started to plunder the town and to search the houses, forcing open the doors with axes and iron bars. There was a large quantity of cotton cloth for Sofala in the town, for the whole coast gets its cotton cloth from here. So the Grand-Captain got a good share of the trade of Sofala for himself. A large quantity of rich silk and gold embroidered clothes was seized, and carpets also; one of these, which was without equal for beauty, was sent to the King of Portugal together with many other valuables.[4]

The Portuguese built stone fortresses at Kilwa, Sofala, and Mozambique to protect themselves on their journeys to their colony of Goa in India. In 1529, they completed the construction of Fort Jesus at Mombasa in order to control the Indian Ocean trade. The Swahili city–states were destroyed, but their culture, especially the Kiswahili language, has survived till today.

NOTES

1. Quoted in Basil Davidson, *African Civilization Revisited* (Trenton, N.J.: Africa World Press, 1991), p. 133.

2. Quoted in Kevin Shillington, *History of Africa* (New York: St Martin's, 1999), p. 134.
3. Ibid.
4. Ibid., p. 136.

SUGGESTIONS FOR FURTHER READING

Beachey, R.W. *A History of East Africa, 1592–1902*. London: I.B. Tauris, 1995.

Collins, Robert O. *African History in Documents: Eastern African History*. New York: Markus Wiener, 1990.

Davidson, Basil. *Africa in History: Themes and Outlines*. New York: Simon and Schuster, 1995.

Falola, Toyin, ed. *Africa*. Vol. 1, *African History before 1885*. Durham, N.C.: Carolina Academic Press, 2000. Chapter 8.

Marsh, Zoe, and G.W. Kingsnorth. *A History of East Africa: An Introductory Survey*. Cambridge: Cambridge University Press, 1972.

Mazrui, Ali A., and Alamin Mazrui, eds. *Swahili, State and Society: The Political Economy of an African Language*. London: James Currey, 1995.

Nicholls, C.S. *The Swahili Coast*. London: George Allen and Unwin, 1971.

Odhiambo, E.S. Atieno. *A History of East Africa*. London: Longman, 1978.

Were, Gideon S., and Derek A. Wilson. *East Africa through a Thousand Years: A History of the Years A.D. 1000 to the Present Day*. 3rd reprint ed. New York: Africana Publishers, 1987.

11

The Atlantic Slave Trade,
1440–1870

The slave trade began in the mid-fifteenth century with a small number of slaves acquired by the Portuguese. By about 1870, when the slave trade ended, what had started as a small traffic had led to the forced enslavement of over 13 million Africans. The scale and intensity of the trade were unmatched in human history. The consequences were disastrous for Africa. In exchange for productive labor that produced tropical products and bullion in the New World, Africa received in return goods of less significance, for instance, firearms to fight more wars and make more slaves, and liquor to be consumed by the trading and political elite.

EUROPEAN CONTACTS

Europeans began to visit different parts of the African coast, from the fifteenth century onward. Improved navigational techniques and shipbuilding facilitated the European expansion. The pioneers were the Portuguese who visited different parts of Africa between 1440 and 1475. By 1480, they had reached areas south of the equator, setting up trading stations along the coast (e.g., the Gold Coast) and on islands (e.g., Fernando Po).

The motives of the early expeditions were economic (to find the production centers for the West African gold that reached North Africa and Europe and to discover an alternative route to Asia without having to pass through the Middle East, which was controlled by Arab Muslim trading rivals), religious (to spread Christianity in Africa), and scientific (to gain more knowledge about Africa).

The Portuguese engaged in trade with the coastal peoples, buying African products such as gold, pepper, ivory, and slaves in exchange for cheap European items.

The Portuguese were challenged by other Europeans, notably the English and the Dutch who joined them during the sixteenth century and also established their own trading forts. By the mid-seventeenth century, the Portuguese had lost almost all their West African posts to the Dutch. Trade was all they cared about—their conversion efforts were feeble and mainly unsuccessful, and they had little or no interest in political control. The African states along the coast were powerful enough to protect themselves from aggression and to negotiate trade terms. Competition among the European traders was fierce, and they did not hesitate to engage in bitter conflicts.

By the mid-sixteenth century, the trade was dominated by one product: slaves. Africans had no control over the commodities that Europeans wanted. The demand for slaves was consistently high, and the wealthy European merchants who sponsored the trade were able to reduce the conflicts among their traders in order to ensure regular profits.

THE SLAVE TRADE

The need for labor in the Americas and Caribbean expanded the volume of the trans-Atlantic slave trade, and the primary interest of Europeans in Africa was only to obtain slaves. The French, Dutch, English, Spanish, and Danes were now established in the Caribbean islands, the Portuguese in Brazil, and the Spanish in different parts of the mainland of South, Central, and North America. They all needed a large amount of labor to develop the economies of these areas. After the decimation of the local population, they turned to West Africa. In 1518, the Spanish shipped their first slave cargo to the West Indies, the first direct shipment. As the plantations in the Americas and the Caribbean expanded, so too did the slave trade. In 1532, the Portuguese also made a direct shipment to the West Indies. In the second half of the sixteenth century, the English and Dutch became participants in the trade.

The volume of trade increased substantially from the mid-sixteenth century onward, reaching its greatest volume during the eighteenth century. The leading European traders were the Portuguese, Dutch, and English. Africa became integrated into an international economic system, the "triangular trade," which contributed to the industrial and economic growth of Europe. It was called a "triangular" trade because it had three stages (or sides) to it, all lucrative. In the first stage, European merchants would take manufactured goods such as knives, jewelry, cloths, spirits, tobacco, metalware, guns, and metal bars to Africa to exchange them for slaves. In the second stage of the trade, the slaves were taken across the Atlantic to the Americas, where they were sold to plantation owners in exchange for sugar, tobacco, indigo, cotton, rum, and other items. To complete the "triangle," the European merchants would take the products obtained in the Americas to Europe.

Forced packing of slaves in a ship.

To elaborate on the African side, many slave-trading castles were created along the seaboard of West and central Africa. In West Africa alone, there were forty-one of them, devoted to buying slaves. Altogether, ten leading slave centers emerged in Africa, with the following markets: Arguin Island, St. Louis, and Gorée in Senegambia; the Isles de Los, Sherbro Island, and Bance Island in Sierra Leone; Anomabu on the Gold Coast; Whydah and Lagos in the Bight of Benin; Bonny, New Calabar, and Old Calabar on the Bight of Biafra; Loango Bay, Malemba, and Cabinda in Loango; Mpinda, Luanda, and Benguela in Angola; and Mozambique, Kilwa Kivinje, Ibo, and Quelimane in the Mozambique region. The European traders were confined to these slave ports, and some stayed on their ships. They did not deal with many Africans, but with a group of selected merchants and especially powerful chiefs and kings, from whom they obtained the slaves.

The slave ports were linked to the interior markets. The slaves came from the hinterland and from further and further inland as the trade grew. Middlemen, mainly coastal merchants, exchanged European imported goods for slaves from

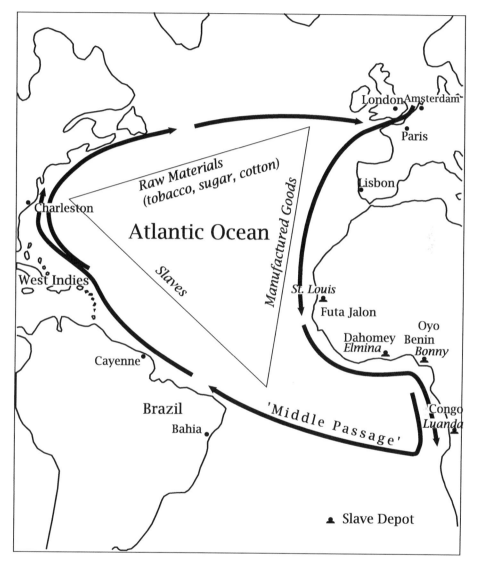

The Atlantic triangle.

Slave castle, Senegal.

the interior. A number of merchants grew rich and powerful through the trade. By the eighteenth century, virtually all the coastal groups in West and central Africa were involved in the slave trade, and they absorbed their hinterlands into the trading network. Established trade routes were used for imported commodities and slaves.

Although a number of Africans opposed the trade, members of the political and merchant class succumbed to the European demands. The slave trade ensured a regular and abundant supply of guns and gunpowder for powerful kings and chiefs. Muskets were more effective than other weapons. Firearms had to be imported, since they could not be produced locally, and Europeans insisted on supplying them mainly in exchange for slaves. The pressure on African rulers to obtain firearms was intense—not to have them was to open oneself to attack from neighbors. Chiefs and kings needed firearms to consolidate themselves in power, raid for slaves, or expand their territories.

Slaves were obtained in a variety of ways, many of which were associated with violence. A few slaves were criminals or offenders who were sold into slavery as punishment. Laws and punishments were changed to meet the needs of the trans-Atlantic slave trade. In the years before the Atlantic slave trade, such slaves would have worked as domestics, farmers, and artisans for their owners. They would have been members of the households of their owners and would have been able to redeem themselves. The trans-Atlantic slave trade involved them in relocation to a strange land, maximum exploitation, and denial of freedom and privileges.

However, as the demand for slaves grew, the trade came to rely on slaves captured in wars or in slave raiding expeditions. In West Africa, the majority of wars were motivated by political considerations, not slave raiding. In a number of areas, states were expanding, incorporating weaker neighbors, and extending their authority. Kanem-Borno, Oyo, Dahomey, Benin, and Asante expanded during the era of the slave trade. The wars associated with state building and political expansion made captives available on a large scale. In the eighteenth and nineteenth centuries, the number of wars increased, and so did the number of captives.

SLAVE RESISTANCE

Whenever the opportunity provided itself, slaves revolted. Whether in Africa or during the Middle Passage, many struggled to free themselves. Heroism characterized slave resistance. When slaves mutinied and failed, they were severely punished. Some slaves chose to die, as in the case of those who were able to jump overboard in order to drown themselves.

A number of attempts were made in Africa to either stop the trade or cut it down significantly, although pressure from European demands and the greed of African slave merchants prevented these efforts from succeeding. One famous example was the attempt in 1526 by King Nzinga Mbemba (also known as Alfonso) of the Bakongo kingdom, located close to the mouth of the River Congo, who asked the king of Portugal to stop the trade because it was ruining his people and their economy. He described slave dealers as "thieves and men of evil conscience" engaged in a destructive economy:

[W]e cannot reckon how great the damage is, since the [slave] merchants daily seize our subjects, sons of the land and sons of our noblemen and vassals and our relatives. . . . Thieves and men of evil conscience take them . . . and cause them to be sold: and so great, Sir, is their corruption and licentiousness that our country is being utterly depopulated. . . . And to avoid it we need from [your country] no more than some priests and a few people to teach in schools, and no other goods except wine and flour for the holy sacrament. That is why we beg of Your Highness to help and assist us in this matter, commanding your factors that they should not send here either merchants or wares, because it is our will that in these Kingdoms there should not be any trade of slaves nor outlet for them.[1]

Yet another unsuccessful attempt was made in the 1780s when the king of Futa Toro in the Senegal River region passed a law stopping the slave trade in the area he controlled. The French slave traders in the area found the means to trade elsewhere.

We may never learn of all the cases of resistance to the slave trade. We know, however, that the trade continued for a long time. The consideration of profits made it very difficult to stop. The slave trade was an integral part of world trade, and African chiefs could not just stop it unless there was a change in the economic system that had created the need for massive amounts of labor in the New World.

THE IMPACT OF THE SLAVE TRADE

The European contacts with Africa and the primary focus on human traffic had many consequences. Trade links widened, with goods coming to Africa from Europe. Gold, ivory, pepper, gum, and ostrich feathers were among the African exports, although the major exports were slaves. To promote this trade, the European traders established their presence in Africa. European languages spread to a few coastal areas, partly in order to facilitate commerce. New crops such as cassava, maize, and sweet potatoes found their way to Africa from the Americas.

The most important consequences were associated with the trade in slaves. The main calamity was a loss of population, as more than 13 million people were taken out of the continent. We will never know the number who died in Africa itself, during wars and raiding expeditions, nor the number who died on the sea on their way to the Americas. One estimate in the mid-nineteenth century concluded that Africa's population would have doubled, had the slave trade not occurred.

Demographic changes varied from one region to another, depending on where slaves were captured. In areas without strong centralized political authorities, as in the case of small, weak societies in the "Middle Belt" between the coastal and the savanna states, a high enough number of slaves was taken that population decline was noticeable. Where female captives were retained in Africa, as in Dahomey, they were able to minimize the population loss by producing more children.

The experience of slavery was one of human suffering that is hard to describe. The wars that produced the captives sold into slavery were traumatizing. Then came the Middle Passage—when the slaves were transported across the sea. Stripped, dehumanized, and branded, they were packed into small spaces and fed contaminated food and water. Dysentery, smallpox, and measles were among the diseases that afflicted a huge number. Many did not make it—one out of six never survived the journey. Those who made it arrived "looking like skeletons," to use the words of a Jesuit priest who saw a group of slaves in Cartagena in Spanish America. He observed that they were "completely naked, and are shut up in a large court or enclosure . . . for as a rule they are left to lie on the ground, naked and without shelter."[2] Buyers examined and auctioned them like cattle. Then came the experience on the plantations where they were treated as property, regarded as no better than cattle.

The slave trade contributed to the spread of racist stereotypes about Africans. In order to justify enslaving human beings and treating them as "property," Europeans had to dehumanize them. Africans were presented as savages, and slavery was justified as an effort to rescue them from savagery. When slavery ended, people of African descent in Europe and Africa continued to suffer racism for a long time—as the "wretched of the earth," they experienced economic marginalization and exclusion from power.

The importation of firearms in exchange for slaves had devastating consequences on society. While it enabled African states to build professional armies, withstand possible European invasions, and expand their territories, firearms encouraged wars, the destruction of villages and towns, and the making of more captives to be sold into slavery. In some cases raiding expeditions were organized to obtain captives. The slave trade thus affected African politics, by producing more ruin, more wars, and more captives.

The slave trade affected the economy in many ways, especially in production. First, Africa lost labor, its most important economic and social asset. As each person departed, wealth was lost. Next, human labor was exchanged for manufactured products, an unequal exchange that added to the growth of America and Europe but the underdevelopment of Africa. The slave trade incorporated Africa into the network of international trade as a weak member. Between the sixteenth century and the first half of the nineteenth century, slaves dominated the commercial transactions between Europeans and Africans, decreasing the importance of other commodities. Whereas Europe and the Americas grew prosperous from foreign trade and became economically developed by the time the slave trade ended, Africa moved in the opposite direction, toward underdevelopment. Losing the benefits of foreign trade in productive goods and entangled in the devastation caused by slavery, Africa's economy lacked the means to transform itself in positive ways.

The loss of productive labor translated into reduced consumption and production of many commodities on the continent. Craftsmen and farmers, notably young people, left many parts of West and central Africa, with a devastating impact on the economy. The rulers that profited from the trade also contributed to damaging the economy. They believed that the economy had to be oriented to the capture and sale of slaves. In addition, they used access to firearms to threaten weak groups and dominate poor farmers and artisans. The goods they received in exchange for slaves, essentially consumer goods and firearms, did not stimulate further development.

Where political instability occurred, even if temporarily, famine could follow. In West Africa's Middle Belt, the effects on agriculture, manufacturing, and trade were devastating. Unable to protect themselves from wars and slave raiding, many groups had to abandon their homes and search for more secure places in mountains and remote areas. Production became highly unstable.

Finally, the slave trade created the African Diaspora—the extensive relocation of a people away from their homeland. Today, blacks can be found in the United States, the Caribbean, Latin America, Europe, and Asia. This Diaspora was mainly created by the slave trade. In the nineteenth century when the trans-Atlantic trade ended, people of African origins constituted half of the population of Brazil and Venezuela and also much of the population of the Caribbean islands. In all these places, blacks contributed substantially to the economy and industrialization, as farmers, miners, artisans, and domestics. They resisted slavery whenever they could, even setting up their own autonomous states such as Palmares in northeastern Brazil, which was created in 1605 and lasted for a hundred years, and Haiti, which emerged from the 1791 revolution of blacks in St. Domingue.

In spite of great suffering and marginalization, African culture spread in the Diaspora, as the slaves and their free successors kept alive many aspects of their old cultures or created new cultures that retained elements of what they had had before. In language, economy, and politics, the impact of people of African descent is indelible. In Spanish America, people of African descent established self-help associations for members of the same neighborhood or religion, each with its own "chiefs," to assist one another and even to organize protests. In Brazil, African culture mixed with the cultures of the Portuguese and American Indians to create a new hybrid, involving child-rearing practices, folktales, food, and *samba* music. In North America, blacks made many contributions to colonial society. On southern plantations, Africans maintained many aspects of their culture, in such areas as songs, cuisine, and folktales. African languages influenced the dialects of the Geechee and Gullah in South Carolina. Africans also introduced better techniques of growing cotton, indigo, and rice.

The slave trade ended in the second half of the nineteenth century. The process that led to its abolition began much earlier. A combination of factors led to the demise of the slave trade: A greater need developed for tropical products to supply European industries, thereby making it profitable to leave Africans in Africa in order to produce; slave rebellions were becoming common in some colonies, thereby creating insecurity; and liberal opposition to slavery was growing in Europe and the Americas as more and more people criticized the injustice and exploitation of slavery.

NOTES

1. Quoted in Basil Davidson, *African Civilization Revisited* (Trenton, N.J.: Africa World Press, 1991), p. 223.
2. Quoted in William Travis Hanes III, *World History: Continuity and Change* (Austin: Holt, Rinehart and Winston, 1997), p. 445.

SUGGESTIONS FOR FURTHER READING

Falola, Toyin, ed. *Africa*. Vol. 1, *African History before 1885*. Durham, N.C.: Carolina Academic Press, 2000. Chapter 17.

Genovese, Eugene. *Roll Jordan Roll: The World the Slaves Made*. New York: Pantheon Books, 1974.

Inikori, J.E., ed. *Forced Migration: The Impact of the Export Trade on African Societies*. London: Hutchinson, 1982.

Lovejoy, Paul. *Transformations in Slavery: A History of Slavery in Africa*. Cambridge: Cambridge University Press, 1983.

Meillassoux, Claude. *The Anthropology of Slavery: The Womb of Iron and Gold*. Chicago: University of Chicago Press, 1991.

Meirs, S., and I. Kopytoff, eds. *Slavery in Africa: Historical and Anthropological Perspectives*. Madison: University of Wisconsin Press, 1977.

Searing, James F. *West African Slavery and Atlantic Commerce: The Senegal River Valley, 1700–1860*. Cambridge: Cambridge University Press, 1993.

Thornton, John. *Africa and Africans in the Making of the Atlantic World, 1400–1800*. 2nd ed. Cambridge: Cambridge University Press, 1998.

12

The Organization of Societies, Fifteenth Century A.D. Onward

Many of the preceding chapters clearly show the success of Africans in adapting to their environments, creating economic and political institutions, and establishing large-scale political units such as kingdoms. Over time, Africans also evolved ways of managing societies at the family and community levels. The institutions of society covered many aspects of life, all in the attempt to regulate human interactions and manage the relations between human beings and the environment, on the one hand, and between human beings and spiritual forces, on the other hand. The most important institutions are those concerning the family, religion, and politics.

KINSHIP, MARRIAGE, AND FAMILY LIFE

Human beings are related by marriage or birth—relations based on marriage are known as affinal, and those based on blood as consanguineal. A consanguineal relationship is based on common ancestry, determined in one of four ways. The most common is patrilineal ancestry, traced to a male ancestor, through one's father. In matrilineal descent, relations are traced through the mother's side. Both of these are unilineal systems. There are also examples of bilineal or duolineal systems, which trace descent through both parents, and bilateral systems, which trace descent through the grandparents.

In precolonial Africa, descent formed the basis of laws on inheritance, marital domicile, and the definition of identity. In a patrilineal system, the child would live in the household of the father, and boys had inheritance rights. In a matrilineal system, children could not inherit their father's property but only that of their uncles. Descent lines constituted a lineage, with members tracing their origin to a common ancestor. Two or more lineages would constitute a clan. When a clan became too big, a faction might relocate to establish a new unit.

Kin groups also included members who were related by marriage. Marriage was partly defined as the union of two large extended families. Elders and families had a say in the choice of partners. In many societies, the payment of bridewealth by the family of the husband was part of the requirements for the completion of a marriage ceremony. Bridewealth comprised money, cattle, crops, and cloths. Among the Kung of South Africa, a man could offer service in lieu of bridewealth—he would stay with his wife's family for a number of years and work for his in-laws. Bridewealth (or brideservice as in the case of the Kung just mentioned) legalized a marriage. It did not mean the purchase of a woman; it was a way to ensure the stability of marriage, involve many family members in the process, and share wealth in a community.

Polygyny—a system in which a man married two or more women—was fairly common. Large families were the ideal, and polygyny ensured that a man would have many children. Where the mortality rate was high, polygyny helped to ensure that some children survived, thus ensuring the continuity of the lineage. The insistence in many areas on having heirs to inherit land and power meant that a man must be survived not just by children but by males. This was more likely if a man had several wives. Where there was an imbalance in the male-female ratio, the system allowed most people to marry. Rules that prevented sexual intercourse during pregnancy or when a woman was nursing a baby promoted polygyny, satisfying the man more than the woman. As most economic activities required the use of household labor, one way to acquire a large labor force was through reproduction. In societies where widow inheritance (the wife of a deceased person being married by one of his relations) existed, polygyny was a form of insurance ensuring that widows and their children were taken care of.

Kinship and marriage forms aimed to produce individuals who would be part of a collectivity and subordinate their personal interests to those of the group. The actions of an individual could bring both praise and condemnation to a kinship or clan. Surviving outside of a group was very difficult—building a house, harvesting extensive crops, and financing marriage and funeral ceremonies were all beyond the capacity of a single person. While the pursuit of individual interests was not necessarily discouraged, the paramount ethos was collectivist.

A family was usually large, comprising a man, his wives, their children, and three generations of relations such as grandparents and uncles, all living close to one another. Children were highly valued, and they were often regarded as the main reason for marriage. One of the major functions of the family was to socialize the children to society and give them occupational skills. Children were trained through the observation and explanation of skills.

NONKINSHIP RELATIONS

Not everybody in a society was related by blood or marriage, and other associations were created to promote interactions. Some were based on bonding through religious and secret societies, whereas others focused on occupations and age. Craft or occupational guilds united members following similar occupations, such as hunting. They helped to disseminate skills, protect members' occupations, and contribute to the overall development of the society. Hunters were respected for their knowledge of the forest and of herbs; medicine men and women were respected for their ability to heal people; mediums and priests served as mediators between people and gods; blacksmiths provided tools; and poets entertained people and recorded histories.

A group of people, men or women, could interact as members of a secret society, such as the Poro and Ogboni of West Africa. Members took oaths of secrecy, protected their beliefs, performed rituals, and initiated new members. In addition to providing opportunities to network and share valuable information, secret societies were involved in the administration of justice, the punishment of those who broke social sanctions, and the selection of chiefs.

Associations based on time of birth, known as age-grades, were by far the most important nonkinship groups in a number of places. A community would have several age-grades, each comprising people of roughly the same age. Members of an age-grade were initiated at the same time and married in the same period. Each age-grade could be assigned a specific function. For instance, among the Afikpo of eastern Nigeria, an expert identified four age-grades, each with different functions: Young men acted as the police and enforced social rules; young married men carried out administrative duties; older men had legislative and adjudicative power; and old men gave advice. Age-grades were also in charge of security and war, while the elders performed initiation ceremonies to welcome the young to adulthood. The most respected and revered age-grades were those of the elders. The elderly were greatly respected, not only for their wisdom and experience but also for their accumulated knowledge. There was an important role for them. Within households, they were involved in raising children and passing on family traditions. They were consulted on a wide variety of issues, from choice of partners to medicines. Their voices carried weight in conflict resolution. Some of them were chiefs, priests, and kings.

LIFE STAGES

Within both kinship and nonkinship groups, individuals celebrated rites of passage. At each turning point, from birth to death, the community was involved in the celebration and in all the necessary rituals. Children were highly valued, and they were welcomed into the world by rituals and festivities. Special names were given to children, and mothers devoted a great deal attention to their children. The child was socialized through informal education offered by the parents, other members of the household, and even neighbors.

The transition to adulthood was marked in many areas by an elaborate initiation ceremony. Initiation for boys could be through circumcision, performed between the ages of twelve and eighteen. This was a common practice among the Kikuyu of Kenya, the Igbo of Nigeria, and the Zulu of South Africa. In some other cultures, such as that of the Hausa of West Africa, marriage was used to initiate young men into adulthood. In almost all cultures, marriage turned girls into adults. A small number of groups, such as the Hausa and the Somali, used female circumcision to initiate girls. Initiation was important for a variety of reasons: It brought the community together to celebrate as a collective; it was a turning point for youths who became adults; it formally instructed young people about adult life, including the responsibilities of married couples and the knowledge required to live in the society; and it gave the participants a sense of achievement through the endurance of pain. Initiation ceremonies enabled the community to reaffirm the identity of its members, while it gave the youth a sexual identity as well.

Initiation practices and marks varied from one place to another, but they included the scarification of the skin, face, or upper torso by tattooing and cicatrization (scar formation at a wound site) and the removal of a few teeth. Where female circumcision was practiced, it involved the surgical removal of the clitoris. In cultures with important initiation practices, failure to perform them would result in the denial of social status and marriage. Circumcision affected women more than men, as it reduced sexual pleasure and possibly sex drive as well. There was a religious side to all initiation ceremonies: An appeal was made to gods and ancestors to bless the new adults and the community, sacrifices were offered to all the major gods, and small quantities of blood were shed to link the initiates with supernatural forces.

RELIGION

Religious beliefs were strong, shaping an understanding of the world, the environment, and mysterious realities. Africans believed in supernatural forces that included a host of gods, spirits, witches, and ancestors. There was a conception of a universe of which the earth was just one part. In some areas, people believed that there were spirits beneath the land, an underworld of strange and powerful objects. There was also the "world above the sky," the abode of yet more forces, including probably a Supreme Being, and such powerful "beings" as the sun, moon, and stars. Human beings linked the various parts of the universe.

In many cultures, the people believed in the existence of a Supreme Being or God. Views on the Supreme Being varied, but it was common to attribute creation and power to God. In many areas, God was invested with superior human attributes. God could be described as gender-based or neutral—in some groups, God was described as a male and in other groups as a female, while still other groups assigned no specific gender.

In worship and sacrifices, the lesser gods and spirits received more attention. Like human beings, the lesser gods were created by the Supreme Being who appointed them as His messengers on earth. Each god also had a specific function or power, as in cases of the god of rain, the god of fertility, and the god of wealth. To ask for children, one might consult the god in charge of reproduction. Farmers would worship the fertility god so that their crops would grow well.

The religious universe was crowded. Some individuals were invested with considerable power to mediate between human beings and supernatural forces. As mediums or priests, they understood the language of the spirits and gods and could relay people's messages to them. There were also people with powers of magic and witchcraft who could do good or evil. Important objects in the environment were identified as powerful, and appropriate sacrifices were made to them at intervals. Major rivers, mountains, farmlands, and some trees were among the objects possessing powerful spirits. As powerful life forces, these natural objects were worshipped because of the protection that they offered to their followers. Human beings and all objects in the universe had origin stories, explaining how they came into being. Not only were human beings expected to recognize the power of the universe; they must also follow moral codes if they wanted to live well. Thus, there were notions of good and evil, laws to be obeyed in relations with the Supreme Being and other gods and spirits, and rules of behavior in interpersonal relations.

Ancestors were also spirits. These could be lineage founders or elderly people who were invested with supernatural power after their death. Ancestors created a chain between the living and God and other unseen forces. As close relations of the living, ancestors were expected to bestow blessings and to answer prayers as quickly as possible.

ECONOMIC ACTIVITIES

Agriculture was the dominant occupation. Most people were farmers. Cattle-keeping societies included the Fulani of West Africa, the Maasai of Kenya, and the Xhosa of South Africa. Production was primarily for family consumption. A secondary aim was to generate surpluses to sell in exchange for both essential and luxury items. Land was available to all lineages, and each household had its own portion. Farm implements were locally manufactured. Each area had a main crop, such as rice and yam in West Africa and maize in South Africa. Other crops were treated as subsidiaries, grown in the same field as the main crop or on other land that was less fertile. Harvest periods were marked by festivals and religious celebrations, held to praise the gods, conduct wedding ceremonies, and exchange gifts. Household work was arranged by gender. Women worked on the farms, performed a host of domestic chores, and took care of their children. Men worked as soldiers to defend the community and in such occupations as hunting, blacksmithing, farming, and carving. Where an activity involved numerous people, members of different households could cooperate with one another.

A host of other occupations were either combined with farming or performed by specialists. Blacksmiths, palace officials, and priests were examples of

Benin plaque.

Ceramic industry.

specialists. Some of them would have small farms. The blacksmith's work was full-time, leaving no time for farming. The blacksmith made tools for the farmers and weapons of war, in addition to domestic utensils. Where blacksmiths also smelted iron ore, they were regarded with considerable respect. The highly skilled nature of iron manufacturing and the need to protect the sources of ore made blacksmiths highly regarded. A variety of items were produced, such as salt, leather items, pottery, textiles, and other craft goods. Manufacturers might form their own guilds.

Trade was a vital economic activity, organized to distribute local items as well as connect towns and villages in regional and international networks. Local and regional trade made possible the distribution of food crops and local manufactures. Essential items such as salt were exchanged for food crops. Farmers and pastoralists exchanged their products. In long-distance and international trade, goods passed through many towns and regions in a relay system. Scarce and expensive products such as iron tools, jewelry, gold, and religious items could travel thousands of miles from their original sources, carried by traders in various caravan systems.

Africa had an extensive network of trade, currencies, and traders, making regional and international commerce a highly developed economic activity. In East and West Africa, the cowrie was a common currency, noted for its small size and durability. Items such as gold and cattle were used in some areas as currencies, while goods could also be exchanged by barter.

POLITICAL SYSTEMS

All African societies, whether large or small, had a form of government. Egypt, Mali, and Songhay were governed by powerful kings. Not all societies were organized on such a large political scale; smaller chiefdoms existed with less powerful chiefs. Lineages were important in all political systems. Management at the lower level involved families and lineage units. Heads of compounds resolved conflicts among their members, ensured that everybody had access to land and shelter, and maintained social cohesion.

In states with kings, power was centralized in a few hands. The state was an agglomeration of many lineages, clans, villages, and towns brought together in a centralized political system with executive, legislative, and judicial power over all important issues. There was also an army, usually of an ad hoc nature, used to ensure that people accepted the authority of the central government. The various communities in a state could be close to one another or separated by great distances. Some examples of monarchies included the Oyo, Benin, and Asante empires in West Africa, the Luanda states in East Africa, and the Zulu kingdom in South Africa. Many of these states emerged because of powerful leaders who brought many communities under their authority; a lineage could grow into a huge clan and incorporate additional lineages and clans to form a larger unit; or one clan or lineage could use military methods to force others to accept its

The king of Kano.

authority and leadership. Irrespective of the method of formation of a state, strong leaders, armed forces, and access to weapons and resources were all necessary.

A powerful king governed in association with a number of prominent chiefs. The king had a specific title. Although there were other chiefs, no one else bore the kingly title. The power of the king could be based on descent from a royal line, possession of ritual or priestly power, or even conquest. The position was justified and legitimized by tradition, the recognition of only one particular lineage that provided leaders, the possession of ritual powers, and control of the army. The people in a state not only respected the king and chiefs but funded the administration. Annual religious festivals united the people and their rulers in celebration and in affirmation of their identity. The king was expected to protect the people from external attack, ensure justice, and cooperate with religious leaders to make necessary sacrifices for rain and good harvests.

Authority could be organized in a pyramid, in which lower chiefs respected and obeyed the senior ones. Kings enjoyed wide powers and were treated as semidivine in many places. A large number of palace officials and others assisted the king to collect tribute, levies, market dues, and other revenues, execute orders, entertain guests, and perform other duties. There was no separation of powers—the king and his chiefs could legislate, give orders, and try offenders all in one meeting. Decisions were arrived at after long deliberations and by consensus, although the king had veto power. There were instances when a king became too powerful and tyrannical. In many states, there were regulations to

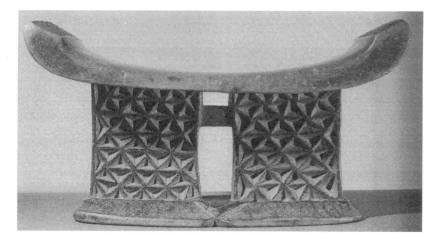

The chief's stool, Zimbabwe.

check the excesses of kings: Angry subjects could migrate elsewhere; the king-makers and secret societies could remove a tyrannical king; and in some kingdoms such as Oyo, the king could be forced to commit suicide.

In some societies power was decentralized. In the absence of a powerful figure such as that of a king, power was not centralized but shared by a number of elders and representatives of kin groups, age-grade associations, and secret societies who maintained law and order, performed public services, and defended their communities when threatened. Bureaucrats, standing armies, and complicated revenue systems were not needed. The village headship was the highest political office. In moments of war and for trade and ritual purposes, many villages could combine and accept the authority of one person, but this would be only temporary.

Examples of African groups with decentralized political authority included the Berbers of North Africa, the Temne of Sierra Leone, the Maasai, Luo, Nandi, and Kikuyu of Kenya, and the Tiv and Igbo of Nigeria. Among the Kikuyu, age-grade associations performed administrative duties, protected village land, collected taxes, and enforced laws. This was a highly democratic system in which both elders and age-grades had a say in the administration of the village. In the case of the Igbo, each village enjoyed political autonomy. A village was an agglomeration of lineages and sublineages, each occupying its own compound. There was a village head, who presided over a village assembly where people were allowed to talk. The assembly performed legislative functions, and the elders would make decisions by consensus. Lineage heads exercised authority among members of their lineages.

In religion, economy, and politics, Africans were able to create institutions suitable to their needs and successfully adapt to their environments. Once established, many practices endured for hundreds of years. Ideas and religions from other parts of the world were subsequently borrowed, modifying some practices and creating new ones, while the essential core values of institutions were retained.

SUGGESTIONS FOR FURTHER READING

Asante, Molefi, and Kariamu Asante, eds. *African Culture: The Rhythms of Unity.* Westport, Conn.: Greenwood Press, 1985.

Austin, R. *African Economic History.* London: James Currey, 1987.

Falola, Toyin, ed. *Africa.* Vol. 2, *African Culture and Societies before 1885.* Durham, N.C.: Carolina Academic Press, 2000.

Kayongo-Male, Diane, and Philista Onyango. *The Sociology of the African Family.* New York: Longman, 1984.

Khapoya, Vincent B. *The African Experience: An Introduction.* Englewood Cliffs, N.J.: Prentice-Hall, 1994.

Ray, Benjamin. *African Religions: Symbol, Ritual and Community.* Englewood Cliffs, N.J.: Prentice-Hall, 1976.

Smith, Andrew. *Pastoralism in Africa: Origins and Development Ecology.* London: Hurst, 1992.

Zeleza, P. Tiyambe. *A Modern Economic History of Africa.* Vol. 1, *The Nineteenth Century.* Dakar, Senegal: CODESRIA, 1993.

PART II

The Nineteenth-Century Period

13

The Outbreak
of Islamic Jihad, 1804

In 1804, a jihad (holy war) broke out in the Hausa states in what is now northern Nigeria and Niger. Also known as the Sokoto jihad, it was the first in a series of jihads that occurred in West Africa during the nineteenth century. The wars had social and political motivations, although these were expressed in religious form. The Sokoto jihad turned out to be a major revolution that revived Islam and created a caliphate (the Sokoto caliphate), a system of government patterned after that of the Prophet Muhammad, and a legal system based on the *sharia*.

According to Islamic belief, a jihad is a war sanctioned by Allah and prosecuted by the followers of Allah to spread or revive Islam. A jihad has a political dimension to it: the leaders of the movement may acquire power by displacing previous power holders, and they also attempt to introduce major political and legal reforms. What factors led to the Sokoto jihad, why was it a success, and what were its consequences? These are the three major questions that this chapter addresses.

UTHMAN DAN FODIO

Islam had been spreading in various parts of West Africa long before the nineteenth century. However, some Islamic religious leaders believed that Islam was not spreading fast enough and that it was being corrupted. They believed that the Hausa political leaders were Muslims only in name. The pressure to reform Islam through a jihad was already building up in West Africa in the eighteenth century, with jihads in the Western Sudan in the 1720s and 1770s. At the forefront of the pressure for change were the Fulani, who included devout

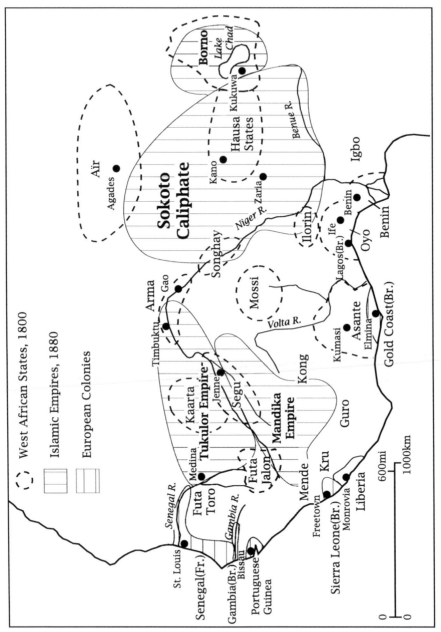

West African Islamic empires.

teachers and preachers. The Fulani originally emerged in the lower Senegal valley, and they migrated to other parts of West Africa from the twelfth century onward. They were concentrated in Hausaland (modern Nigeria and Niger), as well as in the Fouta states and Niger bend area, all areas where jihads occurred during the nineteenth century.

The leader of the Sokoto jihad—the most important of all the jihads—was Uthman dan Fodio. Born in 1754 to Fulani parents based in Gobir (the northwesternmost Hausa state), he studied the *Quran* under famous teachers and took to a life of preaching and teaching at a relatively early age.

In 1774 dan Fodio began to preach in the Hausa states of Gobir and Zamfara, moving from one town to another, while retaining his base in the city of Degel. He criticized the mixture of Islam with local religious practices and called for the reform of Islam and strict adherence to the *sharia*. He was critical of kings and their officials, whom he accused of excesses and corruption. His messages were attractive to the poor, who saw him as a defender against exploitation, and to the youth who studied Islam with him.

His messages threatened the established political order. The king of Gobir had to introduce measures to curtail the growing influence of dan Fodio. In the 1790s, laws were passed to prohibit people from wearing the distinctive Islamic turban and veil in public, while attempts were made to end the conversion of more people to Islam. As the threat to dan Fodio continued, on 21 February 1804, he undertook a withdrawal from the city of Degel to Dugu, a withdrawal known as the *hijra*, similar to the Prophet Muhammad's withdrawal from Mecca to Medina (see Chapter 8).

At Dugu, dan Fodio proclaimed a jihad. He became the *Amir al-Muminin* (the Commander of the Faithful), and his followers were constituted into an army to launch the jihad. The war began in 1804, and dan Fodio and his forces achieved initial victory. Emboldened by their early success, they carried the jihad from one area to another. Support was also given to various Fulani Islamic leaders who rebelled against Hausa kings in different Hausa states. By the time of dan Fodio's death in 1817, a huge Islamic empire had emerged, comprising all the leading Hausa states, areas along the Rivers Benue and Niger (in Nupe and Adamawa), the northern Yoruba city of Ilorin, and parts of the Old Oyo empire.

THE CAUSES OF THE JIHAD

Leadership was a major factor in the jihad—the ability of dan Fodio to preach, to mobilize people, and to build a large army to fight the group in political power. In two manifestos, dan Fodio stated the objectives of the jihad in a way that inspired many Muslims. He strongly believed that the Hausa rulers had established a system of government that Muslims should not tolerate. To quote dan Fodio:

One of the ways of their government is succession to the emirate by hereditary right and by force to the exclusion of consultation. And one of the ways of their government is the building of their sovereignty upon three things: the people's persons, their honor, and their possessions; and whomsoever they wish to kill or exile or violate his honor or devour his wealth they do so in pursuit of their lusts, without any right in the Shari'a. One of the ways of their government is their imposing on the people monies not laid down by the Shari'a . . . intentionally eating whatever food they wish . . . drinking what beverages they wish . . . taking what women they wish without marriage contract . . . compelling people to serve in their armies . . . shutting the door in the face of the needy . . . being occupied with vain things by night or by day.[1]

Dan Fodio was a charismatic leader who inspired his followers to fight for the jihad. The conflict between dan Fodio and the king of Gobir triggered the jihad. However, there were other causes, which were long term in nature.

There were economic and social causes. Indeed, the majority of poor people joined the jihad because they regarded themselves as victims of economic exploitation who paid excessive tax and worked as laborers for the rich. Many of the messages of dan Fodio were directed at excessive taxation and exploitation of the peasantry and slaves. These resonated well with the *talakawa*—a lowly class of farmers and artisans. In addition, the poor expected changes in the legal system, which imposed maximum fines on them and gave preference to the rich.

Existing social hierarchies were a source of worry to the Islamic leaders. They were not happy with the appointment of judges based on considerations other than Islamic knowledge. When the rich and politically connected committed offense, they could pay fines to escape other punishments, a privilege that annoyed Islamic leaders. At the death of an individual, his assets passed to the eldest son, thus denying others access to property and wealth. Those who wanted a change in inheritance practices supported the jihad. In the minds of many, the jihad would bring social justice.

Just as the society was divided by class, it was divided by ethnicity. Dan Fodio was a Fulani, a member of an ethnic group that regarded itself as marginalized by the majority Hausa group. Thus, there was an ethnic dimension to the jihad. The majority of the Fulani supported the jihad for various reasons. To the learned among them, the Fulani Gida who lived in the cities, their exclusion from government was a source of irritation. In addition, they were prevented from carrying arms, owning slaves, or enjoying the privileges associated with the Hausa aristocracy. The Fulani Gida believed in their own skills; they also knew the rules of Islam as they applied to politics. They equated their Islamic devotion with ethnic superiority.

The Fulani who lived in the villages (the Fulani Bororo) were also offended by the taxation laws, especially the imposition of the *jangali* (cattle tax). In addition, they complained that the political leaders confiscated their cattle for no just reason and that they lacked adequate grazing land. Although many among them were not Muslims, they nevertheless saw the jihad as an opportunity to solve long-standing problems.

There were definite political reasons for the jihad. The combination of the social, economic, and ethnic factors identified above led to support of a change in leadership and the overthrow of the existing political class. For the jihadists, Islam could not be separated from politics. By saying that the laws, constitutions, and administration must have the imprint of Islam, the jihadists were making a political demand. The established Hausa kings and dynasties were right to view the message of dan Fodio and the jihad as a political threat. As in this case and in other jihads before and after, a holy war was a means to obtain power.

Finally, the religious factor brought all the other factors together. To dan Fodio, jihad was a religious duty. He himself was pious, and he regarded religious reforms as necessary to change society. To revive and reform Islam, a jihad was necessary. As far as dan Fodio was concerned, a holy war was sanctioned by Allah. The belief was that a jihad was necessary to spread Islam to areas regarded as "pagan." The Hausa kings were accused of ignoring the *sharia* in governing their people and of promoting pagan practices.

FACTORS LEADING TO THE SUCCESS OF THE JIHAD

For a religious leader, untrained in the art of warfare, to lead a small army (later to grow in size) and defeat long-established political dynasties was no small task. To start with, the identification of the masses with dan Fodio and the jihad was important. The Fulani gave their support, for reasons already identified. Even large numbers of poor Hausa ignored their own aristocracy to join the Fulani. Indeed, the majority of poor people, irrespective of their ethnic backgrounds, were eager to support the jihad because they believed that a new political order would bring positive changes in their lives.

The leaders of the jihad were able to motivate their followers. The followers believed that the war was just: Should they survive, they would see changes; should they die, they would enjoy salvation in paradise. Dan Fodio was believed to be a messiah, completely trusted by his numerous followers. His son, Muhammad Bello, and his brother, Abdullahi, were equally respected. The jihadists successfully portrayed the Hausa kings as corrupt infidels who must be overthrown if society was to make any progress. The jihadists also included people who understood military strategies. They were able to train their soldiers within a short time and to instruct them on the techniques of battle. The ambitious among the jihad leaders wanted power, a motivation that drove many of them to work hard.

The Hausa states and their kings had problems that benefited the jihadists. To start with, the various Hausa states failed to unite to present a formidable force against the jihadists. Each state had an experienced army, but long years of interstate conflicts had destroyed their ability to come together. For instance, Gobir had engaged in prolonged wars with three neighboring states, thereby weakening itself and making it hard to call on its neighbors for support. Within each state, the political leaders had alienated their own people, making it difficult to call on their loyalty. To the surprise of some kings, their subjects eagerly joined their enemies. In places with long-standing rivalries for power, one of the factions would invite the jihadists to intervene on its behalf.

THE IMPACT OF THE JIHAD

The consequences of the jihad were revolutionary in many ways. A new theocracy emerged, in the form of the Sokoto caliphate, a huge political entity that united many states. The divided Hausa states were now organized into a united Islamic empire ruled by the Fulani. The expansion of the jihad to the southwest contributed to the fall of the Oyo empire among the Yoruba. The success of the jihad inspired two other leaders to embark on jihads: Seku Ahmadu in Macina (the inland delta area to the west of the River Niger) and al-Hajj Umar, the creator of the Tukulor empire in the area between the Niger bend and the Atlantic.

The jihad contributed to religious and administrative change. As far as dan Fodio was concerned, politics and administration must be based on strict Islamic principles. The *sharia* formed the basis of the legal, administrative, and taxation systems. Islam spread to new areas in northern Nigeria and among the Yoruba to the southwest. Over time, Islam was able to consolidate itself, becoming the dominant religion in the area and remaining dominant ever since.

Quranic education expanded. Many new mosques and schools were built, religious literature spread, and Islamic preachers traveled from one area to another. The jihad leaders were great scholars who authored many books, poems, and essays. Over 300 works authored by dan Fodio, his son Bello, and his brother Abdullahi have been recovered, covering a variety of topics in religion, medicine, politics, diplomacy, and administration. The writers wanted to create a just society through an Islamic revival. They were moralists who criticized society, especially pagan kings.

The large political entity that was created and the stability it offered promoted trade. The security offered by the various political leaders was a boost to long-distance trade. Established market centers such as Zaria and Kano continued to be prominent, and the volume of trade expanded during the nineteenth century. The wars enabled the jihad leaders to take captives in various non-Islamic areas. While many were sold into the trans-Atlantic slave trade in the first half of the nineteenth century, a large number stayed behind and worked on large farms owned by rulers and wealthy merchants.

Demographic changes occurred in some parts of the region, as people responded to the wars by migrating. Where people refused to accept Islam or the new Fulani overlords, they could move elsewhere. New villages were established in the process. Notable examples of migration occurred among the Yoruba, where some groups in the Old Oyo empire moved southward to found new cities.

THE CALIPHATE

A single Fulani empire replaced the old Hausa states and dynasties. The empire (caliphate) was divided into emirates (provinces), each governed by a Fulani emir (king) whose descendants have remained in power ever since. When dan Fodio retired from politics and died in 1817, the caliphate was divided into two. The western half had its capital in Gwandu, under dan Fodio's brother Abdullahi. The larger and more important half was based in the capital city of Sokoto with Bello, dan Fodio's son, as the caliph. Ever since, Sokoto has remained the most important city in the caliphate. Bello was able to complete his father's jihad by preserving unity, overcoming many revolts, and creating an efficient administration that worked well for the rest of the century.

A government led by Muslim leaders was established. At the head in the capital at Sokoto was the caliph, the leader of all Muslims. As the Commander of the Faithful, he was expected to pay attention to Islam and ensure that the laws were in accordance with the *sharia*. He also confirmed the appointments of the emirs who headed the emirates (the provinces of the caliphate). The caliph also settled conflicts between emirates. The caliph served to unite the caliphate, attracting the allegiance of all the kings and chiefs and acting as the religious leader of the Muslims. Uthman dan Fodio provided the criteria with which to judge a good caliph:

[T]he foundations of government are five things: the first is that authority shall not be given to one who seeks it. The second is the necessity for consultation. The third is the abandoning of harshness. The fourth is justice. The fifth is good works.[2]

The caliph was assisted by a number of powerful officials. Notable among them was the *wazir*, who represented the caliph in the emirates and vetted the candidates for emirship. Another was the *kofa*, who handled legal appeals from

Emir's palace, Zaria.

the lower courts. These two and other senior officers were expected to promote the cause of Islam, prevent the exploitation of the poor, and give honest advice to the caliph.

Emirs were powerful kings, heading large political units. They paid allegiance to the caliph by attending the coronation of a new caliph, sending annual tributes, remitting a percentage of the taxes they collected, and contributing to the defense of the empire.

The caliphate experienced a number of major problems. Although it had a clear management structure, it suffered from its large size. People who lived hundreds of miles away from the capital were expected to give their allegiance to the caliph. As they were asked to pay taxes and levies and serve in the army, a large number became unhappy.

Having raised the expectations and hopes of millions of poor people and promised them that social ills and injustice would end, the new leaders failed to keep their promises and thus alienated the people. Like their Hausa predecessors, the new men of power were interested in holding slaves, acquiring large farms, collecting bribes, keeping war booty and captives, and increasing the size of their harems. As the poor noticed this, and saw little or no change in their own conditions, many realized that a just and fair society was simply a dream.

There was power rivalry and there were other political problems. The leaders after Bello, who died in 1837, found it hard to impose their will on all the emirs and officials. Rivalries among some emirates led to war. Given its large size, the caliphate lacked the resources to police all the emirates. Some emirs in distant areas refused to carry out the instructions of the caliph. A number of emirates even organized revolts against the caliph, and four of these revolts became widespread.

Finally, there were external enemies. There were groups that fled when the jihad broke out, later on to reorganize themselves for revenge. Attacks came from such centers as Maradi, Gobir, and Gawakuke. The caliphate had to negotiate peaceful relations with its powerful neighbor to the northeast, the Kanem-Borno empire, where a new dynasty (founded by al-Kanemi) emerged in the process. Since Kanem-Borno's rulers regarded themselves as devout Muslims, the caliphate had problems justifying the extension of the jihad to this area. The army of the Kanem-Borno empire was formidable enough to resist the caliphate. The last enemies were the Europeans who, in the second half of the nineteenth century, began to establish their influence. The European traders began to negotiate with emirs independently of the caliph. Through treaties and military conquests, the British incorporated the caliphate into the modern country of Nigeria early in the twentieth century.

NOTES

1. Quoted in Basil Davidson, *African Civilization Revisited* (Trenton, N.J.: Africa World Press, 1991), p. 376.
2. Ibid., p. 377.

SUGGESTIONS FOR FURTHER READING

Adeleye, R.A. *Power and Diplomacy in Northern Nigeria, 1804–1906*. London: Longman, 1971.

Clarke, P.B. *West Africa and Islam: A Study of Religious Development from the Eighth to the Twentieth Century*. London: Edward Arnold, 1982.

Falola, Toyin, ed. *Africa*. Vol. 1, *African History before 1885*. Durham, N.C.: Carolina Academic Press, 2000. Chapter 13.

Hiskett, M. *The Development of Islam in West Africa*. London: Longman, 1984.

Last, M. *The Sokoto Caliphate*. London: Longman, 1967.

Loimeier, Roman. *Islamic Reform and Political Change in Northern Nigeria*. Evanston, Ill. Northwestern University Press, 1997.

Smaldone, J.P. *Warfare in the Sokoto Caliphate*. Cambridge: Cambridge University Press, 1977.

Wars and Revolution among the Yoruba, 1817–93

Formidable as a massive wooden door
Most senior chief of war
Capable of cutting anybody down to size
Great warrior chieftain
As sure of himself as the dawn itself.
He does what pleases him like God.

Poem in honor of a Yoruba general

In 1817, a major war broke out among the Yoruba. It lasted till 1824. Thereafter, other wars followed, and the Yoruba entered a century of warfare. In all, the major wars lasted twenty-eight years, but they were accompanied by a host of smaller wars and raiding expeditions. Parts of Yorubaland were also invaded by external forces: Dahomey from the west and the Fulani from the north. Professional warriors and generals emerged, heroes of their kingdoms who received high praises such as the poem quoted above in praise of Chief Ibikunle, an Ibadan war leader. The Yoruba also used imported firearms more than ever before, and states had to produce raw materials in order to pay for them. The wars affected virtually all aspects of society. Why did the Yoruba have to fight for so long, and how did the wars affect them?

THE YORUBA AND THEIR WARS

The Yoruba occupy areas of modern southwestern Nigeria and some areas of the Republic of Benin. They have an ancient history, and they regard the city of

Yoruba sculpture.

Ile-Ife as their original homeland and Oduduwa as their ancestor. According to their origin stories, it was from Ile-Ife that princes migrated with their followers to establish other kingdoms. Subethnic groups (and kingdoms) emerged, such as the Ife, Ekiti, Ijesa, Oyo, Akoko, Ondo, Owo, Egba, Egbado, and Ijebu, each with its principal cities and government. The Yoruba were not politically united under one king. Rather, the people developed loyalty to their groups and kings. The belief in a common ancestor and the ability to communicate with one another did not prevent wars among them.

The leading Yoruba state was Oyo. With an effective military organization, access to horses from the north, a unified center, and a reliable revenue system, Oyo was able to grow and expand its influence over other Yoruba kingdoms. Governed by a powerful king (the *alaafin*), Oyo operated a system of checks and balances that ensured good government and political stability. Rich, extensive, and powerful, Oyo attained the height of its power in the eighteenth century. It was the largest coastal empire in West Africa, with its power extending to its northern neighbors (e.g., Borgu and Nupe) and westward to the states of the Fon, Aja, and Dahomey.

During the nineteenth century, a series of wars began, initiated by the fall of the Oyo empire. Oyo's fall was a gradual process that ended in the 1830s. Its

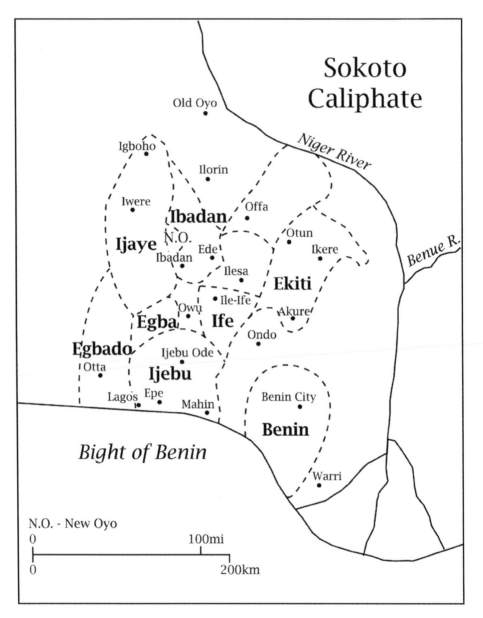

Yoruba states in the nineteenth century.

army suffered a decline, its economy was interrupted by the jihad to the north, it was challenged by the growing power of Dahomey to the west and Nupe to the north, and its principal officers struggled among themselves for power. There were problems within the central government—the leading war general, Afonja, rebelled. With his base in the northern city of Ilorin, Afonja organized a war against Oyo. Then various groups revolted, notably the Egba and Dahomey. The Muslims, too, rebelled, and the Fulani captured power at Ilorin, from where they threatened Oyo. Oyo abandoned its capital, and its rulers moved southward to recreate a much smaller kingdom, now known as New Oyo.

The political instability that led to Oyo's downfall created political upheavals and wars that lasted from around 1813 to 1838. The capital city of Oyo was burned down, its people fled in various directions, many of its former colonies became independent, and its northern frontier was incorporated into the Sokoto caliphate (see Chapter 13). Following the decline of Oyo, other wars ensued. These wars fell into three major phases: the Owu war from 1817 to 1824, the Ijaye war from 1860 to 1865, and the Kiriji (or Ekitiparapo) war from 1877 to 1893. They were accompanied by other wars.

The first major war, which broke out in 1817, started as a small-scale conflict over the control of the market town of Apomu. Other groups and warriors fleeing from Oyo joined in the war, and a major alliance formed against the Owu. In the 1820s, the anti-Owu forces became strong enough to attack Owu, which became the first Yoruba city to be completely destroyed by war. The Egba towns that supported Owu were also attacked, and they were forced to relocate to found the new city of Abeokuta. After the war, the Oyo refugees established a camp at Ibadan in about 1829, and this camp later grew to become the largest Yoruba city–state.

Ibadan became an empire within a period of twenty years. Its main rival in central Yorubaland was Ijaye, a city–state also established by Oyo refugees. Competition between the two states led to war in the 1860s. The ambition of both Ijaye and Ibadan was the same—to create an empire in the same region and collect revenues from the colonies. Although Ijaye was able to form an alliance with the powerful Egba of Abeokuta, it lost the war so comprehensively that the kingdom collapsed and its people dispersed.

With the collapse of Ijaye, no other power was able to rival Ibadan. However, its colonies were resentful. A major war broke out in 1877, the biggest of them all, with Ibadan fighting on several fronts. With regard to its Egba and Ijebu neighbors to the south, Ibadan's goal was to end their control of trade routes and access to the Lagos market, in order to procure firearms and other imported items. As Ibadan calculated, the southern strategy would be "the war to win all wars" since its victory would mean limitless access to firearms. In the east, the problem was to suppress rebellions in Ibadan's colonies. Individually, the Ekiti and Ijesa towns appeared weak, but they creatively forged the largest alliance ever, involving the majority of the groups in the east and northeast of Yoruba-land. Known as the Ekitiparapo, the allies resolved in 1878 to end Ibadan's rule.

Other states also joined the Ekitiparapo, notably Ile-Ife in the center and Ilorin to the north.

Ibadan had to defend its supremacy. Its army had become large and powerful, and a long succession of successful wars had made its warriors the most prestigious and arrogant in the region. Indeed, Ibadan had become the training ground for the warriors of other kingdoms, and some of the leaders now opposed to it were actually trained at Ibadan. For the Ekiti and Ijesa, this was a war of liberation. For years, their people had complained against the excessive collection of tributes by Ibadan and the abuse of power by the Ibadan agents stationed among them. Were they to lose the war, their leaders would pay with their lives, and their people would bear the cost. For the Ijebu and Egba, the increasing power of Ibadan meant that ultimately they too would become colonies and lose their privileged control of trade. For Ilorin, it was an opportunity to avenge its defeat in the 1830s. The stakes were high—the war went on until all the parties became tired of it, and the British successfully negotiated a peace treaty in 1893.

THE CAUSES OF WARS

Failure to provide political stability and impose peace often induces kingdoms to go to war. For many years, the Oyo empire was powerful enough to ensure stability and peace in the region. In the early years of the nineteenth century, the Oyo empire declined and collapsed. Until the rise to power of Ibadan in the 1840s, no Yoruba kingdom was powerful enough to provide political stability.

State building and expansion were important causes of the wars. The struggles to fill the political vacuum created by the fall of Oyo empire were intense. The massive migration of people from the north to the south of Yorubaland led to the creation of new cities—Ijaye, Abeokuta, and Ibadan. These regarded themselves as rivals. The new and older cities competed for political supremacy in the region. All of them acquired territories and imposed control over outlying areas. The quest for colonies meant either that people would voluntarily surrender or that they would be conquered. An example of a state-building war was that between Ibadan and Ijaye in the 1860s.

There were resistance wars, as in the case of the Kiriji wars in the late 1870s. The Ekiti and Ijesa in eastern Yorubaland formed a formidable alliance with their neighbors to end the imperial rule of Ibadan. Colonies of large kingdoms such as Ibadan usually complained of excessive economic and political domination and would struggle to regain their independence.

Protection of economic interests was vital, even if such interests were not primary causes of the wars. Slaves were needed to work on large farms, to carry palm oil and palm kernels to coastal markets, and to sell them in exchange for firearms. The best way to produce slaves was by capturing them as war booty. Equally important was access to the trade routes that passed through the hinterland to Lagos where trade with Europeans was conducted. The people of Lagos, the Egba, and the Ijebu, by their location close to the coast or as gateways to the interior Yoruba, were privileged in the trade. They profited as middlemen, selling imported items to interior traders in exchange for local products. For the interior states, their success in wars was dependent on access to the coastal markets to obtain guns and gunpowder, in addition to other products. The power of the Egba and Ijebu rested on their ability to control access to the coastal markets and even to close the trade routes in order to maximize their political advantages. Thus, the control of trade routes generated its own intense politics and conflicts. When trade routes were closed, European traders in Lagos, who feared a loss of profit, would become involved in pressure to reopen them.

Finally, it was not difficult for professional warriors to provoke wars for both state and personal interests. To win a war was to come home with hundreds of captives, livestock, cloths, and other booty.

THE CHARACTERISTICS OF WARS

The war practices of the nineteenth century were fairly established and well known. Professional warriors emerged. The continuing wars created a group of people dedicated to warfare. Warriors regarded themselves as men of high social status. They lived in big compounds, and they had large households with many wives, children, and other dependents. To maintain their expensive lifestyles, they engaged in large-scale production, growing food crops as well as export items, notably palm oil and palm kernels.

The warriors practiced the skills of mobilizing the people for war, procuring arms, providing a commissariat, and developing tactics and strategies. Every major warrior had his own private army, comprising trained members of his household, dependents, and followers. The soldiers in an area might also fall under the command of the leading warrior in that area. The city had a chain of military command, with the highest titled officers at the top. Each soldier had his own weapons. Where firearms were used, the soldiers provided their own, but the commanders supplied the powder.

Weapons of war were both local (machetes, swords, clubs, slings, javelins, bows and arrows) and imported. In Ilorin, the use of horses was facilitated by imports from the north. Both firearms and horses required trade and access to resources to procure them. Where horses and firearms were used, their control was vested in the leading generals and civil officers of state.

The uniforms of Yoruba soldiers carried all sorts of charms and amulets. A soldier prepared himself with magic to survive a war. The belief was that with the right charms one could become invisible, escape danger, and anticipate problems. There were war rituals as well, some carried out by the entire army and some performed by individual warriors. The god of war, Ogun, was worshipped by many soldiers. Charm makers and herbalists could accompany the army to battle, to supply charms and spiritual guidance.

Normal activities continued in areas without wars. Not all the Yoruba regions were drawn into the wars at the same time. A war could be fought between the armies of two cities, engaging others as allies only for diplomatic purposes or to ensure the continuity of trade. In general, economic activities continued during wars, although with major inconvenience. Long-distance and local trade were conducted, and kingdoms protected markets, trade routes, and women traders. Farming, the major occupation, continued as well.

Wars involved the formation of alliances. A prolonged conflict such as the Kiriji war was fought between coalitions of Yoruba groups. Such coalitions required diplomacy to put them together. Alliances could also be between two groups, as in the case of the Egba and Ijaye against Ibadan in the 1860s. Diplomacy was an important aspect of warfare. Wars were ended with the negotiation of terms, and relations were maintained in peacetime to facilitate trade, build alliances, and maintain cordial intergroup relations. Every major city had its diplomats and seasoned officers to relay messages.

Success in wars was judged by the reasons that led to them. Ibadan regarded its wars as successful because it was able to create an empire. For Ilorin, the Oyo empire was destroyed and the Fulani established a political dynasty that has lasted to this day. For the Ekitiparapo, the peace treaty of 1893 brought to an end their status as colonies of Ibadan. Contrary to the European records of the period, the wars were not irrational but motivated by serious political and economic reasons that could not be resolved by diplomacy.

THE CONSEQUENCES OF WARS

A class of professional warriors emerged, self-made men who rose to prominence because of the insecurity of the age. Rich, powerful, and influential, they became the men with the highest social status among their people. Their prestige was so great that many wanted to identify with the households of such men. Established warriors trained their own soldiers as well as others in the art of war. Everywhere, warriors were needed to fight wars, to defend cities against possible invasion, and to struggle for independence if colonized by an imperial power. The warriors were involved in major domestic and external policies, and they participated in the negotiation of peace.

The warriors gained political influence and acquired far more power than the prewar governments had expected. For instance, at Ijaye, Kurunmi, a leading warrior, established a military dictatorship. His word was law, and his authority could not be challenged. He was the most wealthy individual in the city–state, collecting and keeping most of the tributes from the colonies, dues from the traders, and gifts from the people. The traditional Yoruba political system had never concentrated so much power and wealth in one person. Kurunmi also added religious power to the political, by making himself the chief priest of the leading cults. At Ibadan, where warriors were equally influential, they established a republican system: A handful of warriors governed the city–state in alliance with the heads of various lineages. In other new settlements, political changes occurred in such a way as to give honor to the leading warriors, who were believed to be risking their lives to save others.

The economy benefited in some ways. For traders in guns and gunpowder, the wars ensured a steady demand and accumulation of profits. The leading merchants were able to exploit this demand to enrich themselves. The need to generate resources to procure firearms contributed to the expansion of agricultural production and domestic trade. The successful warriors were able to maintain extensive plantations, with hundreds of slaves working for them.

The wars created mistrust and hostility among various Yoruba groups. The divisions survived the nineteenth century, making it difficult to build strong, widespread political movements. The wars disrupted families, damaged cities, and destroyed farmlands and houses. They produced thousands of captives who served as domestic slaves in various places, notably in the military state of Ibadan.

The wars created an upsurge of refugees, especially in the first half of the nineteenth century. Whole villages and towns were forced to relocate to different areas. Without relief agencies, the refugees became dependent on their hosts for shelter and land on which to farm and build. They had to adapt to new environments.

The refugees contributed to the spread of ideas and culture. Just as they absorbed the practices of their hosts, they contributed their own. For instance, the spread of Oyo culture, in the form of masquerades, drums, and long looms for cloth weaving, to many parts of southwestern Nigeria was associated with the spread of refugees. Similarly, Islam spread as refugees from areas that had previously accepted Islam moved to new areas. The refugees also contributed to the evolution of new ideas on politics that privileged the military and gave consideration to security and defense.

The wars contributed to the creation of new cities such as Ibadan, Ogbomoso, Aiyede, and Abeokuta. More and more people were drawn into these cities because of the security they offered. Many of the cities were able to protect their citizens by creating powerful military forces that prevented invasions. Ibadan was heterogenous, attracting people from various other Yoruba towns and groups.

The security that some cities offered came at a price in terms of personal freedom. The wars were unfair to the war captives who were enslaved. Many people were driven away from their homelands and forced to relocate. Where the military generals were powerful, as in Ibadan, they became patrons to people who had to serve as clients, supplying tributes and gifts to pay for their protection.

SUGGESTIONS FOR FURTHER READING

Akintoye, S.A. *Revolution and Power Politics in Yorubaland, 1840–1893*. London: Longman, 1971.

Falola, Toyin. *The Political Economy of a Pre-colonial African State: Ibadan, ca. 1830–1900*. Ile-Ife, Nigeria: University of Ife Press, 1984.

Falola, Toyin, and Dare Oguntomisin. *The Military in Nineteenth Century Yoruba Politics*. Ile-Ife, Nigeria: University of Ife Press, 1984.

Falola, Toyin, and G.O. Oguntomisin. *Yoruba Warlords of the Nineteenth Century*. Trenton, N.J.: Africa World Press, 2001.

Smith, Robert. *Kingdoms of the Yoruba*. 3rd ed. London: James Currey, 1988.

15

The Spread of Christianity, 1804 Onward

A HISTORY OF CHRISTIANITY

Christianity is an old religion in Africa, even if it is sometimes presented as new and foreign. In the first century A.D., Christianity was introduced to Egypt, from where it spread to Nubia and Ethiopia (see Chapter 5). The rise of Islam in the seventh century and the Muslim achievement of control of areas from the west of Egypt to the Atlantic Ocean led to the spread and domination of Islam in North Africa. During the fifteenth and sixteenth centuries, the Portuguese attempted to spread Christianity and establish mission stations in São Tomé, the Azores, the Cape Verde islands, Benin, the Congo, and areas along the East African coast (Mombasa, Malindi, and Sofala). Most of the Portuguese efforts produced limited results: Many converts reverted to indigenous religions as soon as the Portuguese left, and Islam dominated on the East African coast. Success in spreading Christianity had to wait until the nineteenth century.

Although the slave trade was abolished during the nineteenth century, Europeans continued to come to Africa for three main reasons. First, there was an extensive and lucrative trade in raw materials such as peanuts, cocoa, palm oil, and palm kernels. Many European companies established themselves in various areas along the African coastline in order to take advantage of the trade. The Africans in these areas served as middlemen in the trade between the Europeans and the peoples of the hinterland. Second, there was an interest in learning more about African geography, including its rivers and minerals, and in exploring trade opportunities. A number of European expeditions visited Africa. These included

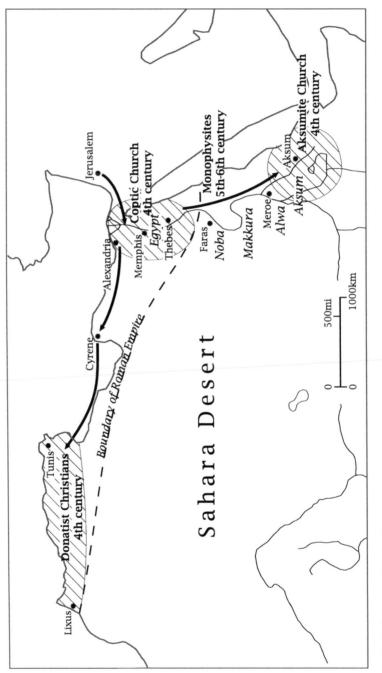

Early Christianity in North Africa.

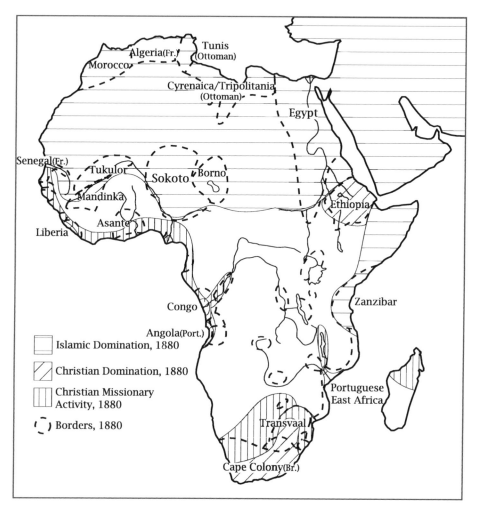

Christianity and Islam in Africa, nineteenth century.

the expeditions of James Bruce, who sought the sources of the Nile River; Mungo Park, who wanted to follow the River Niger to its mouth; and David Livingstone, who traveled in central Africa.

The third reason was the vigorous ambition to spread Christianity. The idea of a "civilizing mission" gained widespread currency; this was the view that the conversion of Africans to Christianity was necessary to combat the evils of slavery and turn Africans into "civilized beings." To become "civilized," not only must Africans become Christians, but they should also go to school, develop their agriculture, and consume imported items. In the late eighteenth century, Christianity was revived in Europe and America, with many religious leaders and social reformers advocating evangelization among their own people and abroad. Reformers called for the abolition of the slave trade, the resettlement of emancipated slaves in Africa, and the exploration of Africa in order to collect data on agriculture and commerce to create an economy that would replace that of the slave trade. Many missionary societies emerged and were determined to sponsor agents to go to Africa to evangelize and collect valuable information. The pioneer missions were Protestant, from Germany, Britain, and the United States. The Roman Catholics, mainly from France and Italy, joined from the 1830s onward.

Christian missionaries from Europe and the United States went to different parts of Africa during the nineteenth century. The missionaries wanted to convert Africans to Christianity, thereby expanding the frontier of their religion into a huge continent. Many among them believed that conversion would halt the spread of Islam and help to end the slave trade.

MISSIONARY WORK IN SIERRA LEONE

Sierra Leone and Liberia were two West African countries connected with the rise of Christianity. In both, important settlements were created for liberated slaves following the abolition of the slave trade in the early nineteenth century. The first set of settlers arrived from Britain in May 1787, settling around an estuary in a place that was given the name "Province of Freedom" and was later known as Freetown. Other settlers came from Nova Scotia, Canada, in 1792; the Maroons came from the Caribbean in 1800; and many others were slaves redeemed in West Africa. Similarly, Liberia (which means "freedom") became a settlement for freed slaves in 1822.

It was among the settlers in Sierra Leone and Liberia that Christian missionaries chose to start their mission. This was a successful strategy—the liberated slaves were receptive to the new religion, and they wanted to create a new social and economic identity for themselves. Among the notable religious bodies that sent missionaries to Sierra Leone were the Church Missionary Society (CMS) and the Society for the Propagation of the Gospel, both Anglican, plus the Baptists, the German Basel Mission, the Glasgow Missionary Society, the London Missionary Society, the Roman Catholics, the Wesleyan Methodist Missionary

Society, and the Presbyterian Church of Scotland. While the missionaries came from abroad, the African converts (known as African agents) became active in spreading Christianity among their people.

The CMS was one of the most successful missions. From 1804 onward, it began to send missionaries to Sierra Leone, where they preached, established schools, and began to translate the Holy Bible into a number of African languages. Many of the European pioneers found it hard to survive, with some losing their lives to diseases, notably malaria fever. However, many Africans were converted, and a Christian elite that imitated European culture in dress, language, and customs eventually emerged. It was from the African elite that the missions recruited their agents who spread the gospel and revitalized missionary fervor. The Rev. Ajayi Crowther became the first African to be ordained into the Anglican ministry in 1843. An ex-slave, Crowther later rose to become the first African bishop, working in the Niger area of modern eastern Nigeria.

In addition to evangelization, the missionaries were successful in establishing elementary and grammar schools for children and even adults. Teachers' colleges were also established to produce Africans who would go to various areas to train others. By the 1850s, the CMS had produced the initial core of the African elite, which included doctors and lawyers. The elite went to other parts of West Africa, where they served as missionaries, traders, administrators, and teachers.

The spread of Christianity in Sierra Leone was successful in part because the number of missions and staff involved was high. In Freetown, the missionaries could use English to communicate with many people who already understood the language. Many liberated slaves were no longer fully committed to traditional religions and were thus receptive to a new religion.

MISSIONARIES IN OTHER AREAS

Gradually, the missionaries penetrated many parts of Africa from the mid-nineteenth century onward. The CMS was successful in Liberia and other parts of West Africa. With a large number of Africans working for the church and with many missions committed to coming to Africa, more and more areas were reached by aggressive evangelists. A few examples should suffice. The Wesleyan Methodist Society sent Thomas Birch Freeman to the Gold Coast (now Ghana) in 1838. Through him, many were converted, and churches and schools were established. The Methodist, Basel, Roman Catholic, CMS, and Bremen missions were all successful in the Gold Coast.

From the 1830s onward, many Yoruba ex-slaves residing in Sierra Leone (known as Creole or Saro) began to emigrate to Nigeria. In the process, they contributed to the spread of Christianity. They invited missionaries to follow them. In 1841, the CMS and the Basel Mission established the Niger Mission to determine the means to spread the gospel and promote trade. Missionaries began to settle among the Yoruba from the 1840s, in such cities as Lagos, Badagri, Abeokuta, Ijaye, and Ibadan. The Roman Catholics built a church in Lagos in

A cathedral in Lagos, Nigeria.

1868, and it was from here that the Catholic mission expanded into the Yoruba hinterland. In what is now eastern Nigeria, Christianity was extended to the Igbo from 1856 onward. In all the places where the missionaries operated in Nigeria, they were associated with the establishment of schools.

In North, East, and West Africa, the French Holy Ghost and White Fathers had an impact. In South Africa, the London Missionary Society, an interdenominational agency, enjoyed a tremendous success. A large number of missionaries went to the Cape in South Africa, from where Christianity was extended to the east and north and later to Madagascar and central Africa.

THE IMPACT OF CHRISTIANITY

A new religion was introduced to the continent, with consequences for Africans' understanding of themselves and their society. A number of communities began to experience a religious divide, between the new Christian converts and the traditionalists who retained their old religious practices and way of life.

Christianity was accompanied by Western education, as the missions established schools to teach their converts the skills of reading, writing, and arithmetic. Indeed, many Africans were drawn to Christianity because it gave them access to Western education, which enabled them to work as teachers, clerks, and technicians. A number of vocational training schools were established by the missions to teach courses in printing, tailoring, and carpentry. The aim was to teach new trades, with the understanding that the economy would become more diversified.

Indigenous languages were promoted in areas where the Bible was translated, and attempts were made to study and preserve many languages such as Mandingo, Sere, Efik, Hausa, Igbo, and Yoruba. As the African languages acquired a written form, they were used by Africans to promote the knowledge of their history and culture.

The use of European languages became a status symbol and also facilitated communication among the members of the elite and people of diverse ethnic backgrounds. Given the small size of the elite in the nineteenth century, those with Western education could travel far and wide for jobs, as in the case of the Creole of Sierra Leone who went to work in Nigeria, the Gambia, and Ghana.

The provision of Western education was not without limits. As far as the missionaries were concerned the goal was to produce an African who would become a Christian, preach the gospel to others, read the Bible, and speak in a European language. As important as the teaching profession was to the missions, many missionary groups were unwilling to provide long periods of training. By and large, would-be teachers were expected to learn simply elementary science, grammar, and mathematics. The CMS and the Wesleyans created a few

African church ministers.

opportunities for higher training, for example, at Islington, England, and Fourah Bay College in Sierra Leone.

Similarly, the missionaries contributed to the introduction of Western medicine. They built dispensaries and hospitals, not just to cure diseases but also to impress upon the people the benefits of conversion to Christianity. Lessons were also offered on cleanliness and hygiene. The prevention and cure of some diseases improved, while the child mortality rate was reduced in some areas. Where traditional medicine was slow or ineffective, Africans now had an alternative in Western medicine. When Western medicine worked, it undermined both indigenous medicine and indigenous religion. However, the shortcomings of Western medicine meant that traditional healing practices were able to continue and survive till the present time.

Christianity and Western education brought many social changes. To the new elite, it was a mark of prestige to dress like Europeans, to speak in European languages, and to assume that they were the only civilized Africans. The elite became the symbol of a new age. The educated Africans of the period were proud of their achievements. For instance, the elite members from Sierra Leone were highly regarded in West Africa—they were associated with high culture and the best jobs, and they boasted that they understood the world outside of Africa.

New values and morality spread in such a way that those who retained indigenous values (traditionalists) began to express the fear that Western culture would displace African culture. The traditionalists believed that the elite and the Christian converts were too interested in wealth and material objects, disrespectful of elders, and arrogant. To many elite members and Christian converts, identification with change was more important than retention of the old culture. They believed that there was no need to promote the use of indigenous languages and religion. Christianity even offered an opportunity for some members of society to revolt against established practices. The Christian missionaries were active in condemning many aspects of African culture as inferior and barbaric. Images and shrines of gods were destroyed, and many songs and dances were criticized as primitive. The African Christians who accepted the criticisms of their people's practices became agents of a new culture and lost respect for what was African.

One area in which cultural change was particularly encouraged was polygyny (the marrying of two or more wives). Whereas African societies promoted a culture of polygyny, Christianity supported monogamy. The missionaries wanted their African converts to create a new nuclear family life that resembled that of the Europeans. Whereas some of their converts accepted this idea, many did not, while Africans in general saw nothing wrong in polygyny. As far as the Africans were concerned, large families enhanced a man's social standing and enabled him to have many children who could assist with farmwork. Where the missionaries insisted on monogamy, converting Africans was difficult. Indeed, among those who became converted, not a few refused to give up the practice.

The missionaries also had an impact on the economy. They arrived in large numbers at a time when the "legitimate" trade in raw materials was replacing the slave trade. Africa supplied Europe with products such as cocoa, rubber, cotton, palm oil, palm kernels, and timber. The missionaries were active in promoting the cultivation of all these products and the expansion of craft industries, all with the aim of ending the trans-Atlantic slave trade and creating an African middle class. Crowther, one of the most distinguished African Christian leaders of the nineteenth century, showed the connection between Christianity and the economy in a remark he made in 1847: "When trade and agriculture engage the attention of the people, and with the gentle and peaceful teaching of Christianity, the minds of people will gradually be won from war and marauding expeditions to peaceful trade and commerce."[1] What the missionaries failed to see is that Africans were sending their products to Europe in an economic arrangement that ultimately undermined them and led to dependence.

Finally, the missionaries were connected with political developments during the nineteenth century. Some Christian missions contributed to the imposition of imperial rule. Many among them encouraged their governments to impose colonial rule so that they could freely convert Africans. In the ideology of the "civilizing mission," the imposition of colonial rule was actually seen as a charitable or philanthropic venture to liberate Africans from their age-old primitive ideas.

The African Christian elite occupied a prominent role in society, serving as lawyers, engineers, administrators, and doctors and in other prestigious positions. These occupations enhanced the political visibility of the new elite, turning them into thinkers and modernizers for Africa. They began to talk about the future of Africa, drawing ideas from Christianity and constructing an image of a Christianized continent. Until the formal imposition of colonial rule when they were marginalized by the European officers, the African elite regarded themselves as the most enlightened and progressive group. A good number among them wanted Africans to become Christians, and the government to run along modern lines, with ideas from Europe and with the elite as the main managers. The Christian elite regarded the kings and chiefs as illiterates. While they did not call for the abolition of the kingship system, they wanted kings and chiefs to be literate or to surrender their power to legislative councils comprising literate members. In the early colonial period, many of them called on Europeans to give power to Africans.

Later in the twentieth century, the African elite were to constitute the leaders of the anticolonial nationalists who pressured the various European governments to embark upon reforms. They had become disappointed by the colonial officers who did not want to share power with them, as well as by the foreign missions that excluded them from high-ranking positions in the church.

NOTE

1. J.F. Ade Ajayi, *A Patriot to the Core: Bishop Ajayi Crowther* (Ibadan: Spectrum, 2002), p. 76.

16

The Rise of Muhammad Ali
of Egypt, 1811–47

From 1811 to 1847, Muhammad Ali, originally from the port city of Kavala in the Ottoman province of Albania, served as the preeminent leader of Egypt. He acquired enormous power, initiated far-reaching changes, and implemented a number of policies to transform Egypt. So successful was he that his rise to power became one of the most significant events in the history of North Africa during the nineteenth century.

PRELUDE TO THE RISE OF MUHAMMAD ALI

Egypt had long been part of the Mediterranean world, with established dealings with European powers. Egypt participated in the Crusades of the twelfth and thirteenth centuries, contributing to the defeat of the European Christian invaders. In 1798, the Egyptian army was defeated by the French, led by Napoleon Bonaparte, the most successful French general of his era. The aim was to colonize Egypt, prevent the British from establishing any influence in the area, and control the Suez route to India and the Far East. The French defeated the Mamluk army, which was then in control of Egypt. Napoleon promised to promote Islam and cooperate with Egyptian Islamic leaders. He reorganized the administration, and French scholars embarked upon the study of various aspects of Egyptian civilization.

The French occupation of Egypt provoked the anger of Britain, which put pressure on the Ottoman sultan to declare war, which he did on 11 September 1798. Egypt was a colony of the Turkish (or Ottoman) Empire, under the control of the Ottoman sultan. The Ottoman army, joined by the Mamluk beys, marched

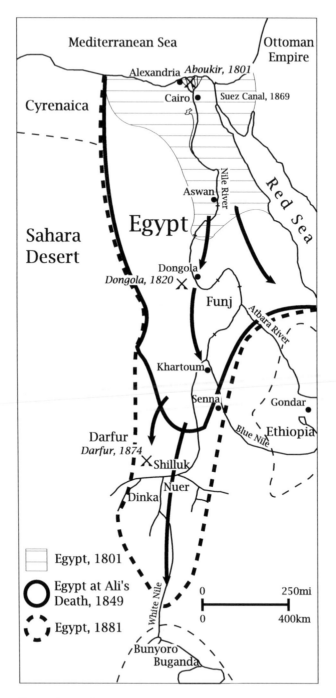

Egypt, nineteenth century.

on Cairo in March 1801, forcing the French to relinquish their control of Egypt in September of that year. The French occupation of Egypt turned out to be a failure. In the view of the British, to allow the French to control Egypt would threaten their route to India. They, too, embarked upon an imperial policy that led to British control of Egypt from 1882 to 1956. The European rivalry for the control of Egypt exposed Egyptians to foreign technologies and helped to initiate a discussion on how to modernize their country.

MUHAMMAD ALI

Ali was born in 1769 to a father who was a commander in the army of the governor of Kavala. A Muslim, he received a limited education but was introduced to the arts of war and horse riding. His fortune changed when the French invaded Egypt. Ali became part of the Albanian contingent that the Ottoman sultan assembled to remove the French from Egypt. When the commander of the contingent returned home, Ali, the second in command, was elevated to the headship of the Kavala forces. In Egypt, his diplomacy and courage earned him yet another promotion, to the position of second in command of the entire Albanian force, the real strength of the Ottoman army.

After the departure of the French and the British troops from Egypt by 1803, there was a power struggle between the Turks and the Mamluks. Muhammad Ali was able to play one group against the other, effectively destroying the leading contenders for power. He endeared himself to the Egyptians, secured the support of the *ulema* (Islamic leaders), obtained the loyalty of the merchants, and promised the people that he was fighting on their behalf. In 1805, his popularity led to his appointment, by the Ottoman sultan, as the wali (viceroy or governor) of Egypt.

After 1805, Ali began the task of consolidating his power. In 1807, his forces defeated the British army that attempted to occupy the port city of Alexandria. This military success added to his reputation. The deposition of the Ottoman sultan in the same year and the political crisis that surrounded this event left Ali free of worry that his overlord would check his growing powers. In 1811, he gained additional power over Egypt when he assassinated most of his leading Mamluk rivals at a banquet that he tricked them into attending. After this date, Ali's ambition was to gain complete control of Egypt by ending its status as a province of the Ottoman Empire, establish a dynasty that would enable him to transfer power to his children, and modernize Egypt. By making Egypt and himself strong, he would be able to gain Egypt's independence. Thus, the programs and activities of Ali revolved around the modernization of Egypt and his relations with the Ottoman Empire.

THE MODERNIZATION OF EGYPT

Ali concentrated on the military, agriculture, education, and industries. He consolidated his power. He introduced a council of ministers and a privy council, a government structure that looked very European. Ministers were appointed to head government departments. Egypt and later the Sudan were divided into provinces, each headed by a governor accountable to Muhammad Ali. Government officials, with regular salaries, worked in the ministries and provinces. The system was not necessarily based on merit. The highest positions were awarded to allies, friends, and family members of Ali, with his son, Ibrahim, acting as an assistant to his father.

With firm control of the economy, the social structure reflected the political structure. At the apex of the society were Ali, the members of his family, and his friends. They were the most influential, with control of fertile land. Next in status were the Turkish-speaking officers. These were followed by the Arabic-speaking officers, mainly junior, and the village heads. At the very bottom of the social ladder were the peasants.

Ali initiated fiscal reforms to obtain resources to finance a host of programs. Like his predecessors, he taxed the peasants. Before him, the Mamluk tax collectors extracted as much tax as they could from the peasants but gave only a fixed amount to the government, retaining large sums of money for themselves. Muhammad Ali decided to end this arrangement by confiscating all the land controlled by the tax collectors in addition to all the farmland controlled by religious leaders. With the state now in control of all land, Ali was able to expand the treasury. Part of the land was given to the peasants, who thus became tenants of the state. A tax was imposed on each village community. It was collected in kind by the village head, who then paid the government. A state monopoly was imposed on sales of agricultural produce. The village head would collect the produce and sell it to the central government. From the proceeds, the peasants paid their rents and taxes. The government would then sell the produce at great profits. In spite of the abuses inherent in the system, the peasants and the government were both able to make more money than before.

A state monopoly was established on the export of all agricultural products, a clever way of accumulating revenues. The government officials bought cheaply from the peasants and sold abroad at higher prices. When Egypt conquered the Sudan, it imposed a similar form of rule, which brought in additional revenue. In 1817, Muhammad Ali also imposed a monopoly on the production of textiles— all factories now belonged to the government—another source of revenues. Imperial conquests brought more wealth. Lebanon supplied timber, Yemen brought coffee, which Egypt exported, and the Sudan provided camels, cattle, and gum arabic. In short, the basis of the fiscal reforms was economic centralization, as Ali became the sole trader with foreign countries and the sole landlord, an arrangement that increased state revenues by almost 300 percent.

Agriculture was also reformed. In 1821, long staple cotton was introduced to Egypt from the Sudan, subsequently becoming a successful crop. By the end of the nineteenth century, 80 percent of exports were provided by cotton. Ali's government found solutions to the irregular flooding of the Nile—excessive flooding in some seasons destroyed houses and crops, while low flood levels in other periods made irrigation difficult. With assistance from European engineers, Egypt constructed canals that supplied sufficient water to the farms when they needed it and reduced the flow of water at times of high flood. The canals regulated the flow of the Nile, making it possible to bring more land under cultivation and work the farms all the year round. Harvests could now be reaped two or more times within a year.

Egypt embarked upon an industrialization policy of import substitution—manufacturing at home items that had previously been imported in order to reduce dependence on Europe. Among the major new industries were those involving sugar, indigo, rice, and textiles. An iron and steel foundry was established, as well as a shipbuilding plant at Alexandria.

This industrialization program ran into problems, ultimately leading to its collapse. The manufactured goods could not be sold abroad, as anticipated, mainly because they were expensive and inferior. Their circulation within Egypt itself was a problem because they were very expensive. The raw materials and machinery were imported, adding to the cost of production. The government had to prevent industrial goods from being imported. Without cheap sources of fuel, the industries relied on costly animal power. The imported machines were serviced by highly paid European technicians. Spare parts were imported as well, and only a few Egyptians knew how to operate the machines.

The state realized the need to reform the educational system, in order to modernize the country and solve the problems of industrialization. Egypt decided to follow the French educational model. A French educator was appointed as the education minister. Elementary, secondary, technical, and medical schools were established. Many Egyptians received training in law, engineering, medicine, and the sciences, and about 200 students were sent to Europe for advanced training. A printing press was established in 1822. Although it was not the government's intention, the educational program accelerated the development of Egyptian nationalism.

MILITARY REFORMS AND WARS

Muhammad Ali needed a strong, loyal army to maintain his power, establish a ruling dynasty, become independent of Turkey, and dominate his neighbors. To attain these objectives, in 1827, he established cavalry and artillery schools to train his soldiers along European lines. European officers were recruited to teach in these schools.

The original plan was to recruit many Africans from the Sudan to form the core of the army, based on a belief that the men would be totally loyal to Ali. The Sudan was invaded, and about 20,000 of its men were captured, but only about 3,000 survived the journey to Egypt; the others were lost to hunger, disease, and fatigue. Ali then turned on the Egyptian peasants, who were conscripted into the army. This was an unpopular policy, with a number of people running away from their villages, some maiming themselves, and rich individuals spending money to buy their freedom.

Through coercion and other means, Ali had, by 1826, built a large army of about 90,000 men, drawn from such groups as Africans, Turks, Albanians, Armenians, and Europeans. French officers were employed to train them, while modern weapons were procured.

Egypt began to put its army to effective use from 1811 onward. The initial military campaigns were directed at the Wahabis of central Arabia. The Wahabis were strong and devoted Muslims who sought the revival of Islam. In the last quarter of the eighteenth century, the Wahabis captured the holy city of Mecca, patrolled the Red Sea and the Indian Ocean, and challenged both British sea power and the Ottoman Empire. Both Britain and Turkey sought the assistance of Egypt in curbing the Wahabis. Ali decided to accept the invitation of the Ottoman sultan to attack the Wahabis. This was a smart move on his part: He appeared to be a loyal officer of the sultan, while hiding his plan for independence. The war enabled Ali to get rid of the Albanian mercenaries in Egypt whose excesses he was finding difficult to check. Without preparing them for the attack, Ali sent the mercenaries against the Wahabis, who killed about two-thirds of them. Thereafter, Ali sent out his own army, which, after a long war that ended in 1818, became victorious.

In the 1820s, Ali turned south to the Sudan where the once powerful Funj sultanate was about to reach its final collapse. The military expeditions against the Sudan were not embarked on solely for imperial expansion but also for the economic exploitation of the material and human resources of the region. The Sudan was reputed to have enormous wealth in gold and ivory, and Ali hoped to discover the sources. In addition, Egypt intended to raid the Sudan for slaves who could be forced to serve in the army and do a host of other menial jobs. Ali also had a personal motive: Many of his Mamluk enemies had escaped to the Sudan, where they possibly hoped to reorganize and regain control of Egypt. The Mamluk remnants in the Sudan had actually blocked access to the Nile waterways for goods and people traveling to Egypt. Ali needed a war to destroy the Mamluks. After a series of hard-fought wars, Egypt took control of the northern parts of the Sudan.

The Sudan expeditions were not as successful as Ali had hoped, mainly because the gains to be made had been exaggerated. The people who might be taken as slaves were located further south, in a swampy region and hard to reach. The gold mines were already exhausted. Sennar, the city Ali's forces had hoped to profit from, was not as big or rich as they had expected. The Egyptian officers and soldiers found heavy rain uncomfortable to deal with. Frustrated and disappointed, Egypt imposed heavy taxation on the Sudanese people and collected it with high-handedness. For sixty years, the Sudanese continued to revolt against Egyptian rule, until they finally became independent.

EGYPT AND THE EUROPEAN POWERS

Meanwhile, Egypt had its own problems, mainly caused by the ambitions of the European powers, which were interested in imperialism and trade. The first problem was posed by Greece seeking its independence from the Turkish Empire. In 1821, the Ottoman sultan called on Egypt for help against Greece in order to retain it as part of the Ottoman Empire. Should Egypt succeed in defeating Greece, Ali was promised control of the two Greek provinces of Crete and the Morea. The offer actually encouraged Ali to create his own autonomous empire. The Egyptian forces defeated Crete in 1823 and the Morea in 1825. The victories alarmed the European powers, who forced Ali to withdraw from Greece, thereby losing considerable resources in men and money without gaining anything.

The clash with Turkey that Ali had expected for so long finally came in 1831. Before then, the Turkish Empire had regarded Egypt and Ali as useful subordinates who could fight its wars. As the Turkish Empire weakened, Ali calculated that it was time for him to become independent. Ali accused Abdullah Pasha, a rival of his and the governor of the Turkish province of Acre in Syria, of offering protection to the Egyptian peasants running away from Egypt to avoid conscription into the army. Ali wanted to control Syria, whose location between Egypt and Turkey would enable it to serve as a buffer zone. The conquest of Syria would also bring control of Jerusalem, Islam's third holy city, as well as Damascus, a leading center of Islamic education and culture. Ali already controlled Mecca and Medina, and adding Jerusalem and Damascus would give him considerable prestige in the Islamic world. Syria also had timber, which Ali could use to build warships.

In the major war that developed, Ali was victorious. In 1839, Syria became a province of Egypt. The Turkish Empire was now in deep crisis, and its navy had to be put under the command of Ali. It was now possible for Ali to acquire the headship of the Turkish Empire, but the European powers intervened to check him once again.

To the Europeans, Ali's leadership of the Turkish Empire posed some problems. The British wanted the survival of the Turkish Empire to safeguard British routes to India and the Far East. Should Ali control Syria for long, he would exercise power over all the major routes, a possibility that frightened the British. Ali's friendship with the French was yet another source of worry to the British, since they regarded both the French and Ali with suspicion. The Russians preferred a weak Ottoman state under the existing sultan, as this would enable them to keep interfering in Ottoman affairs. The European traders interested in Egypt believed that Ali's economic policies imposed too many restrictions on them and prevented them from realizing huge profits.

In 1841, four European powers—Britain, Russia, Prussia, and Austria—all members of the Quadruple Alliance, forced Ali to sign a treaty with the sultan. The size of Ali's army was reduced to a mere 18,000 men, and only the sultan could approve the appointment of military commanders. Ali was to return Syria to the sultan. He was also to agree to all the treaties entered into between the European powers and Turkey, which allowed the powers unrestricted trade in the Turkish Empire. These agreements would not only undermine Ali's military power, but they would destroy his industrialization and trade policies. As if to grant him a small concession, Egypt was recognized as a self-governing province of the Turkish Empire to be administered by Ali and his successors. The heir to the throne would be the most senior member of Ali's family.

In 1841 when the treaty was imposed, Ali was already an old man. In 1847, he transferred power to his son, Ibrahim, and he died on 2 August 1849 at the age of eighty. His successors continued to build on his legacies of economic and political modernization, and they were also forced to deal with the complicated politics of aggressive European attempts at imperial control of Egypt.

SUGGESTIONS FOR FURTHER READING

Falola, Toyin, ed. *Africa*. Vol. 1, *African History before 1885*. Durham, N.C.: Carolina Academic Press, 2000. Chapter 11.

Holt, P.M. *Egypt and the Fertile Crescent, 1516–1922*. Ithaca, N.Y.: Cornell University Press, 1966.

Holt, P.M. *Political and Social Change in Modern Egypt*. Oxford: Oxford University Press, 1968.

Tignor, R.L. *Modernization and British Control in Egypt, 1882–1914*. Princeton, N.J.: Princeton University Press, 1967.

17

The *Mfecane*: Shaka and the Zulu Kingdom, 1816–40

EXPLAINING THE *MFECANE*

Between 1816 and 1840, a series of wars, known as the *Mfecane* ("the crushing"), with the Nguni of southeastern Africa as the most active participants, changed the political landscape of the interior of southern Africa. By the 1820s, the Zulu kingdom and Shaka, its leader, had emerged as the most dominant power. Further wars occurred in the 1820s and 1830s, spreading to other areas in southern and central Africa, leaving massive destruction in their wake.

The European colonialists of the nineteenth century successfully manipulated the wars in propaganda myths designed to justify the colonial conquest and the apartheid system imposed on Africans during the twentieth century. In the eyes of the colonialists, the wars were irrational and useless and created extensive vacant land for white settlers to claim as truly theirs. Contrary to the characterization of the wars as irrational, they were motivated by strong economic and political considerations, and their leaders knew what they wanted to achieve. The wars produced new kingdoms, new political leaders, and new military systems.

The main theater of war was the three northern Nguni kingdoms of Mthethwa, Ndwandwe, and Ngwane in the southern lowveld of southern Africa. The resources with which to graze cattle and to farm began to diminish in the last years of the eighteenth century. A famine also occurred in the last years of the eighteenth century to compound the crisis. Lasting for about ten years, the famine caused untold hardship to people and cattle. The competition for grazing land and patches of fertile land was so intense as to generate insecurity. Villages

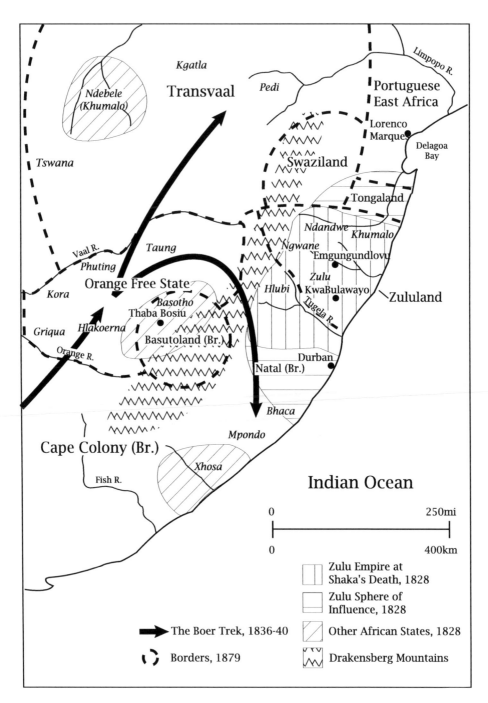

Southeast Africa, nineteenth century.

raided one another for cattle and grain, and regiments had to serve for long periods to keep watch for invaders and hunt game for food. As it became difficult for a village to protect its land and its limited resources, it realized the need to cooperate with other villages and establish larger political units with powerful chiefs.

The Nguni had an established system of initiation ceremonies. People born in the same period were initiated into age-regiments, in order to promote unity among them and to provide people to serve the chiefs. As the competition for resources became intense, the Nguni had to turn their established age-regiments into military forces to watch fields, expand grazing areas, check rivals, and defend cattle. The regiments were also used for hunting wild animals, especially those hosting the tsetse fly that caused the devastating sleeping sickness in cattle. Where elephants were available, the trade in ivory with the European traders stationed at Delagoa Bay further encouraged the use of regiments for hunting. For chiefs and groups to profit from the long-distance trade in ivory, they had to build larger states, which of course meant building larger regiments and fighting with their neighbors.

As the famine devastated many areas, the regiments became full-time armies stationed in the fields to fight neighbors who came in search of grazing land. Stronger kingdoms absorbed smaller ones, and powerful kings emerged to organize regiments for defense. After 1816, the number of wars and raiding expeditions increased, with changes in the political map. The Mthethwa, Ndwandwe, and Ngwane engaged in a number of wars for survival and control of resources—each tried to destroy small chiefdoms in order to recruit their youth into fighting regiments and confiscate their cattle. The Ngwane were expelled from the northern Pongola valley. The contest was now between the Ndwandwe and Mthethwa, with the former initially achieving victory.

The tide was to turn against the Ndwandwe with the emergence on the scene of an astute commander, Shaka, a member of the Zulu chiefdom in the Mthethwa kingdom. After a long and bitter war, Shaka defeated the Ndwandwe, who were forced to relocate north of the Pongola. As the Ndwandwe and others fled to the north, they carried the wars with them, attacking new areas. The collection of the fleeing fighting forces, known as the Nguni, "scattered the war" (another meaning of *Mfecane*) to "crush" smaller groups in eastern central Africa.

SHAKA AND THE ZULU KINGDOM

The rise of Shaka and his accomplishments have been described as among the most important events in the history of South Africa during the nineteenth century. Shaka, one of Africa's most famous generals, was born in about 1787, the son of a minor Zulu chief. Early in life, he was forced to follow his mother into exile, and they resided at the court of another Zulu leader, Dingiswayo. Shaka served as a military commander under Dingiswayo and distinguished himself as a warrior. In 1816, when the head of the Zulu chief died, Shaka, aided by Dingiswayo, seized the throne.

It was Shaka that turned the weak Zulu chiefdom into the most powerful military kingdom in the southern African region. He brought the Mthethwa kingdom under his contol and subdued the Ndwandwe chiefdoms. By 1819, Shaka had emerged as the most powerful force in the region, with control over a Zulu kingdom whose power extended from Tugela to Pongola. From 1819 to 1829, Shaka expanded his kingdom in size and was also powerful enough to collect tribute from many groups in the regions between the Umzimkulu and Tugela Rivers.

The impressive achievements of the Zulu were due to his military innovations, a careful refinement of the methods that the Ndwandwe and Mthethwa had introduced in previous years. Previously, the Zulu had used a long throwing-spear, which was not always effective in overpowering an enemy. Under Shaka, they changed to a short stabbing-spear, known as the *assegai*. In addition to improved weapons, the Zulu regiments maintained rigorous discipline and drill schedules. The army was divided into regiments on the basis of age groups. The wars were ruthless, based on the principle that enemies had to be destroyed unless they surrendered unconditionally. To show signs of reluctance to participate in wars or to show signs of cowardice was costly to the Zulu soldier, who could be executed as a result.

Shaka himself was a brilliant tactician and strategist. He was able to improve upon inherited weapons of war and, more important, to create an efficient and well-trained permanent army. Spies were trained to collect data, and surprise attacks were used to great effect. Shaka believed in a strategy of "total warfare," which would prevent the enemy from ever recovering. The wars before Shaka minimized damage and death—two armies would hurl their long-handled spears at each other until one party surrendered; the victorious army would then seize cattle, burn down the homes of the losers, and leave them alone as long as they paid tribute. For Shaka, wars were not just about cattle and displays of military strength but about the maximum infliction of damage on the enemy—their people would be killed, all their livestock seized, and their homesteads burned to the ground.

Shaka's strategy was dependent on speed, involving a vigorous attack on the opposing forces. The soldiers were active and battle ready. To attain speed, the soldiers ran and fought barefooted—Shaka disallowed the use of leather sandals, which slowed them down. Young boys were involved as baggage carriers, also to help the soldiers achieve speed and concentration. A regular soldier carried two main weapons—a long shield to protect him from spears thrown at him and the short spear to stab the enemy. Zulu soldiers pursued their enemies, many of whom were stabbed. In what is called a "cow-horn" formation, regiments were sent to the left and right of the lead regiment. As the center regiment charged forward, the "horns" on both sides encircled the enemies to prevent any escape.

Shaka successfully used members of his army for economic activities. The regiments were required to farm and produce for the state. The women cultivated the plantations belonging to their kin, while the men sought for ivory and herded cattle belonging to the state. Regimental towns were established in key areas of the Zulu kingdom, each dedicated to military service and economic production. Shaka also engaged in trade. He was entitled to all the ivory collected by hunters, thereby ensuring access to an important source of long-distance trade. He maintained trade contact with Delagoa Bay where he exchanged ivory for cloth and beads. In 1824, a group of British traders were allowed to stay at Port Natal (modern Durban) to engage in the ivory trade.

Shaka also changed the political system, as he combined the various loosely organized homesteads and chieftaincies into a centralized state. The central government revolved around him, as he exercised absolute power. Shaka expected total loyalty and obedience from his subjects and chiefs. In many areas, the chiefs were denied the control of regiments, which meant that they lacked access to military power and the opportunity to challenge the king. Members of a regiment would work for a number of years and must have displayed bravery or, at least, lost their ability to fight before they could be discharged to marry and set up autonomous households.

When a new area was conquered, the existing hereditary chiefs were replaced by loyal palace officers, known as the *indunas*, who were accountable to Shaka. To resist the new political arrangement was to court disaster—not only were the hereditary chiefs destroyed, but a whole village might be wiped out. Where the former chief of a conquered area agreed to surrender and accept the authority of Shaka, he could become an *induna*. All the able-bodied citizens of a conquered area, male and female, were conscripted into the army of King Shaka, and they must not give allegiance to their former chiefs.

The Zulu kingdom was in essence a large military organization. Shaka was the overall commander in chief of the army and kingdom. Although there was a council, comprising the *indunas*, Shaka could ignore their decisions or advice. Members of the council were careful never to antagonize a king who could kill them. The kingdom itself was divided into regimental towns; each was centered on a large cattle enclosure that protected the cattle at night and was used for military training and parades during the day. All adults under the age of thirty-five must belong to a regiment stationed in one of the towns, and they lived in houses around the enclosure. A regiment took care of its cattle, acquired as war booty; the women cultivated food crops (mainly maize and sorghum), while the men took care of the cattle. The regiment lived on the meat and milk.

The regiments were administered by representatives of the king. The *induna* served as the commander of each male regiment, while a female relation of Shaka headed each female regiment. The female leader also served the king as an intelligence officer, observing and reporting the activities of the male soldiers and their *induna*. Close to the regimental towns were the various homesteads of married people with their children. The homesteads paid tribute to the king, collected on his behalf by a chief. This local chief, usually a military commander, was appointed by the king.

In 1828, Shaka was killed by Dingane, his half brother, who declared himself king. Shaka's leadership style had alienated many of his close associates and relations. Although living within the enclosure of royal women, Shaka never married. Indeed, he feared the birth of an heir so much that he executed a number of pregnant women. His power of execution was used to instill fear in many; even the loss of a spear in battle or a display of cowardice could be punished with death. In 1827, Shaka killed a number of people accused of not sufficiently mourning the loss of his mother. As the regiments traveled further and faced the possibility of defeat and possible execution by Shaka, they grew tired of wars and critical of Shaka's excesses. Dingane was able to exploit the anti-Shaka sentiments to stage a coup. He promised to halt the wars and to allow the members of the various regiments to reduce their extended military service period in order to get married. The changes did not, however, mean a surrender of absolute power by the new king.

By 1838, Dingane had virtually wrecked the kingdom that he inherited. Three factors were responsible for the decline of the Zulu kingdom after 1828. First, King Dingane was not as astute or talented as Shaka. The leadership qualities that Shaka had used to hold the kingdom together were lacking in his successor. Dingane initially promised to promote peace but later changed to a policy of war. He broke his promise regarding execution and became far more despotic than Shaka. By allowing regiments to return home, he strengthened the power of local chiefs. To prevent problems of secession, he returned to a policy of centralized regiments and constant warfare. However, the Zulu now found it difficult to defeat some of their enemies such as the Ndebele and the Swazi.

Second, the dependence on constant wars to keep the kingdom together, generate booty, and ensure that the regiments were active was becoming a source of problems. The areas of conflict came to be too far from the center, and many groups had borrowed the Zulu methods of fighting to protect themselves.

Third, Dingane had to confront the most determined invaders in search of land: the Boers of South Africa who left the Cape in 1837–38 in search of land for white settlers in the fertile areas south of the Tugela. The Boers had better armies and weapons than the Zulu. The Boers and the Zulu engaged in wars in which the Zulu were eventually defeated and the expansion of white settlement into the southern African interior was ensured.

THE IMPACT

The *Mfecane* and the rise of Shaka had major consequences. To start with, a Zulu kingdom was established, developing from a small chiefdom into a large territorial political organization. Conquered areas and groups were incorporated into the Zulu kingdom, and various previously existing chieftaincies came to an end. The Zulu kingdom was both powerful and wealthy.

Second, in the process of its creation and expansion, the Zulu kingdom unleashed many wars in the southern Africa region, wars that lasted for about twenty years from 1818 onward. Many people in the foothills of the Drakensberg were forced to relocate elsewhere if they wanted to avoid incorporation into the

Zulu kingdom. Many groups experienced dislocation and sought refuge in various areas that included parts of modern-day Tanzania, Malawi, and Zambia. A great part of the modern-day Kwa Zulu-Natal region was deserted, as its people fled to the mountains and forests. The military conquest of many groups and the destruction of their cattle caused starvation, death, enormous stress, and great anxiety about the future. So confused did many people become that the oral traditions of the period blamed many problems on witchcraft and the anger of their ancestors. Thousands died in the wars, killed in close range-battles in each of which hundreds were stabbed to death. When peace returned, many found themselves citizens of new centralized, powerful nations.

Third, the economy suffered in all the areas that experienced wars and political dislocation. Cattle were central to the economy, but thousands of cattle were killed for food, captured, and recaptured. The wars halted cultivation in a number of areas. Some areas suffered total abandonment. In the attempt to protect themselves, the Zulu established a depopulated zone in the area of present-day Natal, to create a buffer against any invading enemy.

Fourth, the idea of a Zulu identity, which has been sustained to this day, emerged. Drawing soldiers from different towns and villages into a regimental town where they trained, worked, and lived together for a number of years served to promote a sense of commitment to the Zulu nation. Even after their service was over, they could still be called into action by the king. The regiments reduced the people's loyalty to many chiefs, as all were expected to look to King Shaka as the sole leader and defender of the Zulu nation. Once a year, a first-fruit ceremony, the *inxwala*, was performed to affirm the unity and identity of the Zulu. All the regiments and representatives from different parts of the kingdom must attend the event, held in the capital city during the rainy season. The event would celebrate the power of the king and the productivity of agriculture and cattle rearing.

Fifth, the *Mfecane* led to the creation and spread of military innovations. The weapons and the drill strategies of Zulu regiments were carried by the Ndebele and Ngoni people to central Africa, where they subdued many groups in the 1830s and 1840s.

Sixth, many new, large, and powerful states emerged to the north of the Zulu kingdom, and population was redistributed in the region. Before the *Mfecane*, the people were spread over a wide region in the southeast of the highveld, and they lived mainly in many semiautonomous chiefdoms. As a result of the wars, the population became concentrated in secure, compact areas, leaving some areas either unoccupied or sparsely populated.

Among the leading new nations were the Swazi kingdom (located to the north of the Pongola), the Gaza kingdom (in the southern parts of modern Mozambique), and the Ngoni states in central Africa. The most powerful of the new states, that is, in addition to that of the Zulu, was the Sotho kingdom under King Moshoeshoe. Among the Sotho in the southern highveld, the *Mfecane* created a political revolution. The Sotho had lived in many scattered villages whose chiefs were independent of one another. Each village had its regiment used to construct public works and fight small wars only when the need arose. In the early 1820s, the Sotho found themselves prey to their powerful neighbors who exploited their military weakness and lack of unity. Many Sotho villages lost their land and cattle and were forced to relocate. Among the Sotho remnants that survived the wars, there emerged a strong leader, Moshoeshoe, who was able to rally the survivors to found a new Sotho kingdom. The Sotho kingdom was an agglomeration of semi-independent groups, with Moshoeshoe as the king. Sotho villages looking for protection were incorporated into the kingdom. The Sotho were opposed to the Zulu and other invaders. Their determination led to their survival, and they later became the people of the independent state of Lesotho.

SUGGESTIONS FOR FURTHER READING

Beck, Roger B. *The History of South Africa*. Westport, Conn.: Greenwood Press, 2000. Chapter 4.

Falola, Toyin, ed. *Africa*. Vol. 1, *African History before 1885*. Durham, N.C.: Carolina Academic Press, 2000. Chapter 16.

Hamilton, Carolyn. *Terrific Majesty: The Power of Shaka Zulu and the Limits of Historical Invention*. Cambridge, Mass.: Harvard University Press, 1998.

Kunene, Mazisi. *Emperor Shaka the Great: A Zulu Epic*. London: Heinemann, 1979.

Omer-Copper, J.D. *The Zulu Aftermath*. London: Longman, 1966.

Ritter, E.A. *Shaka Zulu*. London: Allen Lane, 1976.

Sanders, P. *Moshweshwe of Lesotho*. London: Heinemann, 1971.

Shillington, Kevin. *History of Southern Africa*. London: Longman, 1987. Chapter 4.

Thompson, Leonard. *A History of South Africa*. New Haven, Conn.: Yale University Press, 1996.

18

European Conquest and African Response, 1885–1900

Whatever happens we have got
The Maxim gun and they have not

English poet Hilaire Belloc

Between 1885 and 1900, most of Africa was taken over as colonies of Europe, a major event that has shaped the course of African history ever since. The long era of free trade and reasonably peaceful relations gave way to one of economic exploitation and political domination. Before the 1880s, very little of Africa was under colonial rule—less than 10 percent, consisting of small areas along the coast where trade was carried out. The greater part of the African interior was unknown to Europeans. The few colonies of the British included areas around Freetown in Sierra Leone, forts in the Gambia, Lagos, a protectorate in the southern Gold Coast (now Ghana), and some areas in South Africa. The French had control in St. Louis and Dakar in Senegal, Grand Bassam and Assini in Côte d'Ivoire, and a small coastal area in Dahomey (now the Republic of Benin). The Portuguese were established in Mozambique and Angola.

By the 1880s, the long-established Afro-European relations based on trade changed to those of colonial domination. By 1900, only Liberia and Ethiopia were free of colonial imposition. What were the reasons for this change, what was the process, and how did Africans respond? This chapter answers these three important questions.

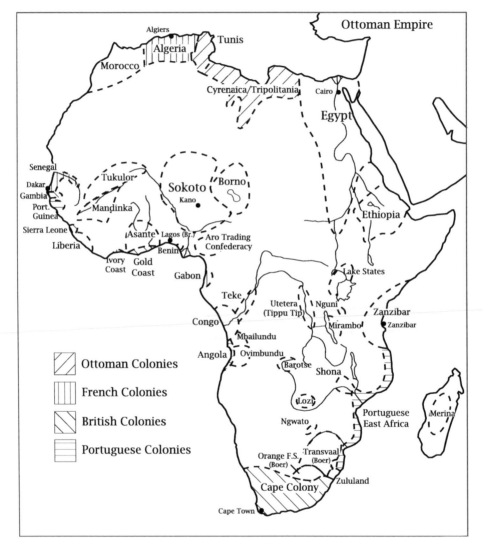

Africa, 1880.

REASONS FOR THE PARTITION

Colonies offered great economic opportunities to Europe. The expansion of capitalism and the desire for profits were the principal motives behind the conquest of Africa. The European merchants who made profits in their business relations with Africa believed that they could make even greater profits by pressuring their governments to involve themselves directly in the management of Africa. Profits could be made in two ways: (1) by obtaining cheap raw materials that would be exported to Europe to manufacture various products and (2) by turning Africa into a huge market to consume imported goods from Europe. As other countries such as Germany, France, and Portugal were catching up with Britain in industrialization, the need for raw materials and markets was greater than ever before. Excess capital was generated by many industries and merchants, and they wanted to spend their money in making more profits. When gold was discovered in South Africa in the 1880s, Africa was seen as offering great promise as a continent in which to invest for quick rewards. The traders already based in Africa began to pressure their home countries to establish economic monopolies in African countries so that they would gain greater access to raw materials and markets.

The fight for Africa was an extension of the intense competition among the European nations. Various elements in this competition can be seen as the "political motives" responsible for Africa's partition. The unification of Germany created a major third power in Europe, in addition to France and Britain. The three were active in maintaining a balance of power and were eager to prevent any one from gaining too much power. Colonial acquisition was interpreted as evidence of a threat to the balance of power. In 1870, France was defeated by Germany, losing two provinces as a result. One way to overcome the humiliation of this and gain more territories was to seek them in Africa. By the 1880s, ambitious European nations had no territories left to acquire within Europe, thus forcing them to look elsewhere. Early in the 1880s, Britain established control of Egypt, thereby also controlling the Suez route to the east. The French and the Germans believed that they too had to seize parts of Africa in order to minimize the advantages that would accrue to Britain. Nationalism was at stake: The extreme passion of the period encouraged the possession of a large empire, if only to show other nations that one was a great country and a great power.

Each European country wanted to claim overseas territories in order to exhibit its military and political strength. The acquisition of a large colony was regarded as evidence of imperial power. Each power wanted to prevent any rival European power from taking an area it was interested in. For instance, the British signed a number of treaties with the chiefs of the Niger Delta in Nigeria in the 1880s, just to prevent the French from encroaching on the area. The European countries believed that they could use acquired territories to build national prestige. For instance, when Britain acquired the Suez Canal in Egypt in 1882, the French and Germans went elsewhere in Africa to assert themselves, partly to build prestige: The French established claims over the north bank of the River Congo, and Germany established claims over four areas along the African coast, in Togo, Cameroon, Tanganyika (now Tanzania), and South West Africa (now Namibia). King Leopold of Belgium decided to annex territory in central Africa, and he created the Congo Free State as his personal estate. The French were interested in possession of the Western Sudan (modern Senegal, Mali, Burkina Faso, and Niger) partly to counteract their humiliation by Germany in the war of 1870–71. Individual European soldiers and officials in Africa regarded territorial possession as a way to gain glory, attention, and promotion.

Evidence of cultural arrogance can be found in the statements of those who participated in the conquest. A belief that Europeans were superior gave rise to the claim that they had a right to conquer Africa. The belief in white superiority was also used to describe the partition as a "civilizing mission"—the idea that a superior race had the right to improve the lives of an inferior one, if necessary through force and colonization. The conquest of "backward races" was even interpreted as a legitimate use of force, as many cited the principle of "Social Darwinism"—only the most able and superior can survive—based on the idea espoused by Charles Darwin in his 1859 book *The Origin of Species by Means of Natural Selection or the Preservation of Favoured Races in the Struggle for Life.* When this idea was expressed in religious terms, aggressive missionaries claimed that evangelization was a way of uplifting the "inferior" people. The partition of Africa was seen as an opportunity to do the same.

THE PROCESS

The principal European countries involved in the partition were Britain, Portugal, France, and Germany. The greatest rewards went to Britain and France. The British and the French participated in trade and the spread of Christianity and maintained control in a few areas before the 1880s. Holland and Denmark withdrew from West Africa and sold their bases to the British. The Germans did not become involved until 1884, but they later annexed the coast of Togoland and the Cameroons. The European countries regarded themselves as competitors and viewed one another with suspicion. In 1876, King Leopold I of Belgium indicated a strong interest in Africa by convening a conference and creating an association to sponsor expeditions to the Congo area. In the same year, Portugal began to send its own expeditions to Africa. France, too, entered an expansionist phase, by exploring some areas in the Congo, participating in dual control, with the British, of Egypt, and indicating that it would use force in the Western Sudan. The tensions of the late 1870s and early 1880s, all showing that the European countries were now strongly interested in colonial expansion, led to a major conference to consider the urgency of their aggression and the fate of Africa.

Now known as the Berlin Conference, it was held from 15 November 1884 to 26 February 1885, with Germany as the host. It was agreed that all the European countries were free to participate in the takeover of Africa, that the navigation of the Congo and Niger Rivers was to be free to all, and that for any country to declare a protectorate over any part of Africa "effective occupation" of the area was required. When a protectorate was declared by one European country, it must notify the others that it had acquired "spheres of influence." The country involved must also give evidence that it would protect certain rights and ensure freedom of trade. The Berlin decisions laid down the rules for partitioning Africa.

After the Berlin Conference, activities aimed at "possessing" Africa became intense. The leading participants wanted to establish "effective occupation" in as many areas as possible. As the Berlin Conference did not make clear whether presence at the coast meant control of the adjoining hinterland, the Europeans challenged one another in areas away from the coast. At another conference, in 1890 at Brussels, they agreed that the principle of effective occupation also applied to the hinterland. Among the evidence that they used to claim an area as belonging to one of them were the settlement of people or traders from the country, exploration of the area, treaties signed with local chiefs, activities of traders and missionaries, and physical occupation.

After 1885, two strategies were used to acquire colonies. The first was the signing of treaties and the second was direct military attack. Treaties were signed between the representatives of a European power and African chiefs or between one European power and another. In the Euro-African treaties, African leaders signed documents to show that they surrendered their power and agreed to promote trade and accept other conditions. There is no evidence that many African chiefs understood the contents of the treaties. Treaties among the European powers demarcated boundaries and defined spheres of influence.

Military attacks involved the deliberate use of armies to subdue areas or at least frighten them into surrender. For instance, the French used their army against groups in the Western Sudan, Gabon, and Madagascar. The British attacked many peoples and places as well, including the Yoruba town of Ijebu Ode and the Asante of Ghana. Germany, Italy, and Portugal also used warfare to acquire their colonies.

The Europeans engaged in various disputes but did not fight many wars among themselves. Their energies were concentrated on sharing Africa among themselves. The British extended their possessions in West Africa and claimed the lucrative and densely populated countries of Nigeria, Ghana, Sierra Leone, and the Gambia. In South Africa, Cecil Rhodes, a private entrepreneur, gained valuable areas for the British. With a fanatical desire to impose British control from the "Cape to Cairo," he was ruthless in attacking African nations in areas that later became Botswana and Rhodesia (now Zimbabwe). The British consolidated their hold during the Boer War (1899–1902), which ended in the absorption of the Boer republics of the Orange Free State and the Transvaal into the Union of South Africa (see Chapter 20). British companies in East and central Africa—the Imperial British East Africa Company and the British South Africa Company—paved the way to the acquisition of Kenya.

The French invaded the Western Sudan in 1879. Using their existing control of coastal areas, the French moved to the hinterland, gaining larger territories and hoping to outflank the British. They moved south from Algeria, northeast from Gabon, and north from Dahomey and Côte d'Ivoire. They also annexed Madagascar and a host of small islands off the coast of East Africa.

With brutal methods, the Congo Free State was expanded. King Leopold treated it as his personal property until 1914 when it was acquired by the Belgian government. The Portuguese and Germans extended their possessions from the coastal areas they controlled prior to 1885. The Italians failed to conquer Ethiopia in 1896 but were able to establish themselves in Eritrea and Somaliland. The Spanish acquired an area on the Guinea Coast (now Equatorial Guinea). By the early 1900s, the definitive map of colonial Africa had emerged. Only a few changes followed. Germany lost its colonies at the end of the First World War, as they were transferred to Belgium, France, South Africa, and Britain to manage on behalf of the League of Nations.

AFRICAN RESPONSE

Many African states and leaders were shocked by the European ambition to colonize them. Many struggled to retain their sovereignty and protect their land, their institutions, and their cultures. While many states wanted to maintain friendship with European traders and missionaries, they rejected the attempts to invade and rule them. Indeed, many refused to compromise, preferring even to die in battle. In a mood typical of many leaders, the king of the Mossi in West Africa told a French leader in 1895:

I know the whites wish to kill me in order to take my country, and yet you claim that they will help me to organize my country. But I find my country good just as it is. I have no need of them. I know what is necessary for me and what I want: I have my own merchants: also, consider yourself fortunate that I do not order your head to be cut off. Go away now, and above all, never come back.[1]

Resistance to European conquest was not isolated or restricted to large kingdoms. Eager to portray their conquest in a glowing light, early European accounts exaggerated their welcome by the Africans and criticized their opponents as bloodthirsty tyrants. However, what the African rulers were struggling to retain was their sovereignty. They resorted to various strategies.

In many areas, the African response took military forms. A state might use its army to fight the European forces, as in the case of the Asante in West Africa or the Zulu in South Africa. Armed resistance could even be prolonged, as in such cases as western Uganda and northern Niger where Africans continued to resist until the 1920s. Samori Toure, the leader of the Mandinka in West Africa, modernized his army and resisted the French for almost seven years.

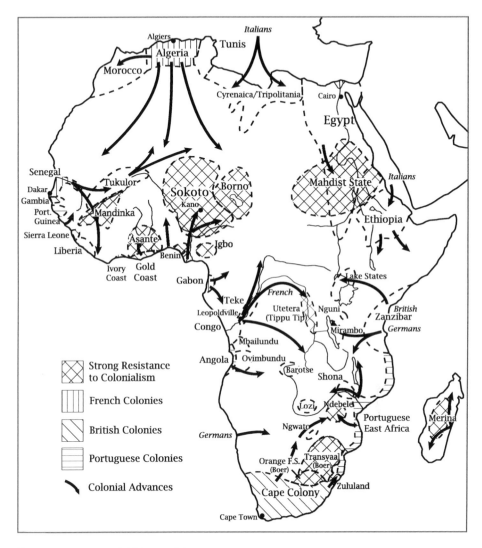

European conquest and African resistance.

Resistant Africans were confident of their ability to succeed, trusting their military experience, spiritual forces, and sheer determination to survive. The appeal to religious and magical forces was one way to win the wars but also a way to seek help from the spiritual realm against the European enemy. Many people and leaders called on ancestors, gods, and spirits for help. Sacrifices were made, in addition to prayers and the use of charms to ward off the "evil forces" represented by European encroachment.

Diplomacy was yet another option, pursued by forming an alliance or promising to cooperate with the Europeans. Where a group felt threatened by violence, it sought the means to minimize the possibility of European violence. In situations where a people believed that they could benefit from the European presence, they accepted foreign rule. Among the expected benefits were the introduction of Western education, the spread of Christianity, and expanded opportunities for trade. In expecting positive changes to come with European rule, the Africans misunderstood the objectives of the colonial enterprise.

Religion played an important role. To win wars and build morale, leaders and soldiers used charms. Religious leaders also emerged to lead the opposition to Europeans. Religious power could come from indigenous religions, Islam, or Christianity. Religion was used to build unity among people and to mobilize them for war or disobedience. When the conquest became a reality, religion provided one of the sources of nationalism but also enabled Africans to reconcile themselves to the new situation. Finally, other options were pursued in meeting the challenges of European invasion. Some groups or people took to migration.

WHY EUROPEANS WERE SUCCESSFUL

In spite of vigorous resistance by a number of African nations and leaders, only Liberia and Ethiopia escaped the imposition of colonial rule. There were a number of reasons for this. To start with, it is misleading to see all of Africa as a single bloc resisting external invasion. Had this been the case, it would have been difficult for the European powers to easily take over this huge continent. Not only did the Europeans take on one African nation at a time, but there were cases in which some African leaders allied with an invading European power against other Africans. The European armies included hundreds of Africans, recruited from one group to fight another group.

Other reasons for the European success in imposing colonial rule relate to the power of technology and the availability of resources. Compared to the African nations, the European powers had more resources to use. They had the money to buy arms and pay troops. If they lost a battle, they could regroup, benefiting from the knowledge gained and the resources available. Their armies were professional, devoted to full-time warfare. African nations, too, had armies, but in many places they were composed of volunteers who had to abandon their farms and other occupations, without the resources to engage in prolonged warfare.

Due to the records supplied by explorers, missionaries, traders, and representatives of governments, the European invaders possessed valuable information about Africa. More Europeans than before could go to Africa, to serve in the armies and administration. The use of quinine had made it possible to minimize the danger of malaria fever, thus removing the fear of the deadly disease that had frightened off many Europeans in previous years.

The Europeans relied on improved firearms. Africans relied on bows, arrows, and muzzle-loading guns (such as Dane guns), which had to be loaded slowly. The European armies in the era of the partition relied on breech loaders, rifles that could fire at the rate of about ten rounds per minute. Whereas the European armies had adequate modern guns (the Maxim and Gatling), their African rivals lacked access to them. A few nations, such as the Baule of Côte d'Ivoire, had stockpiled large quantities of arms and ammunition, but they were mainly old muskets that were no match for Maxim guns. Where Africans had modern weapons, they did not have access to large quantities of them. The armies of even such large states as the Sokoto caliphate lacked the tactics to deal with an invading army using machine guns. The tactics of the African armies—cavalry charges, the defense of walled cities, the use of large armies carrying bows and arrows—were ineffective in facing an army equipped with machine guns. In areas where Africans had experienced recent wars or catastrophes such as epidemics and famine, they were too weak to organize any serious resistance.

Guns were used to subdue many groups. However, others were forced into surrender by the threat of violence. When some groups saw the fate of their more powerful neighbors, they chose to give up. In some cases, it could well be that the rulers saw the futility of resistance and wanted to avoid bloodshed. In the end, only Emperor Menelik II of Ethiopia was victorious against the mighty European powers. By 1902, the conquest of Africa was almost completed. A new map was created: Instead of hundreds of precolonial nations, there were now about forty political units. As we shall see in Chapter 19, the consequences were many and profound.

NOTE

1. Quoted in Michael Crowder, *West Africa Under Colonial Rule* (London: Hutchinson, 1968), p. 97.

SUGGESTIONS FOR FURTHER READING

Betts, Raymond F., ed. *The "Scramble" for Africa: Causes and Dimensions of Empire.* Boston: Heath, 1966.

Boahen, Adu. *African Perspectives on Colonialism.* Baltimore, Md.: Johns Hopkins University Press, 1985.

Boahen, Adu, ed. *UNESCO General History of Africa.* Vol. 7, *Africa under Colonial Domination 1880–1935.* Abridged ed. Berkeley: University of California Press, 1990.

Crowe, S.E. *The Berlin West African Conference 1884–1885*. Westport, Conn.: Negro University Press, 1970.

Davidson, Basil. *Modern Africa: A Social and Political History*. 2nd ed. New York: Longman, 1989.

Falola, Toyin, ed. *Africa*. Vol. 1, *African History before 1885*. Durham, N.C.: Carolina Academic Press, 2000. Chapter 18.

Falola, Toyin, ed. *Africa*. Vol. 2, *African Cultures and Societies before 1885*. Durham, N.C.: Carolina Academic Press, 2000. Chapter 17.

Hallett, Robin. *The Penetration of Africa: Motives, Method and Impacts, 1970–1865*. New York: Viking Press, 1962.

PART III

The Twentieth-Century Period

19

The Colonial Experience, 1900–1939

Africa experienced colonial rule during the first half of the twentieth century. By 1914, Europeans had consolidated their hold on the continent (see Chapter 18). Between then and 1939, they implemented various policies that defined the colonial era. After 1939, a number of reforms were undertaken to respond to African demands for independence. The colonial era had economic, social, and political impacts. The changes were not only numerous; they were also rapid. And Africans had to learn to deal with them in creative ways.

POLITICS AND ADMINISTRATION

New countries with new boundaries were created. These boundaries were artificial. Preexisting political units and ethnic groups might be divided between two or more countries. For instance, the empire of Kanem-Borno in the Lake Chad area was divided between Nigeria (a British colony), Cameroon (German), and Niger and Chad (French). In spite of the problems associated with them, the boundaries have since been maintained with only minor changes. The colonial experience also aided the formation of an African identity, with a commitment to national boundaries, a sense of unity based on a common experience of colonial domination, and a desire to liberate the continent from oppression and poverty.

The major colonial policies were determined abroad. Colonies were extensions of Europe and must reflect changes in Europe rather than the concerns of African subjects. The colonial officers in Africa regarded themselves as under the control of their governments in Europe. They were expected to carry out the

Africa, 1914.

instructions given to them, making them applicable to their local situations. The number of officers—administrators and soldiers—was small, to keep down the cost. Their duties were simple and clearly defined: They must pursue the colonial economic objectives, and they must maintain law and order. As we shall see in the next chapter, what Africans wanted was different: development, so that they could not be exploited; and power, which would threaten the colonial state.

Africans were involved in the administration. The armies and the police were manned by Africans, and many came to believe that they owed their survival and prestige to the colonial state. Educated Africans served in the civil service, mainly in the lower levels. As many of them enjoyed privileges, they began to imitate European ways of life.

African countries were not all governed in the same way, although the broad patterns were clear. After early efforts to administer areas unknown to them, the colonialists evolved administrative systems suited to their objectives and adaptable to the circumstances of conquest. To take just two examples, the British tried a system of indirect rule, and the French, a system of assimilation.

The British and Indirect Rule

In British colonies, a policy of indirect rule—a method of administering local government—was adopted in many colonies. Indirect rule rested on the assumption that European and African cultures were different, and the best way to govern local communities was through the political system that they had evolved on their own. Above the local government was a central government. Each colony was administered as an autonomous unit, divided into a number of provinces. The governor headed the central administration, aided by executive and legislative councils. The executive councils included only British officers. The legislative councils contained a few Africans, but the power of each council was limited to the colony. The governor was powerful within the colony, but he still obeyed instructions from London. A province was divided into districts, where the system of indirect rule operated.

The British administrator most famous for implementing this idea (in the Sudan and Nigeria) and developing the best manual on it was Lord Lugard, author of *The Dual Mandate in Tropical Africa*. Early in the twentieth century, Lugard faced the task of administering the huge area of Northern Nigeria, formerly part of the extensive Sokoto caliphate, which had a highly developed political system under a sultan and emirs. The British would have required a large number of people and extensive resources to govern such a huge area. What they chose to do was to control the sultan and emirs, who would in turn control their own people. Indirect rule in Northern Nigeria became a model for other places. The system was later extended to other areas in Nigeria and other colonies such as the Gold Coast, Sierra Leone, and the Gambia.

Under indirect rule, existing institutions were modified to meet the needs of the colonial administration. Chiefs, kings, and their officials were used for local administration, to carry out the policies of the colonial government. Indirect rule reduced the cost and numbers of foreign personnel, by using Africans to administer themselves. However, many of the Africans involved owed their appointments to the British officers, who could also remove them. They were expected to carry out instructions, performing the unpopular duties of collecting taxes and recruiting labor for the government. To return to the example of Northern Nigeria, the British officer, a resident or district officer, supervised and advised the local emir, instructed on how to reform and modernize local institutions, and ensured the collection of taxes. The emir was the head of the Native Administration—he appointed district heads, village heads, and tax collectors.

Indirect rule experienced a number of problems and can be criticized on several grounds. Chiefs and kings in many areas actually gained more power than before, thus creating tension between them and their people. Indirect rule proved unsuitable to areas that were previously used to powerful kings and their officials. In areas without established centralized institutions or strong kings, as among the Igbo of Nigeria or the Swahili of Tanganyika, powerful chiefs were created for them. Known as "Warrant Chiefs" among the Igbo, they were given wide powers, they carried out unpopular decisions, and they could be individuals of low social status without much respect in the community.

In the attempt to protect traditional chiefs and institutions, as in Northern Nigeria, the British gave little encouragement to the spread of Christianity and Western education. In some cases, European officers would blame African chiefs for lack of progress, wrongly accusing them of not initiating modernization. In the quest to preserve existing institutions, some officers actually prevented rapid changes, arguing that traditions needed to be preserved at all cost. Finally, where a new African educated elite emerged, indirect rule excluded them from power. The exclusion of the educated Africans from power created a lasting hostility between them and the Europeans.

The French System

Proud of their culture, and with a strong belief that they could spread it, the French opted for a policy of assimilation. Their African subjects were expected to become French in culture and, if possible, in citizenship, and the colonies would be run as provinces of France. Not only did the French think that they had attained the highest possible culture; they believed that Africans could acquire the essence of their civilization as long as the necessary institutions were put in place. Their African subjects should imitate them, and their colonies should become an extension of France.

Senegal in West Africa was the place closer to experiment with this grandiose project of culture transfer, in the areas known as the "Four Communes"— St. Louis, Dakar, Rufisque, and Gorée. A French system of local government and a French school system were introduced, and the African residents were regarded as French citizens, with the right to elect a representative to the Chamber of Deputies in Paris.

Outside these four areas, the French did not fully assimilate their African subjects. Thus, the colony of Senegal was divided between the French citizens and "other Africans." The French citizens enjoyed wide privileges. Unlike the British colonies, where the Christian missionaries developed the education system, the French government took control of the school system in its colonies. Only a small percentage of Africans had the benefit of Western education, and those who received it enjoyed the privileges of citizenship. The noncitizens did not enjoy freedom of speech, movement, and the press; they could be forced to work to build roads and railways; and they paid direct tax, which compelled many of them to take to the production of cash crops in order to raise cash. In a notorious system known as the *indigénat*, a French officer had the power to arrest and jail any non-French African without trial.

Extending the policy of personal assimilation proved difficult, partly because it was difficult to enforce a uniform culture. Cultures and customs varied, and it was hard for the French to impose theirs on all Africans, certainly not on adults who were already formed in their ways. There were profound differences between the cultures of the French and the Africans. Aspects of traditional life such as the lineage system, religion (both indigenous and Islamic), and many others were hard to give up. Great differences also existed in terms of laws, rights, and duties, which were hard for Africans to give up. For instance, an African Muslim married to two wives could not become a French citizen since this would violate the law on monogamy. By implication, assimilation would destroy or undermine many aspects of African culture and traditional authorities.

The French, very early in the twentieth century, began to question the need to extend wide privileges to Africans and make them citizens. There was a fear that over time the number of Africans who were French citizens would outnumber the European French citizens and could even possibly take over power. Also, the attainment of colonial objectives meant that the French needed millions of Africans to contribute to the colonial economy.

The French, like the British, set up central and local governments. The Ministry of the Colonies in Paris controlled the colonies, preferring to treat many of them as a federation rather than as separate, autonomous countries. For instance, all the French colonies in West Africa (Senegal, Mali, Guinea, Côte d'Ivoire, Burkina Faso, Niger, Dahomey, and Mauritania) were administered as a single federation under a governor-general based in Dakar.

Power revolved around the governor-general. He represented France in Africa, accepting instructions and implementing them. Only the governor-general could transact official business with the ministry in France. He had a large budget and was financially independent of the individual territories. He controlled appointments to the civil service, while the security forces, the army and police, were treated as federal matters. Below him were the governors who headed the component territories. The governors executed the orders sent from Paris through the governor-general.

With respect to the local government, the colonies were divided into *cercles*, units that ignored traditional boundaries and were artificially drawn so as to be similar in size and population. Each *cercle* was headed by a *commandant de cercle*. A *cercle* was divided into more manageable units, each administered by a *chef de subdivision* who administered the subdivision. The French used more of their own personnel, who enjoyed a more direct exercise of power than the British. The African chiefs were undermined, left with little or no power, denied judicial power, and reduced to a low status. Many chiefs were removed, and the others became subordinate to French political officers. They were given the most degrading tasks, raising forced labor and collecting tax, tasks they must carry out to avoid being disgraced or even removed.

If the idea of personal assimilation could not be implemented, it was easier to implement administrative and economic assimilation. In the long run, this had a number of negative consequences: In the case of Algeria, the close links with France made the struggle for independence difficult and violent.

THE ECONOMY

The aim of the European powers was to exploit the resources of Africa in various ways: using Africa as a supplier of minerals and cash crops, consumer of finished imported products, and provider of revenues to make the colonies financially self-sufficient. Even when important changes were made, they were connected to the colonial economic objectives of generating a massive transfer of wealth from Africa to Europe. The economy rested narrowly on a few products and was heavily dependent on external demands. New currencies were introduced to replace indigenous ones. Until the dying years of colonial rule, industrialization and economic planning were ignored.

To attain the colonial objectives, a new infrastructure had to be built. Roads and railways appeared in areas with exportable resources in order to facilitate the movement of goods from production centers to port cities, thence to be transported by ships to Europe. The building of the new roads and railways brought hardships to the Africans who were compelled to perform construction work. New and efficient for their purpose, the communication facilities contributed to the massive expansion of the export economy, the penetration of imported items into cities and villages, the mobility of people, the unease in urbanization, and the spread of ideas and religions.

Africans participated in the colonial economy in various ways. The majority were producers, working on their farms. Many others were forced to work for the government or for European ventures. Taxes were imposed, and the need to raise cash in order to pay them compelled many people to seek wage incomes, even as laborers.

Agriculture was the most important sector of the colonial economy. Among the key products developed and exported were peanuts, cocoa, rubber, coffee, palm oil, and timber. Except in the areas with large European settlers, agricultural production was mainly in the hands of Africans. Several measures were put in place to ensure production. A common one was the payment of tax in cash, which forced millions of people to produce and sell in order to obtain money. In some colonies, people were compelled to work. The perceived benefits of obtaining money to buy luxury items, pay for the education of children, and build houses also served to encourage production.

Foreign firms made considerable profits from the exportation of agricultural products. In areas and periods when governments became involved in buying crops or regulating prices, they were able to accumulate huge surpluses by underpaying the farmers. Export crops were favored, as the best land was devoted to them. The cultivation of cotton damaged land by reducing its nutrients. The overall consequence of the emphasis on cash crops was to reduce the quantity of food crops available.

Mining was developed in areas with gold, tin, coal, diamonds, copper, bauxite, and manganese. The sector was totally dominated by a few foreign companies who made huge profits and paid limited taxes. Africans worked mainly as laborers. Wages were low, and the formation of trade unions was disallowed for a long time.

Direct European involvement in the economy occurred in a few sectors and areas. Where there were large numbers of European settlers, they established plantations, such as the sisal farms in Tanganyika and the large farms of the fertile "White Highlands" in Kenya. Mining in South Africa, the Belgian Congo, and Northern Rhodesia also witnessed heavy European investments. In Kenya and Rhodesia, where there were a substantial number of European settlers, the foreigners exercised more power than the Africans. They were thus able to award themselves a number of privileges, including control of trade, access to fertile land, and the use of Africans as domestics and farmworkers. This became a source of great tension.

European involvement forced many Africans off their land to work as laborers for European large-scale farmers. Many also migrated to the cities to obtain other kinds of jobs. In some countries, reserves were created to keep the dispossessed Africans in areas where they could be policed. Some Africans were forced to work in European ventures and rewarded with low wages.

African economies were incorporated into the world economic system, with Africans working as producers supplying raw materials to external industries. So important was this role that African areas without raw materials needed for export were regarded as backward, and many of their people could be found as migrant workers elsewhere. To the colonizers, the ability to produce was evidence of progress. This "progress" became uneven between regions—areas with export raw materials had better infrastructural provisions and social services. Areas without minerals or exportable raw materials were forced to supply their labor to distant areas, in a "contribution" that destroyed many rural areas as farmlands and families were abandoned. Countries such as Mali, Basutoland (now Lesotho), Niger, and Chad were regarded as labor reserve areas. When the people were unwilling to work, they could be forced to do so. The requirement that they must pay tax also ensured that they had to seek wage employment in distant areas.

Control of the lucrative export-import trade was in the hands of non-African businesses. European firms enjoyed great advantages, being able to mobilize the capital to control shipping and make huge bulk purchases. Next came the Indian and Lebanese traders who were able to buy raw materials in bulk, sell imported items in retail stores, and advance credit to small producers. African entrepreneurs were pushed to the margins, surviving mainly as small-scale traders in local markets.

SOCIOCULTURAL CHANGES

There was an increase in the population of the continent, by about 37.5 percent. The pace of urbanization increased. New cities were created, (e.g., Enugu and Port Harcourt in Nigeria, Abidjan in Côte d'Ivoire, Takoradi in Ghana, and Nairobi in Kenya), and some older ones rapidly expanded, because they served as centers of commerce and administration. Although services tended to be inadequate, the cities enjoyed far better facilities than the rural areas in terms of medical services, leisure facilities, and schools.

Western education spread in many areas, as colonial governments and foreign firms needed clerks and other literate people to work for them. Interest was concentrated on elementary education. Where missionaries were allowed to operate, as in British colonies, they established elementary schools and a few secondary schools. Governments saw the participation of missionaries as saving them money. The missionaries were able to use the school system to convert many Africans to Christianity. The size of the educated elite increased, and they increasingly dominated the economy and politics of the continent. European languages spread among the elite.

Christianity and Islam spread, as missionaries took advantage of the railways and roads to travel to many areas. They were able to reach millions of people in the cities, where new mosques and churches were built. Their spread pushed indigenous religions into the background.

Western education, Christianity, and urbanization had a combined impact on social structure. The traditional elite—chiefs, kings, warriors, blacksmiths, and diviners—lost power and prestige to a new educated class. Africans also became divided along spatial lines—between those who lived in cities and those who lived in villages. The cities represented "civilization" and the villages represented "backwardness." Migration to cities became fairly common, especially among the youth who wanted to learn about new cultures and seek wage employment.

Both the cities and villages were stratified. In the cities, at least three major classes could be found. At the bottom were the "urban proletariat" comprising artisans and low-income earners. Because of the scarcity of decent affordable accommodation and the limited social services, many had to live in shanty areas. Among the poor, prostitution, unemployment, crime, and juvenile delinquency were more common. Above them were the "subelite," comprising primary school teachers, clerks, nurses, and others who had higher incomes than the low-income earners but lacked power and connections. At the top were the members of the elite—lawyers, politicians, doctors, senior civil servants—who had the resources to enjoy the facilities of the city and participate in politics as leaders. In the villages, there were landholders and landless farmers. In precolonial Africa, everybody had access to land. In colonial Africa, especially in areas with large numbers of European settlers, many were denied land. In southern and eastern Africa, large numbers of landless people moved about as migrant workers.

POSITIVE OR NEGATIVE CHANGES?

The evaluation of the comprehensive changes of this period has given rise to three major views. First, there are those who see everything as positive. Many missionaries, European officials, and scholars of moderate persuasion regard colonial rule as having been beneficial for the following reasons: Peace replaced wars in many areas; Western education and medicine spread; roads and railways were constructed; Africans sold their products abroad for money; and so on. In short, to them, the colonial era brought "civilization" to a "dark continent."

Second, there are those who regard the changes as negative. Rather than development, they see the exploitation and retardation of the continent. Such changes as the building of roads and railways simply provided the infrastructure needed by the colonial powers to take away resources from Africa to Europe. To scholars of the "Dependency School," colonialism destroyed indigenous economies, removed wealth from Africa to Europe, and created the basis for underdevelopment. In the words of Walter Rodney, a famous critic, "Colonialism had only one hand—it was a one-armed bandit."[1] Other critics of colonial rule do not deny that the era brought positive changes, but they assert that indigenous cultures and environments were damaged in various ways, that women were marginalized in a colonial society dominated by men, that the exploitation of the continent was far greater than the benefits it received, that social services were provided primarily to meet the needs of Europeans and a few privileged Africans who lived in the cities, and that racial dominance by Europeans undermined the self-worth of Africans as a people.

Finally, there are those who see both positive and negative aspects in colonial rule. They agree that some changes had beneficial impacts, such as political stability, the creation of a smaller number of countries with fixed boundaries to replace hundreds of previous states, the creation of a judiciary and civil service, and the creation of conditions that led to African nationalism. On the negative side, they mention, among other aspects: the end of the sovereignty of African states, the weakening of the traditional basis of power, the creation of small and landlocked countries, and the rise of ethnicity. With respect to the economy, they praise the creation of new roads and railways and the development of the mineral and agricultural potential of the continent in such a way that wealth was generated by many people whose purchasing power was enhanced. On the negative side, they point to the inadequacies of the communication system, the commercialization of land, the use of forced labor, the acquisition of fertile land by European settlers, the control of lucrative trade by European firms and Lebanese and Indian traders, and other forms of exploitation.

Irrespective of the conclusions of the various analysts, there is no doubt that the colonial era was one of the most significant events in African history. It brought many changes, such as the creation of new countries, the spread of European languages and institutions, and the introduction of Western education and health services. Many of these changes have had a lasting impact on the continent.

NOTE

1. Walter Rodney, *How Europe Underdeveloped Africa* (Washington, D.C.: Howard University Press, 1974), p. 1.

SUGGESTIONS FOR FURTHER READING

Afigbo, A.E., et al. *The Making of Modern Africa*. Vol. 2, *The Twentieth Century*. London: Longman, 1986.

Clarence-Smith, G. *The Third Portuguese Empire*. Manchester, England: Manchester University Press, 1985.

Crowder, Michael. *West Africa under Colonial Rule*. Evanston, Ill.: Northwestern University Press, 1968.

Falola, Toyin, ed. *Britain and Nigeria: Exploitation or Development*. London: Zed, 1987.

Falola, Toyin, ed. *Africa*. Vol. 3, *Colonial Africa, 1885–1939*. Durham, N.C.: Carolina Academic Press, 2001.

Fanon, Frantz. *A Dying Colonialism*. New York: Grove Press, 1967.

Gann, L.H., and Peter Duignan, eds. *Colonialism in Africa, 1870–1960*. Vols. 1–5. Cambridge: Cambridge University Press, 1969–75.

Parsons, Timothy. *The African Rank-and-File: Social Implications of Colonial Military Service in the King's African Rifles, 1902–1962*. Portsmouth, N.H.: Heinemann, 1999.

Rodney, Walter. *How Europe Underdeveloped Africa*. Washington, D.C.: Howard University Press, 1974.

Suret-Canale, Jean. *French Colonialism in Tropical Africa, 1900–1945*. New York: Universe, 1971.

20

The Entrenchment of Apartheid in South Africa, 1948

The history of South Africa in the first half of the twentieth century was dominated by the establishment of white minority rule over the black population and the institutionalization of an apartheid policy. The growth of the apartheid state from 1948 onward was unusual for its extreme exploitation and oppression based on skin color. Until the apartheid system crumbled in the 1990s, it stood out as unique in African history. How did it emerge, what did apartheid mean, and how did Africans and others respond to such a brutalizing system? These related questions are answered below.

HISTORICAL BACKGROUND

The European contacts with Africa from the fifteenth century involved southern Africa as well as areas further north, with the Portuguese and the Dutch making early contacts with the Cape. From 1498 to 1595, the Portuguese dominated the trade of the region, but they were displaced in the late 1500s by the Dutch, French, English, and Scandinavians. In the mid-seventeenth century, the Dutch began to establish a permanent settlement at the Cape. From 1717, the Dutch allowed the extensive use of slaves, thus laying the foundation of a race-based country. The increasing white population generated a number of conflicts with the indigenous Khoisan population. About the same time, a number of Dutch settlers began to refer to themselves as Afrikaners (a Dutch word meaning "Africans") to distinguish themselves from other Europeans. The Dutch-speaking population later evolved into an Afrikaner society.

The growth in the European population and the need for more food created an expansion in farming, as Dutch and other European farmers (collectively known as Boers) sought more land. In the eighteenth century, the Boers began a process of moving beyond the Cape to the interior. The "Trekboers," as they were known, moved to the east and north where they came into conflict with the established African owners of the land. When they confronted the indigenous San people, a war to exterminate them was pursued. In 1702, Europeans came into direct contact with the Xhosa, a southern Nguni group, leading both to tension and to cooperation.

The arrival of the British in 1795 changed the politics of the area. Between 1795 and 1803, the British occupied the Cape. They had to engage in a number of conflicts for power and land with the Dutch and indigenous populations. More settlers and missionaries arrived. During the nineteenth century, the pressure was to move to the hinterland, to take possession of more territory and cattle.

By the 1830s, the Cape region had become overpopulated, and the frantic search for land and the tension between the British and the Afrikaners eventually culminated in the "Great Trek" of the 1830s and 1840s, which involved about 15,000 Afrikaners leaving the Cape area to move into the South African hinterland. Regarding themselves as pioneers and as a chosen people heading to a promised land, the migrants (*voortrekkers*) wanted to create an independent republic in the areas of Natal, Transorangia, and Transvaal, all areas with fertile land.

The Afrikaners had to engage in wars with the Zulu, with both sides experiencing defeats and victories at different times. A deadly battle on 16 December 1838 cost the Zulu almost 3,000 soldiers, and the Afrikaners turned this into their national holiday (the so-called Day of the Covenant) until a new government in 1995 made this the Day of Reconciliation. The Afrikaners eventually claimed Natal and established the Republic of Natalia with its own constitution. A racialized society was established, with the franchise limited to Dutch-speaking men. Blacks had no political rights and were segregated and badly treated. An "indenture" system was established that entitled each Afrikaner family to have five African families as tenants, while the so-called excess black population was driven to southern Natal. In 1842, the British ended this first Afrikaner republic by annexing it as part of their empire.

However, other republics independent of the British were established, such as the Afrikaner republics of Potchefstroom and Winburg and the Orange Free State. In 1858, the South African Republic was formed with its capital in Pretoria. By 1870, two Afrikaner republics (the Orange Free State and the Transvaal) and two British colonies (Natal and Cape) existed, with an economy dependent on agriculture. The Khoikhoi and Xhosa had lost their independence, but other African groups such as the Zulu, Venda, Swazi, and Tswana remained autonomous until the discovery of diamonds and gold created further complications.

BRITISH IMPERIALISM, 1870–1910

The discovery of diamonds on the bank of the Orange River in April 1867 changed the history of South Africa and the fate of its people forever. With riches of an extent not found in any other part of the world, South Africa became a desired destination, and about 10,000 diggers rushed there from Europe, the United States, and other parts of southern Africa. By the early 1870s, the number of diggers had increased to well over 60,000. As mining became competitive and capital-intensive, Africans were prevented from making claims to land containing diamonds. In 1886, gold was discovered, adding to the competition. Three individuals emerged to dominate the mines—Barney Barnato, Alfred Beit, and Cecil Rhodes.

For these individuals and their companies to make profits, they needed to use cheap African labor. A racially divided mine labor force was created—whites performed the skilled and well-paid jobs, whereas blacks made low wages in unskilled positions. Black workers were prevented from bringing their families to the mines, lived in congested compounds, and had to carry passes. There was an expansion of the migrant labor force hired to work in the mines and other sectors such as catering, transportation, and agriculture.

With its abundance of diamonds and gold, there was no longer any doubt that South Africa would be part of the European Scramble for Africa in the last quarter of the nineteenth century. The British, with cooperation from the Afrikaners, launched the vigorous and sustained conquest of one African group after another, until the last one was subdued in 1897. At the same time, the British also tried to unite South Africa into a confederation. Conflicts were not uncommon between the Afrikaners and the British, ultimately leading to the South African War, also known as the Boer War.

THE SOUTH AFRICAN (OR BOER) WAR AND ITS AFTERMATH

The British resorted to military confrontation to control the Afrikaners and consolidate the British imperial presence. The Afrikaner republics saw the British as threatening their independence. On 11 October 1899, the war, known to the British as the Anglo-Boer War and to the Afrikaners as the Second War of Freedom, began. For the Afrikaners, the war was fought to defend their independence; for the British, it was fought to control the gold and diamond mines and impose colonial rule. The war ultimately involved people of various races, including Africans, and regions. A combination of imperialist war and civil war, it divided South African society for a long time. Thousands of people lost their lives, thousands of farmsteads were destroyed, about 14,000 Africans were killed, and over 100,000 were detained in camps. Africans were divided, with the majority supporting the British. The war ended in 1902, with the Afrikaners surrendering the independence of their republics but retaining the use of their language in the schools and courts. They were promised financial aid to repair places damaged by the war. The contributions of Africans did not bring them much gain as they were not given the franchise, received no significant compensation for damage, and also lost land to white farmers. Africans who returned to the mines found that their wages were reduced. To address a labor shortage in the postwar years, South Africa recruited laborers from China and India, who were used to undermine the claims of African workers to better pay and treatment. Afrikaners were allowed to treat blacks as they wanted.

European domination of the economy and politics was consolidated after the war. The interests of the black population would be ignored, and South Africa could be run like Australia or Canada, with linkages to Britain. The railways of South Africa were unified, and a common customs union established. English became the language of instruction in many areas, although Afrikaner nationalism became more intense. Blacks and whites were segregated—native reserves were established for blacks in rural areas, while their counterparts in cities were confined to specific locations.

In 1908, a National Convention met to discuss a constitution for a united South Africa. Approved by the British Parliament in 1909, the constitution provided for a central government and four provinces with limited powers. Only whites could be members of the Union Parliament. The white minority population was given all the power, whereas the blacks, Indians, and Coloureds were denied any major representation in government. The Afrikaans and English languages received equal status. In 1910, the Union of South Africa was established. It was nominally a British dominion, but British influence was not as strong as that of the Afrikaners, who gained political power in the united South Africa.

MINORITY RULE AND BLACK SEGREGATION

The history of South Africa after 1910 revolved around the use and abuse of power by the white minority government to create opportunities for a few at the expense of the majority. In 1910, the population of South Africa comprised 1.2 million whites, 150,000 Indians, 500,000 Coloureds, and more than 4 million Africans. In terms of the privileges and rights of citizenship, only the whites counted. Now firmly in control, white minority governments passed many laws designed to create a racially divided society. The end result was the apartheid system.

Meanwhile, the mining industry brought incredible prosperity, shared in the main by white English-speakers. The Afrikaners remained essentially farmers, but as their prosperity diminished, thousands moved to the cities. As the Afrikaners were members of the white community and represented more than 50 percent of the electorate, their needs were met by the government, but only at the expense of Africans, Indians, and Coloured people.

After 1910, the South African politics and economy were altered in many ways that hurt Africans. As South Africa was a dominion within the British Empire, its leaders and the white minority population enjoyed enormous control over their internal affairs. The Afrikaners continued to promote their own nationalism and resented the English-speakers. The English-speakers sought the means to consolidate their wealth and power. Both undermined the demands of

Africans. The role of blacks in the society was defined in strictly marginal ways. A racialized economy was created—blacks would supply the needed labor force, mainly unskilled, and whites would take the best positions and privileged status. Access by whites to black labor was assured, and the interests of white landowners, miners, and investors were protected.

Many laws were passed to ensure racial segregation. The major ones include the following:

The *Mines and Works Act* (1911) reserved jobs for whites in mines and on railroads.

The *Natives' Land Act* (1913) restricted Africans to just 7 percent of the land of South Africa, in reserves of just 22 million acres.

The *Defence Act* (1920) set up a White Active Citizen Force, with legal rights for its members to defend themselves.

The *Native Affairs Act* (1920) established separate managements and judicial systems for reserves.

The *Natives (Urban Areas) Act* (1923) restricted the access of blacks to white urban places. Blacks were required in the cities only for their labor. Black townships were to be created away from white areas. Pass laws were used to restrict the entry of blacks to the cities.

The *Native Administration Act* (1927) gave the government absolute authority in dealing with the Africans who lived outside the Cape Province. The British governor could appoint and dismiss African chiefs, define land boundaries, and relocate people.

The segregation policies were further consolidated in the 1930s and 1940s. During the Second World War, the government sent 100,000 blacks to serve as military labor in North Africa, in support of the Allied powers. The South African economy expanded with the growth of the manufacturing sector. New gold deposits were also discovered in the 1940s. Thousands of new jobs were created, and over a million blacks left their impoverished farms to come to the cities. Within a short time, the cities were unable to cope with the black influx— wages were low, housing was difficult to find, and many unemployed young people took to crime and prostitution. Thousands took to "squatting," building their own houses with poor materials. An example was the squatter township of Soweto in Johannesburg, founded in 1944.

The Afrikaners gained in power in the 1940s. The black movement to the cities caused alarm among the whites, who feared competition for jobs and racial conflicts. The white-controlled National Party began to advocate an ideology of "white purity" and warned of an impending "black peril" that would diminish white power. So intense was Afrikaner nationalism that the National Party was able to win the election of 1948. A system of apartheid ("separateness") was both the manifesto and the ideology of the Afrikaners, and the new government decided to pass many new laws to ensure this separateness. So successful were the Afrikaners and the National Party in mobilizing whites against blacks in support of apartheid that they retained power in the 1950s and 1960s.

APARTHEID: THEORY AND PRACTICE AFTER 1948

In the view of the National Party, the survival of whites in South Africa was possible only if the races were separated. The party believed that since the population of whites was small—the 1948 figures were 2 million whites and 8 million blacks—the blacks could use their numerical strength to control economic and political power. Thus, the maintenance of white power and permanent white access to housing and jobs was only possible if the blacks were controlled. The apartheid policy would classify all South Africans by race, as "whites" and "nonwhites." The "nonwhites" were subdivided into "Coloured," "Native" (later called "Bantu"), and Indian. The Natives were further split by "tribe" in order to present them as "tribal minorities."

Each tribe was allocated a number of specific rural reserves—so-called "Homelands" or "Bantustans"—comprising only about 13 percent of the entire country. The whites had control of 86 percent of the land. Africans could only legally live in the Bantustans, even if they were born in cities or on white farms and had never even been to the reserves. Africans could leave their reserves for white areas only because they were temporarily employed by whites. Even then, they must carry passes whenever they left their Homelands. The passes indicated their identity, address, ethnic origins, and employer. An up-to-date pass was needed to move into white areas to work; it would expire with the loss of a job and must be renewed every month. The police checked for passes and even conducted "pass raids" in order to frighten blacks. Thousands of arrests were made every year for various "pass offenses," treated as criminal offenses punishable by imprisonment or fine.

Any open opposition to apartheid was labeled "communism," a serious criminal offence. The *Suppression of Communism Act* (1950) empowered the Minister of Justice to "ban" organizations and individuals defined as communist. When banned, a person was prevented from associating with others or even talking with two or more people at the same time. To be accused of promoting a communist organization was to risk imprisonment for up to ten years. The law was designed to silence opposition to the apartheid government. Other notorious laws of this period include the following:

The *Population Registration Act* (1950) and the *Group Areas Act* (1950) both classified South Africans by race and indicated where they could and could not live.

The *Prohibition of Mixed Marriages Act* (1949) and the *Immorality Act* (1950) aimed at maintaining the "purity of the white race" by preventing marriage or sexual intercourse between them and "nonwhites."

The *Abolition of Passes Act* (1952) reformed the pass system by creating a single "reference book" used to award and check passes.

The *Native Resettlement (Western Areas) Act* (1954) sought to regulate "squatter towns," deport blacks from white areas, and destroy so-called unsightly houses around Johannesburg. Many people were forced to move to Soweto.

The *Promotion of Bantu Self-Government Act* (1959) denied political rights to blacks in white areas, thus limiting such rights to their Homelands.

The *Bantu Education Act* (1953) denied blacks the opportunity to obtain the same education as whites. The Bantu Education Department created "black syllabuses" that limited education to what blacks needed in order to work for whites and promoted ethnic differences among the people.

The *Native Labour Settlement of Disputes Act* (1953) made strikes by black workers a criminal offense. The law ensured that workers received low pay or faced unemployment or were deported from white urban areas.

As would be expected, the exploited and oppressed black population reacted to all these laws with protests. Thus, the defining characteristic of Africans during the twentieth century was protest. They were joined by Indians, Coloureds, and pro-black white elements. Eventually, the antiapartheid struggles became international, a major cause that involved people of all races, religions, and ideologies. To start with the early protests, Mohandas Gandhi, later a famous Indian nationalist, lived in South Africa in the 1890s and organized a number of antidiscrimination protests in 1907 and 1914. The South African Indian Congress was established in 1923 to struggle for Indian rights. Although the majority of the Coloureds identified with the whites, they, too, formed associations to demand better treatment.

As was to be expected, the most sustained resistance was provided by the African majority population. Early nationalism was expressed through black media and churches. In 1912, an articulate elite group established the South African Native Congress, whose name was later changed to the African National Congress (ANC), which remains in existence till today. The early leaders of the ANC demanded a political voice and an end to the color bar. Their demands were ignored. A strike by the ANC in Transvaal in 1919 was brutally put down.

Each new segregation law was met by criticisms. The minority government and the majority of the white population were united in their resolve to create a segregated society, using violence to achieve their goals. Many blacks lost their lives, many were wounded, and many went to prison. The *General Laws Amendment Act* (1963) granted the police the power to arrest and detain people, without charge, for three months (extended to six months in 1965). Police brutality, indiscriminate arrests, suppression of political leaders, and characterization of trade union activities as deliberate acts of economic sabotage all consolidated the power of the South African government and its apartheid policy. It appeared in the mid-1960s that apartheid would last forever. This was not to be.

SUGGESTIONS FOR FURTHER READING

Beck, Roger B. *The History of South Africa.* Westport, Conn.: Greenwood Press, 2000. Chapter 8.

Benson, Mary. *The Struggle for a Birthright.* London: IDAF, 1985.

Dubow, Saul. *Racial Segregation and the Origins of Apartheid in South Africa, 1919–1936*. London: Macmillan, 1989.

Falola, Toyin, ed. *Africa*. Vol. 3, *Colonial Africa, 1885–1939*. Durham, N.C.: Carolina Academic Press, 2001.

Lapping, Brian. *Apartheid: A History*. New York: George Braziller, 1989.

Luthuli, Albert J. *Let My People Go: An Autobiography*. New York: McGraw-Hill, 1962.

Shillington, Kevin. *History of Southern Africa*. London: Longman, 1987. Chapter 16.

21

Africa Drawn into the Second World War, 1940–45

British officer: "Away with Hitler! Down with him!"
African man: "What's wrong with Hitler?"
British officer: "He wants to rule the whole world."
African man: "What's wrong with that?"
British officer: "He is German, you see."
African man: "What's wrong with his being German?"
British officer: "You see, it is not good for one tribe to rule another. Each tribe must rule itself. That's only fair. A German must rule Germans, an Italian, Italians, and a Frenchman, French people."[1]

Although Africans were not involved in the politics and crises that led to the Second World War, they were drawn into the war by their colonial masters. The Second World War was a unique event in colonial history, representing a watershed in politics—it helped to instigate a radical political awakening that ultimately led to independence. The African experience during the war years gave nationalism a tremendous boost. Anticolonial sentiment intensified after the war. Mass political parties emerged, led by radical political leaders, and European powers were forced to reform the colonial system and begin a process of transfer of power.

The Second World War began in September 1939, when Nazi Germany attacked Poland. Later, Nazi Germany attacked Belgium, Holland, France, Britain, and the USSR. Fascist Italy teamed up with Germany in June 1940 and completed the invasion of France. Japan joined Germany and Italy, attacking the American fleet at Pearl Harbor in Hawaii and also invading Southeast Asia, creating a short-lived Japanese empire. Germany, Italy, and Japan—the three Axis powers—won most of their battles from 1939 to late 1942. Thereafter, the Allies—Britain, the USSR, the United States, and other smaller partners—began to record successes. Italy fell to the Allies in September 1943, but Germany withstood the Allied attacks till May 1945. The Allies occupied Germany and destroyed the Nazi system. Japan was subdued in August 1945, after atom bombs were dropped on Hiroshima and Nagasaki. Except for the Horn and North Africa, Africa avoided becoming a battlefield in this horrendous conflict.

AFRICA'S CONTRIBUTIONS TO THE WAR

Africa was affected by the Second World War. A few of the battles between the Axis and Allied powers took place in North Africa. As all the European powers (with the exception of Spain and Portugal) were at war, their colonies were inevitably drawn in. The British, French, and Belgian colonies and the Dominion of South Africa joined the Allies, whereas the Italian colonies sided with the Axis. When France fell to the Germans in 1940, and a neutral French state—Vichy—emerged, the African colonies that came under the Vichy government also became neutral. French Equatorial Africa came under the Free French government, as it declared for de Gaulle. In sub-Saharan Africa, there were campaigns to dislodge the Italians from Ethiopia and from British Somaliland.

In both world wars, Europeans drafted thousands of Africans into their armies. For instance, in the Second World War, about 167,000 were recruited from the British colonies in West Africa. These were organized into seven brigades, and all the brigades but one were sent to the battlefield. Almost 280,000 Africans were also conscripted by the British from their East African colonies and from Somalia, Malawi, and Zimbabwe. African soldiers found themselves in Europe, Asia, the Middle East, and some parts of Africa. Many African soldiers were involved in the North African campaigns where they were used in Egypt to resist the Italians and Germans. The Italian and German forces were also driven out of Libya and Tunisia. Africans were part of the British army that successfully attacked the Italians and drove them out of Somalia. They also engaged in bitter wars with the Italians in Ethiopia and Eritrea, where they destroyed the last of the Italian armies in Africa. Thereafter, the Africans were sent to attack the Japanese in Burma.

Not all African soldiers survived the war. To illustrate the losses, of the 80,000 African soldiers in the French army based in France in 1940, almost 20,000 were killed during the German invasion; many were killed in other battles; and others, even when the war was over, were murdered for supporting the Allies. Thousands were thrown into prison camps, where they suffered a great deal and experienced not just deprivations but also racism. Those who served in the British army also experienced casualties. About 2,358 Africans from Tanganyika were lost.

There were other major African contributions as well. When the war extended to North Africa, the Allies had to use airports in West Africa to land their

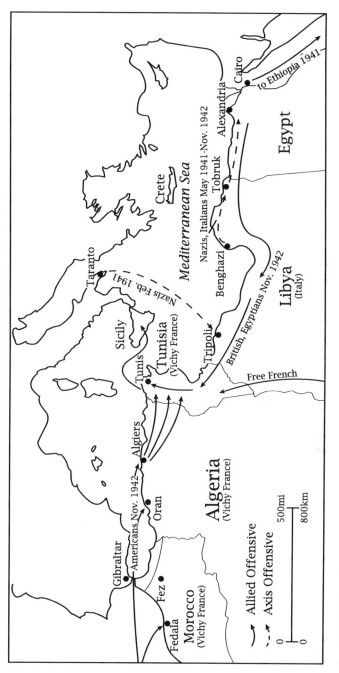

Second World War in North Africa.

airplanes en route to Cairo. West Africa became a major staging post in the funneling of troops and supplies to the eastern war zone. As the use of Mediterranean ports was difficult, the Allies turned to the ports of Lagos, Freetown, Accra, Libreville, Cape Town, and Dar es Salaam. Africans were also called upon to contribute money, with many paying levies and donating part of their wages.

When British Malaya and the Dutch East Indies fell to the Japanese, the Allies turned to Africa to obtain rubber, tin, palm products, and other valuable raw materials. Cocoa and copper were also demanded in greater quantities, thus bringing prosperity to such colonies as the Gold Coast, the Belgian Congo, and Northern Rhodesia.

THE IMPACT OF THE WAR: POLITICS AND NATIONALISM

The war was presented to Africans by the French and the British as being fought for justice, democracy, self-determination, and freedom. The Germans were criticized for their dictatorship and the Japanese for their aggression. This sounded like a contradiction: How could Africans, denied justice and freedom by the Europeans, be asked to fight for justice and freedom against Germany? The contradiction was apparent to many African soldiers and those who stayed at home. Africans had to fight for the same ideals. The war raised the political consciousness of Africans—just as they understood Hitler, Nazi Germany, and the war, they were also able to understand the European powers and what it would take to fight them.

The presentation of the colonial mission as a means to spread civilization was challenged. Here was Europe claiming to civilize others, but it was itself in serious trouble, as its people were killed in the war, its cities were destroyed, and thousands of people languished in death camps. Here was yet another contradiction that was not lost on educated Africans.

By interacting with European soldiers and serving abroad, many Africans broadened their knowledge and vision. A better understanding of Europeans now enabled them to question their long-held belief about white superiority. Like Africans, many Europeans were ordinary and poor. Africans fought side by side with Europeans and realized that all men were vulnerable. Africans saw the Japanese defeat of the Europeans as evidence that non-Europeans were not as powerless as they were often portrayed. And the Europeans defeated the Japanese partly by using African soldiers, a fact not lost on a number of people.

In various ways, the experiences of soldiers aided a greater understanding of the colonial systems. Experiencing a higher standard of living as soldiers, Africans who served in the war tended to expect a continuation of this. When this did not happen, they came to believe that Africans must fight for better conditions or join nationalist forces to demand independence. Many soldiers and anticolonial critics believed that if Nazi domination could be ended by war, the colonial system could be ended in a similar way. Many soldiers acquired valuable skills, including the ability to read and write. Many were to use these skills to demand more freedom for their people.

A document frequently cited during the war was the Atlantic Charter, issued by President Franklin D. Roosevelt of the United States and Winston Churchill of Britain. The Atlantic Charter included a provision stating that after the war independence would be granted to non-self-governing territories. Although Africans expected this to happen, Winston Churchill refused to abide by the provision, saying in 1942 that he would not liquidate the British Empire. Radical Europeans began to question the wisdom of maintaining an African empire, having challenged the ambition of Hitler to create his own empire. Africans regarded the war as one for freedom and believed in the Atlantic Charter. By saying that the Atlantic Charter would not apply to them, Churchill was forcing the African elite to reconsider their strategy of cooperation. For instance, Nnamdi Azikiwe, who would become prominent in Nigerian politics, responded by saying that there could be no "hope for a more prosperous and contented Nigeria under the present colonial status."[2] African Americans joined Africans in demanding a commitment to the Atlantic Charter.

The power of Europe declined with the war. The involvement of the United States was crucial in the victory of the Allied powers. France was defeated by Germany in 1940 and was occupied for four years. It was liberated from Germany in part because of the U.S. involvement. Britain's power and economy were undermined by the war. The balance of power now shifted to the United States, which was also expected to meet possible challenges from the Soviet Union. But the United States had no colonies in Africa and was interested in seeing an end to European rule in Africa in order to gain the opportunity to expand its own trade and political influence there. The changes in the global economy and politics shaped the position of the United States in its attitude toward Africa. Africans also realized that they could use the weakness of Europe to advantage by calling on the United States for help. A number of Asian countries were seeking independence, and the success of India, Burma, and Ceylon (Sri Lanka) gave encouragement to Africans.

The formation of the United Nations Organization (UNO) after the war was also of benefit in the pursuit of anticolonial struggles. The United Nations replaced the discredited League of Nations in 1945, and the two superpowers—the United States and the Soviet Union—were founding members. From its very beginning, the United Nations supported the concept of self-determination—the belief that individual nations should achieve autonomy and the government they desired. Africans read this to mean that the Europeans should leave them alone to establish their own countries and govern themselves. The United Nations took a further step, creating a Decolonization Committee to monitor and report on the transfer of power in areas under colonial rule. The European powers were now asked to render reports on their colonies, putting them in an uncomfortable situation in which they had to clarify their objectives. A number of African politicians and leaders traveled to the UN headquarters in New York to make a case for independence and to mobilize international opinion against colonial rule.

Political changes followed. In the years immediately after the war, the belief among a number of European officers was that Africans should be rewarded for their contributions to victory in the war. Constitutional reforms were undertaken in some places—in French colonies the worst aspects of the administration, notably the use of forced labor and arbitrary arrest and imprisonment, were ended, and French citizenship was granted to the majority of the population. In British colonies, constitutional changes allowed the participation of more Africans in government.

ECONOMIC AND OTHER IMPACTS

African colonies produced more raw materials during the war years in order to meet the demands in Europe created by the pressure of war and to supply goods required by the armies. As the raw materials were required quickly, peasants were called upon to work harder, produce more, and show patriotic concern for the Allied powers. To colonies that supplied valuable raw materials, the war years brought economic prosperity. The war stimulated greater production.

Small-scale industries were established to produce goods that the war prevented Europe from supplying to the colonies and to process some raw materials for export. Thus, import-substituting companies were established, with many later expanding and becoming the core of the pioneer industries in the colonies.

The changes in production affected society. Those who were able to produce and sell or found themselves in wage employment had access to more money. Factory workers and skilled people had access to new business practices and technology. Africans wanted more knowledge, more skills, and better opportunities. Thus, they demanded more reforms, and millions supported new political parties because they expected such parties to bring rapid changes. Trade unions began to proliferate in cities, in mining centers, and among teachers and railway workers. The unions enabled the political parties to reach thousands of people through the workplace and to spread anticolonial literature among those who could read and write. In many cases, trade union leaders also became political leaders, as in the case of Rashid Kawawa of Tanzania and Sekou Toure of Guinea.

African labor was exploited, in programs officially known as "war efforts," to boost production. Labor was conscripted on a large scale to produce a variety of goods in a way that damaged some villages. Farmers in British and Belgian colonies were asked to increase production for export. In some areas, they were organized to produce a list of specific products. In French West Africa, which the British blockaded because a French faction there supported the Nazis, the colonial authorities compelled the farmers to produce goods that had previously been imported. The "war efforts" to increase production forced many people to relocate to the cities, just to escape farmwork or deepening rural poverty. For those who stayed, their family life and farming practices were changed in ways that many did not like or enjoy.

The colonial economic structure established in the prewar years was consolidated during the Second World War. Africans were expected to use their labor in the service of European interests. Farmers and rural areas were useful only to the extent that they could produce, even if family life was undermined and rural society became unstable. An excessive reliance on the production of raw materials consolidated a dependent economy based on exports. Trade enabled a massive transfer of wealth out of the continent.

In East Africa and other areas with large European settler populations, the need to produce to meet the war demands was used by settlers to acquire more land and gain power at the expense of Africans. When the war was over, the tension between the settlers and Africans degenerated into violence.

When the war demands ended, some areas experienced a serious economic downturn. The combined social and economic changes of the war years ultimately weakened the colonial systems and spurred anticolonial movements. Trade union leaders seized the opportunity to energize their members and to organize strikes in some countries. Nationalist politicians exploited the changes of the war years to recruit members for political parties and mobilized a larger number of people for anticolonial protests.

NOTES

1. A modification of a story, originally told by a Zimbabwean, of an attempt to recruit an African into the army in 1940.
2. Nnamdi Azikiwe, *Political Blueprint of Nigeria* (Lagos: Self-published, 1943), p. 72.

SUGGESTIONS FOR FURTHER READING

Falola, Toyin. *Development Planning and Decolonization in Nigeria.* Gainesville: University Press of Florida, 1996.

Falola, Toyin, ed. *Africa.* Vol. 3, *Colonial Africa, 1885–1939.* Durham, N.C.: Carolina Academic Press, 2001.

Hodgkin, T. *Nationalism in Colonial Africa.* London: Muller, 1956.

Olusanya, G.O. *The Second World War and Politics in Nigeria, 1939–1953.* London: Evans, 1973.

22

The End of European Rule, 1951–90

The gaining of independence by African countries was one of the major events in world history during the twentieth century. Independence was gained in three major waves in the course of three decades. The first wave occurred in the 1950s, with the independence of Libya, Morocco, Tunisia, Sudan, Guinea, and Ghana. The second wave in the 1960s saw thirty-one countries obtaining independence. The third wave came in the 1970s, when the five Lusophone countries (Angola, Mozambique, Guinea-Bissau, Cape Verde, and São Tomé and Príncipe) finally became free. Liberia had been independent since 1847, Egypt since 1922, and Ethiopia all through its history except for the short period of imperial control by Italy from 1935 to 1941. After the third major wave, Zimbabwe became free in 1980 and Namibia in 1990.

Independence was the culmination of long struggles by Africans against colonial domination. Africans were joined by blacks in the United States and other parts of the world in criticizing the European powers. It became increasingly difficult to justify colonial rule, while Europe began to think of other means to retain economic control without direct colonial rule.

FOUNDATIONS OF NATIONALISM

European officers in Africa and pro-colonial writers often believed that Africans had accepted European rule without a fight and were happy with all the benefits that came with it. In reality, Africans resisted the imposition of colonial rule. Leaders such as Samori Toure resorted to warfare, whereas some, such as Jaja of Opobo, opted for diplomatic approaches (see Chapter 18).

When colonial rule had become established, protests changed to demands for reforms and later on to demands for the termination of European rule. African nationalism was strengthened by the experience of European domination. Until the 1930s, the attacks on the colonial systems appeared mild. The initial aims of nationalism in Africa were to seek accommodation with the colonial system, make it beneficial to Africans, minimize exploitation and oppression, and deal with assumptions of racial inferiority. The protests by Africans were aimed at ending the use of forced labor, the payment of excessive taxes, land acquisition by European settlers and companies, and racial discrimination. Africans wanted good prices for their agricultural products and more hospitals, schools, and other facilities.

If the traditional political class of kings, chiefs, and warriors led the wars against the imposition of colonial rule, it fell to the new educated elite—products of Western schools—to lead the anticolonial protests. Many of them worked in the very system that they criticized. They used European languages to attack European officers. Many lived in the cities, where they interacted with one another.

Various associations were formed to give expression to nationalist aspirations. These associations included those formed by students (such as the West African Students Union in Britain), religious leaders, alumni of particular schools, people from the same ethnic or regional areas, and people united by occupations. Thus, there were political associations, trade unions, civil servants' clubs, and ethnic clubs.

These associations and leaders adopted a variety of tactics to express themselves: petitions to colonial officers in Africa and abroad, strikes, boycotts, and delegations to the government. They used the media, establishing newspapers where they openly attacked the colonial governments.

PAN-AFRICANISM

The call to end European domination was heard in the Pan-African congresses of the first half of the twentieth century. Pan-Africanism was a movement to unite black people in Africa and other parts of the world to enable them to fight against all forms of domination and exploitation and to use their united strength to develop their economy and politics. Pan-Africanists in the United States during the nineteenth century promoted schemes of black emigration to Africa. In the twentieth century, they continued to advocate emigration, while some organizations sponsored evangelical missions to Africa to convert people to Christianity. Marcus Garvey, a Jamaican, has become one of the heroes of Pan-Africanism. In 1914, he established the Universal Negro Improvement Association and African Communities League (UNIA-ACL) to improve the conditions of black people. Within a short time, Garvey's movement attracted a membership of about 6 million people. Garvey believed in the emigration of black people to

Africa, the establishment of a united government in Africa, and the promotion of entrepreneurship.

Pan-Africanists were quick to criticize the imposition of colonial rule and to demand an end to it. They convened many conferences to criticize the European control of Africa. W.E.B. Du Bois, a famous African American intellectual and political leader, convened many of the Pan-Africanist meetings meant to promote solidarity and liberate black people. In these meetings, African anticolonial leaders had the opportunity to join other blacks in voicing their opinions and considering strategies of gaining power. The resolutions were consistent in their attacks against imperialism, demanding an end to European rule, protecting the independence of Liberia and Ethiopia, and preserving ancient traditions and cultures.

THE ETHIOPIAN CRISIS, 1935–41

In spite of the activities of the nationalists, Europeans maintained strong control in the first thirty years of the twentieth century. Stronger opposition to European rule began in the mid-1930s, instigated by the Ethiopian crisis and then by the Second World War (see Chapter 21). In 1935, Italy, under the fascist government of Mussolini, attacked Ethiopia. This was the second war between Italy and Ethiopia. In the 1890s, Italy had attempted to establish control of Ethiopia, but without success. King Menelik II of Ethiopia was able to withstand the military attack, which ended at the Battle of Adowa in 1896. Ethiopia won and was thereafter a free country until Italy decided on a second attempt in the 1930s. Using the opportunity caused by political troubles in Europe, Italy launched an attack in 1935. Italy ignored the fact that Ethiopia was a member of the League of Nations and an independent country. To appease Italy and avoid a conflict in Europe, other European nations decided not to defend the sovereignty of Ethiopia.

This incident radicalized the nationalist movement in Africa. Other African countries had looked upon Ethiopia as a source of hope. Its long history and culture were impressive. Its independence was used to prove the ability of Africans to conduct their own affairs. In the attack on Ethiopia, the message was sent that colonial rule would last forever. It was clear that the European countries would sacrifice an African country in the pursuit of their own interests. African nationalists and Pan-Africanists everywhere were now united in their condemnation of colonialism and their resolve to seek all possible means to end it. Ethiopian support groups were established in many countries to raise funds, buy food and medicine, engage in anti-Italian propaganda, pressure the League of Nations, and campaign for a boycott of Italian goods. In addition, prayer sessions were held, while violent demonstrations occurred in a number of places.

THE RADICAL PHASE

The Second World War further radicalized Africans who now began to demand nothing less than an end to European rule. Nationalists and freedom fighters became bolder than ever before. New, better-organized political parties were created, such as the Convention People's Party established in Ghana in 1949 and the National Council for Nigeria and the Cameroons created in Nigeria in 1944. In Francophone Africa, political activities intensified, and vigorous demands led to the abolition of forced labor and some discriminatory practices in 1949. Demonstrations, mass strikes, boycotts, and armed conflicts became part of the radical strategies used to bring down European rule.

A number of internal and external developments contributed to the success of the struggles for independence. Internal to Africa were the roles of politicians, labor, and the general populace. Politicians seeking an end to European rule and power resorted to the formation of political parties. The new political parties tried to involve as many people as possible. The strategy was to open party membership to all in order to mobilize millions of people in a country against the colonial overlord. Workers in both public and private agencies established trade union organizations that demanded not only improved working conditions but also political freedom. Students in higher institutions, regarding themselves as future leaders, joined in the political process by playing active roles in nationalist struggles. Economic problems such as low prices for products, control of the import-export sector by foreign companies, and lack of industries all fueled demands for rapid economic development. Africans in the civil service wanted promotion, and many also wanted the power to be able to determine their own fate and the fate of their countries. The spread of Western education had also produced a sizable number of literate and articulate people. Those who received higher education abroad were further radicalized by the experience of racism abroad. Knowledge and skills originally monopolized by the colonizers were now available to the colonized. The media were used to attack the Europeans. As the cities grew, newspapers could circulate among a large number of literate people who also had access to a European language with which to communicate with one another.

Externally, Pan-Africanists continued to demand an end to European rule in Africa. Perhaps the most notable Pan-Africanist Congress was held in 1945 in Manchester, England. Africans attended in large numbers, trade unions were represented, and a socialist ideology was espoused as the best for Africa. The resolutions were radical, including support for the use of force to dislodge Europeans. The Manchester Congress condemned the continuation of European rule in Africa, demanded freedom for the continent, and believed that rapid economic development would accompany the end of colonial rule. Among the radical generation of Africans who attended the conference was Kwame Nkrumah, who later became the first president of Ghana.

World opinion was changing, becoming far more critical of the colonial powers than in the era before the Second World War. Even in Europe, there were a growing number of anticolonialists. The Labour Party, which came to power in Britain at the end of the Second World War, was interested in colonial disengagement.

Yet another external factor was the role of the independence struggles in India, a British colony. From early in the twentieth century, the Indian nationalists had engaged in anticolonial struggles. Through peaceful means, India was able to resist British rule. Mohandas Gandhi promoted a concept of peaceful civil disobedience. India's independence in 1947 served as an example for African countries to follow, and a number of African politicians advocated aspects of Gandhi's civil disobedience.

CASE STUDIES

To illustrate some of the major points mentioned above, a few examples of events in some areas are provided.

West Africa: Ghana and Nigeria

The educated elite were at the forefront of nationalist demands. A number of political associations had emerged in the early years of colonial rule. The earliest was the Aborigines' Rights Protection Society, established in 1897 in Ghana, which successfully protested against government confiscation of unused land. Another protest party, the People's Union, was formed in Lagos in 1908 to oppose the imposition of a water rate. The most broad-based party emerged in 1919; this was the National Council of British West Africa (NCBWA), which held its first congress in Ghana in 1920. The NCBWA demanded the creation of a university, the inclusion of more Africans in the Legislative Councils, and the appointment of senior Africans into the civil service. In Nigeria, Herbert Macaulay and his associates established the first major political party, the Nigerian National Democratic Party. These early parties were dominated by members of the educated elite who focused on reforms. They did not seek the abolition of colonialism.

Events after the Second World War were rapid, marked by constitutional changes and the transfer of power. Ghana was the first West African country to become free. In the years immediately after the war, the strategy of the nationalists was confrontational. In 1947, the United Gold Coast Convention was established by J.B. Danquah and others. A year later, the party invited Kwame Nkrumah to serve as an organizer. Anticolonial riots broke out in 1948, leading to the arrest and imprisonment of Nkrumah and others. The British made a number of constitutional amendments designed to involve more Africans in administration and politics. Nkrumah established his own party, the Convention People's Party (CPP), organized a series of "Positive Action Campaigns," and became a popular leader. His party won the 1951 election, and Nkrumah governed in cooperation with the British. Subsequent elections in 1954 and 1956 consolidated the CPP's position. Ghana became independent in 1957, and Nkrumah used his new power to advance the cause of Pan-Africanism and to call for the complete liberation of the continent.

In Nigeria, the Nigerian Youth Movement was established in 1934, and it became the country's first major national party. It collapsed in 1941. A more modern party emerged in 1944; this was the National Council of Nigeria and the Cameroons (NCNC), led by Nnamdi Azikiwe. Nigeria attained independence through a series of constitutional reforms. The first was the Richards Constitution introduced in 1946, which gave Nigerians more say in the central government and introduced three regional governments. Radical Nigerian nationalists criticized the constitution for offering little by way of a transfer of power.

A constitutional revision took place in 1951, with the introduction of the Macpherson Constitution. It retained the three regions, but the North had as much representation as the other regions combined. Two years earlier, northern politicians had established a regional party, the Northern Peoples Congress, which acquired tremendous influence. In 1951 the Yoruba in the southwest established the Action Group, while the NCNC controlled the Eastern Region. Thus, the Nigerian political parties acquired a regional orientation that shaped the nature of political competition and ultimately led to a civil war in the mid-1960s. In yet another constitutional revision in 1954, expressed in the Lyttelton Constitution, Nigeria became a federation. In 1957, the Eastern and Western Regions attained internal self-government, followed by the North in 1959. Nigeria became independent in 1960.

West Africa: French-Speaking Countries

The expression of nationalism before 1939 was mainly localized in the Four Communes of Senegal—Gorée, Rufisque, St. Louis, and Dakar. In other French territories, Africans could be sent to prison without trial, and they were prohibited from forming or joining political parties. The Four Communes were allowed to elect a deputy to represent them in Paris. In 1914, they chose Blaise Diagne to represent them. At first, he fought for the right of Africans to become French citizens. As he became active in recruiting Africans to serve in the French army during the First World War, he became more loyal to the colonial government. Educated Africans sought the privileges of assimilation.

Other early forms of nationalist expression were similar to those in other parts of the continent. Some people chose to work as teachers, regarding education as a tool of liberation. There were riots, as in Porto Novo in 1923 and Upper Volta in 1934. Although strikes were illegal, a few did occur among railway workers. Religious leaders turned to Islam and Christianity to express protest.

Africans had contributed to the liberation of the French during the Second World War, and many began to make radical statements regarding equality and freedom. Some changes followed after 1946, notably the end of the use of forced labor and the extension of the policy of assimilation (the spread of French culture and citizenship) in the colonies. The most influential party was the Rassemblement Démocratique Africain (RDA) led by Félix Houphouët-Boigny. Other notable politicians were Lamine Guèye and Léopold Senghor. The nationalists were torn between the creation of a federation of French colonies and decentralization. In the end, the countries attained independence as separate nations.

In 1956, the French colonies acquired internal self-government, except that they did not control foreign policy, defense, and economic development. This was a sort of halfway house on the way to full independence. General Charles de Gaulle came to power in France in 1958 and sought the means to grant independence to African countries while at the same time retaining French influence. He proposed the independence of African colonies within a French Community. In a 1958 referendum, Africans were to choose whether they wanted to become independent or become members of a French Union. All the colonies except Guinea voted to stay in the French Union. Thus, Guinea became independent in 1958 and was immediately ostracized by France. However, the mood changed thereafter, and demands for independence by the other countries became vigorous. By 1960, most had become independent, although France continued for a long time to retain close ties with its former colonies and influence over them.

Central Africa: The Belgian Congo

Although rapid changes were taking place in West Africa in the 1950s, the Belgian authorities in the economically rich Congo did not think of granting it independence. The first minor concession did not come until 1957 when municipal government was reformed to allow for the election of councilors and mayors. The first political parties emerged to contest city elections. Rising African politicians began to reject the evolutionary policy of the Belgian government and opted for total independence. In January 1959, riots broke out in the capital city of Léopoldville, resulting in many people being killed or injured.

The Belgian authorities promised that independence would be granted very soon. New political parties emerged, and the unprepared Africans began to think about the transfer of power at very short notice. The Congo became independent in 1960, only three years after the first political change. Unlike West Africa, it had only a small number of educated people, and only a handful of Africans had been exposed to important aspects of the bureaucracy. In a country as large as Europe and containing diverse ethnic groups divided by colonial policies, the challenge of building a national party and understanding the management of government was enormous. The country immediately degenerated into anarchy from which it is yet to fully recover.

North Africa: Morocco

The independence of Morocco revolved around the activities of the Moroccan League, the Istiqlal Party, and Sultan Mohammed V in negotiating and fighting for freedom from the French. A Moroccan nationalist elite emerged in the 1920s and founded political movements. In 1926, the Moroccan League (ML) was established to work for freedom. In December 1943, the ML and other smaller groups became the Istiqlal Party (IP), which cooperated with the sultan—the king of Morocco—to work for independence. Sultan Mohammed V, who came

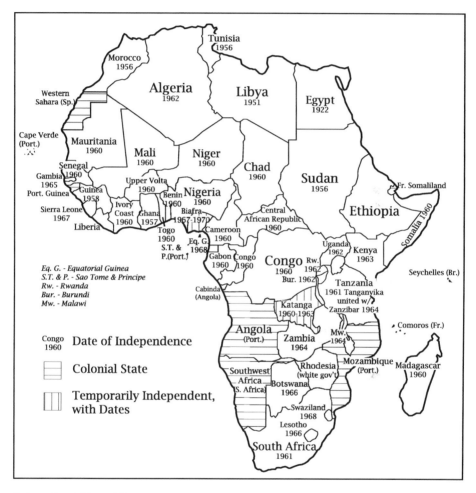

Independent Africa, 1968.

to the throne in 1927, was cautious enough to support the IP and the French at the same time.

Mohammed V continued to promote Islam and indigenous culture without alienating the French. While recognizing the need for Western education, he believed that this should not be at the expense of Islamic education. He supported the Free French and de Gaulle during the Second World War and was disappointed with the limited political concessions that followed.

The friendly relations between the sultan and the French were ruined between 1947 and 1952 when the French attempted to discredit the king for supporting the nationalists. The sultan refused to denounce members of the IP, punish those opposed to the French, or accept the candidates sponsored by the French for important local positions. In 1952, the sultan demanded that he be allowed to form his own government, establish a parliament for Morocco, and end martial law.

The French decided to depose the sultan in 1953 and to replace him with a puppet ruler. The decision was met with widespread protests both in the cities and in the countryside. The Moroccans now believed in the use of violence to win their independence. With the experience of violence in Indochina and Algeria in their minds, the French decided to compromise. Mohammed V was allowed to return home, independence was granted, the IP was allowed to form a government, and Morocco became free in March 1956.

CONCLUSION

When it was all over, Africa's map remained unchanged except in a few areas—Cameroon (the British and French Cameroons became one country), Tanzania (Zanzibar and Tanganyika were merged), Ethiopia (Eritrea was originally integrated with it in 1962 but later became independent), and Morocco (which occupied the Spanish Sahara). Some names of countries or cities were changed—the Gold Coast became Ghana, and Bathurst became Banjul. Africans now controlled the states the Europeans had created, not the indigenous nations the Europeans had overthrown. Africans now assumed control of politics and governmental agencies. They inherited the institutions and structures created by the Europeans. The challenge of independence is to manage the new states.

SUGGESTIONS FOR FURTHER READING

Afigbo, A.E., et al. *The Making of Modern Africa.* Vol. 2, *The Twentieth Century.* London: Longman, 1985.

Davidson, Basil. *Let Freedom Come: Africa in Modern History.* Boston: Little, Brown, 1978.

Falola, Toyin, ed. *Africa.* Vol. 3, *Colonial Africa, 1885–1939.* Durham, N.C.: Carolina Academic Press, 2002.

Falola, Toyin, ed. *Africa.* Vol. 4, *The End of Colonial Rule: Nationalism and Decolonization.* Durham, N.C.: Carolina Academic Press, 2002.

Hargraves, John. *Decolonization in Africa.* London: Longman, 1988.

23

Violence to Gain National Liberation, 1952–62

Where the European powers were unwilling to leave or where large numbers of European settlers rejected the idea of self-determination and independence, Africans resorted to violence to attain their goals. Most colonies attained independence through peaceful means (see Chapter 22), but there were notable exceptions: Kenya and Algeria (discussed in this Chapter), South Africa (see Chapter 20), and the Portuguese colonies (see Chapter 29). The use of violence to gain freedom was a key event in the modern history of Africa. The violence in Algeria also provided much evidence to be analyzed in the scholarship of Frantz Fanon, who became one of the foremost theoreticians of decolonization and colonial legacies.

NATIONALIST POLITICS IN KENYA

Between about 1952 and 1958, the Mau Mau uprising took place in Kenya, the participants aiming to regain their lost land and freedom. The Mau Mau forced the British to introduce reforms and changes that ultimately led to Kenya's independence. As in other parts of the continent, the background to this event was colonial rule and African resistance.

Nationalist politics in Kenya was more intense than in most other parts of East Africa. As early as the 1920s, the Kikuyu Central Association (KCA) had been active in politics, and in later years it received support from other nationalist organizations. Grievances against the British government were also expressed by educational and religious associations, and the membership of the KCA continued to grow.

Land shortage was the cause of anger among many Kenyans. In some areas, the land was inadequate for an expanding population. In some other cases, soil erosion in densely populated areas diminished the amount of fertile land. Overcropping and cattle herding also damaged land and destroyed pastures. The large number of European settlers requiring access to land created more competition. From the 1930s onward, the European settlers began to complicate the land crisis by displacing Africans from their ancestral land, turning away Africans from rented farms, and regarding Kenya as a permanent home. Rather than use Africans as tenant farmers, the settlers wanted Africans to work as laborers.

Kenyans who had looked to the colonial authorities for help and salvation were greatly disappointed. The government was careful not to alienate European settlers or reduce crop and livestock production. An official commission in the 1930s demarcated the boundaries between the land belonging to the settlers and the land belonging to the Kenyans, thus further antagonizing Kenyans who regarded the settlers' land as theirs. The efforts by the government to promote the cattle industry created additional problems. By destroying some herds, the government alienated many Kenyan farmers who protested in the 1930s and 1940s and organized a number of riots. Policies of soil conservation also created problems. By 1945, the atmosphere had become tense; many demobilized soldiers had no jobs, local entrepreneurs complained of limited access to capital, and farmers were unhappy with the European settlers who had taken their land.

Jomo Kenyatta emerged on the scene in 1946 to play a leadership role that would unite many anticolonial associations. He was an educated man, with connections to local traditions and Kikuyu customs. In the 1920s, he served as the general secretary of the KCA, as well as the editor of its newspaper. He traveled to Britain and Russia to explain the grievances of his people, and he wrote *Facing Mount Kenya*, a book that popularized the culture of his Kikuyu people. In 1947, he was appointed the president of the Kenya African Union (KAU), and he began to mobilize various segments of the population for nationalist struggles. What would energize the population was the Mau Mau rising.

THE MAU MAU REBELLION

The Mau Mau was independent of the KAU and was organized in secret. Members of the Mau Mau had to swear an oath to support the organization and its members and fight till independence was attained. The Mau Mau engaged in underground activities directed at paralyzing the economy and frightening the European settlers. The Mau Mau was regarded by the government as dangerous, and it was proscribed in 1951. By October 1952, the Mau Mau's activities were causing so much havoc that the government had to declare a state of emergency. British troops were mobilized to look for members of the Mau Mau, arrest its leaders, and destroy the organization.

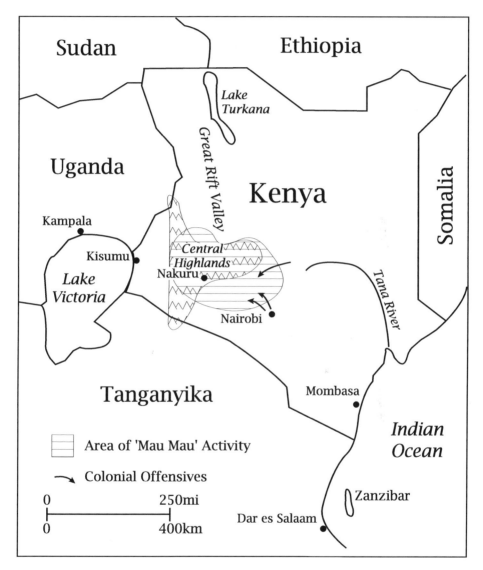

The Mau Mau in Kenya.

The Mau Mau grew into a very powerful organization among the Kikuyu. Its members believed in the use of violence to attain their objectives. Thousands of people lost their lives, some in retaliation for helping the government to destroy the Mau Mau. The organization received widespread support among the people, especially the poor.

The Mau Mau created many war camps in the forest and mountains where it was difficult for government forces to find them. Sympathizers in the villages and cities sent food, arms, and ammunition. In the capital city, Nairobi, a number of small local arms factories manufactured weapons to supply the Mau Mau, while some people even stole guns from security forces to give to the protesters.

The Mau Mau were not easily defeated or cowed as the government had expected. Many people joined the organization, swearing the oath of violence and liberation. When the government closed the independent African schools, many more youths were drawn to the Mau Mau. Unemployed city dwellers, including criminals, went to the bush to join the Mau Mau, some among them motivated by the sheer adventure of underground warfare. The government became more vengeful, using armored vehicles and artillery to destroy and kill. War camps in the mountains were bombed. Villages on the way to the camps were relocated, just to ensure that food and arms supply lines to the Mau Mau were cut off. While the government forces lost about 500 men, they were able to kill almost 8,000 Mau Mau.

In spite of the heavy-handed approach of the government, the Mau Mau kept to one strategy: defensive battles. They attacked only to obtain arms, they spared many settler farms, and only thirty European civilians were killed. The mobilization of a large number of people was an achievement. The oath-swearing ceremonies that rejected colonial domination provided psychological liberation. It took the powerful government forces three years to dislodge most of the Mau Mau from the mountains, but guerrilla warfare continued till 1960, when the state of emergency was lifted.

THE IMPACT OF THE MAU MAU

The Mau Mau struggles brought independence closer. Kenyans had discovered the power of protest. The Mau Mau revealed the vulnerability of the European settlers, who had been planning never to leave Kenya. They were forced to depend on the government to protect their land and privileges. The use of British troops was costly for the government. The anti–Mau Mau campaigns cost almost £50 million at a time when the British economy was still recovering from the devastation caused by the Second World War. The British were forced to concentrate their troops in a single area for a long time, and they could not risk an uprising in another African country. A political approach of negotiation with African nationalists became the preferred option.

The Mau Mau struggles divided Kenyan society. The colonial authorities arrested about 200 Kenyan political leaders, including Kenyatta, who was accused of collaborating with the Mau Mau and then tried and imprisoned. Political parties were banned, and political activities were paralyzed from 1953 to 1955.

The colonial government announced a multiracial constitution that did not give political dominance to any one group. The European settlers were warned by the government to abandon their idea of imposing their control on Kenya. The settlers were divided between a faction that wanted some power given to Africans and a faction that did not.

The Africans, too, were divided. Those associated with the Mau Mau were removed from power, while Kenyans who helped the colonial government were rewarded with promotion. The Kikuyu ethnic group was isolated as punishment for causing the Mau Mau rebellion, a deliberate way of creating ethnic antagonism, and efforts were made to limit the Kikuyu's participation in politics and their rise to senior positions in the army, police, and civil service.

Despite the divisions, Kenyan political leaders recognized the need to unite and demand independence. The Kenya Federation of Labour organized strikes and demanded improvements in living standards. Many Kenyans called for the release of Kenyatta from prison. By the time he was freed in August 1961, he had become a national hero.

Kenya moved rapidly to independence in the early 1960s. The Kenya African National Union (KANU) was established in 1960 as a successor to the KAU. The settlers began to send their assets out of Kenya, realizing that Africans would come to power. Kenyatta was able to bring many rival political associations together and to establish a coalition of two major political parties. In the general election of May 1963, KANU won, and Kenyatta became the country's first prime minister. Ministerial appointments were shared, and the remnants of the Mau Mau in the mountains were invited to accept peace. By the end of 1963, Kenya had become independent of British rule.

ALGERIA: BACKGROUND TO VIOLENCE

Morocco in North Africa (see Chapter 22) won its independence through negotiations. In Algeria, however, a prolonged guerrilla war was fought against the French from 1952 to 1962. In Morocco, the French relied on the sultan and other traditional rulers to govern. Once the traditional rulers and educated nationalists became united, it was difficult for the French to halt the progress toward independence. In the case of Algeria, the power of the traditional rulers had been destroyed by a violent conquest and the presence of large numbers of European settlers (known as the *colons*). For nationalism to be effective in Algeria, the leaders had to mobilize the people against the French colonial authorities and the *colons*.

In 1954, the liberal French prime minister, Pierre Mendès-France, declared that "Algeria is France," a statement intended to mean that Algerian independence was out of the question. France regarded Algeria as an integral part of itself. The *colons* maintained strong family and friendship ties with France. The close proximity between Algeria and France also meant that the *colons* and the

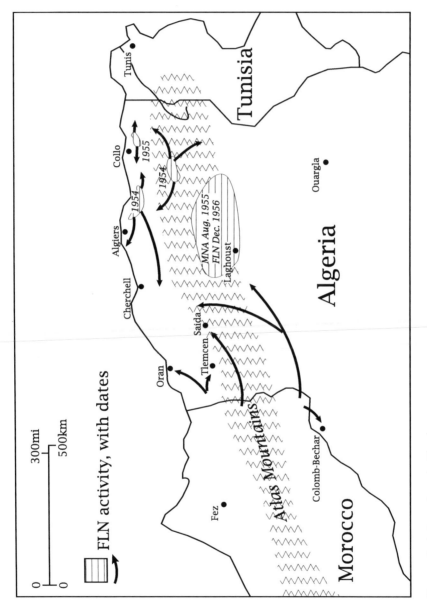

The war for independence in Algeria.

French people living in France could travel with ease and maintain their relationships. The struggle for independence took place against the background of France's reluctance to relinquish control.

The French had attempted to delay the growth of Algerian nationalism by a policy of gradual reforms and the extension of French citizenship to a number of people. About 300,000 Algerians assisted the French during the First World War as soldiers and workers. After the war, minor reforms were introduced, notably the abolition of taxes on Arabs, the extension of French citizenship to many Muslims, and greater representation of Muslims in local assemblies. The Algerians who wanted to enjoy the privileges of French citizenship—notably the Westernized elite—tended to want reforms that would allow more people to become assimilated. Known as the "yes-men," they were large landowners, educated in French, and serving in the local assemblies. The French believed that promoting the interests of assimilated Africans would prevent them from seeking total independence.

A number of radical Algerian nationalists began to emerge after 1914, and they called for more changes or even independence. An early figure was Amir Khalid, who established the Federation of Elected Muslim Officials but was deported in 1924. By the 1940s, many were beginning to doubt the need for a policy of assimilation. Instead, they demanded a new constitution, land reform, equal political rights with the *colons* and other French citizens, the right to form trade unions and political parties, the use of Arabic as the official language, freedom of the press, and a policy of free, compulsory education.

Realizing the popularity of these demands, the French attempted some reforms in March 1944. An ordinance allowed Muslims to vote, while they could become French citizens without renouncing their religion. The *indigénat*, a system of arbitrary arrest and summary trial, was ended. In a new assembly to be established, half of its members would be appointed by Muslims and the other half by the *colons* and assimilated Algerians.

The *colons* were unhappy with the changes. Shortly before they came into effect, violence broke out in 1945. In an unorganized uprising, about one hundred *colons* lost their lives. The French army retaliated, killing almost 20,000 Algerians. Some Algerian leaders were arrested, many fled into exile, and others went underground. A secret movement, the Special Organization (OS), was established by Algerian nationalists. This organization procured arms and ammunition and prepared for war.

THE ALGERIAN WAR, 1954–62

The war broke out in November 1954, and it became Africa's bloodiest war of independence since the beginning of the anticolonial struggles. By the time it was over, 2 million people had suffered relocation, over 250,000 Algerians had lost their lives, and over 250,000 Algerians had become refugees.

The war divided the country. The *colons*, numbering almost a million, did not want to leave Algeria and were very bitter toward the Muslims. The war acquired a racist dimension, with the *colons* displaying arrogance and a superiority complex. While many nationalists supported the war, a small number remained aloof.

The Algerians were able to gather about 20,000 guerrilla fighters to face a French army of a million people bent on destroying them. The French army was brutal and destructive. The leaders of the Algerian nationalist army were former soldiers trained by the French. They were not well educated and were of peasant backgrounds. The majority of their followers were peasants. Unlike the earlier generation of Algerian nationalists, those of the 1950s were not impressed by France, whose glory they did not see. Rather, they were aware of the politics of division in France and France's failure to withstand the military might of Germany in the early 1940s. They were committed to the independence of Algeria, and they believed that war could bring this about. Although they have been characterized as Islamic fundamentalists, they did not see themselves as such. They identified with Muslim concerns and respected Islamic scholars (*ulema*), but they did not present the war as a religious one.

Notable among the Algerian leaders was Ahmed Ben Bella, who later became the first president of Algeria. He had served in the French army during the Second World War and received a decoration for bravery. He returned to Algeria in 1946 and won election to a municipal council. His nationalist concerns led to problems with the French authorities, and he was driven underground as a member of the OS. In 1949, he fled to Egypt when the OS was thrown into disorder by the police and its leaders hunted down. In the early 1950s, Gamal Abdel Nasser, an Egyptian officer, seized power in Egypt. Nasser gave immediate support to the Algerian exiles who established the Revolutionary Committee for Unity and Action (later called the Front de Libération Nationale [FLN; National Liberation Front]). Support also came from Morocco, Tunisia, and the Arab League.

A number of countries trained Algerian soldiers, notably Egypt, Morocco, Tunisia, Yugoslavia, and East Germany. The FLN was well organized, and in 1958 it established an Algerian provisional government in exile. It also became a socialist party. The FLN leaders regarded the war as a revolution—they were interested not merely in acquiring power but also in creating social, cultural, and economic changes that would redistribute land and empower the masses. In Algeria, the FLN was able to call for a boycott of tobacco and alcohol, to deny the government revenue from taxes. Although the FLN was overwhelmed by French equipment and soldiers, the tactics it employed caused great losses to the French in both men and resources. Bombs were planted in public places, schools were damaged, and *colon* farms were raided and destroyed.

The war had a significant political impact. The French parliamentary government was discredited. The army and the *colons* organized to overthrow the Fourth Republic in May 1958, and General de Gaulle came to power. The *colons* had hoped that de Gaulle would support them in creating an "Algérie Française," but he was to disappoint them. The emergence of de Gaulle as the leader of the

Fifth Republic eventually led to the end of the violence. In May 1958, de Gaulle made known his plan to accelerate political changes in Algeria. In the following year, he promised that Algeria would have political self-determination and made three competing offers: integration with France, diluted independence with cooperation with France, or complete independence. Only full independence would satisfy the FLN. The *colons* wanted no such thing. In 1960, the *colons* collaborated with a number of French generals in an attempt to overthrow de Gaulle, and they established the Secret Army Organization (OAS). Enjoying enormous prestige at home, de Gaulle ignored the *colons* and their armed opposition.

In December 1960, de Gaulle visited Algeria and realized that the FLN represented the majority of the Algerian people and was well organized for guerrilla warfare and opposition to the government. In 1961, de Gaulle began a dialogue with the Algerian provisional government, a move that angered the *colons* and the OAS. A cease-fire agreement was signed in March 1962. A referendum on Algerian independence was held in France in April, with 90 percent of the population voting in favor of independence. In Algeria itself, almost 6 million voters wanted independence, as against only 16,531 who did not. Algeria became independent on 3 July 1962, ending a long period of bitter struggles.

FRANZT FANON AND THE ALGERIAN REVOLUTION

Franzt Fanon was a notable scholar who publicized the Algerian revolution and wrote influential books on power, racism, and the African educated elite. His writings brought international attention to the atrocities of the French army in Algeria.

Fanon was born in Martinique, in the West Indies, in 1925. He went to school in the West Indies and France and served in the French army during the Second World War. He later took degrees in psychiatry and medicine and was an activist for black causes while in college at Lyons. In 1953, he published his first book, *Black Skin, White Masks*, about race relations in Martinique. In 1953, he became the head of the psychiatric department in an Algerian hospital. He witnessed the Algerian War of Independence and decided to support the Algerians' cause with enthusiasm. He resigned his position in 1956 and became the editor of the FLN's newspaper, *El Moudjahid*, based in Tunis. A mine injured him at the Algerian-Moroccan frontier, but he continued to write. In 1959, he published his second book, *A Dying Colonialism*, about the Algerian revolution. In 1960, the Algerian government in exile appointed Fanon as its ambassador to Ghana. A year later, he was diagnosed with leukemia, just at the time when his intellectual fame reached its peak with the publication of a bestseller, *The Wretched of the Earth*. He died at the age of thirty-six, and his last book, *The African Revolution*, was published posthumously in 1964.

Since the 1950s, Fanon's works have attracted considerable international attention. He combines knowledge from medicine, psychiatry, and personal observations of war to reflect on race, colonialism, and elitism. From his observations of colonial society in Martinique, he shows in *Black Skin, White Masks* how blacks have been made to feel inferior to whites and even guilty for being blacks. From his medical training and experiences, he shows how colonialism generated a psychology of alienation, to the extent that colonial subjects are robbed of their humanity. To regain this humanity and connection to society, Fanon argues that they must liberate themselves from their masters. In *A Dying Colonialism* he praises the wars in Algeria as a way to overcome alienation and create the opportunities to build a new society. He calls on all societies under colonial rule to struggle for independence if they want to become human. *The Wretched of the Earth* became the bible of the liberation movement and a powerful statement on the need to resort to a socialist ideology to construct a better future. Fanon anticipated the postcolonial crises in Africa. He warned that Africans who easily inherited power from Europeans would abuse the opportunity, oppress the poor, and look after their own interests only. He was opposed to authoritarianism, corruption, and excesses.

SUGGESTIONS FOR FURTHER READING

Falola, Toyin, ed. *Africa.* Vol. 3, *Colonial Africa, 1885–1939.* Durham, N.C.: Carolina Academic Press, 2002.

Falola, Toyin, ed. *Africa.* Vol. 4, *The End of Colonial Rule: Nationalism and Decolonization.* Durham, N.C.: Carolina Academic Press, 2002.

Fanon, Frantz. *The Wretched of the Earth.* Paris: Présence Africaine, 1963.

Kinyatti, Maina Wa. *Thunder from the Mountains: Mau Mau Patriotic Songs.* London: Zed, 1980.

Mboya, Tom. *Freedom and After.* London: Andre Deutsch, 1963.

Quandt, William B. *Revolution and Political Leadership: Algeria, 1954–1968.* Cambridge, Mass.: MIT Press, 1969.

Ruedy, John. *Modern Algeria: The Origins and Development of a Nation.* Bloomington: Indiana University Press, 1992.

Suret-Canale, Jean. *French Colonialism in Tropical Africa 1900–1945.* London: Hurst, 1971.

24

Confrontation with the Gains and Pains of Independence, 1958–70

A rapid shift from the euphoria of independence to the pains of freedom marks the history of Africa in the mid-twentieth century. The change from an optimistic mood to a cautious one was so rapid that many people even began to question whether the independence struggles were worth all the trouble. To illustrate this point: Kwame Nkrumah was in power in Ghana in 1957, but by 1966 he had been driven into exile in Guinea, where he later died. Nigeria obtained its independence in October 1960, but in 1967 it began a civil war that lasted three years. The Belgians hurriedly left the Congo in 1960; two years later, the country was torn apart by war and an authoritarian government that lasted till the 1990s came to power. By the mid-1960s, the democratic experiment was failing, and the military were taking over power in many countries. This chapter will present the major gains and hopes of independence, as well as its pains and troubles.

THE GAINS OF INDEPENDENCE

The year 1960 marked yet another watershed in the modern history of Africa, as seventeen countries obtained their independence in that year. It was a glorious era in Africa, marked by the hope and optimism that political liberation would bring rapid economic changes. The leaders exaggerated what independence would accomplish, but outsiders, too, expected that the resources of the African countries would bring development to their people. The late 1950s and early 1960s were years of great excitement. "Seek ye first the political kingdom," Kwame Nkrumah told all Africans in the 1950s, and all other good things would follow.

The gains of independence were varied. To the nationalists and other Africans who now inherited power, it was a dream come true. The politicians, civil servants, and scholars now had the opportunity to establish new political parties, formulate national policies and development plans for their country's future, review constitutions and political systems, and consider the means to minimize foreign control over their people. True, the leaders made many mistakes, but the opportunity to make mistakes was itself an achievement made possible by political freedom.

While the colonial boundaries were retained in most cases, some countries and capital cities were renamed. Seven countries were renamed at independence: Rhodesia became Zimbabwe; Bechunaland is now Botswana; Northern Rhodesia has been changed to Zambia; Nyasaland to Malawi; Basutoland to Lesotho; the Gold Coast to Ghana; and French Somaliland to Djibouti. In later years, some countries also changed their names: Dahomey to Benin, Upper Volta to Burkina Faso, Malagasy Republic to Madagascar, Congo-Kinshasa to Zaire, and Tanganyika and Zanzibar to Tanzania. The names of five capital cities were changed: Bathurst (Gambia) became Banjul; Salisbury (Zimbabwe) was changed to Harare; Léopoldville (Zaire) was renamed Kinshasa; Fort Lamy (Chad) became N'Djamena; and Lorenço Marques (Mozambique) became Maputo. In later years, four countries created new capital cities: Yamoussoukro in Côte d'Ivoire replaced Abidjan; Lilongwe in Malawi replaced Zomba; Abuja in Nigeria replaced Lagos; and Dodoma in Tanzania replaced Dar es Salaam.

One area where the newly acquired power was put to good use was in the formation of a continental organization, the Organization of African Unity (see Chapter 25). Relations between African countries on a regional and continental level were minimal during the colonial era. The new power holders could also think about forging unity among their various peoples, who were divided by religion, ethnicity, and levels of modernization.

As far as the majority of the citizens were concerned, independence was less about power and more about the enhancement of living standards. The advantage of independence was the power given to Africans to reshape the economy in the interests of their own people. The politicians could formulate national plans that would use resources to meet the needs of their people. It was important for them to take command of their national resources, especially their valuable raw materials, and manage them to minimize dependence on Western countries. A great optimism was expressed about the possibility of reducing the transfer of wealth abroad in the form of profits made by multinational companies, exports of principal products, and payments of wages and benefits to expatriates.

African entrepreneurs could create new businesses and compete with foreigners. Africans could now operate banks, insurance companies, manufacturing industries, and many businesses in which their participation was either barred or restricted during the colonial period. The universities created new courses in economics, public administration, and business management. Many people were content to serve as agents of foreign companies, rising to positions of power and

Modern city of Dakar, Senegal.

influence. Others did more by establishing new businesses, seeking profits in sectors previously dominated by foreign companies. The governments were able to release capital for the entrepreneurs to invest. Where the capital required was extensive, the governments established government-controlled businesses. In rich countries, the groundwork was laid to transfer business control to Africans.

There were many social and welfare needs, notably in terms of schools, health services, and water supplies. Among the majority of Africans who lived in rural areas, expectations were high that improvements would come with independence. The new leaders began to build more schools, dispensaries, roads, and hospitals, although these were never enough. Africans dreamed of increasing access to social facilities in order to create equality. Many people gained access to "modern" items such as Western attire, shoes, bicycles, trucks, cars, wristwatches, radios, and televisions.

In the sphere of culture, independence was mentally liberating. White racism was demolished in many countries. The use of indigenous languages received a boost, especially in schools where they were taught as autonomous subjects. Consideration was also given to the use of some African languages as official languages, either to replace or to complement European languages. Arabic became widely used in North Africa and some other Islamic areas. The Somali language, ignored by the colonial powers, became prominent among the Somali people. After 1972, the Somali language acquired a popular written form and the status of a national language. Swahili was also adopted as a national language in some East African countries.

Cultural creativity was expressed in various ways, using multiple media. The skills of carving, painting, drawing, and other forms of artistic expression were revived and their products sold to other parts of the world. New forms of cultural expression in drama, music, and dance were created, some to express the feelings associated with independence. A pioneer generation began to write poems, plays, and novels in European languages. Some achieved fame, including writers such as Ngugi Wa Thiong'o, Wole Soyinka, and Chinua Achebe. Singers, writers, musicians, and others sought to blend elements of the past with the present and to present their works to diverse audiences of Africans and non-Africans.

Education received the utmost priority. Before independence, the number of schools was small, and the colonial education system assumed that Africans were inferior. Independence created the need for a revolution in education, in the numbers of schools, in the content of the subjects, values taught, and in the giving of special attention to girls, who had long been denied opportunities. School attendance was doubled in many African countries within a decade of independence. Facilities to educate girls were greatly expanded in comparison with those that existed under colonial rule when women were treated as inferior. The establishment of new universities was regarded as a major achievement, while the ambition was to make elementary schools free, universal, and compulsory. Engineering, the sciences, nursing, and medicine were treated as important new fields, all associated with the need to develop the continent and reduce reliance on foreigners. Literacy campaigns also enabled a large number of adults to read and write.

The content of education was changed from the previous concern with European ideas and values to a concern with making Africa the center of knowledge and producing learned graduates with the ideas and visions needed to liberate the continent. Subjects such as African literature, philosophy, religion, music, languages, drama, and sociology were given emphasis in the new universities. New examination bodies set up to test students in the elementary and secondary schools responded creatively by requiring new Africa-based materials and subjects. Africans could now express themselves in creative ways without the need to apologize for basing their knowledge on their own people. Their scholars could use new methodologies to investigate various issues. Teachers and students sought to use the school system to promote national unity and relate education to the primary concerns of their countries.

Within their own countries, they could now act and behave as citizens rather than as colonial subjects. They believed that persecution was over, and there was no need for political violence, as in the Algerian wars or the Mau Mau rebellion (see Chapter 23). They would no longer regard themselves as a people meant to occupy the lower rungs of the ladder while Europeans stayed at the top. Some changes appeared small, but they had a major impact on self-esteem—for instance, in Kenya, Africans could now grow coffee and drink it; in the Belgian Congo, Africans could now travel from one city to another without police permission, which they had needed to obtain when Europeans were in power. The educated among them were now able to occupy the most important positions in the civil service and initiate policies for their own people. Confidence, optimism, and euphoria—all these followed the new freedom, the demolition of colonial racism, and the acquisition of self-respect.

Africa acquired recognition in world affairs. Membership of the United Nations was expanded in the 1960s by the addition of a large number of independent African countries. More and more Africans began to travel to other parts of the world for meetings, business affairs, and negotiations.

THE PAINS OF INDEPENDENCE

Sustaining the gains of independence was not easy, but no one in 1960 anticipated the human and natural disasters that followed in later years. The population increased faster than economic growth. The execution of all the good programs called for a committed leadership, enduring political institutions, a stable political system, a united country, and hardworking citizens. Some of these conditions were lacking. In addition, as both leaders and people realized, Africa was part of the world system existing at the time of the Cold War. Foreign countries wanted to sell goods and ideologies, even when this was not in the best interest of Africa. The various problems are discussed below, and the continuance of the challenges in the following decades is discussed in Chapter 32.

Unfulfilled Promises

The nationalists had raised the hope of their people that political freedom would bring with it major changes in all the important aspects of society. The politicians promised to create jobs for the majority of the population, educate the children, and provide shelter, health services, and the other good things of life. In Algeria and Kenya, where Africans had to struggle with European settlers, many had hoped that the settlers' departure would bring Africans greater access to land and even access to the settlers' former houses.

Popular expectation itself became a problem everywhere. The politicians had exaggerated what they could accomplish with power. Houses and schools could not be constructed as rapidly as expected, and wage employment could not be made available to all. Although the expectations were based on a utopian ideology of equitable distribution, Africans in power regarded themselves as part of an upper class separate from the poor. The politicians, professionals, and businesspeople used their privileges to acquire more wealth and to consolidate their positions. Rather than redistribute land to all, they took the best land for themselves. Well-planned areas vacated by the Europeans were occupied by the privileged elite. By the mid-1960s, the people had realized that the politicians had merely manipulated them in order to attain power by replacing the Europeans.

Political Crises

The problem was, however, far greater than simply the disappointment of the masses by those in power. There was no sufficiency of wealth to be distributed in the first instance, and competition for power was intense among the political actors who wanted to benefit from what little existed or to take control of the most important sectors of the economy.

Politics became unstable right from the very beginning. Without the mechanisms with which to build a united country out of an agglomeration of different ethnic groups, each with its own language, culture, and history, society and politics became prone to conflicts. Military coups became endemic (see Chapter 26), and the transfer of power posed a problem, as whoever was able to gain power refused to relinquish it. Among the causes of political instability in the 1960s were the following: the fear of domination by one ethnic group; the use of power to make money, which made it rewarding to hang on to power; the bitter rivalries among competing members of the political class; and the failure to give an opportunity to opposition groups to express themselves.

The independence constitutions of the new nations were democratic, based on the European multiparty system. Elections were held in many places before the Europeans departed and in some cases shortly after independence. However, the multiparty political system collapsed in most countries soon after independence. This collapse is one of the tragedies of Africa's political history, with consequences lasting until today.

Why did the multiparty system collapse so soon, at a time when Africans were jubilant that the European colonial authorities had left? The stage had been set for ethnic divisions to consume the new nations. Ethnic tensions were rife, as in the case of the bitter regional and ethnic rivalries in Nigeria that led to its civil war. During colonial rule, the various ethnic groups were not only disunited; they were set against one another by colonial governments that deliberately promoted the differences that separated them. The nationalists and politicians had also mobilized their ethnic constituencies to build support and to compete with one another. It was difficult to build the national unity needed to sustain nationalism and political stability.

Creating a culture of political opposition was very hard in the 1960s. As the party in power pursued a policy of winner-takes-all, members of opposition parties left to join the party in power in order to benefit from government patronage and corruption. In other cases, the party in power destroyed the opposition by using violence and state power to arrest, detain, and jail opposition leaders.

The first set of members of the political class (as well as their successors) turned politics into a lucrative business. Many of them were corrupt. When inefficiency and mismanagement were added, it became obvious to their people that their leaders were unworthy. Unfortunately, the beneficiaries of the problems were military officers who used all this as the excuse to take over power.

Where military coups did not occur, one-party rule became common, as in the case of Kenya, Côte d'Ivoire, Senegal, and Guinea. Advocates of the one-party state argued that it would provide strong leadership, continuity in policy, and unity among diverse ethnic groups. In reality, the one-party state destroyed the growth of opposition forces, promoted the idea that force and violence were needed to change leadership, put particular ethnic groups in power at the expense of others, marginalized nonmembers of the party in power in the distribution of resources, and promoted a culture of corruption and inefficiency.

Economic and Social Issues

Economic underdevelopment was a bigger problem than exaggerated expectations. To start with, the colonial economy was dependent on exports. African countries were unable to diversify their economies, and they continued to rely on the export of raw materials. To complicate this dependence, the numbers of products were few, and some countries relied on just one or two, as in the case of Ghana, which was dependent on cocoa. The links between former colonial masters and African countries were strong. The lucrative trade sector was controlled by large foreign companies. The railway and road networks were largely designed to facilitate the export of goods to Europe. Trade between African countries was on a small scale. Industrial development was minimal, and attempts were not made to modernize indigenous craft industries. In the early years, a move toward a socialized economy was believed to be one of the best options to overcome the economic crisis. The number of Africans with the formal education needed to manage the modern economy and politics was rather limited.

A BRIGHT FUTURE?

In spite of the worsening conditions, many Africans living in the 1960s were still expecting a better future. Africans now realized that progress and problems could go together. How could liberation from colonial rule be made valuable? Could the setbacks of the early years become lessons? Ideas were generated by a broad spectrum of the population and various social classes about what to do. Africans understood themselves and their continent better than ever before. Would the solutions be derived solely within the continent, or would foreign ideas become necessary? In a sense, the frantic search for answers positively reconnected to the optimism of the early years of independence to give hope to Africans in the 1960s that progress would come in a not-too-distant future and that a lost continent would rediscover itself.

SUGGESTIONS FOR FURTHER READING

Azevedo, Mario, ed. *Africana Studies: A Survey of Africa and the African Diaspora.* Durham, N.C.: Carolina Academic Press, 1993. Chapter 11.

Davidson, Basil. *Modern Africa: A Social and Political History.* 3rd ed. New York: Longman, 1995. Chapter 17.

Falola, Toyin, ed. *Africa.* Vol. 3, *Colonial Africa, 1885–1939.* Durham, N.C.: Carolina Academic Press, 2002.

Falola, Toyin, ed. *Africa.* Vol. 4, *The End of Colonial Rule: Nationalism and Decoloniza-*
tion. Durham, N.C.: Carolina Academic Press, 2002.
Gailey, A. Harry, Jr. *Africa: Troubled Continent (A Problems Approach).* Malabar, Fla.:
Robert E. Krieger, 1983.
Gailey, A. Harry, Jr. *History of Africa.* Vol. 3, *From 1945 to the Present.* Malabar, Fla.:
Robert E. Krieger, 1989.

25

The Formation of the Organization
of African Unity, 1963

In 1963, the Organization of African Unity (OAU) was established, an event that marked the victory of the protracted Pan-Africanist efforts (see Chapter 22) to unite Africans in order for them to speak with a common voice. Whereas the early Pan-Africanist congresses had been held outside Africa because the colonial powers would not allow such meetings in Africa, the independence of Ghana in 1957 and Kwame Nkrumah's Pan-Africanist vision shifted the center of Pan-Africanism to Africa. Pan-Africanist conferences were held in Africa in 1958, 1960, 1961, and 1963.

The formation of the OAU was one of the achievements of Pan-Africanism, and its survival, in spite of differences among its members, attests to the continued relevance of this continental body. It gave African countries an organization that could bring their leaders together; resolve disputes between nations; enable members to discuss political, cultural, and economic policies; examine the options available to deal with various problems; and in the 1960s and 1970s, find the means to assist countries still under colonial rule to fight for their freedom.

MISSION OF THE OAU

The Charter of the OAU was signed by thirty-one independent African countries on 25 May 1963 in Addis Ababa, the capital of Ethiopia. The objectives were arrived at as a compromise between two competing groups. On the one hand were members known as the Casablanca Group (a name derived from their conference held in Morocco in 1961), comprising Morocco, Mali, Ghana,

Guinea, Algeria, and Libya. The Casablanca Group wanted the immediate unification of Africa. On the other hand were members who wanted a gradual approach to continental unification and who preferred stronger regional associations. Known as the Monrovia Group (named after their conference held in May 1961 in Monrovia, Liberia), this group comprised Somalia, Nigeria, Liberia, Sierra Leone, Congo-Brazzaville, Ethiopia, Tunisia, and many French-speaking countries.

Although the representatives of these two groups had previously disagreed on how to unite Africa, they were all passionately committed to a continental organization. All the speeches by the leaders at the 1963 meeting were inspiring in calling for consensus and for creating a means by which they could all contribute ideas and resources to end imperialism in Africa, control their destiny, and prevent wars among themselves. According to the compromise charter, the OAU would

Promote unity and solidarity of the African States; coordinate and intensify their cooperation and efforts to achieve a better life for the peoples of Africa; defend their sovereignty, their territorial integrity, and independence; eradicate all forms of colonialism from Africa; and promote international cooperation having due regard to the Charter of the United Nations and the Universal Declaration of Human Rights.[1]

The charter provided a number of important principles to guide the member states:

i. Equality of all the member-states with each other;

ii. Non-interference in the internal affairs of member states;

iii. Respect for the existing frontiers of member states; and

iv. Peaceful settlement of all disputes between member states.[2]

In addition, the OAU Charter was opposed to the subverting of African leadership and the assassination of its leaders by external and internal forces. Members were enjoined not to identify with either the Eastern socialist bloc or the Western capitalist bloc but to promote instead a policy of nonalignment. Members were also enjoined to work to end the apartheid system in South Africa and liberate the entire continent from European rule. To prevent conflicts among the member countries, they agreed to promote equal rights and not to give advantages to the big, rich countries that would enable them to dominate the smaller, poorer ones.

AGENCIES AND FUNCTIONS

To fulfill its mission, the OAU established an administration and various guidelines on management and finances. Addis Ababa was made its headquarters, with a secretary-general as its head. As with the United Nations, the money to run the organization would come from the member states, each paying according to its resources. The OAU started out with four major agencies designed to run its affairs and ensure that its objectives were fulfilled: These were the Assembly of Heads of State and Government; the Council of Ministers; the General Secretariat; and the Commission of Mediation, Arbitration and Conciliation.

The Assembly of Heads of State and Government comprises all the heads of state and their representatives. The assembly meets once a year, although it can call an emergency meeting at any time as long as two-thirds of the member states want one. The assembly is empowered to act as the supreme organ of the OAU, coordinates the general policy of the OAU, appoints important officers, such as the chairman and the secretary-general, considers reports from the General Secretariat, and discusses all matters of importance to the continent.

The second most powerful agency is the Council of Ministers, composed of all the foreign ministers of the member states and any other minister selected for that purpose. The council meets twice a year, but it can also meet on an emergency basis. It approves the budget of the OAU and coordinates inter-African affairs. It prepares the agenda of the Assembly of Heads of State and Government, implements the decisions of the assembly, and deals with all matters referred to it by the assembly.

The General Secretariat is headed by a secretary-general appointed by the assembly on the recommendation of the Council of Ministers. The secretariat is responsible for day-by-day administration, budget preparation and management, the organization of meetings, and the implementation of decisions made by the heads of state and ministers.

Finally, there are special commissions designed to carry out specific tasks. In the 1960s, the most active and important was the Liberation Committee, with its headquarters in Dar es Salaam in Tanzania. It was to seek the means to end all forms of colonialism in Africa and give financial and material assistance to liberation movements. By and large, all the agencies of the OAU have functioned well.

CONTRIBUTIONS

The OAU contributed to liberation struggles in South Africa, Namibia, and the Portuguese colonies to ensure that Africa became free. It was consistent in attacking the apartheid policy in South Africa as cruel and unjust. Its fight against apartheid was vigorous and consistent. A policy of boycotting South Africa was imposed on its members. When some members raised the possibility of maintaining dialogue with South Africa, they were defeated by those who advocated a strategy of opposition. The OAU was also at the forefront of the struggle to end Portuguese rule in Africa.

The organization established a special liberation committee to mobilize resources to support independence movements with money and arms. A special liberation fund was created to assist freedom fighters. All areas under colonial rule received assurances that their volunteers would be trained in the art of war.

Angola, Mozambique, Zimbabwe, and South Africa were among the countries whose freedom fighters received generous assistance.

In cases where African countries have gone to war—both within countries, as in the case of the Nigerian Civil War, and between countries, as in the case of the Congo—the OAU has intervened to bring about peace. Although the OAU does not have an army of its own, there have been occasions when it has been able to ask members to send soldiers to represent it in keeping peace. Conflict management has also been extended to issues dealing with complicated rivalries for power. The OAU intervened in the Somali-Ethiopian war in 1977–78, in the crisis in Chad in 1981, in the Western Sahara in the 1980s, and in many other cases. Frontier conflicts also attracted the attention of the OAU, and its mediation was successful in some cases. The earliest was in October 1963 when a war broke out between Morocco and Algeria over a territory claimed by the latter. The OAU arranged a cease-fire, and the two countries signed a peace agreement in February 1964. While Algeria and Morocco agreed on a number of items, Morocco remained unsatisfied, and the OAU had to continue to mediate until 1970. A number of other small disputes have been resolved by the organization.

The liberation struggles, the interstate conflicts, and the apartheid policy in South Africa created refugees who had to live in countries other than their own. The number of refugees grew from a few thousands to about a million by 1976. In association with the United Nations High Commission for Refugees, the OAU established a commission on refugee problems in 1964. Four years later, all the OAU members signed an important convention to assist with refugee problems and to prevent the settlement of refugees from creating wars between two or more countries. The OAU has assisted in the resettlement and support of refugees at different periods.

Issues of economic development and regional cooperation have also occupied the attention of the OAU. In 1964, the OAU established the African Development Bank (ADB) to generate development funds and use them in major enterprises. The member states are aware of the underdeveloped nature of their economies and have used various meetings to discuss strategies. The consensus has always been that a bigger market in Africa will reduce dependence on developed countries. The OAU has contributed to successful negotiations on bilateral and multilateral groupings and agreements on the use of some rivers.

The OAU has enabled the leaders, administrators, scholars, and representatives of the African countries to interact and get to know one another. In its early years, it represented the best forum for the meetings of leaders. The OAU has also sponsored and encouraged cooperation in fields such as education, culture, and sports. Collaborative research projects have been sponsored, such as the effort to find solutions to livestock diseases and the use of African herbs to cure illnesses. In the 1990s, the OAU established a committee to demand reparation for the trans-Atlantic slave trade. It has become a reliable forum in which African leaders can discuss African and world affairs. The topics and solutions have been wide-ranging, even if there have also been many disagreements.

The OAU has enhanced the role of Africa in world affairs. There have been occasions when members have taken a common stand at the General Assembly of the United Nations. During the Cold War, the OAU was courted by the ideologically divided camps of the Eastern and Western powers. After the end of the Cold War, the OAU successfully worked toward the appointment of an African as the secretary-general of the United Nations. Efforts to direct international attention to the AIDS and HIV (human immunodeficiency virus) epidemics in some areas have been coordinated by OAU members.

LIMITATIONS AND PROBLEMS

In the view of revolutionary Pan-Africanists, the OAU has not been active enough in mobilizing Africans to overcome Western domination and economic exploitation. It has also been accused of failing to create a united continent as envisioned by Pan-Africanist leaders such as Marcus Garvey, George Padmore, C.L.R. James, W.E.B. Du Bois, and Kwame Nkrumah. Those who wanted a more activist OAU remain disappointed. Perhaps they had expected too much from such a large organization without representatives of the grassroots, political parties, and elected leaders. The OAU is yet to establish a connection with the majority of Africans.

It is not always easy for the OAU to arrive at a consensus or to implement its decisions and resolutions. The reasons for this include disagreements among member countries, personality conflicts among leaders, the failure of many leaders to attend meetings and pay their dues, ideological differences especially during the Cold War, the organization's lack of power and authority to enforce its decisions, and external intervention in African affairs, notably by France and the United States. The OAU's peacekeeping force has met with failure on several occasions, and the organization was unable to send a force to war-torn Liberia in the 1990s. The OAU is yet to find solutions to many of the continent's problems or to play a more assertive and creative role.

In large-scale disputes, the OAU has always found itself either in difficulties or unable to play a decisive role. The complicated fight between Morocco and Mauritania over the Western Sahara was difficult to resolve. The nationalists in the Western Sahara also established a liberation movement, called POLISARIO (*Frente Popular para la Liberación de Saguia El-Hamra, y Rio de Oro*), which demanded the formation of an autonomous country. Members of the OAU were divided, with the majority in support of POLISARIO. An even bigger conflict was in the Horn of Africa where some areas regarded as provinces of Ethiopia struggled for independence. In 1976, the Somali of the Ogaden rebelled. The Eritreans, too, rebelled and fought until they became independent of Ethiopia in 1991. Also in Ethiopia, the Oromo people began a revolt in 1974. In all of these conflicts, the OAU was unable to stop the wars or persuade the parties to reach agreement on their future.

As with most supranational organizations such as the United Nations, there is always a limit to what the OAU can accomplish. As an assembly representing various governments, the OAU's mandate and authority cannot move beyond the wishes and interests of the leaders of the various member countries. The executive power enjoyed by the secretariat is not strong enough. Thus, the OAU often behaves like a bullying dog that can bark but not bite. Without its own army and self-generated finances, it has limited power to enforce its own recommendations.

It is important to stress the point about the competing loyalties and nationalisms of those who emphasize national identity and those who emphasize continental unity. Some see nationalism (commitment to the nation–state) as difficult to reconcile with Pan-Africanism (commitment to the OAU). The political leaders in each country want the survival of their sovereignty, the success of their independence, and a sense of autonomy. They want their citizens to show patriotism with regard to the nation, rather than to their ethnic group or religion. The belief is that strong central governments and leaders are necessary to attain this. As they seek the strategy to promote nationalism, they tend to exhibit particularistic tendencies, even threatening other African countries.

Pan-Africanists want a strong OAU that will lead a united continent to a greater future. They argue that the problems facing all the African countries are similar, that the common experience of the slave trade and colonial domination are strong enough to strengthen their union, and that without a united continent, each country will be a victim of external exploitation. Although there is no African leader who has not expressed a desire for African unity, each has tended to be engrossed by the problems in his own country.

The political instability of member nations has affected the OAU. In countries that are governed by insecure rulers, military leaders who use force to stay in power, and in which opposition is strong, the heads of state cannot travel to OAU meetings for fear of being toppled in their absence. The overthrow of governments creates its own problems, as new leaders are not necessarily committed to the agreements signed by their predecessors.

In spite of its problems, the OAU has managed to meet some of the aspirations of the founding figures of Pan-Africanism. Its formation demonstrated a recognition of the need to unite to solve common problems. Conflicts between different countries can be minimized or resolved by a continental organization. While the OAU does not prevent nationalism built around the nation–state, it offers the possibility of a continental solidarity and nationalism in which Africans can see themselves as one. It contributed to anticolonial struggles in Africa, and it continues to promote the ideas of African unity.

The experience of its limitations has emboldened a number of Africans, including leaders, to call for a more activist continental union. It has now been agreed that a new organization, the Africa Union, should replace the OAU, in order to create a more effective supranational political organ that will be more involved in intervening in conflicts, promoting stability, and fighting instability. The OAU had its last meeting in Lusaka, Zambia, where the Africa Union was formally inaugurated on 26 May 2001. It is too early to evaluate the impact of the new union. Perhaps, it will be less of a "talking shop" than the OAU.

NOTES

1. Organization of African Unity, *OAU Charter*, 1963, p. 1.
2. Ibid.

SUGGESTIONS FOR FURTHER READING

Amate, C.O.C. *Inside the OAU: Pan-Africanism in Practice*. London: Macmillan, 1986.

Cervanka, Zdenek. *The Unfinished Quest for Unity: Africa and the OAU*. New York: Africana, 1978.

Falola, Toyin, ed. *Africa*. Vol. 5, *Contemporary Africa*. Durham, N.C.: Carolina Academic Press, in press.

Langley, J. Ayo. *Ideologies of Liberation in Black Africa, 1856–1970: Documents on Modern African Political Thought from Colonial Times to the Present*. London: Rex Collins, 1979.

Thompson, Vincent B. *Africa and Unity: The Evolution of Pan-Africanism*. London: Longman, 1969.

26

Coups, Counter Coups, and Military Regimes, 1963 Onward

The cars are the same, only the drivers are different.[1]

Soon after many African countries had gained their independence, that is, between 1960 and 1966, there were military coups and army mutinies in at least fourteen countries. In 1963, the military took power by force in Togo, Dahomey (now the Republic of Benin), Burundi, and Congo-Brazzaville. In 1964, army mutinies occurred in Kenya, Tanzania, and Uganda, and there was a coup in Gabon. In the following years, military coups became rampant in the continent. For example, in 1965, the military overthrew the governments in Dahomey and Zaire (now the Democratic Republic of the Congo). Dahomey witnessed further coups in 1967 and 1972. In 1966, Nigeria, the Central African Republic, Ghana, and Upper Volta (now Burkina Faso) experienced military takeovers. Coups became a fashion, and by 1975, twenty-one countries were under military rule. Between 1960 and 1992, Africa recorded seventy cases of successful military coups in thirty-one countries. Unsuccessful coups and counter coups were equally frequent, all involving the killing of many people.

The military may overthrow a civilian regime or more commonly another military government. When the military are in power, disgruntled officers may strike in a counter coup to seize power. When a coup is successful, a legitimate government is constituted; when it is not, the officers are treated as rebels and summarily executed. By the 1980s, the military had become an integral part of

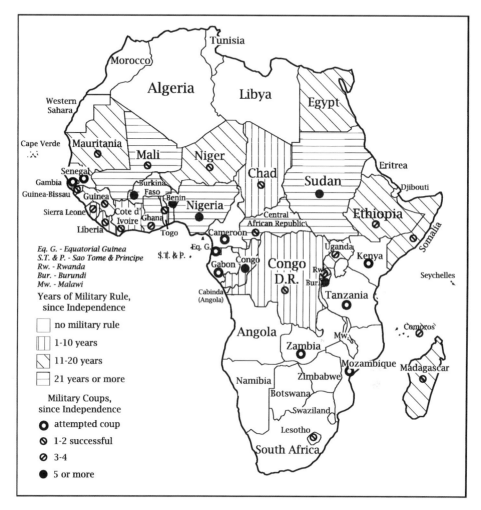

Military rule in independent Africa.

the political problem of Africa. Military coups follow a pattern:

- Soldiers take over the radio, television, and major telephone stations.
- They kill or arrest the important political figures in the national capital.
- They base their claims on the failure of the previous government and ask for public support.
- The reasons they give for their action are a combination of the following: the failure of the preceding government to bring about development, disagreement over policies, corruption, financial mismanagement, the extravagance of political leaders, ethnic rivalries, political schism, the failure to relinquish power, reduction in military budgets, lack of promotion in the army, and the possible disintegration of the country.
- They promise a return to civilian government as soon as possible, although they almost never mean this.

CAUSES OF MILITARY INTERVENTION

Military coups and regimes in different African countries have been justified on similar grounds. Military officers use civilian politicians' failure, ethnicity, and general instability to assume power. Where corruption and economic mismanagement are endemic, a further opportunity is provided for the military to intervene. In cases of rivalries among competing ethnic groups and members of the political class, the military will base its intervention on the need to protect the country's unity and prevent anarchy. Military officers claim to have acted to preserve political unity and stability in almost all cases of intervention, although in actuality they tend to add to existing problems. To give an example, all the aforementioned reasons were used in the overthrow of the first government in Nigeria after independence. The first federal government after independence in 1960 was described by the military as incompetent, corrupt, and inefficient. In a major radio address, one of the coup leaders, Major Chukwuma Nzeogwu, remarked:

Our enemies are the political profiteers, the swindlers, the men in high and low places that seek bribes and demand ten percent, those that seek to keep the country divided permanently so that they can remain in office as Ministers and VIPs of waste, the tribalists, the nepotists, those that make the country look big for nothing before the international circle, those that have corrupted our society and put the Nigerian political calendar backwards. We promise that you will no more be ashamed to say that you are a Nigerian.[2]

The pioneer Nigerian civilian politicians disagreed over many issues, they raised ethnic differences to the level of protracted conflicts, they could not conduct a satisfactory census, and they rigged elections in order to retain power. However, Nzeogwu's promise remained unfulfilled. Nzeogwu himself did not come to power, other coups occurred in the years that followed, the military left a legacy of ruin, and the country's situation went from bad to worse.

All the various manifestations of political instability or failure of democratic regimes have been used by the military as a reason to seize political control, rather than as a contributor to the search for enduring solutions. In the 1960s (and up to the present), most African governments have been unresponsive to the needs and aspirations of their people. The transition from colonial rule to independence did not create conditions conducive to political stability. During the colonial era, in the first half of the twentieth century, there were no democratic institutions that Africans could participate in and learn from, and the majority of people had no knowledge of the workings of the European-derived political systems that were set up before independence. When the Europeans were leaving, they chose to hand over power to their allies in many countries to preserve the links that were beneficial to them. The Africans in power wanted to deny trade unions, students, and political rivals the opportunity to express themselves. Many leaders portrayed themselves as the political saviors needed by their countries. The unity among Africans created by anticolonial struggles began to disappear soon after independence. Profound differences and divisions began to develop along religious, regional, and ethnic lines. All these political problems and the failure to develop a strong culture of political opposition have enabled the military to seize power in many countries. Examples of military intervention based on the preceding reasons are common, and the case of Ghana is sufficient to serve as an illustration. A coup occurred on 24 February 1966. According to General Joseph Ankrah, the soldiers wanted to "banish privilege, overlordism, political opportunism, wasteful pompousness, and incompetence." He promised that the military would restore "liberty, justice and human dignity."[3] As in the case of Nigeria, this turned out to be an empty promise, and other coups followed.

An inept and corrupt civilian government needs the military to keep it in power. To curb the opposition and prevent popular uprisings, the army and the police are used to threaten the people and to stop antigovernment activities. This involvement of the army may lead to coups, either as officers become reluctant to carry out the wishes of the civilians in government, or as they come to believe that they can do a better job of political management. The officers often believe that the army is better organized than a political party and should be able to intervene in politics. According to this line of thinking, some officers actually regard themselves as messiahs who deserve to be worshipped.

Another common reason for coups is economic underdevelopment. Africans expected independence to bring rapid changes. Instead, what followed was a scarcity of housing, food, and health facilities, inflation, and high unemployment. When the people protested, governments reacted with excessive use of police power to suppress them. That the majority of countries are poor and struggling there can be no doubt (see Chapter 32), and the military capitalizes on this by promising to bring rapid progress. Such a promise is hollow, but it buys immediate public support. In addition, the military adds reform and efficiency to its reasons for intervention. The assumption is that the military officers will be fast, decisive, and reformist, in contrast to the rather slow pace of activities carried out by their predecessors. On coming to power, they make some sweeping changes in the first few weeks, then relax into the routine that they previously criticized.

The sheer control of firepower is enough to instigate coups and counter coups, with other reasons given merely to rationalize greed and personal ambition for power. Creating important functions and daily routines for the African army has never been easy. African armies were initially established by colonial governments to maintain law and order among colonial subjects and to prevent external aggression. Since independence, the aim has been to create national armies that will attract the confidence of the people and contribute to stability and development. However, the leading officers in the army believe that they can use their control of weapons to take over political positions, thereby changing the major role of the army from the maintenance of security to the exercise of political power.

There have also been situations where the need to protect established privileges enjoyed by officers and soldiers has caused coups or mutinies that ended in changes of government. For instance, in the coups in Ghana in 1966 and 1972, the officers added the poor treatment of soldiers to their list of reasons. They complained of lack of adequate funds to support them, the possible retirement of some officers, the interference by civilians in military affairs, the loss of some allowances, a reduction in the military budget, the erosion in purchasing power because of inflation, and the slow pace of promotion. When soldiers use their conditions of service to justify their intervention, they tend to forget that people in other sectors of society experience similar problems.

Ideas supporting military coups may come from abroad. The influence can be indirect, as in the case of officers in one country trying to imitate their colleagues in other countries. In a few cases during the Cold War, external powers indirectly encouraged some officers to overthrow a government that was promoting a policy the external powers did not like.

Finally, there are cases in which a military takeover has been justified on ideological reasons. Whereas most military leaders avoid ideologies, the coups in Libya in 1969 and Morocco in 1971 were based on ideological reasons. When Colonel Muammar al-Qaddafi came to power in Libya, he announced that he would create an Arab socialism, one that would combine Islam with Marxism. He later published a socialist manifesto, called the *Green Book*, to specify what he meant. In the case of Morocco, the unsuccessful coup was based on opposition to the rule of a king in a modern world and the desire to introduce a socialist ideology.

THE IMPACT

Not many military regimes are either benevolent or successful. Some have provided stable governments, but usually for only a few years, as in the case of Nigeria in the 1970s. Using force and a centralized administration, a few military leaders in Nigeria temporarily prevented secession and the collapse of the country. In two cases, the Nigerian military handed over power to civilian governments. There are also some cases in which military regimes use the control of arms and the abolition of the constitution to remove unpopular leaders and end one-party regimes or take some decisions that the previous politicians have found difficult.

However, the record of most military regimes is negative. Rather than solve the problems of political instability, military regimes have complicated them. In the majority of cases, they lead to oppressive and tyrannical rule. As the military becomes involved in politics, the officers see their major role in political participation rather than in security and defense. They tend to be disrespectful of civilian politicians, thereby ignoring the constitutional provision that the army is merely one agency of the government, subordinate to law and constituted order.

A small number of officers assume a monopoly of power and of ideas on how to govern complex societies. Yet it is always clear that military officers lack the knowledge, intelligence, and temperament for governance. Where they have political skills, they do not possess the ability to manage the modern economy. Almost invariably, military regimes incorporate civilian members, drawing precisely from members of the group they have criticized or replaced in power. In other cases, they rely on established bureaucracies that are not necessarily development oriented.

In areas where wars and conflicts have occurred (as in Nigeria and Sudan), the armies have grown larger, far larger than the countries need or can maintain. A large army drains the country's resources in salaries, benefits, and procurement of arms. Significant expenditures on the military mean that key areas of development are ignored. It is not unusual for defense expenditure to be higher than expenditure on education and health.

The military can rarely create political stability. There are occasions when temporary stability has been created, as in the cases of Nigeria, Zaire, and Togo in the 1970s. However, in many cases, the military actually creates more instability, as in Congo-Brazzaville, Uganda, Ethiopia, and Burundi in the 1970s. When military leaders stay too long, they create the conditions to mobilize opposition against them, which can degenerate into warfare, anarchy, or underground activities. Some leaders set one ethnic group against another, thereby unleashing brutal rivalries and conflicts.

By and large, military regimes are corrupt. Their policies and behavior reflect abuse of power, nepotism, and reckless theft of public money. As they are accountable to no one but themselves, they are able to steal more than the civilians they criticize. Government contracts and favors are distributed to relations and loyalists. The government agencies and their staff usually remain the same, which makes it even more difficult to reform society. As in the case of Nigeria and some other countries, corrupt military leaders do not desire to relinquish power. When they are forced to leave power, and civilian regimes are installed, the former military officers use stolen money to buy their way into power. This explains the prominence of former military officers in the Nigerian civilian government after 1998.

The military has damaged democratic institutions. On coming to power, military regimes suspend constitutions, disregard the rule of law, and ignore regulations on accountability. Military leaders are dictators, and many of them unleash a rule of terrorism, killing those who oppose them. Military regimes discourage opposition to the government and do not allow alternative policy options to be discussed or tried. Violence and counter coups become the only ways to change the group in power. Discontented army officers may create a temporary alliance with civilians to overthrow the government.

The promise to bring about change is hardly ever fulfilled. The military men are not revolutionaries with the capacity and commitment to do what they promise. Many promise revolutionary changes, but they make only a few modifications and, in most cases, actually cause additional economic problems. The changes they make, some in hurried manner just to impress the public, are hardly lasting. While many officers think about how to obtain power through force, they rarely engage in serious consideration of what to do with the power they gain. Once they possess the power, they are consumed by the need for survival in order to retain their power. Many realize that the qualities required by an army commander are far different from those required to manage a nation. Economic development cannot be realized overnight, and the palliatives applied by the military usually end in disaster.

The style, personality, and degree of dictatorship of military officers do vary. Some military dictators have been benevolent, like General Yakubu Gowon of Nigeria, and some excessive, like General Sanni Abacha, also of Nigeria. Some have ruled for long periods, like Mobutu Sese Seko of Zaire, Jerry Rawlings of Ghana, and Gnassingbe Eyadema of Togo. A few have been notorious to an extreme, as in the case of General Idi Amin of Uganda, whose power was based on terror and violence. Idi Amin came to power in 1971. He appointed himself president for life and governed like a king possessed by a demon. He killed thousands of people, from the ordinary to the powerful, while thousands of others were forced to flee from Uganda. In 1972, he expelled about 50,000 Asians living in Uganda. Over time, the basis of his support weakened, the economy collapsed, and an external attack by the Ugandan National Liberation Front and the Tanzanian government toppled his repressive government on 11 April 1979.

CONCLUSION

Whether benevolent or cruel, military regimes are abnormal. All over Africa, it is now realized that military regimes cannot solve problems, and they actually create new ones. While in power, the ranks of military officers are divided, as each officer struggles for more power and more money. A few officers centralize power in themselves, virtually destroy opposition forces, and marginalize local communities. They create dozens of advisory committees to make all sorts of recommendations that are implemented in a haphazard manner. They use force to implement their policies, even the most mundane ones.

Although they promise, on assuming power, to cleanse society of its ills and generate development, it is clear that they do the opposite. In general, there is very little distinction between the civilians and the military when it comes to development, political stability, and corruption.

Opposition to military rule has become common, not just among the civilian politicians who seek power but among students, workers, and other members of the civil society who strongly believe that the future of Africa lies in the creation and maintenance of democratic institutions and governments accountable to the people. Although the mood and aspiration are for democracy, coups will continue to take place as long as there are officers with ambitions for wealth and power. The conditions to justify the coups will remain—a slow pace of development and political crises among the civilian politicians—although the military in power will not be able to solve these problems.

NOTES

1. A Ghanaian song composed in 1968 to point out that the military are no different from civilian leaders.
2. Part of a speech broadcast by Radio Kaduna, 15 January 1966.
3. General J. Ankrah, "The Future of the Military in Ghana," *African Forum* 11, no. 1 (1996), p. 5.

SUGGESTIONS FOR FURTHER READING

Decalo, Samuel. *Coups and Army Rule in Africa: Studies in Military Style.* New Haven, Conn.: Yale University Press, 1976.

Falola, Toyin, ed. *Africa.* Vol. 5, *Contemporary Africa.* Durham, N.C.: Carolina Academic Press, in press.

Falola, Toyin, et al. *The Military Factor in Nigeria.* Lewiston, N.Y.: Edwin Mellen, 1994.

First, Ruth. *The Barrel of a Gun: Political Power in Africa and the Coup d'Etat.* London: Penguin, 1970.

Gutteridge, W.F. *Military Regimes in Africa.* London: Methuen, 1975.

Lee, J.M. *African Armies and Civil Order.* New York: Praeger, 1969.

27

Ujamaa and Policy Choices, 1967 Onward

Independence did not bring as many changes as had been anticipated (see Chapter 24), and the mood of many Africans by the mid-1960s was beginning to change to one of doubt and despair. A number of politicians, administrators, scholars, and policy experts began to review history and past failures, in order to come up with new ideas. These ideas involved economy and politics. Many were about ideological choices: Should African countries retain the capitalist model created by the colonial powers, or should they experiment with socialism? Among the leading African initiators of new ideas were Julius Nyerere of Tanzania, Kwame Nkrumah of Ghana, Sekou Toure of Guinea, Amilcar Cabral of Guinea-Bissau, and Léopold Senghor of Senegal, all of whom leaned toward socialism. The belief was that socialism would enable farmers and workers to earn good incomes and that society should promote principles of equality, justice, and fairness. Not all countries and leaders believed in socialism, and many continued with the capitalist economic practices inherited from colonial rule. The search for and implementation of economic models, ideas, and ideologies to transform the continent constitutes one of the major events of the postindependence era.

Irrespective of the choice of ideologies, all African countries had to deal with similar problems of development and had to confront competing options. For centuries, African economies had revolved around agriculture. Rural areas were self-sufficient, and they survived without an industrial revolution, massive importation of food, or reliance on heavy machines. After independence, Africa had to face the challenge of modernizing its economy—it could no longer return to the past. However, to move forward, African governments in the 1960s and beyond had to deal with some of the following complicated issues:

- Should they reject or retain the colonial legacies? In colonial Africa, the European powers had used various strategies to drain Africa of its resources. Through international trade, involvement in the world economy, and the use of imported technologies, dependence on Western countries continued after independence. Africa supplied raw materials without the power to determine the prices and the quantity of goods to sell. How could they break their dependence on Western countries? This would involve finding alternative domestic uses for items that they were exporting to obtain hard currency.
- Should they promote the cultivation of export crops or food crops? Their governments relied on export crops for money to pay for the administration and to fund development projects. However, focusing on exports meant that they began to experience food shortages. By the mid-1960s, many countries were finding it difficult to feed their growing population.
- Should they concentrate development in cities or rural areas? The majority of the population were farmers, but the members of the political class, the bureaucrats, and the educated elite preferred to live in cities. Concentrating development in cities meant that most of the nation's resources were absorbed by the minority of the population.

In trying to resolve these and other issues, the leaders had to consider the ideologies of economic development that would work for the majority of the population. The governments had to seek the means to generate wealth and use it for the majority. The search for and disbursement of wealth were issues of development: How could they overcome the colonial legacies? How could they use their national resources, even when these were few, to enhance living standards? How could they build an infrastructure to support the desired changes, and how could they develop such vital sectors as banking and foreign trade, sectors that were necessary for development? They had to choose a strategy: Should it be that of socialism and central planning or that of capitalism? They tried various approaches, but the results were not always as positive as they had expected.

UJAMAA IN TANZANIA

Between 1967 and 1973, Julius Nyerere implemented his ideology of *Ujamaa*, which means "familyhood" in the Swahili language. In the colonial period, before Africans came to power, some thinkers had been discussing the economic and political ideology of "African socialism." As Nyerere understood it, *Ujamaa* was the adoption of the African principle of the extended family in a modern economic model. According to him, before the coming of the Europeans, Africans belonged to large extended families whose members collectively owned land, worked together to produce and share, promoted the interests of all members, and developed the ethic of cooperation. To Nyerere, the principle of the extended family meant that there were no exploited members, as all had to work, and there was no class division as was promoted by capitalism. Only the elderly and the infirm were excused from contributing their labor, and idlers were few and constituted a disgrace to themselves. According to Nyerere, those who had more than enough shared it with others and freely gave away what they had in times of disaster or famine.

In Nyerere's view, the penetration of colonial rule threatened the ideology of the extended family. However, he argued in 1962 that the conditions existed to revive it and turn it into modern socialist principles—the people were still rural, dependent on farming, and preindustrial; kinship groups were still important; class interests were undeveloped; and land and labor were abundant. Tanzanians should return to the ideology of the past, they should believe in "Human Brotherhood and in the Unity of Africa," they must not divide their society into classes of rich and poor, and they should promote "true African socialism." *Ujamaa* would be opposed to capitalism and the exploitation of one person by another. At the same time, it would be opposed to the type of socialism that is based on class conflict. *Ujamaa* would draw the best from the social institutions and ethics of old and blend them with the modernization quest of the new Tanzania.

In the Arusha Declaration of 1967, the objectives that *Ujamaa* would attain were clearly stated:

(i) Complete human equality and the absence of economic classes with wide disparities in income and benefits.

(ii) Political democracy in which individuals would be allowed to vote in open elections for candidates of their choice, and in which anyone, within certain rules, could run for elective office at the local, regional, or national level.

(iii) Just and fair wages for work performed.

(iv) The eradication of all forms of exploitation and the prevention of accumulation of wealth incompatible with the nature of a classless society.

(v) Public ownership of the economy, i.e., all firms, factories, industries were to be owned by the state in order to advance economic justice for everyone.

(vi) Respect for a certain amount of private property such as personal belongings and household goods, so long as the amount was not enough to give the owner undue influence or the ability to exploit other people.

(vii) Basic political freedoms of speech, association, movement, and worship, within the context of law.[1]

The implementation of *Ujamaa* gave a large role to the government in restructuring the society. Tanzania established a one-party state. The selection of candidates for parliamentary seats was open and competitive, although the candidates all belonged to the same party, the Tanganyika African National Union (TANU), later renamed the Chama cha Mapinduzi (CCM—the Revolutionary Party). The members of the executive organ of the party were drawn from various associations and interest groups, such as the National Women's Organization and the Cooperative Union of Tanzania.

The party discouraged accumulative tendencies among its leading members. Leading party members and government officials were prevented from becoming landlords, holding stock in any private company, serving as members of the board of directors of any private company, and having more than one source of income.

The development of the rural areas—the "villagization" policy—constituted the core program in the implementation of *Ujamaa*. The premise was that Tanzania had a shortage of capital but an abundance of land and labor. Its people were mainly rural, and they would profit from the development of agriculture. *Ujamaa* villages would be created by peasant families who would form cooperative societies to produce and sell as collectives and take decisions affecting their economies and lives. In the early years, the role of the government was limited to supporting the establishment of the villages, providing the guidelines for their establishment, and monitoring performance. Government and party officials also regulated the production and sales of the principal products, sisal, tea, and coffee.

Tanzania received financial and technical assistance from other countries, notably the Scandinavian countries. The assistance was wisely used for the improvement of social services, especially in the rural areas. Clean water supplies and free medical centers were made available in the development villages. The education system was reformed in 1967, and a massive expansion in enrollment followed. By 1980, over 90 percent of children of school age were enrolled, a truly impressive achievement. Adult literacy was also promoted, to the extent that about 80 percent of the population learned to read and write, making Tanzania one of the most literate countries in Africa. An attempt was also made to close the gap between rich and poor. In official wages that the government could control, the gap between the best paid and the minimum income earners stood at a ratio of 6:1.

In the 1970s, more and more bureaucrats became central planners and interfered in the management of *Ujamaa*. From 1974 onward, the government supervised the establishment of new villages, moving hundreds of people from their age-old land to new "development villages." A new *Ujamaa* village was connected by roads to other villages and had some modern amenities.

The massive relocation of farmers to new villages met with opposition from the very people that the policy was supposed to help. First, the majority of people were attached to their ancestral land, which had been passed down for hundreds of years from one generation to another. Second, the new villages created for them were in areas that were not necessarily productive. Third, they resented the educated bureaucrats who were seen as treating them like children to be ordered around and instructed about what to do. Many of the bureaucrats were perceived as arrogant, further alienating the farmers. More bureaucrats became involved in marketing and transportation, as state agencies replaced member-run cooperatives. This further alienated local producers who felt that the government was exercising too much power over them and that state officials were corrupt.

The farmers failed to cooperate or behave as expected, and productivity declined in the 1970s. Falling productivity meant a significant loss in national income, with resultant difficulties in maintaining social services. By 1980, the economy had slowed down, recording a downward growth trend. The currency lost its value, the rate of inflation increased, and public morale began to wane, with many beginning to question the relevance of *Ujamaa*. Interest on foreign loans went unpaid, and the country found it hard to acquire new loans. By the 1980s, the economy was in serious trouble: Development began to stagnate, and many existing projects were abandoned. The country found it difficult to pay for its invasion of Uganda in 1979, which was embarked upon to end the brutal regime of Idi Amin (see Chapter 26) and to pay for expensive petroleum products. The farmers and other rural residents grew extremely resentful of government officials—they believed that their hard work brought them little gain, that the officials had taken away from them the power to control their lives and farms, and that the officials were living well and earning a good income based on the farmers' sweat. Nyerere resigned as president in 1985, leaving a legacy of bankruptcy.

OTHER SOCIALIST THINKERS

Ujamaa was not the only idea that was discussed and tried in Africa in the postindependence years. Kwame Nkrumah of Ghana was another socialist, but he did not believe that there were no classes in precolonial Africa or that there was indeed such a thing as "African socialism." "Colonialism deserves to be blamed for many evils in Africa," Nkrumah concluded, "but surely it was not preceded by an African Golden Age or paradise. A return to the pre-colonial African society is evidently not worthy of the ingenuity and efforts of our people."[2] He believed, however, that colonialism had increased social inequalities in Africa. Nkrumah wrote as a revolutionary Marxist: Africa should seek the means to disengage from Western dependency and capitalism, and violence should be used to impose the socialist ideology.

Nkrumah was unable to develop an ideology as coherent as that of *Ujamaa*. He believed in charismatic leadership, and he took pains to make himself both respected and feared. He wanted to turn his political party into a mass-based party, but he did not succeed. In the Ghanaian economy, public enterprises were allowed to collaborate with foreign ones. By using state agencies to buy and market cocoa, the leading export commodity, the government was able to make a profit by underpaying the farmers. Angry and disappointed by the excessive government control, many farmers cut down on cocoa production. In the early 1960s, cocoa prices declined on the world market, the economy of Ghana began to suffer a decline, and the country resorted to external borrowing. By 1966 when Nkrumah was overthrown, the price of cocoa was low and the economy was in serious trouble.

Léopold Senghor, the president of Senegal from 1960 to 1980, advocated a socialist ideology based on the idea of *négritude* (blackness). The idea of *négritude* was developed in reaction to the European characterization of Africans as inferior, having no history, and contributing nothing to civilization. Senghor celebrated the contributions of Africans to civilization, their humanity, and their spirituality. He regarded *négritude* as a foundation for the development of African socialism. To Senghor, Africa before the imposition of colonial rule was based on spiritual freedom and economic equality and was community oriented. Policies in modern Africa must prevent exploitation and emphasize community sharing.

THE CAPITALIST OPTION

Many countries and leaders did not opt for the socialist approach; instead, they adopted the capitalist options of mixed economies or the free market system or variations of both. Côte d'Ivoire, Nigeria, Kenya, and Senegal were among the countries that stayed with the capitalist approach. A number of weak or poor countries (for example, Niger), which could not risk offending external powers, accepted foreign control and ran their economies as dictated by Western countries. The countries formerly under French rule, with the exception of Guinea, also accepted the advice and leadership of France, which tied their currencies to the franc.

A number of countries were able to decide on their own options. For instance, Nigeria opted for a mixed economy in which the government would spend money on the infrastructure and create some businesses, while allowing private enterprises to flourish. In the case of Côte d'Ivoire, which also opted for capitalism, the country allowed considerable opportunities to foreign companies and relied on migrant labor from Burkina Faso to work on farms.

Some countries, such as Kenya, presented their capitalist approach as an example of African socialism. At about the time that Nyerere was putting together the idea of *Ujamaa*, Kenya under President Jomo Kenyatta issued in 1965 a policy paper, "African Socialism and Its Application to Planning in Kenya." According to this policy, Kenya would choose a policy of "positive non-alignment" based on a rejection of Eastern communism and Western capitalism and the adoption of what it called a "philosophy of Democratic African Socialism." However, in practice, Kenya pursued a capitalist ideology. Throughout the first half of the twentieth century, Kenya was integrated with the European capitalist economy, its land was farmed by European settlers and Africans, and participation in trade involved Asians, Europeans, and others. If Kenya rejected capitalism, it would have to embark on a policy of nationalizing foreign companies, reclaiming land from foreign holders, and attacking Asian merchants.

Kenya actually sought foreign investments, facilitated the means for European and Asian businesses in the country to send their profits abroad, and passed laws to encourage foreign companies to stay in the country. At the same time, the country would encourage the participation of Kenyans in the economy in various ways. Africans would replace the departing British and other foreigners in management positions. Capital would be provided to Kenyans to acquire businesses, while the government would establish some businesses. The government acquired some land from Europeans and redistributed it, while allowing those Europeans who wanted to retain their mechanized farms to do so.

Kenya solicited Western aid and assistance in the form of money, skilled personnel, loans at low interest, grants, and technicians and engineers, many of whom were paid with funds raised from external sources. The government used many of these resources as well as those it generated to establish public agencies in such areas as the manufacturing of coffee and the promotion of tourism. The government also formed business partnerships with foreign firms. Government participation created jobs, provided opportunities for Kenyans to acquire valuable business skills, and reduced foreign control of the economy. In addition, government participation provided support in areas avoided by investors because they were not too profitable—for example, in the provision of transportation, hospitals, and houses for the poor and for rural areas. As in most of Africa, the government also had to build roads and provide social services for its people.

In many African countries, including Kenya, government-run enterprises tend to be inefficient and wasteful. As they request additional funding to improve upon their performance, they drain the country's resources. Political leaders use them to create jobs for their followers and award contracts to favored businessmen. Due to the poor performance of these enterprises, it has often been suggested that they should be privatized.

CONCLUSION

In the final analysis, the ideological options did not resolve the crises identified above. Growth was experienced in some countries such as Nigeria, Kenya, and Côte d'Ivoire, but this was not sustained in later years and did not necessarily lead to development. In most countries, the gap between the rich and the poor widened, the cities were developed at the expense of the rural areas, and social facilities never became adequate. Although great efforts were made to manage the economy, the continent entered the 1970s without having solved its major problems.

NOTES

1. J.K. Nyerere, "The Arusha Declaration," in Julius K. Nyerere, *Ujamaa: Essays on Socialism* (New York: Oxford University Press, 1968), p. 13.
2. Kwame Nkrumah, "African Socialism Revisited," in Wilfred Cartey and Martin Kilson, eds., *The Africa Reader: Independent Africa* (New York: Vintage Books, 1970), p. 203.

SUGGESTIONS FOR FURTHER READING

Clarke, W. Edmund. *Socialist Development and Public Investment in Tanzania, 1964–73.* Toronto: University of Toronto Press, 1978.

Davidson, Basil. *Can Africa Survive? Arguments against Growth without Development.* Boston: Little, Brown, 1974.

Falola, Toyin. *Nationalism and African Intellectuals.* Rochester, N.Y.: University of Rochester Press, 2001.

Hyden, Goran. *Beyond Ujamaa in Tanzania.* Berkeley: University of California Press, 1980.

Leys, Colin. *Underdevelopment in Kenya: The Political Economy of Neo-Colonialism, 1964–1971.* Berkeley: University of California Press, 1974.

Nyerere, Julius K. *Ujamaa: Essays on Socialism.* New York: Oxford University Press, 1968.

28

The Creation of the Economic Community of West African States, 1975

The treaty that established the Economic Community of West African States (ECOWAS) was signed in Lagos on 28 May 1975. In the following year, its five major protocols were signed in Lomé, the capital of Togo. While the Organization of African Unity, or OAU (see Chapter 25), is a continental union, ECOWAS is a regional union of West African countries. It is an economic union, based on the need to integrate West Africa into a big market and create better conditions for development. Sixteen West African countries (Republic of Benin, Cape Verde, Gambia, Ghana, Guinea, Guinea-Bissau, Côte d'Ivoire, Liberia, Mali, Mauritania, Niger, Nigeria, Senegal, Sierra Leone, Togo, and Burkina Faso) formed the union in order to promote greater economic interaction by integrating their markets and pooling their resources. The members pledged to use ECOWAS to create self-reliant regional economies, pursue cooperation in many areas, and trade with one another.

ECOWAS is an example of what is generally described as the phenomenon of regional integration, the process of bringing together two or more countries in a union with the intention of pursuing specific objectives. In the mid-1960s when Africans were pondering their future, the formation of regional organizations was at the top of their priority list. Among the reasons advanced by proponents of regional integration were that it would help Africa to secure full political independence, maintain economic growth and development, safeguard the region from external aggression and unnecessary external influence, and secure for the region a fair share of world resources. The belief was that West Africa should be

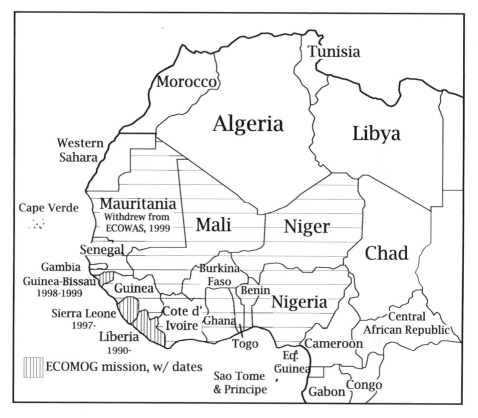

ECOWAS and ECOMOG (Economic Community of West African States Monitoring Group).

strong enough to become not just a major political actor on the international scene but an attractive market in the global economy. To attain successful integration, member states would have to remove many restrictions that separated them, trade freely among themselves while controlling trade with the outside world, create a customs union that would enable them to impose a common external tariff on outsiders, free the movement of capital and labor among the members, and harmonize the monetary, fiscal, and tax policies of the region.

The formation of ECOWAS was a major move. Given the failures of economic management in the 1960s (see Chapter 24), regional cooperation became one of the new strategies to overcome underdevelopment. It was also realized that the OAU deserved to be complemented with smaller regional units that would have more focused and manageable objectives. It was feared that without these smaller regional units the continent would remain a victim of global domination and exploitation. Upon signing the ECOWAS treaty, an excited head of state of Ghana, General Ignatius Acheampong, remarked:

By our signature and subsequent ratification of the treaty we have raised in our citizens the vision of a vast, homogenous society linked together by a complicated network of roads, connected by a direct, efficient and rational system of communications, enriched by a steady flow of commerce and sustained by common ventures in agriculture, industry, energy, mineral resources, and other fields of common activities.[1]

OBJECTIVES

ECOWAS is an economic union, designed to promote cooperation among its members and sponsor development in various fields including transport, industry, energy, telecommunications, agriculture, natural resources, and monetary and financial areas. Members also agreed to seek areas of cooperation in cultural and social matters, all in order to increase the standards of living of their people, increase and maintain economic stability in the region, foster closer relations among members, and contribute to the progress and development of Africa. According to its treaty, ECOWAS is to ensure the following:

- The elimination of customs duties and other charges of equivalent effect in respect of the importation and exportation of goods.
- The abolition of quantitative and administrative restrictions on trade among the member states.
- The establishment of a common customs tariff and a common commercial policy toward Third World countries.
- The abolition, as between member states, of the obstacles to the free movement of persons, services, and capital.
- The harmonization of the agricultural policies and the promotion of common projects in the member states, notably in the fields of marketing research and agroindustrial enterprises.
- The implementation of a scheme for the joint development of transport, communication, energy and other infrastructural facilities, as well as the evolution of a common policy in these fields.

- The harmonization of the economic and industrial policies of the member states and the elimination of disparities in the level of development of member states.
- The harmonization required for the proper functioning of the community of the monetary policies of member states.
- The establishment of funds for cooperation, compensation, and development.
- Such other activities calculated to further the aims of the community as the member states may from time to time undertake in common.

A special office was created in Lomé for the Funds for Cooperation, Compensation and Development, with the responsibility to

- Finance projects in member states;
- Provide compensation to member states that have suffered losses as a result of community enterprises;
- Provide compensation and other forms of assistance to member states that have suffered losses arising from trade liberalization within the community;
- Guarantee foreign investments made by the member states in respect of enterprises established in pursuance of the harmonization of industrial policies;
- Provide appropriate means to facilitate the sustained mobilization of internal and external financial resources for the member states and the community; and
- Promote development projects in the less developed member states of the community.[2]

The funds have their own separate governing board, comprising the representatives of cabinet ministers from all the member states. The board appoints the managing director who sees to the daily administration of the office and funds. Initially, the funds were to operate with capital of $500 million, with a first capitalization of $50 million.

The Executive Secretariat of ECOWAS is in Lagos, Nigeria, and its funds headquarters are in Lomé. The secretariat, headed by an executive secretary appointed by West African heads of state, is the principal administrative organ in charge of the implementation and monitoring of various programs. The secretariat can also initiate new ideas and seek the approval of the various member governments.

ECOWAS represents a bold initiative to unite to develop the West African region. If its treaty can be followed to the letter, ECOWAS will protect the interests of the region and the continent. Countries that were previously divided by competing European powers now have a forum in which to interact. Thus, French-, Portuguese-, and English-speaking countries came together, although their former masters had separated them. This unity is a strength that can be used to protect regional interests against external powers and other competing groups. With a population close to 200 million, ECOWAS is a large grouping with tremendous potential.

To realize the potential, gradual steps have to be taken to create a "common market" similar to that of the European Economic Community. This requires overcoming the obstacles posed by hundreds of languages and loyalties to individual countries. In 1984, the members agreed to coordinate many of their economic programs so that they can complement one another. They plan to create a monetary zone as well as a customs union. The ECOWAS Funds have made small efforts to finance some projects.

Member states have allowed easy movement of labor and goods; they agree on many economic issues; they have prevented conflicts over the use of the River Niger, which passes through many countries; and they have encouraged the foundation of a regional bank. They even established a joint peacekeeping force that intervened to bring peace in Liberia and Sierra Leone.

PROBLEMS

The integration of modern West Africa remains in its preliminary stages. It is not that the people do not want to travel or trade, but communication facilities are still underdeveloped. Telephone links are scarce, and air travel is expensive.

It has not been easy to alter the traditional trade links between each country and its Western trading partners. The principal raw materials are not sold within the region, where there are no industries extensive enough to utilize them, but to Western countries. As all the West African countries also need the products of modern industries and machines, they rely on imports from outside of Africa. Thus, rather than minimizing dependence and the transfer of wealth abroad, the need for external trade has meant the marginalization of ECOWAS.

The resources and wealth of the member nations are varied. There are wealthy countries (notably Nigeria) and poor ones such as Burkina Faso. This affects the funding of the community. Some members do not pay their dues on a regular basis.

Migration and mobility of people have posed some problems, even leading to the expulsion of noncitizens from such countries as Ghana and Nigeria, contrary to the treaty and to the idea of the free flow of people. In the case of Nigeria, its declining economy since the 1980s makes it less receptive to migrants from the ECOWAS member states. The migrants have been criticized for taking jobs from citizens; disregarding the laws of the country; promoting immoral behavior; contributing to inflation, especially high prices of basic food items; and increasing crime, especially armed robbery and car theft, as the criminals and their stolen goods can easily cross the borders.

The treaty providing for free movement without restrictions occasionally runs into trouble. There have been cases when a country has arrested migrants, as in the case of forty-six Ghanaians who died in a prison in Côte d'Ivoire in 1981. Following this incident, diplomatic relations between the two countries broke down for some months.

In Liberia, Sierra Leone, and other countries that have experienced civil war or prolonged political disorder, neighboring countries have been accused of sponsoring rebels and dissidents, harboring fugitives, and training soldiers. Interference in the internal political affairs of member states has been a source of problems.

Nigeria, the regional power and the biggest country, tends to see some aspects of ECOWAS as a nuisance. Some Nigerians are inclined to argue that other ECOWAS members have exploited the country and threatened its economy.

Nigeria bears a large part of the burden of funding ECOWAS, and a number of its citizens think that the benefit is not worth the expense. As with all regional unions in other parts of the world, a country may worry about the economic and political consequences of losing part of its sovereignty. Some Nigerians think that through ECOWAS, their country may lose control over its destiny. However, ECOWAS has not been a hindrance to the development of Nigeria.

REGIONAL UNITY FOR DEVELOPMENT

What ECOWAS has demonstrated is the need for unity to enhance economic development and remove the obstacles in the way of realizing this goal. Building unity within each country is not enough, and such efforts have to be supplemented with the equally important effort to create cooperation among nations. Many countries are either small or poor, but they will be able to compete and survive if they organize powerful cooperation among themselves. Such regional groupings as ECOWAS will minimize conflicts among countries and provide a forum in which to resolve tensions. Africans realize that the colonial boundaries can weaken them, unless they find the means to come together. Pan-Africanism, the formation of the Organization of African Unity, and the foundation of ECOWAS demonstrate the advantages of unity, even if progress is slow.

Other groupings have also emerged. In 1980, nine countries in southern Africa (Botswana, Lesotho, Swaziland, Zimbabwe, Zambia, Malawi, Tanzania, Angola, and Mozambique) established the Southern African Development Coordination Conference (SADCC), with objectives similar to those of ECOWAS, in addition to struggling to end apartheid in South Africa. The much older Arab League (established in 1944) brings together North African countries and nations with large Muslim populations such as Sudan and Somalia. There are also smaller unions, such as the Mano River Union between Guinea, Liberia, and Sierra Leone, formed to discuss issues of common interest.

To take the case of SADCC, formed a few years after ECOWAS, this regional union was established with the signing, in 1980, of the Lusaka Declaration on "Southern Africa: Towards Economic Liberation." In its preamble, the declaration described the countries in southern Africa as "fragmented, grossly exploited and subject to economic manipulation by outsiders." As with ECOWAS, the members resolved to attain economic liberation, based on the pursuit of the following objectives:

- Reduction of economic dependence, particularly, but not only, on the Republic of South Africa.
- Forging of links to create a genuine and equitable regional integration.
- Mobilization of resources to promote the implementation of national, interstate, and regional policies.
- Concerted action to secure international cooperation within the framework of a strategy for economic liberation.

The members agreed to prioritize on the development of communication and transportation in order to link their countries and promote trade. They recognized that trade among the members was small; less than 10 percent of their external trade was conducted between them, while their trade with South Africa was far more important.

As with ECOWAS, poor transport and communication linkages and weak national economies created obstacles to the realization of trade growth among the members. However, significant changes were recorded after 1980. Zimbabwe substantially improved its trade relations with other members, as it was able to export more goods to them and improve its industrial sector. After 1992, the members also agreed to work toward the creation of a regional common market, similar to that of ECOWAS.

SADCC was able to coordinate a number of development efforts and relate to external agencies. It established a number of smaller professional and cultural organizations to further unite the member countries. For external companies looking for investment opportunities, the emphasis on the improvement of transportation opened fresh avenues. In the 1980s when sanctions were being imposed on South Africa, the external companies also hoped to be able to divert their business to other parts of the region. The members of SADCC met regularly to discuss issues of importance and to coordinate some of their activities with external donors.

One area where SADCC recorded greater success than ECOWAS was the coordination of its activities with foreign donors and lenders. The members agreed among themselves as to the development projects they needed and then negotiated with donors to fund them. By 1990, SADCC had received about $2.5 billion to fund almost 500 projects in communication, energy, transportation, food supply, training and research in agriculture, and rehabilitation of railways and ports. The member states were also able to link some of their power grids. So that each country would benefit from the proposed projects, the offices were decentralized: The tourism office was located in Lesotho, energy in Angola, food security in Mozambique, and mining in Zambia.

With the fall of apartheid in South Africa in the 1990s, SADCC has had to face adjustments to a new political reality in which it has to promote friendship with a former enemy. South Africa may emerge as the regional powerhouse in the region, with the means to assist in the development of its neighbors.

THE RELEVANCE OF REGIONAL INTEGRATION

It is true that ECOWAS and SADCC have yet to reduce the problems of underdevelopment and dependence on Western countries. Trade contacts with developed nations remain strong, while the commercial benefits of regional interaction are not fully reaped. Regional economic policies are yet to be fully harmonized. SADCC has acquired substantial external debts in order to finance many projects, thereby consolidating its dependency relations. All these problems notwithstanding, ECOWAS, SADCC, and other regional groupings remain important and deserve to be strengthened, rather than abandoned, as some critics have suggested. The contributions of regional integration are many, including the following:

- Different countries, peoples, and leaders have an organization that can enable them to meet and cooperate. Over time, trust and productive interactions are generated.
- The creation of a regional identity is important, as it can serve various political purposes, such as speaking with a common voice in moments of crisis and preventing the outbreak and spread of conflicts.
- As the example of SADCC has demonstrated, a larger regional union has improved the chances of obtaining external funding. The individual countries would have received far less had they negotiated separately. The debts, in the case of external loans, can be shared.
- Economic benefits can accrue, notably the expansion of the market, trade diversification, monetary stability, import saving, and increased savings. Regional integration offers the possibility of greater regional trade, if member states can exchange goods among themselves. For instance, South Africa can supply other countries in the region with industrial goods. Nigeria can supply oil products to other West African countries. When new industries are established, they can be protected by a common external tariff.

NOTES

1. *West Africa*, 2 August 1976, p.1091.
2. *ECOWAS Final Communiqué*, ECW/HS9/1/21/REv/, Lagos, April 1978.

SUGGESTIONS FOR FURTHER READING

Amin, S.D. Chitala, and I. Mandaza, eds. *SADCC: Prospects for Disengagement and Development in Southern Africa*. London: Zed, 1987.

Falola, Toyin, and Jide Olagbaju. "Economic Cooperation: The ECOWAS Example." In G.O. Ogunremi and E.K. Faluyi, eds., *An Economic History of West Africa since 1750*. Ibadan, Nigeria: Rex Charles, in association with Connel Publications, 1996. Pp. 246–56.

Falola, Toyin, and S.A. Olanrewaju. "Development through Integration: The Politics and Problems of ECOWAS." In O. Akinrinade and J.K. Barling, eds., *Economic Development in Africa: International Efforts, Issues and Prospects*. London: Pinter, 1987. Pp. 52–76.

Lee, M. *SADCC: The Political Economy of Development in Southern Africa*. Nashville, Tenn.: Winston-Derek Publishers, 1989.

Onwuka, I. Ralph. *Development and Integration: The Case of the Economic Community of West African States*. Ile-Ife, Nigeria: University of Ife Press, 1982.

29

Portuguese Colonies Attain Freedom, 1975

If the majority of African countries had long since attained independence and were struggling with its gains and pains by the early 1970s (see Chapter 24), the areas controlled by the Portuguese were still under an oppressive colonial system. Guinea-Bissau, the Cape Verde Islands, São Tomé and Príncipe, Angola, and Mozambique did not become independent until the mid-1970s, an event that closed a long chapter in Luso-African relations. The independence struggles in the Portuguese colonies were noted for the extensive use of violence in armed struggles that lasted for many years. Ideology was important, as the African leaders opted for a socialist option, which displeased the countries interested in the advancement of capitalism. The liberation of Portuguese colonies and the end of apartheid in South Africa became the principal goals of the foreign policy of the majority of African states during the 1970s. Portuguese rule reminded Africans of the brutality of the colonial system.

LONG RETENTION

The Portuguese were the earliest Europeans to reach Africa, exploring the western and eastern coasts in the fifteenth and sixteenth centuries. They embarked upon trade and established control over some areas along the coast. When the Scramble for Africa began in the 1880s, the Portuguese extended their claims in the hinterlands of the coastal areas they already controlled. Their largest colonies were Mozambique, Angola, and Guinea-Bissau, which, in most of the

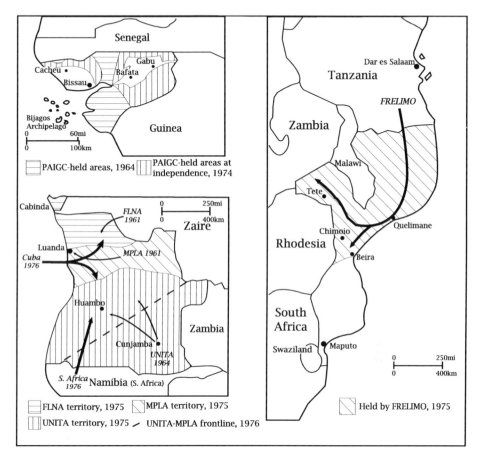

Wars of liberation in Angola, Mozambique, and Guinea-Bissau.

literature, is regarded as including the Cape Verde Islands. As it turned out, this earliest European power was also among the very last to leave Africa.

The Portuguese African colonies were brutally exploited and for much longer than most other parts of Africa. Why were these colonies repressed for so long? To start with, Portugal derived many benefits from the exploitation of its African colonies. For over 300 years, beginning in the sixteenth century, the Portuguese treated their coastal possessions as lucrative sources of slaves to be sold across the Atlantic. The possession of African territories became a way for Portuguese kings to reward their families, friends, and associates, who were given large colonial estates. Military expeditions were raised to conquer these estates, and their owners regarded Africans as subjects and sources of free labor. Estate owners were brutal and repressive. When these areas became colonies during the twentieth century, the older practices were only slightly modified. The Portuguese government continued to give large grants of colonial lands to foreign companies that exercised complete control over these lands and used them for whatever they wanted. The use of Africans as forced labor simply replaced their being shipped abroad as slaves.

Yet another reason for treating the Africans so badly and for so long was that Portugal itself was badly governed for most of the twentieth century. The unsavory politics and mismanagement at home were reflected abroad. In 1910, Portugal became a republic, but a mediocre record of achievement provided an excuse for the army to take over in 1926. Seven years later, Antonio de Oliveira Salazar became dictator. Promising to reform the society and improve the economy, Salazar concentrated all power in his hands and abolished civil liberties. Portugal became a police state, and the ruthlessness exhibited at home was extended to its colonies in Africa. As far as Salazar was concerned, the African colonies gave his country an image of greatness among other European nations. In addition, the wealth of Africa could be used to rebuild the economy of Portugal. In 1968, an aging Salazar was replaced by Marcello Caetano, but Caetano merely continued with most of the policies of his predecessor until Portugal was forced by protests to change course in 1974.

A third and final reason for the long and brutal exploitation of its colonies was that Portugal was a rather poor country, and it regarded its African colonies as a source of alleviating its own poverty. The colonies were rich, with fertile soils, rich forests, good climates, rivers to generate hydroelectric power, and minerals such as diamonds, gold, iron, mica, copper, phosphates, manganese, and petroleum. In spite of this, the colonies were poor because Portugal itself was poor and partly relied on them for survival. Portugal lacked the capital to invest in the colonies and had a limited range of manufactured goods to exchange for raw materials. In exploiting its colonies, Portugal had to invite foreign businesses and other European countries to invest in its colonies. These companies were given generous concessions over minerals, land, and labor. Before 1930, to build the ports in Angola and Mozambique and the railway in Angola, Portugal relied on external investors. After 1930, the colonies generated wealth, and their products were in high demand in the world market. The Salazar government regarded the colonies as provinces, so as to make it possible to unify their economies with those of Portugal and live on the colonies' wealth.

Agriculture, forestry, and mining were the three principal sources of wealth in the colonies. Mozambique supplied crops such as cashew nuts, cane sugar, tea, cotton, copra, sisal, maize, peanuts, maize, *kenaf*, and tobacco. Angola had coffee, sisal, maize, cane sugar, cotton, oil palm products, beans, manioc, rice, millet, tobacco, and sorghum. Guinea-Bissau produced rice, peanuts, and oil palm products. In Angola and Mozambique, cattle were raised. All of the colonies also supplied timber. External companies were granted large land concessions to produce many of these items for export. They had the power to recruit African labor, collect taxes from Africans, and make laws and regulations to control them.

Angola became a supplier of diamonds from 1917 onward, with two mining companies formed by investors from the United States, Belgium, and Britain. One-quarter of the country to the northeast was given in concessions to these companies, and a third company received a concession to mine in the coastal areas. After 1955, petroleum exploration began in Angola, carried out by a Portuguese company in partnership with a Belgian one. Investors from Germany, Denmark, Austria, and the United States mined the iron in Angola. In Mozambique, foreign companies exploited iron, coal, and tantalite. Through concessions to foreign companies, hydroelectric works, ports, and railways were built in Mozambique.

The Portuguese authorities forced Africans to work in order to reduce the cost of production, and they were interested in using any profitable resources at little cost. The use of forced labor was the most oppressive of all the Portuguese colonial measures. It started with the so-called Native Labor Regulations of 1899, which stated:

All natives of Portuguese overseas provinces are subject to the obligation, moral and legal, of attempting to obtain through work the means that they lack to subsist and to better their social condition. They have full liberty to choose the method of fulfilling this obligation, but if they do not fulfill it, public authority may force a fulfillment.

What this meant in practice was that the Portuguese colonial authorities could force all Africans to work. Indeed, the use of force was presented as part of the responsibility of Portugal to "civilize" Africans—forced labor was assumed to develop their moral and physical growth and to turn so-called lazy people into productive citizens. In a system known as "corrective labor" or "contract labor," an African could be seized by a company or government official and forced to work for low wages. Contractors went about "hunting" labor, and chiefs were directed to send people to work. An African deemed to be "jobless" was forced to work—Portuguese officers defined what was meant by "joblessness" so that they could round up people whenever labor was needed by companies. Portugal also devised a way of sending its own citizens to Africa, again to solve its internal economic problems. This strategy of exporting its people created additional problems.

PORTUGUESE MIGRANTS AND RACE RELATIONS

The Salazar regime promoted a policy of large-scale emigration of Portuguese citizens to Africa, to add to those who had settled there since the sixteenth century. The Salazar government presented migration as exciting and rewarding and appealed to youth to see living in Africa as a great adventure. The main motive was to reduce the unemployment problems in Portugal.

Between the 1930s and the 1960s, the number of Portuguese settlers in the African colonies increased substantially. To take a few examples, the number of settlers in Angola increased from about 30,000 in 1930 to over 172,000 by 1960. Ten years later, Angola had a settler population of almost 250,000, making it the country with the second largest European settler population on the continent (South Africa came first and Rhodesia third). By 1970, Mozambique had over 130,000 European settlers, the fourth largest concentration in Africa. Only a few, about 2,000, went to Guinea.

From the 1950s onward, the settlers were encouraged to become large-scale farmers in Mozambique and Angola. Large farm colonies or settlements, known as *colonatos*, were established to provide employment for Portuguese settlers. The Portuguese government provided money and selected families in Portugal who were transported to Africa to settle on the *colonatos*. They were provided with land, seeds, and livestock to establish farms. Roads, irrigation works, and electricity were provided in the *colonatos* to make them attractive and profitable. The creation of these settlements took away land from Africans and turned many of them into tenants of Portuguese settlers.

The presence of Portuguese settlers in these colonies created problems in race relations. A new identity group was created, the *mestisos*, products of interracial marriages between Africans and Portuguese. The *mestisos* ran into thousands, and the Portuguese used this to deny evidence of racial discrimination in their colonies. While it is true that Portuguese colonies did not practice apartheid of the form found in South Africa (see Chapter 20), it is equally true that segregation and racial discrimination did exist.

Racial issues are rooted in the history of Luso-African relations. During the era of the slave trade (see Chapter 11), the Portuguese were merciless in their raids for Africans, whom they regarded as animals. When they established their colonies in the 1890s, they passed a series of laws to define the legal status of colonial subjects. Up until the 1950s, Africans were officially known as *indigenas*, meaning uncivilized people who needed a series of measures to "bring them up" and control them. They were actually denied human and civil rights, a denial justified by the need to curtail the "primitive people." The *indigenas* had to carry identification cards at all times, and they had to be able to produce the cards on demand by the colonial authorities. To fail to do so was to risk imprisonment or a term of "corrective labor." The *indigenas* needed official permission to leave their area of abode in search of jobs. They were not allowed to leave their countries without permission, and even with permission they could visit only Rhodesia (now Zimbabwe) and South Africa where Africans were also badly treated. In some areas, a permanent curfew was imposed on the *indigenas* to restrict their movements. Their children were not allowed in public schools. Those who owned cattle were not always allowed to slaughter or give away their cattle without permission. Those who kept their money in banks could not withdraw it without permission.

As many more Portuguese settlers arrived in the colonies, the *indigenas* suffered more problems and economic disabilities. Although many of the Portuguese immigrants were unskilled and uneducated, they took the jobs for which Africans were qualified. Even menial jobs were given to the settlers unless they did not want them.

To escape the indignities of being *indigenas*, individuals had to seek assimilation into the legally and socially higher status of a privileged group, the *assimilados*. To become an *assimilado*, one must be able to write and read in Portuguese, make enough money to support a family, serve in the army when called upon to do so, demonstrate so-called qualities of human interaction and social graces, and persuade the colonial officials that they were of good character and dignified habits. There was a rite of passage—an *indigena* who sought to become an *assimilado* would submit a formal application to the government and be interviewed on a designated date, with probing questions about his public and private life. If deemed successful, he was issued a card reclassifying him as an *assimilado*, which meant that he was now regarded as a Portuguese citizen, with the right to freedom and privileges. He no longer required permission to move about, he could compete for many jobs, he was exempted from forced labor, and his children could attend government schools.

The attempts to force Africans into accepting the imposed identity of the *assimilado* were not without their problems. Many who were qualified refused to apply, just to rebel against an oppressive system and to avoid a humiliating process. Applicants were also required to have gone to school. Up till the 1950s, the Portuguese did not invest in schools and other social services. While they believed that education was necessary to "civilize" Africans, they were afraid that educated Africans would endanger Portuguese interests. Even in Portugal itself, the government was not spending enough to educate its own citizens, with the result that the rate of illiteracy in 1960 was 40 percent, the highest in Europe. In Africa, progress was slow. In Angola, the most developed colony as far as education was concerned, in 1950, there were only about 13,000 children in elementary schools, about 3,000 in secondary schools, and less than 2,000 in technical schools, out of a population of close to 4 million. The Catholic Church dominated the school system, and it concentrated on a "rudimentary education" of three years to teach Portuguese culture and language.

To those who became *assimilados*, it was clear that they were not necessarily treated as equals of the Portuguese, as they could not compete for all jobs or receive the same pay as the Portuguese. Moreover, they paid higher taxes on their incomes. They forfeited certain indigenous rights, such as inheriting family land or becoming chiefs. Not even 1 percent of Africans in all the Portuguese colonies became *assimilados*.

NATIONALISM AND WARS

As with their counterparts in other parts of the continent, Africans in the Portuguese colonies were not happy with the features of the colonial system highlighted above. While it was clear that other European powers would grant independence to their colonies in the 1950s and 1960s, Portugal never intended to leave. Rather, it chose the politics of making concessions to Africans, in order to buy time. The brutalities of its colonial system were also becoming the subject of international attention, thus forcing Portugal to rethink, just to retain investors from the United States and Europe.

In 1953, legislative reforms were introduced to set up a council with a majority of elected members. In practice, this was difficult to attain. Only a few educated Africans were allowed to vote, in addition to nonliterate heads of households. To qualify as a member of the council, one had to be a Portuguese citizen born in the colony where he was seeking power, educated, and with a job. This favored the Portuguese settlers.

Early in the 1960s, "contract labor" was abolished, and everybody was granted Portuguese citizenship, thereby eradicating the distinction between the *indigena* and the *assimilado*. The school system was also expanded. Nevertheless, the established social and racial distinctions remained in place.

The harsh nature of Portuguese rule provoked an equally harsh form of nationalism among Africans in the Portuguese colonies. Resistance to the imposition of Portuguese rule lingered in Angola until 1915, in Mozambique until the 1920s, and in Guinea until the 1930s. As Portuguese rule became established, Africans took to violence in many places. Violent uprisings were common in all the colonies until the 1940s.

Educated Africans began to organize modern nationalist politics in the 1950s. Compared to other parts of the continent, this was rather late, but the reason was again the repressive nature of Portuguese rule, which was hostile to any form of political expression. For a long time, the only associations they tolerated were the ones established by the government itself for the *assimilados*. These *assimilado* associations were mainly social and cultural, they were not allowed to discuss politics, and their activities were closely monitored by the government. In cases where an association indicated an interest in politics, the government would remove its leaders and choose new ones. The watchful eye of the government was such that educated Africans found it almost impossible to establish political associations. As far as the Portuguese authorities were concerned, the African colonies were mere provinces of Portugal, and there was no such thing as a movement for independence. Even after the Second World War when most of Africa moved into a radical nationalist phase (see Chapter 21), the Portuguese refused the freedom of press, association, and expression. Even the settlers were denied the privilege of establishing a political party.

The emerging African nationalists were forced to go underground, mobilizing and meeting in secrecy. They founded cultural and religious associations but met in areas where they could not be seen to talk about politics. Members took great risks. When they were discovered, the penalty was severe. A secret police force was introduced in the colonies in the 1950s, and suspected people were severely repressed. In Angola in 1956, African leaders were arrested and deported. Three years later, the secret police compiled names of hundreds of people involved in politics, and all were arrested and punished. Many were tried in secret and later sent to jail. In Mozambique, many were to suffer arrest, and in 1956, forty-nine protesting dockworkers were shot to death. In 1960, about 600 Maconde people in northern Mozambique were killed for protesting. In Guinea-Bissau, the "Massacre of Pidjiguiti" in 1959, when the Portuguese authorities killed many striking workers, is now regarded as a landmark in nationalist history.

Seeing the brutality of the Portuguese authorities, African nationalists resorted to a single strategy: the use of violence. Acting underground, and later on boldly in public, political parties began to emerge from the mid-1950s onward, with a commitment to use violence to dislodge the Portuguese. In Angola, the United African Party of Angola (abbreviated as the PLUA in Portuguese) called on the people to prepare for war. In 1956, the leaders of the PLUA and other underground associations merged to establish the Popular Movement for the Liberation of Angola (abbreviated as the MPLA in Portuguese), with Agostinho Neto as their leader. In Mozambique, the nationalists in exile in Tanzania and elsewhere began to form nationalist organizations from 1960 onward. In 1962, many of these associations united to form the Mozambique Liberation Front (FRELIMO) and chose as its leader a former university professor, Dr. Eduardo Mondlane. In Guinea-Bissau, the most important of the nationalist associations was the Independence Party of Guinea and Cape Verde (PAIGC) led by Amilcar Cabral, a notable socialist thinker. The parties and leaders in all these colonies exchanged notes and ideas. The Portuguese had to face three major wars of liberation—in Angola from February 1961, in Guinea-Bissau from January 1963, and in Mozambique from September 1964.

When the Congo (Kinshasa) obtained its independence in 1960, it generated excitement in neighboring Angola. The Bakongo people had been divided into two countries, some of them living in southern Congo and others in northern Angola. The Bakongo learned lessons from the independence of their kin in the Congo. In 1960, the MPLA sent a petition to Portugal, asking for dialogue and a peaceful transition to independence. The leaders of the MPLA were immediately arrested, and the police killed protesters who demanded their freedom. With the failure of other petitions to the United Nations and to Western countries, the MPLA began to prepare for war. Early in 1961, the Portuguese authorities killed thousands of people in the districts of Malange and bombed many villages where opposition was expected. In February 1961, the MPLA attacked the radio station, prison, and military barracks in Luanda, the capital, beginning a long and brutal liberation war. In March, a revolt broke out among the coffee planters in Primavera in northern Angola. The revolt spread to other parts of the north. The Portuguese responded with the use of maximum force, killing over 20,000 people and using bombs to destroy many villages. The liberation movement succeeded in driving out the Portuguese from the north in 1961. However, the Portuguese quest to reconquer the northern province led to more wars. In 1962, a new political group emerged, the National Front for the Liberation of Angola (the NFLA), based in northern Angola. The NFLA was able to operate from the Congo where it trained its soldiers to conduct guerrilla activities in Angola. In 1962, Agostinho Neto escaped from prison, and the MPLA began its own guerrilla wars. A third movement also emerged, the National Union for the Total Independence of Angola (UNITA), which operated in the eastern parts of the country.

The experience was similar in the other Portuguese colonies where guerrilla activities were also carried out. In 1964, FRELIMO started its liberation wars in Mozambique, concentrating in areas close to Tanzania where it had its base. In Guinea-Bissau, the PAIGC started its own wars in 1963, with a great deal of determination and courage.

PORTUGAL'S REACTIONS

The Portuguese government did not regard the African nationalists as people fighting for the freedom of their countries but as terrorists who must be destroyed with all available means. Leading Portuguese officials believed that the loss of Portugal's African colonies would simply worsen its economy and lead to more poverty. Portugal was determined to use its army to crush the African liberation movements and to continue its dictatorial colonial rule. The Portuguese forces were enlarged to deal with the situation. As the guerrilla fighters relied on the people in the rural areas to hide them and help them survive, the Portuguese authorities forcibly relocated many people to so-called "fortified villages." If a village was known to support the guerrillas, it was destroyed and its people killed.

Portugal drew support from the United States and some European countries since it lacked the resources to sustain its wars. From France came military helicopters, West Germany and the United States gave bombs and bombers, while the United States also supplied naval vessels. To disguise their intention, the foreign countries maintained that the various supplies were provided to defend Portugal in Europe and not for use in Africa. Apartheid South Africa and racist Rhodesia also gave massive support to Portugal. Indeed, Portugal formed an alliance with South Africa and Rhodesia to coordinate their strategies against African resistance in the southern African region.

To consolidate the support of its foreign allies, Portugal granted a series of additional concessions to America and European countries, who were allowed to make more profit and claim areas rich in minerals. The African liberation movements included a number of foreign companies as targets for destruction.

To divide the Africans and deny popular support to the liberation movements, the Portuguese authorities made some changes. From the 1960s onward, they began to allow a certain level of political discussion in the hope that some assimilated Africans would support Portuguese rule. More Africans were allowed to vote after 1968, again with the idea that this would be interpreted as freedom. More schools were established, and economic and social councils were created to advise the government.

A serious effort was made to fragment the liberation movements and to destroy their unity. In Angola, the Portuguese recruited Africans from the south to fight in the north in order to sow the seeds of ethnic discord. In Mozambique, the Portuguese planted the idea that the Maconde group controlled FRELIMO because its members wanted to dominate other groups in the country. The intense struggles among the various liberation movements and the rivalry among their leaders were exploited to advantage by the Portuguese. Between 1969 and 1973, two principal leaders, Eduardo Mondlane of FRELIMO and Amilcar Cabral of the PAIGC, were assassinated. Successors emerged to carry the wars to a positive conclusion.

THE LAST DAYS OF PORTUGUESE RULE

The wars went on until the 1970s, but the Africans prevailed in the end. By 1970 in Guinea, the PAIGC was already in control of about two-thirds of the country. In Mozambique, FRELIMO controlled the northeast, almost one-third of the country. In 1972, they added parts of the northwest to the areas under their authority. In Angola, the Portuguese were forced to confine themselves to the cities, as the freedom fighters controlled many areas in the countryside.

To draw more people to their side and to show that independence would bring progress, the liberation movements embarked upon changes in areas under their control. Although they had limited funding, they developed projects to improve education. They established schools and enrolled more students in elementary schools. Technical schools were also created. The ideologies of revolution and social change were taught. As the Portuguese had divided the African groups by categorizing them as competing "tribes," the liberation movements had to unite the people as citizens of the same country. The movements also espoused an ideology and plan—notably socialist—to develop their countries and unite their people. They could not accept the society constructed by the Portuguese and had to create an alternative society based on freedom and equality. The liberation movements promised to give power to the people. The Portuguese had forced them not even to consider the option of losing the war, as the consequences would be grave for them and the people.

In 1973, the PAIGC declared the independence of Guinea-Bissau. Many African countries and a few countries outside the continent gave their support and recognition. The colonial wars took a toll on Portugal, dividing its leaders and people. A faction of the army that wanted the wars to end overthrew the government of Caetano in 1974. The new government stopped all the wars and promised to grant independence. Guinea and Cape Verde became independent in 1974, and Mozambique and Angola followed in 1975. Portugal itself became a parliamentary democracy, a change made possible by the wars of liberation in Africa.

SUGGESTIONS FOR FURTHER READING

Akintoye, Stephen Adebanji. *Emergent African States: Topics in Twentieth Century African History*. London: Longman, 1976.

Birmingham, David. *Frontline Nationalism in Angola and Mozambique*. London: James Currey, 1992.

Davidson, Basil. *The Liberation of Guiné*. Baltimore, Md.: Penguin, 1969.

Davidson, Basil. *In the Eye of the Storm: Angola's People*. Garden City, N.Y.: Doubleday, 1973.

Falola, Toyin. "Colonialism and Exploitation." *Lusophone Areas Studies Journal* 1, no. 1 (1982): 41–62.

Falola, Toyin. "Amilcar Cabral on African Economic Development." *Lusophone Areas Studies Journal*, no. 2 (1983): 64–72.

Gibson, Richard. *African Liberation Movements*. London: Oxford University Press, 1972.

Grundy, Kenneth. *Guerilla Struggle in Africa*. New York: Grossman, 1971.

MacQueen, Norrie. *The Decolonization of Portuguese Africa: Metropolitan Revolution and the Dissolution of the Empire*. New York: Addison Wesley Longman, 1997.

Munslow, Barry. *Mozambique: The Revolution and Its Origins*. New York: Longman, 1983.

30

Cultural Revival and Cultural Inventory: The Second World Black Festival of Arts and Culture, 1977

The Second World and African Festival of Arts and Culture will be a momentous event in the annals of our cultural crusade.

Olusegun Obasanjo, 1977[1]

In 1977, Nigeria hosted the Second World Black Festival of Arts and Culture (FESTAC), an event that attracted participants from Africa and other countries with black populations. FESTAC also celebrated African culture and directed world attention to African music, fine art, dance, literature, performing art, religion, philosophy, and other aspects of culture. FESTAC was Africa's biggest cultural event during the twentieth century, one that enabled black people to reassert their definition of the self, emphasize the role of Africa in the black world, and present the various elements of African culture to the world at large. FESTAC also made it possible to analyze the state of knowledge in the understanding of African culture. There was a political side to it: Black people wanted to use their culture to promote identity, draw on FESTAC to express their cultural freedom and demand respect from others, reject the domination of other cultures, and assert the possibility of development without rejecting tradition.

WHAT IS FESTAC?

The first major postindependence cultural event organized by blacks, known as the World Festival of Negro Arts (later changed to the First World Black and African Festival of Arts and Culture, to avoid the negative connotation attached to the word *Negro* in the United States) was held in Dakar, Senegal, in 1966. Nigeria hosted the second and larger festival in 1977. The main objectives of FESTAC were to

- Ensure the revival, resurgence, propagation, and promotion of black and African cultural values and civilization;
- Present black and African culture in its highest and broadest conception;
- Bring to light the diverse contributions of black and African peoples to the universal currents of thought and the arts;
- Promote black and African artists, performers, and writers and facilitate their world acceptance and their access to world outlets;
- Promote better international and interracial understanding; and
- Facilitate a periodic "return to origin" in Africa by black artists, writers, and performers uprooted and living in other continents.

Lagos, then the capital city of Nigeria, was the main venue, although a major event, the parade of horses and their riders known as the *durbar*, took place in the northern city of Kaduna. Seventy-five countries were represented, with thousands of participants in various aspects of culture. The festival emblem was a sixteenth-century ivory mask from Benin, worn as a pectoral mask by Benin kings. In 1897, the original was seized by the British, following their invasion of the Benin empire, and later deposited in the British Museum. The festival flag consisted of three rectangles—the two on the outside were black to represent the black people, and the one in the middle was gold to represent the wealth of culture and the nonblack peoples associated with FESTAC. The major festival events included the following:

- Exhibitions on African history, the black contribution to science, technology, and invention, books, costumes, domestic arts, handicrafts, animals, musical instruments, the influence of African art on European art, and many others.
- Dances, including traditional African dances, African American, Caribbean, and Australasian dances, ballet, modern dance, and contemporary dance theater.
- Music, including traditional African, African American, African-Latin, Afro-Caribbean, and Australasian music, and modern music from all parts of Africa and the African Diaspora.
- Drama, including tragedy, comedy, poetic recitals, presentations revolving around fables and legends, children's shows, and pantomime.
- Films, notably feature films, short-length films, children's films, cartoons, and documentaries.

• Literature, including poetry, essays, novels, short stories, fables and legends, and texts for children.

• A colloquium on the theme of "Black Civilization and Education" covering such aspects as arts, philosophy, literature, languages, history, pedagogy, religion, arts and sciences, government, and the mass media.

BLACKNESS AND CULTURE

The events and lectures were meant to celebrate black culture and its relevance in the modern world. The assumption was that people and culture cannot be separated and that following a period of European rule (see Chapter 19) Africans and black people worldwide should invest in the rediscovery of their past and the ties that bind them, explore the contributions of blacks to their societies and to civilization in general, encourage the coexistence of different cultures, and use culture to reduce global violence and ease world tensions. In the words of Olusegun Obasanjo, the patron of FESTAC:

The Festival will help obliterate erroneous ideas regarding the cultural values of the Black and African race. The occasion will surely lead to the abandonment of the "museum approach" to our culture by which men of other cultures consider our culture only in terms of pre-historic objects to be occasionally dusted, displayed and studied instead as a living thing containing and portraying the ethos of our peoples.[2]

The promotion of black culture was also regarded as crucial in order to protect its destruction by other cultures. The belief was that external influences had had a damaging impact on Africans, creating a crisis in their social life, destroying behavior patterns and attitudes on marriage, education, family systems, and religion, and promoting private and public vices.

Léopold Senghor, the leading exponent of the idea of blackness (*négritude*) and African personality and the convener of the first festival in 1966, was another leading voice in the campaign for FESTAC. In his view, Africans have deep values that FESTAC must celebrate. Senghor asserted that there was a black culture and a black civilization, original to blacks, and expressed in their politics, arts, literature, language, tapestry, sculpture, and religion. In identifying what is typically black culture, Senghor remarked that it includes "fundamentally, the sense of communion between the visible and the invisible, man, nature and God; the sense of analogical images, which expresses this communion and finally, the sense of rhythm."[3] What FESTAC focused attention on was the link between race and culture and the necessity of relying on culture in the development of black people.

CULTURAL HERITAGE

The cultural heritage that was displayed covered the fine arts, songs, dances, drama, history, humanism, and religion, just to mention a few areas. FESTAC also enabled African scholars to review the state of knowledge in various disciplines. The focus here was on the documentation of culture by the scholars and others in an attempt to identify the crucial components of African culture. Just a few of the ideas and issues that emerged from the works and papers presented during FESTAC are used as illustrations here.

Cultural Identity

Africans have always had their culture, defined as the totality of their experiences, including all social and political institutions, material items, habits, philosophy, religion, art, aesthetics, theater, dress, and agricultural practices. Society and its culture are integrated—all institutions are knitted together, and religion runs through all aspects. An individual is regarded as an integral part of a community, and a feeling of belonging within a kinship system is promoted. The principles of collective sharing, social justice, and the welfare of all members of the society are promoted. There is a social hierarchy based on age, while values emphasize wisdom, responsibility, and accomplishments. Religion is important, as the community engages in collective worship and encourages individuals to focus on the spiritual, and all seek the intervention of unseen forces in their lives. The impact of external influences is recognized as well as the rapid spread of cultural ideas from other places. Many people expressed the fear that the African continent was moving from a community culture to a culture of the market, that the old sanctions and sense of community were weakening, and that new classes and social tensions were emerging. In spite of the changes, many participants at FESTAC believed that there are peculiarly African cultural features, such as the values of generosity, brotherhood, affection to others, and spirituality. Aspects of African culture have been carried elsewhere, notably Latin America, the Caribbean, the United States, and Europe, by Africans who now constitute a Black Diaspora.

Cosmology

The rich African view of the universe has suffered from limited written documentation but is well expressed in proverbs, idioms, wise sayings, legends, and myths and in art, symbols, and dances. Africans believe that the universe was created by God, whose existence is generally taken for granted. As a created universe, it belongs to God, the creator. It is a two-tier universe, in which God lives in heaven together with other beings. While human beings may die, there is no idea of an end to time or the universe. The universe is believed to be governed by laws of nature, by a religious order, a moral order among people, and the existence of evil can be conquered by the intervention of spiritual forces. Human beings occupy the center of the universe, but they have to worship God and respect nature in order to survive.

Art

The feeling at FESTAC was that it was necessary to preserve objects that had not been lost and to promote new talents. In spite of the abundance of traditional arts and the survival of many old skills, many aspects of the African heritage have been lost. More than 75 percent of African art and craft objects are made of wood, which cannot survive fire, termites, fungus, or woodworm. Many works, great and small, have perished as a result. The best preserved works are in metal, but not a few have also been lost due to the practice of melting down metal objects and recasting them. There is also the great impact of social change. As the traditional order based on indigenous religion, farming, and community cohesion disintegrates, this affects the quantity and quality of production. The need to produce artworks used in the worship of many gods has declined. The new religions of Islam and Christianity are hostile to these art objects. In many cases, converts are told to destroy them.

FESTAC successfully presented African art as the creative aspect of culture and not as the "fetish" portrayed by missionaries and colonial officers. Art objects are connected with religion and rituals and with the representation of all aspects of life. Production skills can be passed down in families and can also be acquired through education. Many objects try to invoke the spirits of gods and the ancestors, to give form to them, so that they can be appreciated or worshipped by the living.

Benin brass plaque.

African art has traveled to other places. The European artists at the turn of the twentieth century borrowed ideas from what they regarded as exotic African pieces. European visitors took many artworks back with them and made them part of private and public collections. Not a few were stolen, including masterpieces from various parts of the continent. Participants at FESTAC called on their governments to demand the return of many of these pieces and buy those put up for auction.

Traditional Music

Traditional music, with its idiom and orientation, has survived into the modern world. New musical genres have arisen, while traditional music has been transformed in many ways. The ethnic idioms of various groups affect traditional music, although there are common themes and patterns. In general, there is no traditional musical notation. Music is an oral practice, and the apprentice has to be in close touch with the master. Music is performed from memory. Rhythm and tone are very important. Hand clapping, drums, and other percussive instruments are common. Instruments are used to convey signals and imitate human speech. Most music is a combination of instruments and voices. Traditional music uses the language, rhythm, and intonations of the people who created the songs. Vocal qualities vary, as well as instruments.

Musical activities are commonly integrated with other activities and occupations, social events, political activities, and religion. The verbal text and the form are very much influenced by the context. Improvisation is the key, as the composer adjusts to the context. Thus, musical performance can be used for ritual, recreation, ceremonies, and a host of social functions. Music can be used for historical documentation, to keep important community records, and even to relay news and information. It is a key component in the socialization and education process, as it aids the acquisition and spread of knowledge on a variety of issues.

Music can be generated privately for individual pleasure. In many cases, music production is socially controlled, and there are songs specific to contexts such as festivals and ceremonies, the coronation of kings, and burial rites. Musical instruments, too, may be tied to context, as in the use of special drums for the worship of gods or instruments played only for kings. For instance, in Ugandan circumcision rites, percussion sticks are used. Among the Tutsi of central Africa, drums are reserved for the king and queen mother. Cult societies use bull roarers, diviners use bells, and trumpets are associated with kings.

Performances are generally given outdoors, which explains the extensive use of drums and other percussion instruments that produce intense sounds rather than the soft sounds of indoor music. The musicians display great feeling and dramatic expression and expect the members of the audience to participate with them. Age and sex may affect musical organization: Some songs are associated with youth, women may specialize in recreational songs and dirges, and men's songs may be about labor and hunting.

Oral and Written Literature

Oral literature was dominant where no written script was used. Even after writing became fashionable, oral methods still document and narrate history, stories, parables, and all forms of knowledge. Creativity can be expressed in various ways. Oral literature provides an outlet for creativity, and many works become community property. Oral literature provides entertainment in the form of humor, descriptions of marvels, and riddles. The histories of people and nations are narrated in stories and myths. The stories mirror life—they show what people do, how they live and think, and which values they hold dear. African oral literature reveals many things about African religion, philosophy, and customs. FESTAC provided an opportunity to showcase various aspects of African literature. It was also an occasion to discuss the preservation of oral literature. The participants were worried that many forms of oral literature may be lost, as society changes and emphasizes written literature, as the habit telling stories by moonlight dies, and as radio and television take over the role of storytelling. The struggle for survival in the modern world can also undermine the interest in oral literature, while knowledgeable people will be reduced in number as old folk die. To remedy the situation, the leading suggestion has been that as many examples of oral literature as possible should be collected and recorded for posterity.

Works of modern African literature, especially those written in European languages, have circulated widely and form the subject of studies in many university departments. Modern African literature grew in the colonial era as a protest literature criticizing the European cultural domination and economic exploitation of Africa. However, by the time of FESTAC, writers also had to direct their protest against African leaders who had failed to deliver on their promises. The writers are interested in culture, but they also want to draw attention to the plight of their people. They do not glorify or idealize the past, but they want to bring out elements in it that are useful to the present.

The first generation of authors that acquired prominence, such as Camara Laye, Ngugi Wa Thiong'o, Lechi Ahmadi, Okot p'Bitek, Mazisi Kunene, Lofi Awoonor, Wole Soyinka, and Chinua Achebe, were among the elite created during colonial rule and exposed to European literature. They want to use the acquired foreign languages to popularize the cultural values of their people and express their desire for a great future. The African character, concluded the famous Kenyan writer Ngugi Wa Thiong'o, must be restored to its history. Creative writers regard Africans' survival of the slave trade and colonial rule as heroic. There are multiple visions of the presentation of the past and the strategies needed to reform the future. But the writers seem to agree that Africans have enormous capabilities to survive oppression, to resist bad leadership, and to dream of a better future. The writers capture changes. To Senghor, "the Africa of Empires is dying."[4] But what will replace the dying continent is unclear. As Abioseh Nicol of Sierra Leone said in his poem, Africa is "but an idea" and its peoples still nurse "separate fears" while they "dream . . . separate dreams."[5] The dream at the time of FESTAC was still about development and how culture would contribute to it. "Is Africa, your Africa, growing again?" asked the Senegalese poet David Diop.[6] The assembly at FESTAC believed that it would grow, without losing its "soul," its "African personality," and its "blackness."

CONCLUSION

Africans and black people in the Diaspora recognize the role of culture in the formation of their identity. Many look back on FESTAC as a turning point in the development of a global black consciousness and look forward to a time when there will be a repeat performance. The idea of cultural propagation and revival has taken hold, although large-scale festivals are hard and expensive to organize. FESTAC was an opportunity to talk about identity, to bring together blacks from different countries to discuss issues of cultural awakening and awareness, and to urge them to work hard and carefully for their collective survival. There was also a recognition of the role of Africa in the world, as it imports and exports ideas and culture. While FESTAC celebrated the past, it also looked forward by presenting the means to blend the cultures of the past with the cultures of the present. Africa will not reject other cultures but play host to them and accepts aspects that are useful to its peoples. Africa will not forsake development, and it will promote education and technology for its progress, but without destroying its traditions.

NOTES

1. Lt-General Olusegun Obasanjo, head of the Federal Military Government of Nigeria and patron of the Second World Black and African Festival of Arts and Culture, *FESTAC Souvenir* (Lagos: CBACC, 1977).
2. Ibid.
3. President Leopold S. Senghor of Senegal, "Black Culture," in ibid.
4. Ibid.
5. Ibid., p. 81.
6. Ibid., p. 85.

SUGGESTIONS FOR FURTHER READING

Falola, Toyin. *The Culture and Customs of Nigeria*. Westport, Conn.: Greenwood Press, 2001.
International Festival Committee. *Festac '77*. Lagos: Author, 1977.
Mbiti, John S. *African Religions and Philosophy*. London: Praeger, 1970.
Mbiti, John S. *Introduction to African Religion*. New York: Grove Press, 1975.
Nketia, J.H. Kwabena. *The Music of Africa*. New York: Norton, 1974.
Owomoyela, Oyekan. *Yoruba Trickster Tales*. Lincoln: University of Nebraska Press, 1997.

31

The Women's Decade, 1975–85

The United Nations declared a decade dedicated to women's issues to discuss issues of gender equality and peace. The 1975 International Women's Year opened the Women's Decade (WD) with many activities sponsored by different countries. The WD closed with the International Conference on Women in Nairobi in 1985. Africa was involved in many of the events. The aims were to enhance the visibility of women in the economy, in politics, and in society. Women's associations were formed in order to embark on a number of small-scale projects, notably handicraft production and small cooperative farms. Many governments promised to increase the level of funding for women's activities and improve their access to loans, land, training, and technology. In a few countries, some old laws were reformed in ways that favored women. Ethiopia, Kenya, and Côte d'Ivoire changed their laws to allow women to own and also inherit property. Polygyny (the marriage of two or more wives by one man) was disallowed in Tunisia and Côte d'Ivoire. In Senegal, where polygyny is still allowed, men were told to seek the consent of their wives before marrying another.

The focus of international attention on women generated scholarly interest, most especially because women's and gender issues had previously been ignored in much of the literature, while governments have tended to assume that economic and political developments include everybody, irrespective of gender, even when the male bias has been glaring. Many women were able to raise their voices and to insist that their concerns not only should be taken seriously but should form the core of development programs. Above all, the contribution of women to development received recognition. There are areas of disagreement as yet unresolved. The most well known is the desirability or otherwise of female circumcision (popularized in the Western media as female genital mutilation). Opinions are divided between those who want the practice to end and those who want it to be modified. The WD also generated discussion of the right age for girls to marry, in view of the value of Western education. While some see nothing wrong in marriage before the age of twenty, others argue that it prevents women from receiving higher education and competing with men.

During the Women's Decade, various African governments established bureaus or ministries of women's affairs. Political positions were given to a number of leading women to demonstrate a commitment to involve women in formal political systems. There was a proliferation of nongovernmental women's organizations (with national and international affiliations) that mobilized women, educated the public about all forms of discrimination against women, and informed women on how to achieve economic and political empowerment. The Association of African Women's Research and Documentation (AAWORD) was established, based in Dakar, Senegal. It was made Africa-wide and bilingual in order to bring scholars and activists together to talk about a variety of women's issues. Scholars devoted considerable attention to the study of women's issues, including women and resistance in African history, women and liberation movements, and women's role in wars, leadership, religion, the economy, and politics. Other issues received attention, such as widowhood practices, marriage and family roles, and motherhood. The impact of the Structural Adjustment Programs introduced in the 1980s and Africa's declining economies (see Chapter 32) on women was yet another main topic. Female circumcision became a major issue in politics, as feminists and radicals began to mobilize support to oppose this age-old practice. From the point of view of history, the women's decade provided an opportunity to review the role of women in Africa over a long historical period. The concern in this chapter is with this broad review, now a major theme in African history.

WOMEN'S CONDITIONS

As in many other parts of the world, African women have lower status and fewer privileges and opportunities than men. Yet women work more hours than men. They carry multiple workloads in production and reproduction. Those with education and skills work in the formal sectors and also do virtually all the domestic work. Those without education are productive as farmers or craftswomen, rear children, and of course carry the burden of domestic activities. Women are active in the informal sector, as traders, food-sellers, repairers of small crafts items, and so on. Many of these activities, especially child rearing and domestic work, go unrewarded.

The activities connected with the Women's Decade highlighted the issues, pointing to the marginalization of women in politics, business, the professions, and other aspects of life. There were many women members of the elite in the 1970s and 1980s, indicating the progress that had been made in the education of women and in their recruitment to many modern professions. In spite of these gains, however, men control power, both in the public and private domains. In poor economies, men and women suffer alike. Thus, some problems are related not to gender inequalities but to issues of underdevelopment. Peasants and poor women experience more problems than elite women. The incorporation of Africa into the world economy and the spread of Western influence also have their impact, in some cases actually providing better opportunities for men, thus widening the gender gap. The chapter traces the changing role of women in order to provide a broad historical context.

WOMEN IN PRECOLONIAL SOCIETIES

Women's conditions were different in many ways before the imposition of European rule. In some societies, they were deeply involved in politics, both in formal and in informal institutions. They could become influential chiefs among some groups, as in the case of the Mende in Sierra Leone or the Tonga of Zambia. Where the institution of the queen mother existed, as in some West African communities, women held power as regents, advisers to kings, and kingmakers. Women warriors were found in Dahomey and Angola, where they distinguished themselves in wars. Women created their own powerful and influential organizations, which enabled them to be actively involved in politics and the management of affairs important to them, such as trade. Thus, there were women's secret societies, age-grade associations, and market clubs. In these associations as well as in community life, female titled chiefs were appointed as leaders. A number of titleholders exercised considerable influence on issues that pertained to women, while they were involved in the overall management of cities and kingdoms. In the religious sphere, women priests and titleholders played the crucial role of mediating between human beings and supernatural forces.

A number of privileges enabled women to enjoy autonomy. Where they had access to land, livestock, and labor, they could create dynamic economic opportunities and empower themselves. In places where occupations were divided along sex lines, women controlled some areas. They could produce, control local trade, and serve as key participants in a variety of small industries and businesses. Above all, they had reproductive power, producing children in societies that cherished large families. Ultimately, women were protected by their adult children, who were also expected to take great care of them in their old age.

In spite of the prominent roles that many women were able to play, and the autonomy that they enjoyed, male dominance was still common. More men were rulers and chiefs, and they controlled the majority of prestigious titles. In many cases, women had to rely on their acquired economic power and family connections to be able to attain a significant degree of success. Where the trans-Atlantic slave trade created social dislocation and population loss, women were probably pressured to produce more children, thereby undermining some of their other roles.

CHANGES BROUGHT BY COLONIALISM

Some of the changes brought by European rule discussed in Chapter 19 affected gender relations in a way that favored men at the expense of women. Colonial institutions were male dominated. Europeans brought with them the idea that men were more important than women, the Victorian belief that the place of women was in the home to cook and look after their children, the idea that economic and political changes were shaped and controlled by men, and that African men were the people they needed the most to achieve their aims. As the colonialists' policies unfolded, more and more women lost access to old resources and failed to gain access to new resources.

While it is true that Africans were exploited by colonial rule, men had greater access than women to power, education, land, wage incomes, and new skills. The colonial economy was dependent on export crops such as cocoa and peanuts, which were cultivated by men. Women were mainly connected with food production, which generated a smaller income. While women were confined to households and rural economies, men worked for wages in various sectors and were often forced to leave their wives in the villages. The colonial authorities regarded men as the essential power holders. In recruitment of Africans to work in the civil service and in European companies, men were the chosen ones. Proceeds from the production of cash crops and wages were not evenly distributed within the household; men regarded themselves as the legitimate creators of the wealth and took the lion's share. Many among them chose to use their excess wealth to marry additional wives to demonstrate their status.

As land became commercialized for building and production, men struggled hard to claim far more than women. In some areas, traditional practices of sharing the inheritance were abandoned in favor of men. Access to labor was generally competitive. Men were lured or forced to work for companies and government, leaving their wives behind in rural areas to concentrate on raising children. Not all women located in the cities found legitimate employment, and many were forced to perform domestic duties or do menial and less-rewarding jobs to sustain themselves.

THE CONTEMPORARY REALITY

By the 1970s, gender relations in Africa had become unequal—men had more access to many privileges and opportunities. The colonial political and economic structures continued to exist after independence, in conditions that put women in relations of dependency to men. Leadership, important occupations, jobs, land, wealth, prestige, and property were monopolized by men. Although women were involved in the liberation wars and political struggles that led to independence, they did not reap rewards equal to those enjoyed by men.

The attention given to women in the Women's Decade exposed the reality of exploitation, their conditions in the 1970s and 1980s, the ways in which exploitative gender relations are frequently justified, and the changes that are necessary to attain a better society. Each of these major issues is highlighted in turn.

CONDITIONS AND GENDER DIFFERENCES

If women were able to share power in precolonial Africa and were able to exercise a considerable degree of informal influence, the situation in postcolonial Africa would be greatly different. Power has become excessively centralized and mainly male dominated. Women have not been able to rise to become heads of state or to control the legislative assemblies or the judiciaries. As the informal institutions where women have traditionally exercised power have declined in their importance, so, too, has women's power been considerably eroded. Bureaucracies, rather than families and community organizations, control power in ways that do not necessarily involve dialogue with the people. Since the bureaucracies are dominated by men and are not democratic, women have been put at a serious disadvantage, being unable to influence many decisions. Where access to politicians and bureaucrats is crucial to obtain jobs and favors, the arrangement works in favor of men with patrons in the right places. In distributing national resources and creating opportunities, most policies tend to favor men.

As the majority of the African population are farmers, it can be argued that the role of the government should not be exaggerated. Even then, the gender disparities in informal economic activities are clear. Women constitute more than 40 percent of the agricultural labor force and do more work than men but earn smaller incomes. In addition to farmwork, they do most of the domestic chores. Farm earnings go mainly to men, who spend the lion's share on themselves and their own needs, while women spend the bulk of their incomes on their children and households. Women lack access to legal title to land, which means they cannot raise loans or claim land when they divorce or lose their husbands. Assistance in the supply of farm equipment and machines goes mainly to men. Where government and external agencies spend money on rural areas, the main beneficiaries tend to be men.

African development policies are urban oriented, which means that farmers, irrespective of gender, are marginalized. Consequently, the rate of rural-urban migration is high. Women also migrate, although in smaller numbers than men. However, because many women are less well educated than men, they face more obstacles in obtaining jobs.

Although tremendous improvements have been made in the education of women, a number of trends suggest gender differences. In a number of countries, more boys than girls go to school. More women than men are nurses, secretaries, and teachers; these are important jobs but with incomes that are not comparable to those in fields dominated by men. Women do not have sufficient time, capital, or education to compete with men or even create successful women's organizations to promote their interests.

RATIONALIZATION OF GENDER RELATIONS

Many of the established relations of inequality and dependency are regarded by men as part of the "African tradition." Both old and new dependency relations are described as "traditional" by men who wish to retain their established privileges. Leading political offices and senior positions in the civil service and army are controlled by men. When women press for inclusion, they are told that men were kings and chiefs in traditional Africa or that the Islamic religion does not favor the appointment of a woman as the country's leader. Women are expected to be submissive and focus on raising good children. Daniel arap Moi, Kenya's president, reminded women at the International Conference on Women, held in 1985 to close the Women's Decade, that "God made man the head of the family." Feminists and radical scholars interpreted this to mean that the struggles for change had achieved little in ten years. Traditionalists supported Moi for wanting Africa to progress without destroying its basic values.

There is a perception that if women can rise to higher positions and earn good incomes, it will damage the status and power of men. Asking men to give up their privileges is bitterly resented as an effort to destroy society and unleash unnecessary gender competition. Those who advocate far-reaching changes can be accused of wanton disregard for culture or of being agents of Western cultural imperialism.

Men are presented as agents of change. The theory may be that if the head of the household is happy and prosperous, everybody else is fine and doing well. Projects are supposed to be directed at those who will make the most gain and transform society. If men are not satisfied, so goes another rationalization, society would become disorderly and ungovernable. On the other hand, women are presented as easy to satisfy or control in moments of protest. Religious preachers present men as the legitimate and divinely sanctioned leaders of households and society. In some areas, men are entitled to take the earnings of their wives and to spend their own incomes without being questioned by their spouses.

The school system, popular culture, and the media institutionalize gender relations. Men are presented as "bread winners," heads of households, strong, intelligent, and courageous. Women are presented as docile, gentle, subordinate, weak, and less adaptable to change. In large families with limited resources to spend on education, the boys are sent to school, while the girls may be asked to stay at home and to marry at an early age. Since they have been constructed as subordinate, it is believed that they need not pursue courses or aim for occupations that will lead to wealth and prestige. Thus, domesticity is presented as the main arena for women. So successful has been the popular conception of the subordinate female role that many women have actually come to accept it. Many elite women propagate the view that the role of women is to raise successful children and make their husbands happy. Married to men who can support them, they tend to accept the view that if men can provide adequate incomes, women should be contented with taking care of domestic issues.

TRENDS AND CHANGES

Many of the arguments in support of male domination are being questioned and challenged. Like men, women also seek status, prestige, and power, and all people seek survival. Even the basic skills of survival require competition and access to education, income, and the means to make a living. Thus, the demands made during the Women's Decade included access to the means to survival by women in different social classes and locations.

Women also want changes within households that will bring them respect, authority, and security. In many areas, women are entitled to few or no privileges when they divorce or lose their husbands. Women seek legal rights to protect themselves, give them a share of the family's inheritance, and give them custody of their children. Women control local markets, especially in terms of the distribution of food and many small manufactured items. This is one area that the government can invest in to further empower women. Farmers demand access to land and capital so that they can become better farmers, produce more crops, and increase their earning power. Women in trade seek access to capital as well, so that they can expand their businesses. Without access to capital, many will continue to pursue the option of marrying men who can support them financially, a situation that will keep men in their dominant positions.

A number of nongovernmental organizations (NGOs) are raising various issues related to the empowerment of women. Foreign donors and the World Bank have been successfully pressured to consider the impact of their policies on women and to allocate resources in such a way that more women will benefit from them. Within the continent, millions of women's organizations, small and large, create opportunities to improve women's lives. They save and provide resources for self-help, contribute time and money to help members to expand their businesses, educate their children, minimize exploitation by men, and seek assistance from government agencies. The organizations of educated women seek improvements in the education of girls, assistance to working mothers, the creation of women-friendly work environments, and access to bank loans. Collaboration among women raises their levels of consciousness.

Elite women fight for their own rights in seeking access to higher incomes and promotion in the workplace. In many countries, women are now represented in some cabinet positions. They demand changes in inheritance and divorce laws to give women access to higher income. In educating their children, they do not discriminate between boys and girls. For women's position to change, the struggles for economic and political equality will have to intensify. More women have to acquire power so that they can change existing policies in their favor.

SUGGESTIONS FOR FURTHER READING

Cutrufelli, Maria R. *Women of Africa: Roots of Oppression*. London: Zed, 1983.
Emecheta, Buchi. *Second Class Citizen*. London: Fontana, 1974.

Gordon, April A., and Donald L. Gordon. *Understanding Contemporary Africa.* Boulder, Colo.: Lynne Rienner, 1992. Chapter 9.

House-Midamba, Bessie, and Felix K. Ekechi, eds. *African Market and Economic Power: The Role of Women in African Economic Development.* Westport, Conn.: Greenwood Press, 1995.

Obbo, Christine. *African Women: Their Struggle for Economic Independence.* London: Zed, 1980.

Oppong, Christine, ed. *Female and Male in West Africa.* London: George Allen and Unwin, 1983.

32

A Continent in Deep Crisis, 1980 Onward

By the 1980s, the failure of the majority of African states had become glaring. Indeed, it was even expected that some states such as Sierra Leone, Liberia, Chad, Rwanda, and Zaire would collapse. Many countries acquired debts from external sources and were forced to implement a Structural Adjustment Program, with stringent conditions imposed by the International Monetary fund (IMF) and the World Bank. The gains of independence had disappeared in many places, and many Africans became very distrustful of the government and even began to lose hope in their future. Those who had the opportunities and the credentials to do so, especially leading scholars and professionals such as medical doctors and nurses, migrated to more prosperous countries in Europe and to the United States.

In 1989, the World Bank issued a document concluding that Africans had become poorer than ever before. The growing poverty and the possibility of total collapse became the major economic event of the twentieth century. What are the conditions and causes of Africa's economic and political failure, a calamity that threatens to destroy a continent that started its history as a leader? The answers can be found not just in the 1980s but long before then, as well as in the cumulative failure of leadership since independence.

UNDERDEVELOPMENT

Millions of Africans became poorer than ever before, and the World Bank warned in the 1980s that poverty would increase. The economy was in decline for many years, reaching an annual growth rate of only 0.8 percent by the mid-1980s. The majority of African countries do not have the industrial capacity to produce large amounts of goods and generate income. Industries often lack the machinery or the spare parts to run at full capacity. African countries continue to produce raw materials for export, as they have done for years, but prices in the world market are unstable. Whenever prices fall, national incomes are reduced, and social and welfare services suffer. Since the countries are dependent on foreign reserves to pay for their imports, a reduction in world commodity prices immediately affects their ability to buy food, drugs, and technology.

So high is the level of external debts, close to $200 billion, that the continent is the most indebted in the world if the amount is related to national income. If the debt was to be shared by the citizens, it would be higher than the annual per capita income. In the 1980s, most countries were forced to implement SAPs imposed by the lending agencies, notably the World Bank and the IMF. The conditions imposed by SAPs were stringent: devaluation of currencies, wage freeze, price determination of food and cash crops by market forces rather than prices imposed by the government, reduction in the labor force, reduction in the number admitted to colleges and universities, and so on. The SAP was a total failure in most countries: The level of external debts increased, more people became poor, the rate of unemployment increased to double digits, inflation became uncontrollable, the middle class was devastated, and social services and infrastructure collapsed. As the people took to violence to protest the economic failures, the government took to drastic dictatorial policies and used the army and police in very brutal ways. Notable among the declining sectors are the following.

Agriculture and Food Crisis

In a continent largely dependent on agriculture, the performance of this sector has become so appalling that almost 70 percent of the population lack adequate food to eat. The food crisis of the 1980s has continued ever since, as the level of agricultural productivity is too low to sustain an ever-increasing population. In a number of places, droughts devastated communities, forcing them to become refugees. During the 1980s, famine occurred in not less than twenty-two countries, and they had to depend on food charity to be able to survive. Chronic undernutrition occurs each year, as each region witnesses food deficits. Famine is not uncommon whenever food deficits become chronic due to war, crop failures, or natural disasters. Hunger afflicts many people, because they are too poor to buy or grow food.

According to the World Bank, the African agricultural and food crisis includes at least four major aspects. To begin with, the rate of population growth is faster than the growth rate of agriculture in almost all African countries. Second, dependence on the imports of food such as rice and wheat have changed the African preference from local foods to foreign ones. The importation of food grains has increased at a rate three times faster than that of population growth. Importation contributes to dependency on other continents, thus draining scarce resources that otherwise could be used for other development purposes. Third, the

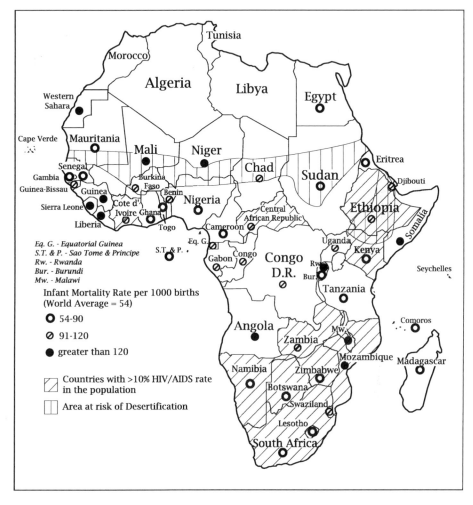

Health and environmental issues.

exports of agricultural products for foreign reserves have suffered, thus compli-
cating the overall economy. For instance, while Nigeria had for many years sold
cocoa, peanuts, rubber, and palm products, the country is now solely dependent
on the export of oil, thus losing the opportunity to diversify its economy. Fourth,
food aid has also increased, especially during periods of famine and drought.

Why is a continent so large and rich in land unable to feed itself? In some cases,
the problems are due to ecological reasons such as drought and desertification. Soil
and vegetation are deteriorating in some places, leading to drought. In some other
cases, political instability and conflicts force farmers out of their lands and paralyze
production. Where population grows at a rate faster than agricultural productivity, it
also creates problems. There are a host of other reasons: Colonial rule turned Africa
into a producer of export crops at the expense of food production; postcolonial planning and development strategies have favored the nonagricultural sectors; rural
farmers are generally ignored and treated as lacking knowledge; some cultivation
practices tend to destroy trees and soil; and large-scale rural-urban migrations strip
the farming areas of the youthful population who could produce.

Environmental degradation has become another serious problem. The continent has been turned into a dumping ground for toxic waste from Europe. As fuel
becomes expensive, trees and shrubs are cut down indiscriminately. Desertification threatens almost 85 percent of Africa's drylands. For instance, the Sahara
Desert keeps expanding, diminishing the areas for farming and grazing in West
Africa. Evidence of global warming can be seen in the drier and hotter climate in
the semidesert and savanna areas of Africa.

It was not that efforts were not made to increase agricultural productivity. Indeed, many countries embarked upon irrigation schemes, committed huge public
expenditure to agriculture, undertook land tenure reforms, encouraged the extensive use of fertilizers, and established new farming projects. In spite of these and
other efforts, food scarcity and general decline in agricultural productivity re-
curred for the following reasons: erosion in a number of areas that destroyed the
topsoil, drought, locust infestations, poor prices for raw materials in the world
market, population increase, poor transportation to distribute crops, a lack of adequate storage facilities for harvested products, and the declining interest of the
younger generation in agriculture.

Health

Since the 1980s, it has been difficult to buy medicinal drugs, maintain existing
health facilities, build new hospitals, and train personnel. Diseases, old and new,
continue to spread as poor nutrition weakens people's immunity. Initially ignored, AIDS has affected a large number of people. Cholera and malaria fever
have devastated millions of people. Expenditures on health services are grossly
inadequate, and diseases that kill in large numbers, notably malaria, have not
been effectively targeted for eradication. Expenditures on curative medicine are
higher than those on preventative ones, such as the vaccination of children, the

maintenance of friendly environments, and the provision of safe water. Health services have declined since the 1980s, due in part to the overall decline in the economy and the repayment of interest on external loans. In countries where AIDS has spread, it has been difficult to pay attention to this devastating disease because of limited resources.

If Western medicine is proving difficult to acquire or facilities hard to manage, ethnomedicine is filling the gap in many areas. Spiritual healing by religious organizations and established herbal practices used by traditional diviners, mid-wives, bone-setters, "medicine-men," and others are gaining widespread cur-rency. "Alternative medicine" is not just a rural phenomenon in areas where there are no Western medicinal facilities but even in cities and among the edu-cated elite. Alternative medicine tends to be cheaper, more readily available, and more efficient in the cure of well-established diseases such as malaria. Although practices are unregulated and there are many fake practitioners, "alternative medicine" is no longer dismissed as "primitive" or "unreliable," and efforts are being made to improve its delivery.

Population Growth

If development had occurred as expected, many of the questions regarding population growth would have been unnecessary. However, it is clear that the rate of economic growth lags behind that of population increase, and available resources are not being managed in such a way as to take care of the majority of the population. Africa has the highest rate of population growth in the world. From 1985 to 1990, the annual population growth was 3 percent, whereas that of South America was 2.1 percent; Asia, 1.6 percent; and Europe, 0.3 percent. The consequences of high growth rates include the inability to meet the social and educational needs of people, rural-urban migration, food scarcity, and high rates of unemployment. Growing at an annual rate of 3.1 percent, Africa's population may double every twenty-three years, in spite of a high death rate. Over 40 per-cent of the people are under the age of fifteen, and the expectation is that they will contribute further to population increase through reproduction.

The high fertility rate is due primarily to the preference for large families. A woman can give birth to six or more children; a man can have two or more wives. The preference for large families is due to the social status attached to a household with many children, the security rendered to the elderly by their chil-dren, and the help that children render in the various occupations of their parents.

The infant mortality rate in Africa is one of the highest in the world. Poor nu-trition and sanitation, diseases (e.g., malaria, polio, coughs, and measles), and widespread poverty lead to the death of many children. Life expectancies are lower than in many other parts of the world. In general, life expectancy is under sixty years. The high level of mortality is due to unhealthy environments, poverty, and diseases. The most deadly diseases are malaria (transmitted by the anopheles mosquito), schistosomiasis, cholera, and measles.

REASONS FOR ECONOMIC PROBLEMS

Africa did not suddenly reach its sorry condition in the mid-1980s—the foundations were laid in previous years, but they were complicated by bad leadership and mismanagement. The resources of the continent have been used not to benefit the great majority of the population but to benefit a minority of privileged Africans in power and the external investors. The blame for Africa's problems has to be shared between external and internal forces.

To start with the external forces, the contacts that foreign countries had established over hundreds of years were solely motivated by profit, a desire to drain the continent of its wealth. Millions of slaves were taken, thereby reducing the productive and consumption capacity of many places. During the nineteenth century, the emphasis shifted to agricultural products for export. Then colonial rule was established, and the level of exploitation was intensified. Important minerals and agricultural products were exported, with minimal benefits to the majority of the population (see Chapter 19).

Although colonial rule in many areas was already over by the 1980s, the economic system in place was based on the long-established relations with the external world. Thus, Africa moved from a colonial to a neocolonial phase, with similar economic conditions. The essentials of the economic system, devastating in its impact, included the following:

- The African economy was operated to the advantage of Western markets. African farmers planted coffee, cocoa, rubber, peanuts, and other products for processing in Western factories. Where European settlers went to Africa during colonial rule (and later) to grow these crops, they often took the best land.

- The minerals, too, were mined for external markets. During colonial rule, foreign companies extracted the minerals and kept most of the companies. After independence, foreign profits still dominated the sector, with their capital and technology. African countries received royalties and other forms of compensation.

- The producers responded to the external markets by supplying what they required, by abandoning food production in favor of the more lucrative cash crops, and by migrating from their original homelands to other areas where they could work in mines.

- African countries became dependent on the world market and external forces that they could not manipulate or shape. They could not determine the quantity and prices of goods they supplied, they lacked control over interest rates charged by foreign banks, and they had no means to check the impact of inflation in Western countries on their own economies. They paid high prices for manufactured imported items and received low prices for their own exports.

There have been many internal problems as well. A major factor has always been that of bad government and leadership. The problems of political instability are identified below, but they impact the economy and society in many negative ways. State-run agencies are inefficient, and corruption is rampant. Excessive government intervention often constitutes a great barrier to economic development.

Governments have tried different economic models without success. Many started with the inherited capitalist ideology, but they were unable to expand the market or create the conditions to generate capital. Some turned to the Soviet Union and China to borrow the socialist or Marxist/Leninist economic model. The socialist model turned out to be a disaster as well, as it simply enabled political leaders to acquire excessive power and ruin many private initiatives (see Chapter 27).

POLITICAL WOES

Political instability was endemic in the 1980s and beyond. This was manifested in military regimes, with coups and counter coups in many countries (see Chapter 26). Political problems could also include the excessive use of power by those in government. Yet another common feature was for those in power to refuse to relinquish it. Transition from one head of state to another in a peaceful manner became highly unusual.

Power struggles among the representatives of different ethnic groups led to wars in a number of countries. In the 1970s and 1980s, about 2 million Africans died in various wars, including wars of liberation from European powers. By the mid-1980s, the following countries had experienced armed conflicts: Chad, Eritrea, Mozambique, Ethiopia, Uganda, Sudan, Somalia, Angola, Djibouti, Liberia, Sierra Leone, and Rwanda. These conflicts destroyed the economy of these countries and created millions of refugees.

There were more countries with undemocratic arrangements than countries with governments with leaders chosen by free and fair elections. Where elections were held, the results were manipulated by those in power. Even in countries with so-called multiparty systems (e.g., Tunisia, Egypt, Morocco, Liberia) the elections were controlled by those already in power. In most places, opposition forces were intimidated, and their leaders were destroyed or jailed. The majority of countries were ruled either by single parties (thirty-five countries by 1989) or by military regimes.

The reasons for political instability and related crises are many and varied. The majority of African countries were artificially created by Europeans, without the involvement of Africans in the process. Various preexisting groups and governments were lumped together within the same country. There were even cases of preexisting groups divided among two or more new countries. These countries have come to stay, but the divisions within them have not been resolved. One division is that of ethnicity. In the majority of African countries, people belong to a variety of ethnic groups—those of the nations that existed before the colonial conquest. The people could express nationalism both in support of their country and in support of their ethnic group. A problem arises when the commitment to the ethnic group is greater than that to the country. The management of an ethnically divided country, usually referred to as the politics of pluralism, is rather complicated. Divisions can also be along religious lines, in countries with both Christians and Muslims. In Nigeria, for instance, there were many cases of religious violence during the 1980s.

In managing the divisions, governments in many countries resorted to drastic measures. The army and the police were used to curb legitimate protest, even to kill innocent people. Such antidemocratic arrangements as the one-party state or military rule were promoted by using the divisions as an excuse to impose authoritarian rule and to disregard the principle of accountability and the rule of law. The government resembled a police unit. Indeed, throughout the twentieth century, many countries in Africa were run as "police states," with severe limits on self-determination and freedom of expression. Opposition forces were curtailed, elections were unknown, and the police and army kept a close eye on the people.

During the Cold War, when the Western bloc (the United States and Western Europe) and the Eastern bloc (the Soviet Union and the socialist regimes) were competing with each other, Africa was drawn into the rivalry. External intervention during the Cold War added to Africa's political problems. To secure the loyalty of an African government, an external power could provide military and financial aid. Once it had a friend in power, an external power would help to retain that person in power, even when his people did not like him. For instance, as bad as Joseph Mobutu Sese Seko of Zaire was, the United States and its Western allies, were happy to retain him in power for a long period in order to maintain their vested economic interests. The Soviet Union also supported dictators, as long as they claimed to be implementing socialist policies, as in the case of Ethiopia, Burundi, and Guinea-Bissau.

Economic underdevelopment had its impact on politics as well. Poverty was an excuse for corruption. To army officers seeking wealth, coups and political participation were lucrative options. In the case of poor people, the failure of governments could force them to take to crime and violence. The inability to provide jobs and basic human needs tended to undermine the political system. Many of the problems of the 1980s still remain, although many countries now have democratic governments and various interest groups are organizing to demand changes, as in Nigeria and Zambia.

SUGGESTIONS FOR FURTHER READING

Harrison, Paul. *The Greening of Africa: Breaking Through in the Battle for Land and Food*. London: Paladin, 1987.

Knight, C.G, and R.P. Wilcox. *Triumph or Triage: The World Food Problem in Geographical Perspective*. Washington, D.C.: Association of American Geographers, 1976.

Lawrence, P., ed. *World Recession and the Food Crisis in Africa*. Boulder, Colo.: Westview Press, 1986.

Stock, Robert. *Africa South of the Sahara: A Geographical Interpretation*. New York: Guilford Press, 1995.

World Bank. *Accelerated Development in Sub-Saharan Africa: An Agenda for Action*. Washington, D.C.: World Bank, 1981.

World Bank. *Sub-Saharan Africa: From Crisis to Sustainable Growth*. Washington, D.C.: World Bank, 1989.

33

Environmental Challenges, 1980s Onward

The concerns about environmental problems expressed in the 1970s began to be repeated with extra force in the 1980s. By the mid-1980s, a number of people were actually raising the alarm about many problems. By the 1990s, there was no longer any need to persuade Africans and the world that the environment had become a central issue in Africa's underdevelopment. Events and crises that were ignored in previous years have now come to the limelight. If the concerns in the United States are about the damaging impact of industrialization on the environment (e.g., air pollution, the dumping of chemicals into rivers), the concerns in Africa are both about natural disasters and about the consequences of the exploitation of trees. The notable problems include soil erosion, desertification, drought, and global warming. The drought of the 1970s directed world attention to such issues as reduced soil fertility in many places, diminishing rainfall, and the overall decline in agricultural productivity. The most serious environmental problems in Africa include the following.

SOIL DEGRADATION AND EROSION

Africa is an old continent, with soils of ancient origin, and a stable geology. Human activities have been intense for centuries, with the result that some areas have been overused. In some areas, the soils have lost their nutrients due to human activities and natural causes. Where rainfall is heavy or temperatures are too high, the soil loses its nutrients to leaching. About 75 percent of the continent is located in the tropics. Areas outside of the tropics are dry, notably the Kalahari

Desert in southwestern Africa and the Sahara Desert in northwestern and northern Africa. Less than 10 percent of the continent falls outside of the tropical climate zone, and the rest experiences high annual temperatures, which may have an impact on the land. Over half of Africa's land is not arable, while large areas cannot support field crop cultivation for too long a time. There are extensive dryland areas, and the richest alluvial soils are limited to just 7 percent of the total land area.

The problem of deforestation, discussed below, creates soil erosion in many areas. Once trees disappear, rain and wind damage the topsoil and overall soil fertility is greatly reduced. Leached soil becomes further exposed to high temperatures and can be baked into laterite. Lateritic soil is hard to penetrate, and such land can only support stunted trees or shrubs.

Among the countries that have experienced problems of erosion are Tanzania, eastern Nigeria, Ethiopia, and Mozambique. Ethiopia suffers the most—it is a hilly country that suffers from floods when rainfall is heavy. Soil erosion, drought, famine, and population displacement have all been experienced in Ethiopia. One devastating report puts the annual loss of Ethiopia's topsoil at 1 billion tons, due to a lack of forest cover, which would protect the soil from heavy rains. With damaged topsoil, cultivation becomes a problem. A three-year drought occurred in the early 1980s in highland Ethiopia. But when it rained in May 1984, the rains poured heavily for four days and caused erosion.

DEFORESTATION

If human beings must learn to adjust to problems of precipitation (wet and dry seasons) and natural phenomena that they cannot control, their activities and methods of survival can create environmental problems that are even harder to deal with. Deforestation is caused by human beings, because of failure to create a sustainable society, manage resources efficiently, and use only renewable energy sources. Reliance on the use of firewood for energy and of timber for building has led to massive felling of trees; this has exposed soils to greater erosion and damage. Excessive grazing by cattle as well as bush clearing for cultivation also destroy the forest and create more problems. Without an effective policy in place to coordinate human activities in terms of cultivation and energy use, many areas in Africa cannot sustain the relationship between society and environment.

Since the middle of the twentieth century, the areas covered by forest have been shrinking. The United Nations Environmental Program (UNEP) has alerted the world to the shrinking forest in the Congo, to annual cases of forest destruction, and to the possibility that closed forests (rain forests with tight canopy, in areas with high annual rainfall) may disappear in Africa by the end of the current millennium. Madagascar has lost more than half of its rain forest, the Congo is losing its own at an annual rate of 0.2 percent, and Côte d'Ivoire loses as much as 7 percent a year.

Firewood is used extensively at great risk to the environment.

Forest clearing is the factor primarily responsible for the destruction of the African forest and land. The majority of the population, as high as 90 percent, rely on firewood for domestic and commercial cooking. The rate at which trees are cut is faster than the rate of growth of new trees. The expansion of cities and population increase in turn lead to the use of more firewood in cooking for large numbers of people. In a number of cities, the surrounding countryside has been completely denuded of trees, as city dwellers demand wood and charcoal for cooking.

Yet another human activity is crop cultivation, which entails extensive land clearing. The production of cash crops for export and food crops to feed an ever-growing population has led to the use of more land for agriculture. In many areas, farming is based on shifting cultivation—the farmer will clear and burn a plot, use it for a few years, and then move on to another plot to allow the older one to regenerate. When land was abundant in relation to population, land was allowed to lie fallow for many years, which enabled it to regain its forest growth and nutrients. As population expands and greater demands are placed on farmers, the fallow duration becomes too short to allow the land to regenerate. Farmers also penetrate new areas, burning more land in the process. The consequences of shifting cultivation based on a short fallow duration are devastating: Trees do not grow back in many areas, the soil loses its nutrients, and new crops do not grow well. The rate at which new areas are put under cultivation and ultimately destroyed is so high that it has now reached crisis level.

DESERTIFICATION OR WASTELAND

The destruction of the forest creates other problems for the environment. As more and more land loses its nutrients and fails to sustain agriculture and farming communities, the ecosystem becomes damaged. Deforestation promotes desertification. Wasteland replaces formerly productive land, due in part to overgrazing, destruction of the forest, and overcultivation of crops. The desert is expanding, and about 700 square kilometers (270 square miles) of land have become wasteland in the last fifty years. A recent estimate puts the loss of good land at the staggering figure of 36,000 square kilometers (13,900 square miles) a year. Countries that continue to be affected by the expansion of desert land include Egypt, Sudan, Nigeria, Niger, Mali, Burkina Faso, Mauritania, Ghana, Senegal, Gambia, and Chad. Six countries (Nigeria, Angola, Uganda, Madagascar, Cameroon, and Benin) have less than 30 percent semiarid and arid lands. Countries with more than 30 percent arid and semiarid lands are Zimbabwe, Burkina Faso, Ethiopia, Zambia, Gambia, Mozambique, Senegal, Tanzania, and Sudan. Countries with close to 70 percent arid lands include Botswana, Cape Verde, Chad, Djibouti, Kenya, Mali, Mauritania, Niger, and Somalia. Arid areas cannot support large populations, and vast areas are empty. Dry areas are occupied, but they tend to support nomadic pastoralism or the production of limited quantities of grain crops.

Drought and desertification are linked. Changes in climate and lack of adequate rainfall create drought, which in turns leads to desertification. The water in parts of Lake Chad has evaporated over the years, forcing settlers to move elsewhere. In the Western Sahel, comprising countries such as Mauritania and Senegal, rainfall has declined over the years, with devastating consequences for the land.

INDUSTRIALIZATION AND URBANIZATION

Although Africa is mainly rural and nonindustrial, many areas are experiencing the problems of industrialization and uncontrollable growth of cities. In places with modern industries, both local and foreign companies ignore environmental regulations. In the rush to attract foreign investors in the early years of independence, there was a failure to formulate adequate laws to protect the environment. Where laws were established, the need for economic growth has prevented any rigorous implementation of them. Corrupt bureaucrats may also collude with business enterprises to ignore the laws. To give an example, the oil industry in Nigeria has created a host of environmental problems, notably pollution. Gas is flared into the environment, pipeline leakages have occurred, many farms have been damaged, and soil is degraded in areas near oil production sites. So widespread is the environmental damage in many parts of the Niger Delta region in southeastern Nigeria that a number of villages have been destroyed. The oil companies and the Nigerian government have collaborated to underplay the complaints by many communities in the oil-producing areas, and when the Ogoni people radicalized their protest, the military government killed their leaders.

The rate of urban growth after independence has been phenomenal. In the 1940s, less than 20 percent of Africans lived in cities. By the 1980s, about a quarter of the population lived in many cities. Cities such as Lagos in Nigeria and Kinshasa in the Congo keep growing. In 1960, Lagos contained less than a million people, but by 1980 it contained over 4 million people, and by 2000 close to 10 million. Nowhere is environmental degradation more noticeable than in the cities. Housing is usually so scarce that people sleep in any available space. Many people crowd into a room, and squatter settlements are common. Large areas are slums, and even the areas inhabited by the most privileged members of society are not always clean. Schools, hospitals, water supplies, sewage systems, transportation, and other facilities are grossly inadequate. The rate of unemployment is high—there are more workers than jobs in the formal economy, thus depressing wages, pushing a high majority into informal jobs, and lowering living standards. The policies pursued to solve urban problems are contradictory. On the one hand, policies are intended to reduce migration to the cities, mainly by making farming and rural areas attractive. On the other hand, there is a focus on improving conditions in the cities. Any small improvement in the cities makes them more attractive to migrants. When new migrants arrive, they worsen urban problems by congesting living spaces and adding to the slums. One of the greatest challenges is to supply safe drinking water and improve the sewers so that malaria-carrying mosquitoes will have limited breeding places.

ENVIRONMENT AND DEVELOPMENT

Until the 1980s, many African governments failed to make the connection between economic development and the environment. Not only were issues of environmental protection ignored, but some people believed that economic development could be retarded by paying too much attention to the management of the environment. For instance, to build more schools and hospitals, they had to cut timber from the forests. To expand the cities, they had to destroy the countryside. Western countries also divorced the interests of Africa from their concerns. Although scientists and various environmentalist pressure groups have pointed to the interconnectedness of the universe and the "global environment," planners in the West have generally ignored Africa. In the 1990s, many more people began to realize that global warming, the ability of the dust in the Sahara Desert to travel as far as Austin in Texas and New Orleans in Louisiana, the sea waves from West Africa that create hurricanes in the United States, and the international spread of AIDS and other disease all mean that environmental problems in one part of the world can affect other places. It is now realized that the outbreak of "mad cow disease" in Britain can become a global phenomenon through the agency of human migration and trade.

The environmental problems will not only slow down the rate of national economic growth but also devastate Africa's rural population. Over 70 percent of Africa's population is dependent on forests, trees, and other plants for a number of basic necessities, such as shelter, food, and medicine. Women collect fruits and process all kinds of products to sell in the markets. Without wood and grazing land, many will become poorer. Fodder sustains cattle-rearing communities, and fuelwood is the main source of energy. The loss of the forest will translate into loss of income for millions of rural dwellers. Should they be pushed into cities to seek survival, more negative consequences will follow.

Soil erosion and loss of nutrients have reduced crop yield and overall land capacity for production. Since the 1970s, the annual yields of important crops such as millet, wheat, peanuts, maize, and cotton have declined. This poses a problem of hunger and poverty for the majority of Africans.

The preference for export production that was promoted during the colonial era and inherited after independence has posed its own dangers to the environment and the people. As most countries depend on export crops for foreign exchange, they have encouraged farmers to cultivate these crops at the expense of food crops. When the economy suffers a decline, and additional external revenues are required, more land is devoted to cash crops, again at the expense of food crops. The best lands are devoted to cotton, coffee, tea, sugar, and cocoa. Over time, the land is overused, and crop yields decline. Research is concentrated on export crops, and irrigated land is devoted to them. When drought strikes, as in Sudan in 1985, little or no contingency planning is in place to feed starving and displaced people.

The poverty of some countries has been exploited by foreign companies looking for places to dump toxic products. Recipients of toxic waste see this as an easy means of access to foreign currencies, failing to consider the great health risk. By 1988, at least ten countries had legally agreed to accept toxic waste, although regional and continental agencies pressured them not to conclude ongoing negotiations and to renege on signed agreements. As such contracts are concluded in secrecy, records of official transactions are not even available to members of the public.

Wildlife is another aspect connected to the external market. Botswana, Tanzania, Zimbabwe, and Kenya earn hard currency from foreign tourists interested in wildlife. In the case of Kenya, tourism is extensive, attracting close to a million visitors each year and providing the best source of foreign exchange. However, the external market is also interested in animal products such as ivory, rhinoceros horn, and leopard skins. Poachers kill the desired animals in an indiscriminate manner. In Kenya in the 1980s, the elephant population faced extinction, until vigorous antipoaching measures saved the animals. In Zimbabwe and Botswana where the elephant population keeps increasing, the problem is to maintain a balance between the needs of the growing human and animal populations. In these two countries, the government wants to kill animals to raise money for conservation and to manage land and natural resources for the benefit both of animals and of human beings. Many continue to argue that the needs of human beings and concerns for economic growth are more important than saving animals.

In areas with drier land, the ability to sustain large populations will depend on the application of science and technology to agriculture. Extensive irrigation may minimize the damage caused by the encroachment of the Sahara Desert, while the use of fertilizers may solve the problem of poor soils. However, in seeking solutions in modern science, Africa experiences some contradictions. On the one hand, irrigation and fertilizers will lead to greater food production and an ability to meet the needs of the population. On the other hand, irrigation and fertilizer use can create a host of new problems due to the use of dangerous pesticides, the abuse of even good pesticides, and food and crop poisoning. Irrigation poses its own problems as well—the energy to power machines has to be paid for, and in dry climates, irrigation can increase the alkaline and salt levels of soil. Efforts have to be made to minimize damage to Africa's topsoil, halt the spread of the desert, minimize the hunger and displacement caused by occasional droughts, prohibit the dumping of toxic waste, and check the activities of industries that cause pollution.

SUGGESTIONS FOR FURTHER READING

Anderson, Dennis. *The Economics of Afforestation: A Case Study in Africa*. Baltimore, Md.: Johns Hopkins University Press, 1987.

Gordon, April A., and Donald L. Gordon, eds. *Understanding Contemporary Africa*. Boulder, Colo.: Lynne Rienner, 1992. Chapter 7.

Ives, Jane H. *The Export of Hazard: Transnational Corporations and Environmental Control Issues*. Boston: Routledge and Kegan Paul, 1985.

Leonard, H. Jeffrey, ed. *Divesting Nature's Capital: The Political Economy of Environmental Abuse in the Third World*. New York: Holmes and Meier, 1985.

Lewis, L.A., and L. Berry. *African Environments and Resources*. Boston: Unwin Hyman, 1988.

Timberlake, Lloyd. *Africa in Crisis: The Causes, the Cures of Environmental Bankruptcy*. Washington, D.C.: Earthscan, 1986.

Watts, M. *Silent Violence: Food, Famine and Peasantry in Northern Nigeria*. Berkeley: University of California Press, 1983.

34

African Refugees, 1980 Onward

During the 1980s and 1990s, Africa produced one-third of the world's refugees. In the early 1990s, there were more than 5 million African refugees, enough to populate an entire country. As ethnic and other armed conflicts have become endemic, Africa has witnessed a massive increase in the number of refugees and other forced migrants. In addition, there were over 10 million people displaced people who were not classified as refugees but who lived in refugeelike conditions during the 1980s and 1990s. The creation of this enormous population of refugees has become a phenomenon in global history, bringing into sharp focus Africa's economic and political problems and the suffering of its people. Millions of people have been displaced from their homelands by wars, political persecution, poverty, and famine. Authoritarian governments use violence to solve problems; they suppress the expression of political freedom, deny people's right to political participation, and fail to promote economic development, thereby providing the circumstances that force people to flee their country.

Refugees seek shelter, food, justice, and security, and the majority hope to return to their original homelands when conditions change. Forced migrations raise issues of resettlement, tension with host societies, repatriation, and the need for economic development to overcome the poverty and famine that have led to some of the population movements.

CAUSES AND CASES

Refugees are created by different circumstances, notably wars, leadership rivalries, interethnic conflicts and hatreds, environmental crises, and poverty.

Refugee crisis in Africa, 1990s.

Countries that have produced refugees include South Africa, Ghana, Kenya, Chad, Angola, Rwanda, Burundi, Mozambique, Ethiopia, Somalia, and Sudan. The last three countries have become known in the American media for the images they have provided of starving children and desperately ill adults.

In the first decade following independence, the majority of refugees were created by wars of liberation and political conflicts. Conflicts between two or more African countries, clashes over boundaries, rivalry for territories, guerrilla warfare, and internal strife should be added to the political factors. Among the political crises that have caused forced migrations are the Algerian War of Independence in the 1950s, the civil wars in Nigeria, Chad, Sudan, Sierra Leone, and Liberia, the anti-apartheid struggles in South Africa, the territorial wars in the Horn of Africa, the ethnic conflicts between the Hutu and Tutsi in Rwanda and Burundi, and the competition for power in Somalia and Sierra Leone. The wars of liberation against the Portuguese in Angola and Mozambique also produced refugees.

Wars of national liberation and internal conflicts influenced the definition of refugees by the Organization of African Unity (OAU) and other agencies. In order not to confuse refugees with other migrants, the OAU came up with a working definition in 1969:

The term "refugee" shall mean every person who, owing to well-founded fear of being persecuted for reasons of race, religion, nationality, membership of a particular social group or political opinion, is outside the country of his nationality and is unable, or owing to such fear, is unwilling to avail himself of the protection of that country, or, who, not having a nationality and being outside the country of his former habitual residence as a result of such events is unable or, owing to such fear, is unwilling to return to it. The term "refugee" shall also apply to every person who, owing to external aggression, occupation, foreign domination or events seriously disturbing public order in either part or whole of his country of origin or nationality, is compelled to leave his place of habitual residence in order to seek refuge in another place outside his country of origin or nationality.[1]

As broad as this definition is, it was based on the assumption that many refugees will be driven by political considerations. Written in 1969, the OAU definition was concerned with Africans running away from South Africa and areas still under European control. However, by the 1980s, economic circumstances had also become important. Children, women, elderly people, and the disabled were among the refugees. Taking care of displaced people who were not classified as refugees by the OAU became a source of problems. If displaced people live within their own countries, it is difficult for international aid agencies to take care of them, for fear of offending the government.

Drought, volcanic eruptions, famine, and resource depletion have pushed many people out of their homelands, as in the case of Tigray, Ethiopia. After all strategies have failed to cope with food shortage, migration can become the last available option. In areas affected by political conflicts, decline or failure of production leads to food shortage, which in turn will force the people to migrate.

Food distribution can be used as a weapon by a government in an unstable area to reward loyalists and drive away enemies. In the Horn of Africa where relief agencies have distributed food to starving populations, some governments or "warlords" have prevented the distribution of food to so-called enemies, in order to punish them and force population displacement.

The number of refugees has been on the increase since the 1950s. In 1964 when the first statistics were compiled by the OAU, there were 700,000 refugees. Five years later, there were about 900,000. Over a million were reported in 1977. Between 1977 and 1979, the number doubled. In 1981, the number was over 3 million, and in 1987, well over 5 million. The crises in Liberia and Somalia in 1990 generated additional numbers of refugees. The refugee population in Africa by 1990 can be broken down by region: southern region (1.2 million), eastern region (2.6 million), central region (743,000), western region (734,000), and northern region (171,000). These figures are most likely to be grossly underestimated. Countless numbers of refugees do not register with the United Nations High Commission for Refugees, which supplied the data. Neither do they necessarily even report to their host government, as many simply relocate to local communities, especially if they share the same culture and ethnicity with their hosts. The figures also exclude those who do not cross the borders of their own countries.

A number of trends have emerged over the years. Some countries have become noted for producing or receiving refugees. In the 1980s, Ethiopia was the largest refugee-generating region, although it also received the highest number of refugees, from the Sudan. Ten countries dominate the list of those creating and receiving refugees, with Somalia and Rwanda having up to 10 percent of their population as refugees. Since 1980, more than half of the African continent has experienced a refugee problem, either losing or receiving people. In West Africa, Liberia, Sierra Leone, and Mauritania top the list of countries that have created refugees. The greatest number of refugees has been produced in the Horn of Africa and in central and southern Africa. Sudan is a notable case, for the large number it has received and created and for the persistent nature of the problem. Southern Sudan has lost many of its people to its neighbors due to a prolonged war with the north. With religious conflict between the Christians in the south and the Muslims in the north, the war has become one for religious freedom and regional autonomy. On the other hand, Sudan itself has received millions of refugees from Chad, Ethiopia, Uganda, and the Congo, all victims of serious political conflicts. Sudan has created a number of government farms where the refugees can live semipermanently. The refugee problem is not about statistics but about human tragedy involving great losses to communities and individuals.

CARE, CONCERNS, AND PROBLEMS

How to shelter, feed, and protect refugees are all serious problems. Host countries show compassion and generosity to refugees, although there are cases of tension, mutual suspicion, and hostility. Local people and government agencies respond to the situation in spite of limited resources. The United Nations Disaster Relief Organization (UNDRO), the OAU, and many nongovernmental organizations are also involved in taking care of refugees.

The resources available to assist refugees are not always sufficient for the large numbers. In the early stages of a crisis, thousands of refugees may show up, unannounced, in an area within a few days and deplete available water and food resources. Relief is generally inadequate for such large numbers. Aid agencies do not always find it easy to deliver materials and assistance to refugees scattered over vast areas. Among the issues that refugees confront are inadequate shelter, water, food, infrastructure, communication, and land to cultivate crops, plus a lack of self-esteem. The children of refugees have few or no educational or apprenticeship opportunities.

Where refugees have stayed in an area for a long time, they have embarked upon self-help projects, creating semipermanent farming communities. Creating self-sufficient refugee camps is always a problem, but where self-help and aid have been combined this has tended to ease the pain of relocation. If international relief agencies give too much food, medicine, and other resources to refugees, they may attain a standard of living higher than that of their hosts and thus create some resentment among their hosts. When host communities are called upon to assist refugees who want to farm, there may not be sufficient land, or the land given may require the use of water, fertilizers, and equipment that are not available.

When most refugees were driven out by apartheid (as in the case of South Africa) or wars of liberation (as in the case of a million Mozambicans in Zambia in the 1970s), the host societies tended to be sympathetic, regarding the care they gave as a contribution to the anticolonial struggles. However, in the 1980s and 1990s, when refugees were created by power and ethnic rivalries among Africans, host communities tended to resent their guests. When food materials run out and aid is slow to come, hosts are critical of refugees, blaming a handful of people for creating the problems.

There are many other problems. Political leaders in host societies can be fearful of refugees, thinking that they may become involved in politics and schemes to destabilize the host countries. Political relations between refugee-receiving and refugee-generating countries can also degenerate into tension and conflict, as in the conflicts between Uganda and Tanzania and Angola and the Congo. Thus, in locating refugee camps, issues of security and safety have to be considered. Refugees want to be close to their relations, which may mean that they do not want to be too far away from the borders of their home country. As far as aid agencies are concerned, the best location is a place where it is easy for them to distribute food, water, medicine, and other necessities. In some cases, aid workers may have to be accompanied by soldiers, as in Somalia in 1992 and 1993 when ethnic leaders competed for power.

To host societies, refugees represent both an economic asset and a burden. Host communities want to take advantage of the situation in terms of providing people to serve as aid workers, selling some items, and using cheap refugee labor. Thus, the refugees are denied the opportunity to participate in politics by the host government and denied the opportunity to engage in economic activities by competing host communities. This is often a source of trouble. The healthy and active among the refugees lead a life of inactivity. In cases where refugees flee due to political problems, they are not wanted back home. Thus, to deny them political and economic participation in their temporary home is to further alienate them by treating them as people that nobody wants or cares about. In response to this marginalization, refugees can become restless, fighting or criticizing their hosts. The desire to return to their homelands where they have self-worth and dignity may turn many into rebels, fighting just in order to return. Either for challenging their host or becoming armed warriors, they risk repatriation, and some refugees have been forcefully repatriated. The Tutsi of Rwanda who settled in Uganda in the 1980s decided to self-repatriate, even when this involved armed conflict with their Hutu rivals. Where refugees are restless, measures are taken to confine them to designated areas and to police their movements. Sometimes the management of refugee camps is authoritarian, and the refugees are denied freedom of political expression.

Where refugees are created by ethnic and religious hostilities, the problem is complicated by their determination to take revenge and seek all possible means to return home. Notable examples include the refugees who fled from Idi Amin's regime in Uganda in the 1980s, the Hutu and Tutsi of Rwanda in the 1980s and 1990s, and the southern Sudanese since the 1970s. Refugees may turn themselves into armed militias to fight for their rights. When refugees form armies, fresh troubles are created: The nation that forced them out and the one that receives them become enemies; the environment and economy of host communities may be devastated by insecurity and conflict; aid workers helping the refugees may be treated as mercenaries; convoys taking food and medicine to the refugees may be attacked in order to divert these materials elsewhere or simply to deny the refugees the means to survive. In this kind of atmosphere, more people are displaced, humanitarian efforts are undermined, and local conflicts are internationalized.

The future of refugees is always uncertain. They and their hosts prefer the option of repatriation and resettlement in their homeland. However, there are always obstacles to this. To start with, the political conditions that created their displacement may still exist. As long as the government that created the problems remains in power, it is difficult for refugees to return. This was the case with the South African exiles during the long apartheid regime. To take another example, the war in Sierra Leone in the 1980s and 1990s lasted so long that it was difficult to convince refugees to return home without fearing that they would lose their lives. Where armed conflicts are protracted, as in the warfare and ethnic hostilities in Rwanda and the Congo, it is always difficult to ask refugees to return. Indeed, the army of a refugee-generating country may even pursue those in flight, killing as many of them as possible in order to prevent them from forming a guerrilla movement. In some cases, repatriation has to be negotiated by various governments and interested parties, and arriving at a consensus can prove impossible. One of the parties may anticipate future conflicts and not want the refugees to become armed warriors. Finally, the concerns of the refugees may cause anxiety among them and affect their decisions: How will they readapt? What jobs will be available for them? Will their children be happy?

Permanent settlement in the host country is another option, where the chances of repatriation are minimal. This is not an easy undertaking, as both the refugees and the host communities may resist. Permanent settlement involves allocation of land, competition for jobs, and the sharing of scarce resources. Aid agencies have to provide resources both to the refugees and to their hosts in order to avert crises. The coexistence of two cultural identities within the same area also causes fear, especially among host communities, who may be resistant to the settlement of another group in their area. Host communities fear tension based on ethnic and cultural differences, an increase in crime, excessive overloading of limited social facilities and infrastructure, and intense competition for jobs. Obtaining citizenship in a new country is usually a complicated matter.

CONCLUSION

Refugees still exist in Africa, and conditions conducive to the creation of new ones are always present. In the final analysis, both the creation and the management of refugees are very much tied to the economic development and political stability of Africa. Cases instigated by drought and famine can be solved by the development of agriculture and other economic sectors that can create jobs for millions of people. Whether an area loses or receives refugees, its development witnesses a major setback. The people become poorer.

If enduring solutions to political instability, ethnic rivalries, and religious conflicts are not found, many African countries will produce more refugees in the future. Authoritarian governments lay the foundation for the production of refugees. Even when people do not leave their countries, they may still be displaced internally.

The care of refugees can be facilitated if host societies are sufficiently developed to cope with a sudden population influx. Host communities resent refugees in part because they reduce access to water supplies, land, housing, schools, and other amenities that are in short supply to start with. Repatriation, rather than integration into host societies, is the best option to resolve the refugee situation. While awaiting repatriation, many of the problems experienced by refugees can be minimized if hosts do not limit assistance to food, water, and medicine but encourage the acquisition of skills, the productive use of time, and the creation of self-help projects, provide opportunities for refugees to go to school and form cultural and religious associations, and offer citizenship to those who ask for it. Refugees should be involved in decisions relating to their existence and future options. Powerlessness is one of the conditions that has produced the refugees; empowering them in the management of their lives will restore a sense of hope and optimism in their future.

NOTE

1. Organization of African Unity, *Convention Governing the Specific Aspects of Refugee Problems in Africa*, 10 September 1969 (Addis-Ababa: OAU, 1969).

SUGGESTIONS FOR FURTHER READING

Adelman, Howard, and John Sorenson, eds. *African Refugee: Development Aid and Repatriation*. Boulder, Colo.: Westview Press, 1994.

Falola, Toyin. "Nigeria in the Global Context of Refugees: Historical and Comparative Perspectives." *Journal of Asian and African Studies* 32, nos. 1–2 (June 1997): 5–21.

Gorman, Robert. *Coping with Africa's Refugee Burden: A Time for Solutions*. New York: Martinus-Nijhoff and UNITAR, 1987.

Harrel-Bond, B.E. *Imposing Aid: Emergency Assistance to Refugees*. Oxford: Oxford University Press, 1986.

Refugee Policy Group. *International Conference on Assistance to Refugees in Africa II: Future Directions for Assistance to Refugees in Africa*. Washington, D.C.: Author, 1984.

United Nations. *Protocol Relating to the Status of Refugees*. New York: United Nations, 31 January 1967.

Zolberg, Aristide R., Astri Suhrke, and Sergio Aguayo. *Escape from Violence: Conflict and the Refugee Crisis in the Developing World*. Oxford: Oxford University Press, 1989.

35

Africa in World Politics in Transition, 1980s Onward

African relations with the outside world entered a period of transition in the late 1980s, from the politics of the Cold War to those of the post–Cold War period. From the 1960s to the collapse of the Soviet Union in 1991, Africa had to operate in a bipolar global environment, in addition to negotiating with former European colonial powers. The optimism in the early years of independence that the continent would be influential in world politics quickly gave way to despair as the politics of the Cold War unfolded. Africans were not allowed to have full control of their destinies—foreign powers interfered to pursue their interests and maintain their spheres of influence. African countries were weak in relation to the Western powers. With the fall of the Soviet Union, however, the international environment was radically altered. The conflicts over ideological choices between capitalism and socialism changed to conflicts over the acceptance of the free market. The agony of choosing between satisfying the Soviet bloc or the Western bloc changed to that of coping with the hegemonic power of the United States in world politics. As Africa lost its place in the strategic interests of the Western powers, the need to keep some dictators in power disappeared and political reforms occurred in a number of countries. Economic underdevelopment and dependence on the West for imports and technology have weakened the role of Africa in world politics. The changes in African relations with the rest of the world constitute a major historical event with profound consequences for the economy and politics.

Political conflicts in the 1990s.

EURO-AFRICAN RELATIONS

Africa's relations with Europe have a long history. There was the history of trade, dominated by the traffic in slaves from the sixteenth century to the nineteenth century. Slaves were replaced by raw materials during the nineteenth century (see Chapter 11). Trade gave way to colonial domination in the first half of the twentieth century (see Chapter 19). The achievement of independence by African countries did not terminate these relations. A number of further developments occurred, notably the following:

- France maintained close, almost supervisory relations with its former colonies, far more so than any other European country. Britain, the second major European colonial power, did not pursue a policy as all-embracing as that of France.

- The United States, the Soviet Union, and to a lesser extent China involved Africa in their superpower rivalries. The United States wanted to spread its ideologies of democracy and capitalism, minimize the global role of the Soviet Union, and trade with Africa. The Soviet Union was interested in spreading socialism and reducing the number of countries in the Western orbit. There was a crisis in the Congo in 1960, in which the superpowers were involved, and socialist-leaning leader Patrice Lumumba was murdered and replaced by a "friend of the West," Mobutu Sese Seko. In the 1970s, there were tensions in Ethiopia, Somalia, South Africa, Mozambique, and Angola, as the superpowers intervened to obtain political and economic advantages. In the mid-1980s, South Africa and Libya offered opportunities for superpower conflicts.

- As part of their response to the Cold War, African countries sought identification with other developing countries, notably the members of the Nonaligned Movement, in order to develop a collective diplomacy and strategy to deal with the developed countries. Since most countries were weak, they believed that alliances with other countries would enhance their ability to bargain. While external powers sought to intervene in Africa when it suited them, African countries wanted to defend their independence and improve trade relations.

AFRICA AND THE SUPERPOWERS

After the Second World War, two new powers—the United States and the Soviet Union—entered Africa as major actors, joining the established European colonial powers. The new actors brought with them their interests in trade, ideology, and military strength. More important, they brought their deep hatred of one another: Africa was important to them only as they calculated their Cold War rivalry and policy. African leaders in search of assistance or troubled by internal opposition sought to identify with one of these two powers or even to manipulate them when it was possible to do so.

The Soviet Union's strategy was based on an anti-imperialist ideology and the promotion of a socialist economic system. The Soviets had no colonies in Africa, which enabled them to promote a philosophy of anti-imperialism that appealed to pioneer African nationalists and leaders. The initial contacts of the Soviets in post–World War II Africa were with Egypt under Nasser, who received arms denied to him by Western Europe. Nasser was, however, unsympathetic to communist ideas. The next contact was with Guinea under Sekou Toure, an anti-French labor union leader. Neither early cooperation nor the Soviets' supply of arms led to any close friendship. Mali under Modibo Keita, Algeria under Ahmed Ben Bella, and Ghana under Kwame Nkrumah also befriended the Soviets. But socialism failed to take any real root in these places. Nevertheless, the Soviet Union continued to develop relations with many African countries, if only to demonstrate to them that it was a great power. Faced with competition from China, the Soviets declared their support for socialist-leaning African leaders and assisted the anti-apartheid movement in South Africa. In the 1970s, the Soviets sold considerable quantities of arms to Angola and Ethiopia and supported the socialist regimes in Angola, Guinea-Bissau, and Mozambique. Socialist policies did not succeed as anticipated, and the contributions of the Soviets were limited to supplying arms and facilitating anticolonial wars in a few places. The Soviet Union was able to use anti-imperialism to win friends in Africa and demonstrate its strength as a world power.

For the United States, identifying with former colonial powers was important, and so was developing fresh trade and political relations. The United States also wanted to prevent the Soviets from selling socialism to Africans. To achieve its objectives, the United States established commercial and diplomatic relations with many countries. Although U.S. policy toward Africa has been very consistent, Africa has never been a major priority. However, people in the United States have been able to acquire considerable knowledge of Africa through college courses and research. In addition, the technical assistance provided through the Peace Corps program has enabled many Americans to live in African cities and villages and interact with African people.

After the Second World War, the United States presented an anticolonial image but without alienating its European allies. Where a European country was heavily involved in an African country, as in the case of France and its former colonies discussed below or Britain and Nigeria, the United States did not become deeply involved. When the United States intervened in Africa, it was to halt the spread of Soviet influence and benefit from trade. In 1960, the United States was involved in the killing of the first premier of the Congo, the left-leaning Patrice Lumumba. This inaugurated a policy of hostility to socialist movements and radical African leaders. Africa was regarded as part of the Cold War politics, with the energy of the United States focused on halting the spread of communism, even if it meant supporting repressive governments and corrupt leaders. The repressive and corrupt Mobutu of the Congo was treated as a valuable friend, and his country was the second largest market in Africa for U.S. arms. The United States was able to benefit from Congolese minerals. The United States was also involved in Ethiopia and Somalia, mainly to curtail Soviet influence. Similarly, the United States was opposed to the anti-Portuguese organizations in Angola and Mozambique because these were regarded as allies of the Soviet Union and Cuba.

In the case of South Africa, the United States failed to condemn apartheid for many years, regarding the minority government as insurance against the spread of communism. It was not until the Jimmy Carter administration that the policy was revised to condemn human rights abuses in South Africa and to pressure the apartheid regime to accept the independence of Namibia. U.S. policy was still cautious, largely because of the heavy capital investments of U.S. companies in South Africa. Trade with South Africa was also important, running to $4 billion a year in the 1980s. International protest and violence in South Africa led to a shift in U.S. policy after 1986—the United States now joined others in demanding the reform of the apartheid system and supporting the imposition of sanctions.

THE ROLE OF FRANCE

The French attitude to Africa was consistent for a long time—the conquest of large areas was regarded as a national achievement. The majority of the African leaders that inherited power from France also had a strong attachment to French culture and ideas. France regarded itself as Africa's metropole, with a policy of developing dependency relations labeled *coopération*. From 1973 onward, there was an annual Franco-African summit, a major international event to review affairs and decide on a common stand on a number of issues. Relations between French and African leaders were personalized. The African leaders were showered with praise and attention. Through technical and financial arrangements, France was able to maintain a considerable influence over its former colonies. France sent to Africa teachers, technicians, engineers, and others to offer basic services. France also contributed to the development of government agencies and supported the CFA (Coopération financière africaine) franc as the common currency. In addition, France trained the police and armed forces in Francophone Africa.

Although its policy was presented as one of helping Africa, it was actually one of self-interest. French goods were sold to Africa, while French capital investment was supported and encouraged. The use of the common CFA franc enabled France to impose tight financial control. France maintained military bases to protect its interests and to assist other Western countries in the fight against the Soviet Union. France was the main supplier of arms to many African countries and led the Western countries as an arms merchant.

France intervened in the internal affairs of the Francophone countries and even helped unpopular governments to stay in power. France supported such brutal dictators as Mobutu of the Congo, Omar Bongo of Gabon, and Jean-Bédel Bokassa, self-appointed emperor of the Central African Republic. The French military presence was a reminder to opposition forces and civil society that their campaigns for change could be repressed by African leaders in cooperation with their French sponsors. France established security agreements with Côte d'Ivoire, Senegal, Gabon, Djibouti, and the Central African Republic.

France's relations with its former colonies are a classic example of neocolonialism—the ability to retain dominance even when the colonies have become independent. It was not the interests of the mass of the African people that were paramount but those of the political leaders and business community. Dictators and autocrats were supported as long as they cooperated with France, and issues of human rights were regarded as unimportant. France even sold arms to South Africa.

France was very successful in its domination of its former colonies in Africa. To start with, other Western countries and even the Soviet Union all conceded that France had the most dominant influence in all its former colonies. Leaders of the poor and struggling African countries needed assistance from France, in spite of the dependency that would come from it. Presiding over weak economies based on the export of a few crops, these leaders regarded France as contributing to their search for development. Those in power and the elite already assimilated to French culture benefited from the French connection by way of access to jobs, travel abroad, and education of their children. France's military assistance enabled many leaders to stay in power. There were occasional profound tensions and disagreements, mainly with Libya and Algeria, which wanted to assert their political autonomy and negotiate better trade relations.

POST–COLD WAR RELATIONS

While established relations of dependency have continued, some changes are noticeable. In the 1990s, European countries began to warn that financial and technical assistance would be linked to good governance and democratization. They began to demand that African leaders should be more accountable to their people. However, many of these wishes were expressed largely as mere political rhetoric. It was during this period that Nigeria suffered under its worst dictator, General Sani Abacha.

France, Britain, Portugal, and Belgium, all former colonial powers in Africa, together with other European nations are now members of the European Union, which enables them to coordinate their policies on economics, politics, and immigration. While each country continues to maintain its individual relations with African countries, the European Union also provides its members with an instrument to impose and facilitate their dominance over Africa.

The East-West ideological rivalry has ended. The United States no longer has to pursue a policy of preventing African countries from adopting the socialist ideology. In the 1980s, the Soviet Union under Mikhail Gorbachev began a series of reforms—perestroika—that changed the country profoundly and the international environment as well. A period of detente followed, marked by international cooperation and also withdrawal. In 1988, the United States and the Soviet Union agreed on peaceful solutions to African conflicts, and they ended their rivalries over Angola and Namibia. The Soviet Union began to pressure the anti-apartheid movement in South Africa to pursue a strategy of dialogue with the government, instead of violence. By 1990, the Soviet Union and the United States were advocating the same policy in South Africa, that of dialogue and reform. Similarly, the

Soviet Union asked Ethiopia to solve its problems with Eritrea peacefully, and it scaled back its military and financial assistance. When African socialist regimes such as Mozambique wanted to seek assistance in the West or raise loans from Western institutions, the Soviet Union did not stand in their way or even criticize them. The Soviets were no longer expecting any socialist revolution in Africa.

Now free of the Soviet challenge, the United States, too, began to change its policy. The Bush administration was now eager to see the end of apartheid. In addition, the administration began to talk about democratization and good governance in Africa. Authoritarian regimes and one-party states were worried about this development, fearing that the United States would no longer support them. Interference in African crises was also reduced, although this had terrible consequences in Rwanda, Liberia, Ethiopia, and Sierra Leone where ethnic conflicts and wars led to the deaths of thousands of people.

As the West searched for new markets in Asia and Latin America and the Europeans created a stronger economic union, Africa increasingly became marginalized in world politics. Obtaining concessions from Russia, the United States, and Europe has become far more difficult. It is clear that small, weak nations may have little or no major influence in world politics, but regional powers such as Egypt, Algeria, Nigeria, and South Africa have tremendous opportunities to develop stronger continental and regional unions that will promote better trade among Africans.

THE DETERMINANTS OF FOREIGN POLICY

A number of factors have shaped Africa's role in world politics, many of which underscore its weakness and dependency. The main determinants include the colonial impact, the economy, the Cold War, and Africa's nonalignment, political instability, and united front against the apartheid regime in South Africa. The former colonial masters have exerted the greatest influence on postcolonial Africa. The role of France has been discussed above, while the British continued to hold a leadership position in the Commonwealth, an association of former British colonies.

Arguably the most important determinant of foreign policy as well as a major constraint on it has been economic underdevelopment. Africa has been incorporated into the world system to supply resources—labor, raw materials, minerals, and so on—to Western countries. The interest of the West in Africa has never been in the development of Africans but in markets, investment, and access to important raw materials. Thus, Africa is exploited. At the same time, Africa has become dependent on the West for industrial products, technology, and even luxury items such as cigarettes and alcohol.

The problems of economic dependency are too numerous to be listed here. African countries want to overcome their fragility, and they seek various forms of support and assistance from the international community. When aid is offered, it comes with many strings attached. France, for instance, has maintained almost permanent control over such countries as Côte d'Ivoire and Gabon. The expectation that some countries with valuable resources would use them to establish considerable influence has largely been unfulfilled. For instance, it was thought that Nigeria could use oil, Botswana diamonds, and South Africa gold to create effective diplomacy for power. But these countries have failed to establish a powerful influence because the buyers control the market, the terms of trade may deteriorate, and the suppliers are unable to use their minerals to diversify their economies and reduce dependency.

External powers exploit political problems to intervene in Africa. Secession struggles, civil wars, annexation, wars of independence, and other problems were used during the Cold War to justify interference in the internal affairs of the Congo, Angola, Ethiopia, Somalia, Morocco, Chad, Sierra Leone, and Liberia, to mention just a few cases. Cases of interference during the Cold War also brought Africa onto the center stage of superpower rivalries.

As Africa enters a new millennium, under the leadership of its own people, its role in world politics will be affected by its ability to democratize its key institutions, transform its economies, minimize dependence on the West, develop appropriate local technologies, and foster a spirit of patriotism and nationalism. Continental and regional organizations must be strengthened to play an active role in empowering Africans and creating a voice worthy of respect in foreign affairs.

SUGGESTIONS FOR FURTHER READING

Albright, David E., ed. *Communism in Africa.* Bloomington: Indiana University Press, 1980.

Aluko, Olajide, ed. *The Foreign Policies of African States.* London: Hodder and Stoughton, 1977.

Chazan, Naomi, et al. *Politics and Society in Contemporary Africa.* Boulder, Colo.: Lynne Rienner, 1992. Chapter 12.

Colletta, Nat J., et al. *The Transition from War to Peace in Sub-Saharan Africa.* Washington, D.C.: World Bank, 1996.

Falola, Toyin. "Africa in Perspective." In Stephen Ellis, ed., *Africa Now: People, Policies and Institutions.* London: James Currey, 1996. Pp. 3–19.

Jackson, Henry. *From the Congo to Soweto.* New York: Morrow, 1982.

Wright, Stephen, ed. *African Foreign Policies.* Boulder, Colo.: Westview Press, 1999.

36

The Fall of Apartheid and the Advent of Nelson Mandela's Government, 1994–99

In 1994, Nelson Mandela became the first black president of South Africa, four years after leaving jail. That apartheid would end and Mandela would move from jail to power was an event no one could anticipate even in the preceding decade. It was also an event that closed the book on European colonial domination of Africa. The background to the event was marked by long resistance to the injustice and racial discrimination of the apartheid system (see Chapter 20).

BLACK RADICALISM

Resistance to apartheid has a long history. In 1944, Nelson Mandela, Oliver Tambo, and some other students expelled from Fort Hare College formed the Youth League of the African National Congress (ANC). The Youth Leaguers were radicals who demanded national and political freedom and an end to all segregationist laws and white leadership. By 1949, some of the members of the Youth League had become members of the executive of the ANC. In 1952 and 1953, the ANC organized a series of defiance campaigns—blacks used facilities reserved for whites, about 8,000 of them were arrested, and black leaders were arrested or banned from political participation. In 1956, the Federation of South African Women organized a mass demonstration to protest the law that mandated black women to carry passes. Women were actively involved in anti-apartheid struggles. The resistance strategy was to organize mass defiance.

On 21 March 1960, the Pan Africanist Congress (PAC), another radical black organization, embarked on a ten-day protest, burning passes and inciting the police to arrest thousands of protesters. About 4,000 blacks marched to the police station in the city of Sharpeville, thinking that they would be arrested. Instead, the police opened fire, killed 69, and wounded 180. The South African government was condemned for its excesses. But it responded with more force: A "state of emergency" was declared to give the government more power; the ANC and PAC were proscribed; and thousands of blacks were arrested. The United Nations condemned all the actions of the South African government, but both the United States and Britain blocked the imposition of sanctions. In 1961, the South African government declared South Africa a republic and withdrew from the Commonwealth, in order to break all constitutional links with Britain.

Black political activities went underground, using sabotage and guerrilla tactics to make their points. Oliver Tambo went into exile to organize political struggles, and a number of blacks went to China and other countries for military training. In 1961, the ANC established Umkhonto we Sizwe ("Spear of the Nation"), a military wing that would sabotage economic, communication, and political targets such as government offices, railway lines, post offices, and electricity pylons. The PAC also embarked upon guerrilla activities, but the police infiltrated the organization and arrested some 3,000 of its members.

In 1962, Nelson Mandela was arrested and sent to prison for leaving the country without an approved passport. A year later, eight other prominent members of the military wing of the ANC were arrested. Mandela and the others were tried from December 1963 to July 1964. At the trial, Mandela defended himself, showed how peaceful means had failed, and ended his closing speech to the judge with words that have become famous:

During my lifetime I have dedicated myself to this struggle of the African people. I have fought against white domination, and I have fought against black domination. I have cherished the ideal of a democratic and free society in which all persons live together in harmony and with equal opportunities. It is an ideal which I hope to live for and to achieve. But if needs be it is an ideal for which I am prepared to die.

All but one of the defendants were sentenced to life imprisonment.

Black radicalism intensified, as did the violence intended to destroy it. The government continued to pursue its "Bantustan" policy of confining Africans to self-governing "Homelands" in order to control labor recruitment, monitor black entry into white areas, curb black nationalism, and weaken the ranks of black leaders and their followers by dividing them into various "tribal minorities." Thousands were forced to relocate to Bantustans, generally in areas without sufficient land to support them.

The ANC received support from the Soviet Union, Scandinavia, and Eastern European countries. It established a military camp in Tanzania. In the 1970s, trade unions became active and were able to organize a series of strikes.

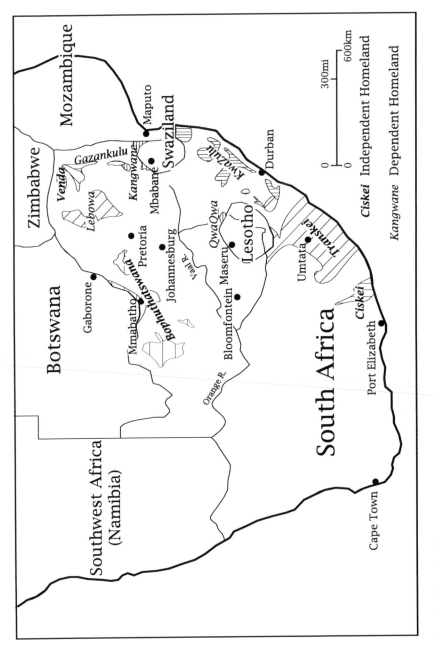

South African black homelands.

Students, too, became active, with many joining the "Black Consciousness Movement" headed by Steve Biko, who was banned from politics and later killed by the police in 1977.

International attention was diverted to the plight of Africans with the Soweto uprising of 1976–77. On 16 June 1976, the students in Soweto mounted a vigorous challenge to the system. They originally wanted to protest the use of the Afrikaans language to teach social studies and mathematics, a symbol of the inferior "Bantu education," as well as the gross underfunding of their schools. A revolt started after the police teargassed about 15,000 students, killed 2, and injured many more. A mass revolt engulfed the township, later spreading to the rest of the Rand area, Natal, and Cape Town. By the time it ended in 1977, more than 3,000 had been wounded and 600 killed by the police. Thousands of students were dismissed from school, and many fled into exile to become active in the ANC.

South Africa moved into the 1980s with its old problems. Guerrilla activities intensified, and various organizations demanded the release of Mandela, the unbanning of the ANC, and an end to apartheid. More and more whites and Afrikaners were joining blacks to demand reforms, to prevent a revolution. The society was becoming politically divided. While some Afrikaner organizations wanted the survival of apartheid, some began to call for the abolition of the system. The possibility of black majority rule was being discussed in the mid-1980s, if only to avoid a revolution that would destroy the economy. South Africa entered its decade of change in the 1990s as a deeply divided country.

REFORMS

A number of developments in the economy, politics, and international relations forced the minority regime in South Africa to undertake major reforms that led to the end of apartheid. The economic expansion and prosperity of the 1970s called for an increasing use of black labor in many sectors of the economy. Skilled black labor was needed in the industrial sector. The need for skilled, well-paid workers, living with their families in settled areas, contradicted many of the country's segregation laws. A number of businesses that needed black labor became critical of some of the policies of the government. Black trade unions became better organized at pressing their demands and organizing strikes, which became common after 1973.

A climate of black radicalism engulfed the entire southern African region in the 1970s and 1980s. The cost of maintaining the apartheid system was becoming excessive. The Soweto uprising of 1976–77 showed how brutal the system had become but also that it required violence to sustain it. Increasing black militancy forced the minority government to think about possible concessions.

South Africa became more and more isolated in the 1980s. Within Africa, it had enemies far and wide. After 1974, rapid political changes were taking place in the southern African region, leading to the independence of Mozambique and

Angola in 1975. In Zimbabwe, a civil war led to the country's independence in 1980. Although the South African government did all it could to prevent these positive changes, the changes led to its further isolation. The racist policies in South Africa were highlighted by the struggles in other countries.

In 1977, the United Nations imposed an arms embargo on South Africa. The United States, which had for many years been a partner of South Africa, called for a democratic government. As the economy declined, the privileges of the white population began to suffer. Investments declined and the rate of white emigration increased.

Between 1978 and 1989, South Africa pursued a policy of "total strategy" to prevent the imagined potential overthrow of the minority government by black communists aided by other blacks. The government would make a number of "friendly" changes expected to win the trust of the black people. A government commission called for the creation of a black middle class to spread economic benefits to skilled black people, and yet another called for the liberalization of the trade union laws. A number of hotels, universities, and movie theaters previously limited to whites began to let in blacks. Many of these measures were no more than cosmetic changes designed to change the image of South Africa in Western countries.

Pieter Willem Botha came to power in 1978. He was in favor of reform, although many Afrikaners were still in favor of the retention of the apartheid laws. In 1983, a revised constitution allowed the Coloureds and Indians to elect representatives to their own legislative chambers, although this would not give them much power or remove the conditions leading to discrimination. Anti-apartheid organizations among the black population continued to grow stronger and more militant. Spontaneous protests became common, with attacks even directed against many blacks who supported the government or were regarded as supporters of the apartheid system. Young blacks took to violence, making many townships ungovernable. It became risky for any black to be associated with the government. The government, too, responded with violence both within South Africa and in the neighboring countries where the ANC had its military camps. Neither the government nor the ANC and other black organizations used only violence to resolve the crisis. The government had to negotiate. The ANC, too, was being pressured by the Soviet Union, which was experiencing internal problems, to make some compromises and negotiate.

Frederik Willem de Klerk came to power in 1989. A conservative politician before then, he now realized that major changes were necessary if South Africa was to survive. On 2 February 1990, de Klerk announced the unbanning of the ANC and other major black organizations, the unconditional release of Nelson Mandela and other political prisoners, and the formulation of a new constitution that would allow blacks to vote. Nine days later, Mandela left prison, an event that has to be listed as one of the most important milestones of the twentieth century.

Mandela regarded his release as an opportunity to end apartheid. He refused to change his mind on armed struggles, remained committed to the ANC, and called on foreign governments not to lift the sanctions on South Africa. The ANC created a political party with Mandela as its president. The new party operated as an opposition to the minority government in power, but its members were divided on the strategies to pursue in negotiations. Conservative members of the ruling National Party were not happy with the changes and possible loss of power. They found opportunities to sabotage the government and attack the ANC.

Important changes continued. A number of apartheid laws were repealed, and by June 1994 apartheid was being proclaimed as dead. The ANC announced that it would end its armed struggles and would pursue dialogue. Political exiles were allowed to return home. In 1991, many foreign countries lifted their sanctions, and South Africa was allowed to participate in the Olympic Games held in 1992, thus ending a thirty-two-year ban. White fears intensified, as many lost their jobs. Expectations of change by blacks went unfulfilled, as millions of them had no jobs either.

The last major reform was political legislation to give the franchise to blacks. The majority of whites supported the reform measures and gave the mandate to de Klerk to complete the process. The ANC and the National Party agreed on a formula to share power. A date—27 April 1994—was fixed for the first democratic election. In spite of opposition by white conservatives and the black antagonists of the ANC, the election was held, and the ANC won 62.65 percent of the votes. On 10 May 1994, Mandela became the president. South Africa opened a new chapter in its long and complicated history.

PRESIDENT MANDELA IN POWER

The ANC and Nelson Mandela came to power in 1994 with little or no experience in managing a country. They had to move from the politics of resistance to the art of state management. Unlike many other cases, when Europeans left after independence, South Africa had millions of whites in economic strongholds, the police, and the army. The task that the Mandela government had to face was to please the majority of the black people, meeting their demands without losing the support of the white minority.

Mandela became a blessing to the country. He was not bitter and he did not govern as if revenge was necessary. Whites who were originally apprehensive of black rule calmed down, and the majority among them accepted Mandela and his government.

South Africa projected stability. The long-held belief that blacks would introduce a communist ideology and engage in class warfare was proved wrong. State management was pursued with measured changes. In the international arena, South Africa became active; it joined the Organization of African Unity and the Non-Aligned Movement in 1994, rejoined the Commonwealth and UNESCO (United Nations Educational, Scientific, and Cultural Organization) in the same year, and regained its seat in the United Nations General Assembly. After many years of isolation, the country is now treated as a partner in the international arena.

At the domestic level, there were three major issues that Mandela had to deal with—interracial relations, the setting up of a new constitution, and the economy—all in such a way as to correct the problems created by apartheid. To start with, poisoned race relations had to be improved upon. A large number of blacks expected revenge, or at least expected Mandela to be hostile to Afrikaners and other whites associated with their oppression. The Afrikaners were suspicious of Mandela. Among the blacks, the division into "Homelands" had created some division, as seen in the case of Zulu nationalism (on the Zulu, see Chapter 17). The National Party was still represented in the new government, with four cabinet appointments. The army and police had to be reorganized to include many black officers.

Archbishop Desmond Tutu, a South African peace activist and Nobel laureate, called for the creation of a Rainbow Nation that would unite all races and groups. Mandela governed with this spirit of unity and reconciliation in mind. He used the language of compassion and human brotherhood and was hopeful that blacks and Afrikaners would find a common ground to live together in peace. In 1995, the Truth and Reconciliation Commission (TRC) was established for individuals to confess their sins and be granted amnesty. This covered the period from the Sharpeville massacre of 1960 to May 1994 when Mandela assumed power. The sins to be forgiven must be political in nature, and those who refused to appear could be punished. The TRC was to seek the means for South Africans to come to terms with the past, but many were offended that criminals were not punished. The TRC collected an enormous amount of data from over 20,000 people while over 7,000 applied for amnesty.

Interracial relations and mutual suspicion also found expression in discussion of the new constitution to govern the country. First came an interim constitution and later a permanent one, both of them reflecting the need to correct the mistakes of the past and deal with issues that could divide the nation in the future. South Africa would be a "sovereign state," with citizenship granted to all its members, and a democratic government that would promote the goal of equality among people of all races and both genders. The government would ensure civil liberties, freedom, and fundamental rights and prohibit all forms of discrimination. Local and provincial authorities received more power, the police and army were prohibited from excessive meddling in politics on behalf of any political party, and all races were to be represented in the civil service and security forces. A policy of affirmative action was put in place to prevent discrimination on the basis of gender, race, and color. The new constitution was signed on 10 December 1996, and it came into effect in February 1997. The president would be appointed for a five-year term by the leading party in the Parliament, which comprised 90 members of the Senate and 400 members of the National Assembly.

The Mandela government had to face the challenges of the economy. Should it create a new economy or retain the old structure? Mandela and many ANC members were aware of the dangers of capitalism based on apartheid and needed to make changes without creating panic among investors. The government pursued a policy of alleviating poverty and uplifting the black population. A Reconstruction and Development Programme (RDP) was approved in 1994, with the aim of providing free education and making electricity and water available to the majority of the population. A million new homes would also be built. In spite of the changes designed to spread the benefits of economic growth, the rate of unemployment remained high, the gap between the rich and poor remained wide, and the number of skilled and experienced black managers remained low. The radical members of the ANC remained worried that the economic structure and privileges of the apartheid years were yet to be completely dismantled.

In July 1997, Mandela, now seventy-nine, stepped aside as president of the ANC, which later chose Thabo Mbeki as its new leader. Mandela retired in June 1999, the ANC won the national election in the same month, and Thabo Mbeki was selected as the country's second black president. With Mbeki in power, South Africa continues to move away from the apartheid era and to face the problems of managing the economy and politics of a multiracial society.

SUGGESTIONS FOR FURTHER READING

Falola, Toyin. *Africa*. Vol. 5, *Contemporary Africa*. Durham, N.C.: Carolina Academic Press, in press.

Mandela, Nelson. *Long Walk to Freedom: The Autobiography of Nelson Mandela*. Boston: Little, Brown, 1994.

Mbeki, Thabo. *Africa: The Time Has Come*. Cape Town: Tafelberg, 1998.

Sampson, Anthony. *Nelson Mandela: The Authorized Biography*. New York: Harper-Collins, 1999.

Index

About the Author

TOYIN FALOLA is the Frances Higginbothom Nalle Centennial Professor in History at the University of Texas at Austin, and the recipient of the Jean Holloway Award for Teaching Excellence. A distinguished Africanist, Falola serves on the editorial board of many journals, co-edits the *Journal of African Economic History,* and serves as the series editor of the University of Rochester's Studies in African History and the Diaspora. He is also series editor of the Greenwood Press series Culture and Customs of Africa. His publications include many essays and books on Nigeria, including *Decolonization and Development Planning* (1996); *Violence in Nigeria: The Crisis of Religious Politics and Secular Ideologies* (1998); and *The History of Nigeria* (Greenwood, 1999).

Made in the USA
Lexington, KY
30 August 2011